Unemployed Negativity:

Fragments on Philosophy, Politics, and Culture

Jason Read

Published by Mayfly Books. Available in paperback and free online at www.mayflybooks.org in 2024.

© Authors remain the holders of the copyright of their own texts. They may republish their own texts in different contexts, including modified versions of the texts under the condition that proper attribution is given to Unemployed Negativity.

ISBN (Print) 978-1-906948-76-4
ISBN (PDF)   978-1-906948-77-1

This work is licensed under the Creative Commons Attribution-Non commercial-No Derivatives 4.0 International (CC BY-NC-ND 4.0).
To view a copy of this license, visit
http://creativecommons.org/licenses/by-nc-nd/4.0

Layout and cover art work by Jess Parker who retains the image copyright.

For Bento.
My best friend and a true Spinozist.

Contents

Introduction: Why We Write: Or, Blogging as Philosophical Practice — 01

PART I: Movies — 09
Hijacking a Train: Revolution and its Limits in Snowpiercer — 11
Winchester '73: Destiny or Contingency — 17
"You'd be a Beast": Get Out and Race — 23
You Will Not Replace Us: On Jordan Peele's Latest — 29
Between Legacy and History: On Peele's Nope — 37
Ape Like Imitation: Repetition and Difference in the Planet of the Apes — 45
Man is a Wolf to Man: An Appreciation of Wolfen — 53
The Primitive Accumulation of Prehistory: On the Jurassic Park films — 59
Violence and the Common: Truth is Structured Like a (Science) Fiction — 67
How Can It Not Know What It Is? On Blade Runner 2049 — 73
Avenge Me: The Avengers and the Culture Industry — 79
The Use and Abuse of Blockbusters for Life: Movies and Memes in the Age of Viral Collapse — 85
Revenge of the Children of Marx and Coca-Cola: Remarks on Deleuze, Vertov, and Godard — 93
Becoming Spider-Man: Deleuze and the Superhero Film — 101
Shine On: We Are All in Room 237 Now — 111

PART II: Television/Streaming — 119
"Look on my works, ye mighty, and despair!": Breaking Bad as Austerity Allegory — 121
Everybody Loves Kim: Breaking Bad on Better Call Saul — 131
The Devil is in the Details: Twilight Zone's Demonology of Capital — 137
"Live Every Week Like it is Shark Week": Remarks on the Ecology of the Mediasphere — 145
Old Time Religion: On American Gods the book and TV show — 153
The Golden Pig: Okja and the limits of Satire — 159
Man is a Super-Villain to Man: The Boys and the limits of Satire — 165
In Space No One Can Hear You Struggle: On The Expanse — 173
Gonna Leave You All Severed: Initial Reflections on Severance — 181

PART III: Politics 187
The Methlab of Democracy: More on the Micropolitics of Neoliberalism 189
Debt Collectors: The Economics, Politics, and Morality of Debt 195
Starting from Year Zero: Occupy Wall Street and the Transformations of the Socio-Political 205
Trumped: The Ecology of Attention and Affects 227
Must Love Dogs: Animals and Racism in the Age of Trump 233
Reduction to Ignorance: Spinoza in the Age of Conspiracy Theories 239
The Dialectic of Conspiracy and Trust: Hegel and Conspiracy Theories 249
The Spontaneous Ideology of Conspiracy: This One on Marx 255
Woke Capital and Twilight of the Bourgeoisie (How is that for a title?) 263
Despair and Indignation: The Inevitable Reflection on Covid (with Marx and Spinoza) 269

PART IV: Books 279
Personalized Ideology (or Ideology Personified): Silva's Mood Economy 281
Any Bird Whatsoever: on Fujita's Le Ciné-Capital: D'Hitchcock à Ozu 289
It's Competition All the Way Down: On the Spontaneous Anthropology of Contemporary Capitalism 297
Every Day I Write the Book: Macherey on the Quotidian 305
Reworking Hegel: Philosophies of Work in Macherey's Petit Riens 313
The Class Struggle at Home: Jaquet's Transclasses 321
Translating Transclass: Or Teaching Eribon in America 329
What Does it Mean to be a Materialist: Thoughts After Spinoza after Marx 337
"Let Me Tell You of the Time that Something Occurred": On Yves Citton's Mythocratie 345
Meta-Fiction: The Comic Book (Politics and Narrative, Part Two) 351
I Owe You an Explanation: Graeber and Marx on Origin Stories 359
Waiting for the Robots: Benanav and Smith on the Illusions of Automation and Realities of Exploitation 365
Put a Drone on It: Chamayou's A Theory of the Drone 373
The Means of Individuation: Castel on the Dialectics of Individuality 379

PART V: Philosophy 387
Althusser Effects: Philosophical Practices 389
Immanent Cause: Between Reproduction and Nonreproduction 395
Anti-Aesthetics: Or, Towards a Spinozist Theory of Cultural Production 413
Imagination, Fiction, Knowledge: Towards a Spinozist Theory of Cultural Production Part II 421

Nexus Rerum: Spinoza and Marx (again) — 429
Economies of Affect/Affective Economies: Towards A Spinozist Critique of Political Economy — 439
The Imaginary Institution of Society: Spinoza's Version — 451
The General Intellect Personified: Capitalism as a Social Relation — 459
Negative Solidarity: Towards the Definition of a Concept — 467
The Original Sin of Accumulation: Trying to Say Something Original About Ursprüngliche Akkumulation — 473

TRANSLATIONS — 479
Vengez-moi : The Avengers et l'industrie culturelle — 480
L'accumulation primitive de la préhistoire : sur les films de dinosaurs — 484
Blockbusters et mèmes à l'ère de l'effondrement viral — 490
Le diable est dans les détails : la démonologie du capital dans « La Quatrième Dimension » — 498
Le capital « woke » et le crépuscule de la bourgeoisie — 503
En attendant les robots: Benanav et Smith sur les illusions d'automation et les réalités d'exploitation — 508
Te debo una explicación: Graeber y Marx sobre las historias de origen — 514
Colpi preventivi: Marx e Spinoza — 519
Economías del afecto / economías afectivas: hacia una crítica spinozista de la economía política — 529

Why We Write: Or, Blogging as Philosophical Practice

"...no philosopher has held any interest for me as long as I was aware only of hid ideas, and not of his practice."

– Etienne Balibar

There is too much to read. Too many hot takes, blogposts, etc. The last twenty plus years have completely transformed the attention economy of writing. The digitalization of text, combined with the dissemination of social media has led to a proliferation of texts and takes. Every moment from politics to popular culture generates more tweets, blogposts, and comments than anyone can read. There is a fundamental transformation of the attention economy in which it seems that there are more writers than readers.

How can any justify contributing to such a deluge. Does the world really need more takes on *Snowpiercer*, *Breaking Bad*, and Trump? Why write such things, and we reprint them here and now. In short, why blog?

I started the blog Unemployed Negativity in the summer of 2006. I was in JFK airport waiting for an overdue connecting flight to Portland, Maine. I started it during a brief swell in philosophical blogging. I won't list all of the blogs here, and someone should write the history of that period, but for a while it seemed like a new blog was forming every month, and most were being updated repeatedly.

Most of those blogs are no longer updated, lingering on now as digital time capsules of a moment that has passed. The activity has shifted to other spaces, podcasts and substacks. I have kept at it for eighteen years now, a fact that might attest to the persistence of habit more than anything else. It is an important practice for me.

I can only think of my continued engagement with the blog as a particular kind of practice of philosophy. I take this term from Louis Althusser and his students, Pierre Macherey and Etienne Balibar. While there are multiple different definitions and debates about the term and what it means, the fundamental underlying idea is that philosophy is a kind of activity. It is something that one does, an activity, rather something that one is, an identity. I have never really liked the idea that one who studies philosophy is a philosopher, someone who has a reservoir of knowledge and wisdom. One has to do philosophy, and that activity has to be constantly enriched and transformed by an engagement with the outside world. In other words, one has to constantly think and write about the books one reads, the films one sees, the latest news from politics, culture, and society; not just to make sense of them, or to illustrate philosophical concepts, but to put those concepts to the test. In other words, philosophy needs material, without it philosophy risks becoming a dead letter of cliches and stock phrases. It needs a matter to reflect on if it is not to collapse in an endless reflection it itself. This is perhaps always true, but it becomes increasingly so as philosophical reflection comes to us as categorized and pre-digested by all of the various introductions, guides, and articles; if we know the names of different philosophers we know that Spinoza is a rationalist, Louis Althusser a structuralist, Michel Foucault a postmodernist, all of these labels save us the trouble of actually thinking. G.W.F. Hegel outlined this problem two centuries ago:

> The manner of study in ancient times differed from that of the modern age in that the former was the proper and complete formation of natural consciousness. Putting itself to a test at every point of its existence, and philosophizing about everything

that it came across it made itself into a universality that was active through and through. In modern times, however, the individual finds the abstract form ready-made; the effort to grasp and appropriate it is more the direct driving forth of what is within and the truncated generation of the universal than it is the emergence of the latter from the concrete variety of existence. Hence the task nowadays consists not so much in purging the individual of an immediate, sensuous mode of apprehension, and making him into a substance that is an object of thought and that thinks, but rather in just the opposite, in freeing determinate thoughts from their fixity so as to give actuality to the universal, and impart to it spiritual life.[1]

One way to free these thoughts, to remove them from their reification in so many categories, is to put them into contact with something that they could not anticipate: *Snowpiercer* and Althusser's ideas on ideology and repression, Covid and Michel Foucault, Spinoza and conspiracy theories. This is the first sense of what could be called the materiality of philosophical practice: philosophy needs matter in order to matter. This matter must in some ways be alien or foreign to the philosophy at hand. It is precisely because something does not fit into established categories and concepts that it becomes something worth thinking about. At the same time, in order for thinking to have any effect, any transformative relation to not only the world, but any effect on itself it must be materialized, it must be written. Writing is always a transformation of thought, even if the written text never finds an audience beyond the person who wrote it. As anyone who has reread even their journal, or tried to revise something months later, can attest to, the person who reads their own writing is not the same person who wrote it. The text, the words, stay the same, fixed in their meaning, but the thought that created it vacillates and change; or maybe our thinking stays the same, fixed on the same point, but it is the text that seems to vacillate, meaning something else. To write is always to transform

---

1 Hegel, G.W.F. *The Phenomenology of Spirit*, translated by A.V. Miller, Oxford: Oxford, 1977, 20.

what one thinks, fixing the flux of impressions and ideas into words and sentences, and in doing so one transforms oneself. This is the second sense of materiality. The materiality of the letter, of the text, undermines and calls into question the ideality of identity. The difference that one encounters in reading their own writing is nothing compared to being confronted by someone else's interpretation or reading. Interpretations exceed intentions, but these interpretations have an uncanny identity, they are both familiar and unrecognizable.

These two senses of materiality, the matter considered and the materiality of the text, create difference, or two differences, the difference between the concept and its situation and a difference between the text and its interpretation. Writing is not a pure play of difference. There is, even on a blog, an attempt to connect and reconnect the observations and ideas into something that could be called a position, or point of view, I hesitate to use the word, "a philosophy." As Balibar writes, "philosophy constantly endeavors to untie and retie from inside the knot between conjuncture and writing, or if you will, it works from within the element of writing to untie the elements of conjuncture, but it also works under the constraint of the conjuncture to retie the conditions of writing."[2] In blogging the emphasis is on the untying rather than tying, of trying to see what happens when a concept confronts the cultural or political elements of the conjuncture. This collection is an attempt to see if it ties together.

A lot of blogging goes nowhere, become nothing more than a few thoughts that never cohere into an essay or even an idea. It is in part for this reason that I decided to call my blog unemployed negativity. I remember reading about the phrase in some of the discussions of Hegel's end of history brought about by Alexandre Kojéve's influential seminar on the *Phenomenology of Spirit*. The idea was that end of history, when the conflict and struggle for recognition that

---

[2] Etienne Balibar, The infinite contradiction. Trans. J.M, Poisson with J. Lezra *Depositions: Althusser, Balibar, Macherey, and the labor of reading. Yale French Studies*, 142-165. 88,

had defined most of human existence had come to end, conflict, negativity itself would be unemployed, without a use. It seemed a fitting name for a blog. It seemed to be fitting for a bunch of writings that were never conceived to be put to work. Not only were they not planned to be books or articles, they were often in areas that were outside of my official areas of expertise or training. They were posts on television shows, movies, and comic books by someone who did not study or teach on media or film. There was something of a surplus, an excess to these writings. Writing outside the boundaries of academic productive research and writing. Critical thinking, negativity, working off of the clock; thinking does not stop just because one is going to a movie or keeping up with current events. I started this blog as someone who could not imagine publishing on television or movies, leaving these thoughts unemployed, but I should mention that since I started it some of these ideas have been put to work. My book, *The Double Shift: Spinoza and Marx on the Politics of Work* incorporates discussions of movies and television in its argument about representations of work. Blogging transformed the kind of writer that I am.

I wrote often for my own self-clarification. It is worth noting how utterly idiosyncratic some of the posts were, posts on the political subtext of Planet of the Apes films, the economic structure of dinosaur movies. Add to this a collection of philosophical references, Marx, Spinoza, Deleuze, etc., and one has writing so idiosyncratic to almost be unreadable. Part of the appeal of blogging is in the absolute idiosyncratic nature of the writing. I wrote what I wanted. Sometimes I wrote on a film that was being discussed and debated, sometimes on some major issue like a Presidential election on an ongoing pandemic, other times I wrote a review of a book that was recently published in French and would never be translated into English. Part of the unemployed nature of the negativity is that I was not driven by revenue or clicks. I did manage to find readers, and even translators, as posts were translated into French, Spanish, Portuguese, Turkish, and Farsi. This brings me to another thesis that I have written about at length in my published, or employed writing, and that is the concept of transindividuality. I do not plan to go into it here except to say that one aspect of this idea is in rethinking the very relation of the individual and community. It is not a matter of engaging the community by suppressing individuality, by trying to write in a neutral voice, but that idiosyncrasy and individuation is not the opposite of some kind of community, some kind of commonality, but its necessary condition.

One of the clichés of writing is that one always imagines an audience. I am not sure if I ever did that, at least in any specific sense. However, part of the impetus for blogging came from my own experience as a graduate student and that shaped my idea of audience. First, in graduate school I developed the habit of writing a lot, a lot more than I would ever use in papers or classes. I was in a number of reading groups, groups on Marx's *Capital*, on Althusser, on Deleuze, and many more. In these groups we constantly read and wrote small reports for each other, building collective knowledge. Many of my blogposts are modeled on that line, reviews, small book reports to a collective that does not exist, or would perhaps exist in and through reading it. I was in graduate school before the age of blogs, but we did have listservs. These listservs were sometimes the only place that I could read about some of my interests that were outside of the standard philosophy curriculum. I learned a lot about Autonomia and Operaismo from the listserv called AUT-OP-Sy (which I believe stood for Autonomia, Operaismo, and Syndicalism), even Deleuze and Guattari were discussed more on listservs than in classes or books back then—as hard as that is to believe. These listservs made it possible for me to understand things that were not taught at my school or discussed by my peers. Graduate reading groups and listservs were a huge part of my education. They allowed me to engage with ideas and perspectives outside of the expertise of the faculty at my university, setting up lateral communications of knowledge that short-circuited the hierarchies between advisor and student. Blogging was an attempt to continue and maintain the kind of community, both face to face and virtual, that I found in graduate school.

All of this sounds rather self-important for a bunch of pieces written under the hold of insomnia, or while having a cup of coffee in the morning, but I firmly believe that philosophy has accepted the university as its natural environment at its peril. This has excluded a great many people who want to continue to think and reflect, but do not have access to classrooms or teachers, and more importantly this natural environment has proven to be ultimately quite hostile to thinking and reflection. Its focus is an accreditation and jobs training, tasks that often stand in the way of the practice of philosophy. Universities are cutting philosophy programs every year. If philosophy, if thinking the intersection of conjunctures and concepts, is going to continue to have a future, and I think it must, it will have to find new spaces and methods of communication. Blogging might not be all of that, but it is at least a start.

Speaking of community, I would like to thank the editors of Mayfly books for having the idea of publishing this book, and the help of Emrah Ali Karakilic, Charles Barthold, and Jess Parker. I also would like to thank the people who took it upon themselves to translate some of these posts into French (David Buxton), Spanish (Javier Sanz Paz and Jaime Ortega), and Italian (Gigi Roggerro). They are all part of the community referred to above.

MOVIES

Hijacking a Train: Revolution and its Limits in Snowpiercer

Originally posted July 3rd 2014 after a summer afternoon in the cool dark theater.

I scrupulously avoided reading any reviews of *Snowpiercer* once I became intrigued by the basic premise. I was already hooked, and did not want to spoil what seemed like a fun afternoon at the movies. Despite this, I was aware, in that way we become aware of things through an almost social media osmosis, that it was quickly being heralded as a new film about the 99% and the 1%, about social inequality, and, more importantly, about revolution. In what follows I would like to explore these allegories for at least two reasons. The first, and most basic, is that the film openly invites such readings. Its particular premise, that the Earth is plunged into an extreme ice age after a failed attempt to solve global warming with the last surviving remnants of humanity stranded on globe circling super train, is so thin in terms of any pretense at credibility, and yet so packed with allusions and images, I am not sure it is even possible to watch it as "just a movie." Second, and more importantly I am interested in what it means to make or interpret a film as allegory of the present, recognizing of course that the line between making and interpreting can never be rigidly defined. (Spoilers follow)

Initially the film's premise is presented as a kind of freshman essay on dystopia. It turns out that the train was designed by a maligned but gifted engineer, referred to only as Wilford, who somehow foresaw that the attempt to solve global warming would fail horribly resulting in a new ice age. Already we have a kind of John Galt figure filtered through Fox news. Life on the train is a strict hierarchy with the ruler in the front, next to the sacred engine, followed by the elites in first class, the remainder of humanity is stuck in back, crammed in the tail of the train. This hierarchy is fairly static; occasionally guards from the front come looking for someone possessing a particular skill, a violin player, or, more chillingly a few children of the proper size and height. Other than that the people in the back do not seem to work, or serve much of a purpose. They only reproduce, this is the source of both their value to those who run the train and makes them objects of hatred of those in the front of the train. As is so often the case in American popular culture, or even in the media, inequality is much more easy to imagine and discuss than exploitation. It is easier to imagine a world divided into rich and poor than a world in which the rich live off of the work of the poor. Thus, to butcher a phrase that has been quoted all too often, it is easier to imagine some dystopian tyranny than it is to come to grips with actually existing capitalism.

What makes Snowpiercer engaging, however, is precisely how it runs up against these limitations of imagination and representation. First, and to be fair, the film does not entirely present us a world without work. The majority of the people on the train are unemployed and unemployable, doing only the most basic reproductive labor of keeping humanity alive, a kind of surplus population even when humanity only numbers in the hundreds. Overpopulation, surplus, and reserve armies are not natural conditions, a species out of control, but are relative to a given mode of production. On an automated train almost the entire population is surplus, and an arbitrary line separates those unproductively languishing in the cramped rear, and those reveling in the hedonistic excess of first class. There are of course a few workers, making protein bars, teaching kids, doing security, and making sushi, but much of the train, rich and poor, live a life without work. The train is thus predominantly a service economy in which hairstylists outnumber protein bar makers, but overall it is a world in which a small elite governs over a fundamentally expendable population. They are kept alive not because they are exploited, but because they are potentially exploitable, might have some skill or ability that those in the front of the train could use. Viewed this way the film's effacement of labor brings it closer to a picture of the present in which many are unemployed and underemployed hoping to one day to be exploited.

It is when we get to the theme of revolution that things get interesting. First, there is a matter of how the film answers the question, why don't people revolt? What keeps the people in line, besides the few guards, is the recognition that as much as the order on the train subjugates them, keeping them living in crammed, dirty, and dark quarters, living off of a meager diet, it is also the condition of survival. If Tilda Swinton's performance has been compared to Margaret Thatcher it is also fair to say that the train is the very embodiment of "there is no alternative." There is no life outside the train.

As much as we see a classroom where students are interpellated into the ideology of the train, taught to idolize the train and its conductor, all of this ideological indoctrination is a bit superfluous to the way in which the train itself materializes ideology. If people cannot live outside of the train, or can imagine no life outside of its walls, then there is almost no need to venerate it, or to indoctrinate people to love it. Material necessity supplants ideology when it is impossible to imagine other conditions capable of reproducing existence. It is easy, perhaps too easy, to see the train as an image of contemporary capitalism. The inequality is acknowledged by nearly everyone except for the lucky few, but as long as the world outside of it appears frozen and hostile, a gulag in the waiting, then the train just goes on and on.

The back of the train is dominated by what Althusser would call the Repressive State Apparatus (RSA), the masses are kept in line with a gun butt, while the middle is where you find the Ideological State Apparatus (ISA), the school—the children are interpellated in the lessons which treat the train as the condition of survival, and Wilford, its creator, as their savior. Not just a "job creator," but a life creator. Of course these distinctions quickly breakdown in two interesting scenes. We learn that the guns that maintain order in the back are empty and just for show, almost all bullets have been spent repressing past revolutions. Conversely, the loaded guns are hidden in the school, in the baskets of eggs which symbolize rebirth and renewal as the train makes another round. There is always symbolism, ideology, in every RSA, in every appearance of the cops on the street, and there is always violence, exclusion and guns, in every ISA. Every school has its security, and often its police. Breaking the repetition of the existing order entails being able to spot the imaginary dimension of violent force, and the violence and force existing underneath ideological indoctrination. It is a matter of recognizing where belief becomes a force and force becomes just an idea. Even shock troops need black hoods (and must occasionally sacrifice a carp for dramatic effect).

That the train is the necessary condition of existence, or at least appears to be so, puts any revolution are narrow tracks. The revolutionaries can seize the train, but seizing the train risks all too easily reproducing the same relations. In fact we eventually learn that these revolutions are nothing other than the temporary disruptions that keep the order intact. They reduce the population, functioning as a kind of unnatural selection, and they occasionally bring new leaders to the front of the train. Successful revolutionaries are bribed into becoming new leaders, or at least offered the chance. The only solution then is not to seize the train, to claim its engine, but to begin to imagine a life outside of it. The end there are two revolutionaries, two ideas of revolution. One Curtis (played by Chris Evans) wants to make it to the engine to seize control; he reads the signs of power and subjection aboard the train, spotting the ideology that sustains violence and the violence underneath ideology. While the other Namgoong Minsoo(played by Kang-ho Song) wants to escape the train; he reads the signs of the changing conditions outside the train, seeing the possibility of life where others see only death. *Snowpiercer* is very much a film about what people see and cannot see. The visible and the invisible is given not only tactical importance, as in spotting the empty magazine of a rifle or enemies in a the darkened tunnel, but a utopian significance as well. Namgoong can see the snow melting and the world outside of the train thawing, and thus a life outside the train. In the end the future belongs to those who can imagine a life outside of the train and can realize it.

This is ultimately what makes *Snowpiercer* worth viewing, and even timely, it is not that it is particularly imaginative dystopia for our present, but that it stages the dystopia of our current imagination. We are so desperately in need of a vision of life outside of our particular economic and political system; it is clear that the train is going nowhere and we need something more to hope for than becoming a cog in its machinery.

For further reading on ideology see Althusser Effects: Philosophical Practices and Immanent Cause: Between Reproduction and Nonreproduction.

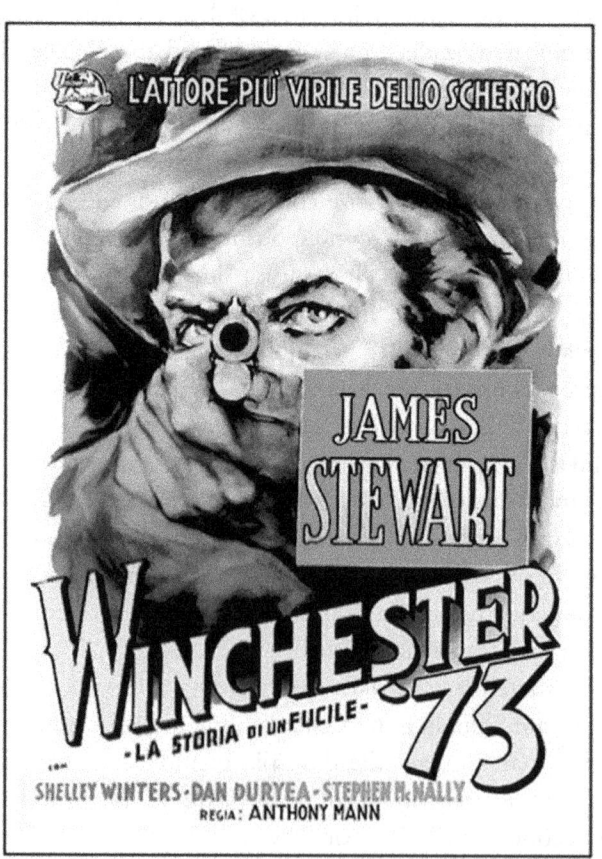

Winchester '73: Destiny or Contingency

Originally written in December of 2010. Anthony Mann's westerns are discussed by both Gilles Deleuze and Jacques Rancière. At the time they were hard to come by, but I found this film at my local videostore.

> "...the American cinema constantly shoots and re-shoots a single fundamental film, which is the birth of a nation-civilization..."
>
> — Gilles Deleuze[1]

I have often thought that one could write something of an history of American ideology in the middle of the last century through the films of Jimmy Stewart. This is in part due to his casting as a sort of "everyman," the generic subject of mass society, but, more importantly, it is the way in which this "everyman" was cast in very different light from the black and white morality of Capra to Hitchcock's infinite shades of grey. The shift of directors is not just a shift of style, but a fundamental shift in the understanding of subjectivity and the world. The Capra, Ford, and Hitchcock films are well known. Perhaps less well known are the Westerns that Stewart made with Anthony Mann. Mann's films are thematically and

---

1 Gilles Deleuze, *Cinema 1: The Movement Image*, Translated by Hugh Tomlinson and Barbara Habberjam, University of Minnesota 148.

chronologically placed between the films of Capra and Hitchcock: Stewart plays the hero but one who is often driven by an obsession, conflicted beneath his generic exterior.

Stewart may seem like an unlikely western hero, especially to anyone who has seen *The Man Who Shot Liberty Valence*. Mann seemed to be aware of this, Jacques Rancière cites him as saying that he found it necessary to follow a "series of precautions" in order to make Stewart, who is not "the broad shouldered type," believable as a man who can take on the world, precautions that define the relationship between what one can do and what one must do within the film.[2] These precautions define the relation between the character and action, a relation that breaks with almost organic connection with a milieu that Deleuze argues defines Ford's and Hawk's westerns. As Rancière writes, "It doesn't much matter whether Mann's hero is a man of justice or a reformed criminal, since that is not the source of his quality. His hero belongs to no place, has no social function and no typical Western role: he is not a sheriff, bandit, ranch owner, cowboy, or officer; he doesn't defend or attack the established order, and he does not conquer or defend any land. He acts and that's it, he does some things."[3]

In *Winchester '73* Stewart plays Lin McAdam a brother pitted against brother, seeking to avenge his father's murder. In this story Cain doesn't so much slay Abel, but his father. This fact, this crucial motivation, is only alluded to in the opening of the film: it is finally explained much later, during the final shootout. Initially we only know that Lin is pursuing a man to Dodge City with determination that borders on the murderous. Narrative completion is only given retroactively in the closing scene. Up to that point we only have a quest, a conflict without a clear sense of its stakes. This quest, with its linear obsessive determination, is immediately displaced and deferred by the rifle of the film's title. The rifle, which is introduced before any character, the subject of the first close up, first appears as the prize

---

2 Jacques Rancière, *Film Fables*, Translated by Emiliano Battista, Oxford: Berg, 2006, 76.
3 Jacques Rancière, Film Fables, 78.

in the fourth of July shooting contest organized by Wyatt Earp in Dodge City. The contest, and Dodge City in general, are presented as ordered and just: the story begins in place order and descends into lawlessness, a reversal of the traditional western narrative.

The contest pits Stewart against his brother, "Dutch Henry" (an alias) as two expert marksmen, both taught by the same man (their father). As Stewart says, hinting at the murder he is seeking to avenge, they were both taught how to shoot, but not why: equal in skill, but distinguished only by a slight moral difference. Just how slight this difference is made clear in the first scene where brother encounters brother. They both simultaneously reach for their guns. There is no difference of hero and villain at the level of basic actions: they are both prepared to shoot the other in (relative) cold blood. They would have shot each other, but there are no guns allowed in the oasis of order that is Dodge City, so all they can do is reach for their holsters, grasping at absent guns. As is so often the case in this film, intention exceeds action, the logic of the film restores one to the other.

Stewart wins the shooting contest, but is ambushed by his brother in his hotel room and the prize gun is stolen. This crime takes place within Dodge City, suggesting as the film does repeatedly that order and authority are only appearances. The plot of the film then follows three series of events. First, there is Stewart doggedly pursuing his brother from Dodge City across the west; then there is Dutch Henry, who isn't so much fleeing pursuit as setting off on his own attempt to rob a bank; and finally there is the gun itself, which travels from the hands of Dutch, to the gun dealer who swindles him out of it, to a Native American chief (played by Rock Hudson), to the soldier who plucks it from the Chief's dead hands, to "Waco Johnny Dean," a member of Henry's gang, eventually back to Henry for the final shootout. In the end Dutch Henry is defeated by Stewart and the gun is returned to its rightful owner.

This trajectory of the rifle's movement, from hand to hand, could be understood as a kind of test, a quest with an object at its center.

Criminals, corrupt gun dealers, "Indians," soldiers, and cowards all try to possess the gun, only to be deemed unworthy in the moral (and racist) logic of the film. Read this way the trajectory of the rifle overlaps with that of the moral quest for vengeance and the restoration of order. It is logic of fate: the murdering brother will be killed, and the gun will return to its rightful owner. However, the gun's trajectory is overdetermined by the events of history itself. The film makes constant reference to the Battle of Little Big Horn, and the role that the Native American's Winchesters played in Custer's last stand. The repeating Winchesters were able to outgun the calvary's single shot rifles. Custer's defeat is presented as a kind of trauma, of a reversal of the established racial order based on the slight difference of a faster rifle. In the final shootout Stewart is able to defeat his brother, despite his superior gun, by tossing pebbles, distracting him to waste ammunition shooting at rocks and shadows. Underneath the moral narrative in which the gun is restored to its proper owner, and justice is dealt, there is the contingency of history, of the slight differences of technology, speed, and skill that simultaneously realize and undermine any intention.

The rifle doesn't just move from hand to hand, passing from Dutch, to the gun dealer, to the chief, and so on, it also passes between two different ways of understanding events; it passes between the moral logic of destiny and the historical logic of contingency.

Mann is most well-known for introducing a noir sensibility to the Western, of bringing the conflicted and ambiguous psyche of the postwar urban milieu into the open spaces of the West. However, what is interesting about *Winchester '73* is the way in which this interior space, Stewart's obsessive drive for vengeance is displaced by the pure exteriority of history. History in this case is indicated by the gun itself: it is an object that is always out of place, despite being named and dated. There is nothing to keep this gun from falling into the wrong hands: materiality is defined as that which simultaneously enables and thwarts the intentions of individuals. The gun might have a rightful owner, and there might be a rightful order of justice, but a faster gun and the luck of finding it can set everything off kilter. In the end the only way to correct this, to right things, is to toss a few pebbles into the air. Slight differences of speed and timing ultimately matter more than official differences of law and order.

Perhaps when Althusser invoked the figure of the cowboy to sketch his portrait of a materialist philosopher, the philosopher of aleatory materialism who catches a moving train, he was thinking of Anthony Mann.

For more on aleatory materialism see "Immanent Cause: Between Reproduction and Nonreproduction."

"You'd be a Beast": Get Out and Race

Originally written in February of 2017. Part of what eventually became an ongoing series on Jordan Peele's films.

As most people reading this already know, the central story of *Get Out* begins when Rose Armitage (Allison Williams) brings her boyfriend Chris Washington (Daniel Kaluuya) home to meet her parents. What begins as a racial comedy of manners, a satire of well-intentioned liberalism, quickly descends into horror, but the question is what kind of horror? what is the dark secret waiting for Chris? The question of narrative is inseparable from the theme of the film. What kind of horror movie it is cannot be separated from what horror of racism it will depict.

At first, the odd mannerisms of the black maid and groundskeeper, as well as one strange party guest, suggests that we are watching *The Stepford Brother* in which the town's black population has been restored to some pre-civil rights fantasy of docile servants and well-dressed dinner guests. As Chris says to his friend on the phone, an America that "missed the movement," left behind by civil rights and the sixties. Initially *Get Out* appears to be another one of those films in which a new person is brought into a community only to become a victim of its dark secret. I am not sure what to call this particularly sub-genre or even if it is one. The best examples of this genre, examples that the writer and director Jordan Peele knows well, are films like *The Stepford Wives* and *Rosemary's Baby* (Both written by Ira Levin).[1] To perhaps take it seriously as both a movie about race and a movie steeped in the genre and subgenre's of horror is to examine the way in which the latter shapes the former. In other words, to take it seriously as an examination of the nightmare of race is to examine the way in which the genre does a kind of dream work, shaping and transforming its primary trauma. (One could even use such a method to examine the various "horror of racism" novels that have appeared in the last year, such as *The Ballad of Black Tom* by Victor Lavalle and *Lovecraft Country* by Matt Ruff, both of which take Lovecraft and thus a different sub-genre of horror as their point of entry).

This would be one horror story about race. Racism as the fantasy of a return to an old hierarchy and order. Racism as nostalgia or vice versa. To take the parlance of our times, America made great again. However, racism as nostalgia is itself anachronistic. It identifies racism with only the most overt and heavy handed assertions of racial superiority and hierarchy. As the film's plot unfolds, as it begins to show that there is more going on than simply brainwashing African Americans to emulate the butlers and maids that populated the homes, and the movies, of the good old days, it also shifts its definition of racism. The shift begins when Rose's brother Jeremy joins the family gathering. He immediately begins to chide Chris for not being interested in Mixed Martial Arts, stating that with his build and genetic makeup he would be "a beast" with proper training. This fetishization and reduction of the black man to his body, continues into the family party the next day, as guests touch Chris, and ask Rose if the rumors they have heard about black men and sex are true. Chris is a photographer, a point that is underscored at practically every moment in the film. His talent and ability is described by white characters as "his eyes." It is somatized,

---

1 Jason Zinoman, "Jordan Peele on a Truly Terrifying Monster: Racism," *New York Times*, February 16, 2017, https://www.nytimes.com/2017/02/16/movies/jordan-peele-interview-get-out.html

made a physical attribute of the body rather than a skill developed by a mind and body, not an achievement of an individual but a fact of nature. This is no longer race as order and hierarchy, but a racism that esteems, admires, and even fears the black body as it reduces individuals to just their body. Jesse Owens can be admired for his physical prowess, but that does not mean equality, or that he is seen as human.

To cite Balibar on the body as the intersection between class and race:

> "This process modifies the status of the human body (the human status of the body): it creates *body-men*, men whose body is a machine-body, that is fragmented and dominated, and used to perform one isolated function or gesture, being both destroyed in its integrity *and* fetishized, atrophied *and* hypertrophed in its 'useful' organs. Like all violence, this is inseparable from a resistance and also a sense of guilt…This is an unbearable process for the worker, but one which is no more 'acceptable,' without ideological and phantasmic elaboration, for the worker's masters: the fact that there are body-men, mean that there are also *men without bodies*. That the body-men are men with fragmented and mutilated bodes (if only by their 'separation' from intelligence) means that the individuals of each of these types have to be equipped with a *superbody*, and that sport and ostentation virility have to be developed, if the threat handing over the human race is to be fended off."[2]

In a seemingly throwaway joke the audio of the United Negro College Fund can be heard while Chris' friend Rod watches TV. This can of course be understood as a joke about mind control (and brain transplants), but minds are also wasted as individuals are reduced to bodies. Being revered as a body, as a skill, a strength, etc., is also always being reduced to it.

---

[2] Etienne Balibar, "Class Racism" Translated by Chris Turner in Etienne Balibar and Immanuel Wallerstein *Race, Nation, Class: Ambiguous Identities*, Verso, 1991, 211.

While Peele's film was initially conceived during the Obama administration, intended as horror film for post-racial times, its focus on the black body, on its skill and prowess extends its critique into the era of Trump and the alt-right. As it has been often noted, the term "cuck" has become a preferred pejorative that the alt-right and its extended online universe uses for its enemies, a term with a complex racial and sexual history, but one that cannot be separated from the envy and fear of black bodies.[3] (As I aside I wonder how much porn informs not only the online world's view of sex, but race as well) Modern racism is less a racism of hierarchy and superiority, than one infused with fear and strange envy of the other.

As the film progresses we learn that the "family's" plan is not simply to reduce black people to maids and servants, but to reduce them to their very body, to make their bodies the substrate for white minds and lives. The hypnotism and mind control is only phase one, the final completion of the plan, phase three, is to transplant aging white brains into healthy black bodies. White lives are extended, and expanded, by not just black labor, but also bodies. Or, if one wanted to read the allegory differently, the recipe for success in a racist society for those with black bodies is to take on white minds, to see themselves and the world as white people do. Peele's film smartly combines this revelation, with its seventies paranoia film trapping, with another much more intimate and contemporary one: Chris' realization that Rose is in on the plan, that he has been betrayed by the person he most intimately trusts. It is this last point, the intimacy of racism as something that enters into every relationship, even one's self conception. This is simultaneously the film's greatest tribute to films like *The Stepford Wives* or *Rosemary's Baby*, which were most frightening when they deal with husbands betraying their wives for some success and control in this world rather than when presenting a science fiction or fantasy world of fembots or devils, and its most trenchant criticism of racism as an

---

[3] Dana Schwartz, "Why Angry White Men Love Calling People "Cucks," *GQ*, August 1, 2016. https://www.gq.com/story/why-angry-white-men-love-calling-people-cucks

intimate relation. As one tagline for the film states, "just because you're invited doesn't mean that you're welcome." Racism is not just exclusion or segregation, but it can include a kind of inclusion that invites the body in, for its talents, but does not welcome the mind or the person.

I do not entirely want to give away the ending, or spoil the joke, but it is worth noting that the last horrifying image that the film gives us is of a police cruiser. This too can be considered a nod to the history of horror films, a reversal of the ending of *Night of the Living Dead*, but it is also the point where the film's allegory collapses into reality. The movie leaves the theater before the audience does, reminding them that the real horrors are not mind control, secret cults, or even racist body snatchers, but red and blue flashing lights and what passes as normal life in contemporary America.

For more on the films of Jordan Peele see "You Will Not Replace Us: On Jordan Peele's Us" and "Between Legacy and History: On Peele's Nope."

You Will Not Replace Us: On Jordan Peele's Latest

Originally written in March of 2019.

Us is a strange title for a horror film. "Them" and "It" are often the go to pronouns for horror, both suggesting something unknown and alien. In contrast to this "us" is often seen as the familiar, that which is generally threatened by some unknown "it" or "them." "Us" suggests unity not division, familiarity rather than fear, and would in general seem a more fitting title for a sappy romance than a horror movie. That Jordan Peele uses this title for his film suggests how uncanny it is, and how much the divisions between us and them are going to come under scrutiny. Jordan Peele's first film, *Get Out* hinged on the terror of the realization that one could be betrayed by their most intimate relationships. While *Us* works with very different subtexts and cultural anxieties it takes that basic uncanny sense of the foreignness and hostility of what is most familiar to new and more twisted levels.

To begin with *Us* opens on a forgotten bit of popular culture history. The Hands Across America charity campaign. This idea, and its image, people linking their hands across the nation to address and assist the forgotten and overlooked, to solve the hunger crisis, takes on an uncanny new significance by the time the film is over. Its initial appearance does not just contextualize the opening scene; it is also the first clue about the nature of the film.

Hands Across America appears as part of a flashback that opens the film. Young Adelaide is visiting the Santa Cruz boardwalk with her parents. She gets separated from them and wanders into a hall of mirrors. There she sees something that terrifies her, but it will take the rest of the film for the audience to figure out what it is. The film jumps to the present day nearly forty years later, as the Wilsons (Adelaide, her husband, Gabe, and their kids Zora and Jason) are returning to Santa Cruz on a family vacation.

Their vacation is soon interrupted by some odd doppelgängers. An entire Bizarro Wilson family, each like a funhouse distortion of their counterparts, breaks into the house. Gabe asks "Who are you people?" of these invaders. The audience can't help but ask the same question, or at least a variation of it. Who are these new monsters, these doppelgängers supposed to be? How is this film supposed to fit into Jordan Peele's announcement that he was planning to make a series of horror films dealing with social issues? Red, the distorted version of Adelaide answers Gabe's question by stating "We are Americans." Or, as the son, Jason, puts it "They're us." Red explains that her life has mirrored that of Adelaide, but in a twisted way. All of the events of Adelaide's life, her marriage to Gabe, her prince, and the birth of her two children were lived by Red as a form of torture, forced to undergo these things against her will and with much suffering. Everything Adelaide takes for granted, sunlight, fresh air, and some degree of freedom have been denied her double. What one assumes the other desperately craves.

It takes a few more twists to reveal what this explanation means. First, we learn that the Wilsons are not alone in having demented doubles. Their friends the Tylers also have murderous doubles. The film then shifts from the subgenre of home invasion horror, films which generally pit us against a strange and hostile them, to a broader "doppelgänger apocalypse" as it is revealed that all of Santa Cruz, and perhaps even the entire country is under attack by these uncanny doubles. They emerge from hidden tunnels, sewers and other forgotten places, kill their doubles, and then in something that is referred to in the film as "strange performance" art, they join hand to bloodied hand across America, a dark and twisted remake of that forgotten bit of eighties feel good trivia.

Red, the bizarro Adelaide, refers to the doubles as "the tethered," explaining that they are part of some forgotten attempt at social control. This attempt has long since been abandoned and the tethered were left in vast underground bunkers, doomed to live out their lives as twisted pantomimes of the real world above. In one of the film's best visual sequences we get a return to Adelaide's initial visit to the Santa Cruz boardwalk. Only now it is intercut with shots of her double walking through the massive underground bunker. We see people playing games, riding the roller coaster, sharing food, doing everything people do at the boardwalk. We also see their doubles go through the same motions, only without the necessary props of roller coasters, tilt-whirls, or whack-a-moles. Deprived of the necessary props, the necessary context and coordinates, the same actions look disturbing and unnerving, like something from a madhouse.

Peele's use of the Santa Cruz boardwalk is significant not just because it gives us such unnerving locales as halls of mirrors necessary to a horror movie but because boardwalks, carnivals, and other vanishing bits of American culture are places where people of different classes, different races, and so on come into contact. These public spaces are places where the comfortable middle classes come face to face with the very people that they otherwise go to great pains to deny even exist.

This brings us to the final revelation, the final twist of the film. Adelaide's horrifying memory from the eighties that opens the film was not just that she encountered her double, encountered Red in the funhouse, but that they switched places. Or, more to the point, Adelaide was dragged to the underworld below and Red took her place, eventually becoming the relatively happy and successful woman who cares for her kids and loves her husband. The real

Adelaide has been trapped beneath ground all along, planning her escape, planning a revolution. *Us* plays out like the darkest possible remake of *The Prince and the Pauper*, of two identical people who switch places. The tethered are oppressed and marginalized to the point of being the stuff of nightmares, and because of their oppression they hate those of us who walk in daylight, breathe fresh air, and go on vacations with a murderous passion. They hate us, but also are us. If things were reversed they would fight desperately to retain their privilege and we would struggle to overturn things, to find our place in the sun.

I have seen many reviews referring to *Us* as a more straight forward horror film, free of the social political subtext that defined *Get Out*. I think that they could not be more wrong. The way I see it, and if I had to answer the question, "What is *Us* about?"or "Who are they?" I would say that it is about the realization that our way of life, our vacation homes, boats, and Alexas, are ultimately unjustified. That as much as "we," the people who have the time and luxury to read blogposts about major motion pictures, tell ourselves we are better than them, than those that we would prefer to keep in the darkness, that we have earned our place in the sun with our hard work and righteous living, the only real difference between us and them is the social system that necessarily divides us from them. That is the real horror. As the old saying goes, "we have met the enemy and they are us."

Concluding Post-Script on Gesture (with obligatory Spinoza reference):

The more I think about this film, and I have been thinking about it a lot since I first watched it, the more I think how much of it hinges on gesture and comportment. Many have noted how well Lupita Nyong'o, Winston Duke, Shahadi Wright Joseph, Evan Alex, and Madison Curry etc. use gesture to embody different characters. However, it also seems to me that Jordan Peele deserves credit as an observer and director of gestures, something that makes sense coming from a comedy background. This is something that could already be seen in *Get Out*. Giorgio Agamben has argued that "Cinema leads images back to the homeland of gesture."[1] Gestures, ways of walking, sitting, standing, etc., are part of human life that film more than any other art form can convey. As Agamben writes "The gesture is the exhibition of mediality: it is the process of making a means visible as such. It allows the emergence of the being-in-a-medium of human beings and thus it opens the ethical dimensions for them."[2]

In *Us* we are constantly confronted with gestures that differentiate people, but also the same gesture presented in different context and situations drawing out different implications. Gestures identify and differentiate. The difference between the normal and the doppelgänger, is found in the way they walk or move. As Gabe Winston Duke moves with an affable and laid back comfort — a "dad bod," but as Abraham, as the tethered, the same body becomes a lumbering monstrosity. The tethered do not just differentiate themselves through comportments they also imitate the movements of the people they resemble. As I indicated above, however, we are also confronted with the same gesture in different contexts and situations. We see a flashback of young Adelaide's dance performance (actually Red), but we also see the same performance taking place in the austere institutional setting of the underground bunker where the tethered live. A space that looks like a nightmare version of an insane asylum. The pirouettes of the dancer on the stage become a psychotic spinning when placed in a different situation. Artistic expression becomes the manifestation of madness. As Spinoza argued the same gesture, raising my fist and extending my arm in the case of throwing a punch becomes something very different in different situations. Or, in the case of the film, killing someone with an outboard motor can be a source of either horrified screams

---

[1] Giorgio Agamben, Means without End: Notes on Politics, Translated by Vincenzo Binetti and Cesare Casarino, Minneapolis: University of Minnesota, 2000, 56.
[2] Ibid., 58.

or celebratory cheer depending on how we perceive the context and motives of the one doing it. Or, to go back to the film's political subtext, the actions we do to get by in this world, to create a better life for our children, look very different depending on what side of the class divide we occupy.

For more on the films of Jordan Peele see "You'd Be a Beast: Get Out and Race" and "Between Legacy and History: On Jordan Peele's *Nope*."

Seeing Nope at the Bridgton Twin Drive In

Between Legacy and History: On Peele's Nope

Originally written in July of 2022 after seeing Nope at a Drive-In movie theater under a starry sky.

Movie critics love puns; they love working the title into their reviews. So it takes a certain amount of confidence to call a film "Nope". It just invites too many titles for negative reviews, say "Nope to nope" and so on. In the case of Peele that confidence is earned. It is the third movie by a director who is developing his own vision in an era where such things as vision or style, even directors as auteurs, are increasingly obsolete in the age of intellectual property. The title of *Nope* recalls the title of Peele's first film, *Get Out* which was an homage to Eddie Murphy's bit about how a haunted house movie would never work with a black family, they would get out at the first warning

   Just as *Get Out* was about a man, Chris who ignored all the warnings and did not "get out" until it was almost too late, *Nope* is a film about saying yes, about going towards the horror rather than away from it. It seems to me that any attempt to understand the film has to begin with that, why do the characters not just say "nope" and walk away.

Nope is about Otis Jr. or "OJ" (Daniel Kaluuya.) and Emerald "Em" Haywood (Keke Palmer) who, at the beginning of the film, inherit Haywood Hollywood Horses a horse ranch that trains and supplies horses for films, television, and commercials when their father is mysteriously struck and killed by a nickel falling from the sky. Metal objects falling from the sky is the first hint that things are amiss in their little valley, but it is not the beginning of the Haywood family problems. Their family business has been in Hollywood since before there was a Hollywood. Their great great great grandfather was the unidentified jockey in Muybridge's famous footage of a horse galloping. It is a secret legacy, one obscured by the official history which remembers Muybridge but forgets the jockey. The Haywood's have no official claim to any real legacy, OJ and Em still have to work and hustle for every job. He handles the horses and she handles the people, he is the craftsman and she is the salesperson. However, when a horse almost injures an actor on the set of a commercial, all of their skills are quickly replaced with a CGI prop horse. What does a legacy, a connection to the past mean in an industry, and in a country, that is constantly retelling its story, reinventing itself. What do skills mean in an economy that is constantly deskilling, replacing knowledge with technology?

This same question burdens the Haywood's neighbor, Ricky "Jupe" Park (Steven Yeun) a former child star who now runs a wild west show capitalizing on his television role as "Kid Sheriff". Jupe was also the star of a short lived but popular show called *Gordy's Home* that ended after one season when its chimpanzee star, the Gordy of the title, went on a rampage on set and killed and mutilated several of its cast members. Jupe was the only person to be unharmed (at least physically) in the attack. Jupe works with one version of the past, a western theme park, one myth, but hidden behind his office is a museum to the tragic history of the show which might be a more lucrative attraction. A Dutch couple once paid thousands just to sleep in the museum.

Television, or memories of television, play a central part in all of

Peele's films from the commercial for the United Negro College Fund that provides the ironic commentary to *Get Out* to the reference to "Hands Across America" that drives the plot of *Us*. This is because Peele understands that our memories, collective and individual, are made as much by what happens on screens than in the so-called real world. Peele's three films, *Get Out*, *Us*, and *Nope*, can be placed in a progression in terms of these video memories. In the first, *Get Out*, we hear the United Negro College Funds' slogan, "A mind is a terrible thing to waste" in the background just as Chris is about to have his mind wasted; in *Us* the image of hands across America is Adelaide/Red's primary memory and the structure of the tethered's revolution; and in *Nope* Jupe's traumatic memory of Gordy proves to be central to the whole film. Peele weaves together the audience's and characters memories of old commercials, media events, and cheesy sitcoms because these things make up our world as much as the clouds and desert of the valley.

OJ, Em, and Jupe are all linked by the way that they deal with a legacy, with the past. In the case of OJ and Em this legacy was recorded but never credited, no one knows the name of the jockey in the famous pictures that created cinema, they are in some sense erased from history. Without ownership of their legacy they need to create their reputation anew, selling their business and their skills. Jupe on the other hand seems tied to a traumatic past that he can neither escape nor entirely live off of. His niche fame or infamy does not provide enough to live on, but it is what people remember.

When what appears to be an alien spaceship appears in the valley OJ, Em, and Jupe all see it as an opportunity to change their condition. Em and OJ decide to photograph the alien spaceship, to get proof of alien life so incontrovertible that it cannot be contested. Proof of alien life will pay off enough to save the ranch and set them up for life. As they are trying to capture the elusive craft on film it turns out that Jupe has already started to profit off of the visitors, incorporating them into his wild west show. He has been buying horses from OJ and offering them to the alien ship. Jupe makes his offerings in front of a paying audience, exchanging the alien's mysterious desire for horses for a spectacle of an otherworldly being. It appears to be a fair trade, horses for a glimpse at the ship, but how can one understand what an alien understands or wants? *Nope* approaches this question by way of another question, how can we know what a non-human animal understands or wants? Understanding how we would communicate with alien minds is answered by asking how do we communicate with minds that are already other, with animals.

This question is approached from two angles. First, there is the traumatic event of Jupe's past, the day that a seemingly trained chimpanzee was startled by the sound of a balloon popping and went on a rampage, killing and mutilating the cast. Jupe hid under the table and was not only spared in the rampage, but Gordy the Chimp was even about to give him his trademark fist bump before he was shot and killed. From his survival Jupe thinks he understands something about human animal communication, and thus, by proxy, how to communicate with aliens, give them what they want in exchange for something you want. In this case horses for a show. Second, there is OJ who does not presume to understand what horses want, but works from the premise that the first thing you need to understand about animals, and thus aliens, is that you do not see or understand how they do. A horse sees things differently, and to tame the horse, to work with it safely on a set, you have to understand that. To this basic principle OJ adds a second caveat he learned from his father, that some animals don't want to be tamed,

a warning that OJ applies specifically to predators. As he argues you cannot tame a predator, the best you can do is collaborate with it, entering into an uneasy partnership.

SPOILER ALERT: It turns out that the alien spacecraft is not a space craft at all but an alien creature. It is not sucking people and horses up to probe them or capture them for an alien zoo, but sucking them up to eat them. It is a predator. This is why it was not satisfied with the offer of a horse when it could gobble up the whole audience. It cannot be bargained with, but it can be appeased. OJ figures out that the only way to avoid the alien is to avoid looking at it—to not appear to be a threat. Incidentally this, and not the fist bump, may have been what actually saved Jupe when Gordy went on a rampage. Hiding under the table he avoided making eye contact with Gordy. Gordy did not spare him because they were friends, but because he did not look Gordy in the eye, did not appear to be a threat.

OJ's strategy to photograph the alien creature without looking at it is a strategy that ties together the two themes of the film. First, and most immediately what could be considered the problem of different minds. In order to understand a different creature you have to understand how it sees things differently. A balloon is just a balloon to us, but a different creature might see it as a threat (or as potential food). Second, the difference between legacy and history is the difference of seeing. A legacy unseen, or unidentified is not a legacy at all. The characters of *Nope* have all been cast out from the spectacle, Jupe is former child star, OJ and Em have a connection with Hollywood history that was never recognized, even Angel, the tech support staff who helps OJ and Em install their cameras, has been discarded in a way, it turns out his girlfriend broke up with him when she got cast in a show on the CW. Hollywood, the spectacle eats people and spits them out, not unlike the way a space monster eats people and spits out the undigestible bits of metal like coins and keys. The spectacle of Hollywood doesn't need to hunt its prey. They are all desperate to get their legacy back, to get control of their image, to capture what Em refers to as the "Oprah shot," the money shot. The spectacle is not just an image that is alienated and separated from us, but in doing so it takes on a life of its own. Muybridge's clip lives independently of the jockey that is filmed in it, just as Gordy's attack lives on even as it is suppressed by the studio. The spectacle ultimately does not just have a life, an existence independent of its creators. It lives by consuming others. As we see with Jupe, OJ, and Emerald, as well as other characters not mentioned, the desire to capture the spectacle and be the spectacle, to get the "Oprah shot," can become an all-consuming passion. Or, as Antlers Holst puts it to Emerald, "This dream you're chasing, where you end up at the top of the mountain, all eyes on you. It's the dream you never wake up from."

Years ago I remember reading that Jordan Peele planned to make five films about what he referred to as social demons. The first, *Get Out* was generally recognized to be about race the second was *Us*, which I argue is about class. *Nope* cannot be neatly situated as an allegory for a specific social issue, or identity; its theme of a spectacle that engulfs everyone and spits them out could be seen as an allegory for Hollywood. No wonder Peele considers it his most personal film. Peele has managed to somehow create a spectacle, this is his most blockbuster film, without being sucked into its maw. The social demon is the spectacle itself, not just the image separated from its conditions, but the desire to possess or be that image. We do not need to wait for an alien to arrive to see what people will do to capture the spectacle. This demon is everywhere, as the unnamed motorcycle rider asks OJ in the film, "Why aren't you filming this?" The spectacle has escaped the confines of Hollywood to become a universal dream, the idea of capturing the perfect image, our own Oprah shot, has consumed all of life.

For more on the films of Jordan Peele see You'd Be a Beast: Get Out and Race" and "You Will Not Replace Us: On Jordan Peele's Us."

Ape Like Imitation: Repetition and Difference in the Planet of the Apes

First posted August 6, 2011 after a viewing of *Rise of the Planet of the Apes*.

The Hollywood tendency towards repetition, towards reproduction of the same, which reaches its culmination in recent reboots and remakes must, despite itself, confront history. History not in the sense of definite dates and events, but the historicity that defines a moment, its structure of feeling—history at the level of subtext rather than text.

There is perhaps no clearer illustration of this than *The Planet of the Apes*. The first version, the novel by Pierre Boulle, used the figure of the ape to express the fear of an inferior species an imitator that can only "ape" the original eventually overcoming its supposed betters. In this way it was resonate of John Stuart Mill's argument. In *On Liberty Mill* refers to those who do not choose, who only conform, as requiring no other faculty than the ape like one of imitation. This criticism takes on a colonialist tinge when Mill describes China and India as parts of the world that once had innovation and individuality, developing culture long before Europe, but have fallen into stagnation through the dominance of custom. "The greater part of the world has, properly speaking, no history, because the despotism of custom is complete." For Mill custom, ape like imitation, ends innovation. Boulle's novel presents us with apes, apes who possess modern technology, rifles, jeeps, and aircraft, but cannot create it. Thus suggesting that "man," or white man, will one day be overwhelmed by cultures which can only imitate and not create. Imitation destroys the original.

The film, written by Rod Serling, removed this subtext of colonial anxiety replacing it with apocalyptic dread. He replaced the novel's strange ending, restored in the ill-conceived remake by Tim Burton, in which the human astronaut returns to an Earth dominated by apes, to make it set on "Earth all along," a point driven home by the iconic image of the Statue of Liberty buried in the sand. The new subtext is one of a humanity destined to destroy itself, and the rebellion of the youth: as Taylor, the astronaut from our world says to a young ape, "never trust anyone over thirty." The lone human finds himself supported by young idealistic apes, tired of the

authority of the older generation. (The movie also presents a society divided into the military, gorillas; religious and political authority, orangutans; and scientists, chimpanzees). The apes still imitated, but what they imitated was our inability to change, to stubbornly hold to our "sacred scrolls" to the point of destruction.

The apocalyptic dread culminates in the second apocalypse of *Beneath the Planet of the Apes*. After this film, the latter movies in the series, which, thanks to the paradoxes of time travel, are both sequels and prequels, play up the connection with rebellion and counter culture. The first, *Escape from the Planet of the Apes* begins with the sympathetic chimps from the first film traveling back in time in the missing human spacecraft only to arrive at Earth in 1973. While this was probably an ingenious way to deal with the dwindling budgets of the later sequels, it also sets up a narrative where the apes are the sympathetic figures, isolated outcasts rather than dominant species, inverting the book's inverted world. The US government is afraid of the apes, symbols of the decline of man, and eventually decides to kill them and their unborn son as a preemptive strike against the ape's eventual dominance. The parents are killed, the infant survives, and humanity reveals itself to be the monster. The film offers everything that we would expect from a paranoid thriller of the seventies: a secretive government that is not above political assassinations and second sniper.

The opposition to "the man" becomes much more explicit in *Conquest of the Planet of the Apes*. Set in what as at the time the distant nineteen nineties it follows the surviving ape from the future into the prehistory of the first *Planet of the Apes*. It is a world in which apes have already become slaves rather than pets: they work as butlers, hairdressers, and store clerks. There are no scenes of apes working in factories or farms: it is entirely a service based economy where everyone seems to be able to afford their own monkey butler. This is supposed to be efficient and beneficial for the humans, but the film constantly shows the apes to either incompetent or unruly, overturning buffet trays, shrieking from the flames of a fondue set, and grabbing the wrong book from the shelf. In contrast to this unruliness of the apes, there is the docility of the humans: one scene shows a group of out of work human waiters, displaced by the ape based slave economy, peacefully protesting their condition. The film offers an opposite message than it would appear to invoke: slavery proves to be a difficult form of domination, lashes and chains are less effective than an interiorized sense of privilege and belonging. The apes are difficult to dominate precisely because their domination is so overt, and their ignorance of the tasks assigned to them always risks spilling over into insurrection. The movie brings together the primitive accumulation of original domestication with the indignities of service work, drawing a straight line that suggests that civilization is nothing other than obedience. Nature is the original strategy of refusal.

The analogy to the history of slavery and racial oppression is so heavy handed as to cease to be subtext. This is especially true in the case of Macdonald, the Governor's African-American assistant. He is presented as someone who must necessarily be sympathetic with the apes, a point which is first uttered by a group of cops, perhaps as proof of their racism; of course they think that the black man must be sympathetic to the apes, but sooner or later in the film everyone makes this equation. The difference between the enslavement of another species, even a highly intelligent one, and the enslavement of humans is barely mentioned in the film, which is either a testament to its concern for animals or evidence of its confused grasp of race. Nevertheless, the constant invocation of racism and the history of slavery paints a rather brutal picture of human history, a picture underscored by cast of ugly, angry, and petty humans. The Ape's revolution doesn't just condemn their treatment, but all of human history, a history of exploitation and domination. The distrust and hatred of humans that the original *Planet of the Apes* presented as prejudice is now reiterated as fact. Dr. Zaius will have been vindicated.

Given that *Rise of the Planet of the Apes* is a remake, or reimagining, of *Conquest*, albeit without the time travel, the question is how will it rewrite the odd anti-racist racism of the original. The focus is now on genetic engineering and the use of apes as research subjects. The tagline states "Evolution becomes Revolution," placing this film in the subgenre of what could be called "Darwinian" horror: films that try to make the extinction of humanity the object of fear and horror. (other examples of the genre include *The War of the Worlds*, *Species*, and the horrible *Godzilla* remake, films which present the conflict between man and a superior species). Such films could be understood as products of a biopolitical era when it is easier to imagine the extinction of mankind as a species than the end of capitalism, but the equivalence that the tagline sets up between "evolution" and "revolution," biology and politics suggests real confusion of nature and culture that is integral to racist thought. In the earlier Ape films the difference of species did not make much of a difference. Yes the apes were harrier, and walked with a slight hunch, but they were mostly hairy humans with different sets of laws and rules. Their evolution was really more of a revolution, an overthrowing of the oppressor. *Rise* is able to utilize the new digital technologies to give us apes that really move like apes, swinging through trees and over the Golden Gate bridge. In doing so it is able to really capture, in a way the earlier films could not, the feeling of being defeated by a smarter, faster, and stronger species. (The New York Times has suggested that form meets content in this case: the story of genetically altered superior apes is mapped at the level of the form with the digitally created characters of Caesar the ape leader. We are watching the make believe extinction of humanity we are watching the actual obsolescence of the actor.)[1]

Where does *Rise* ultimately stand with respect to subtext? Much of the discussion has stressed the role that animal experimentation plays in the film. People for the Ethical Treatment of Animals (PETA) has even come out in favor of the film. This is true, but it overlooks the fact that the movie is no less critical of zoos, circus, shelters, and even the misguided practice of keeping wild animals in homes,

---

[1] Manhola Dargis, "Looking Apocalypse in the Eye," *New York Times*, August 4, 2011, https://www.nytimes.com/2011/08/05/movies/rise-of-the-planet-of-the-apes-stars-james-franco-review.html

domesticated as little children. (The release of this film overlaps with the release of the documentary *Project Nim*, a film about an attempt to raise an ape as a child. The latter also presents the humans as fundamentally misguided in their attempts to domesticate apes). Caesar's rebellious spirit is cultivated in a seemingly unlikely place, an ape sanctuary, where bureaucracy, indifference, and the banality of daytime soap operas drives him against humanity. (One staff member, who appears to be left over from *Conquest*, repeatedly takes out the frustrations of his menial job on the apes). Ultimately the film suggests that the gulf that separates man and animal is unbridgeable: an uncanny gulf separates us from the apes, the more they look like us, think like us, and are like us, the less we can relate to them. We can place neither in our cages nor our homes (itself a kind of cage).

Both *Conquest* and *Rise* suggest that the similarity that links ape with man will be exploited, as servants in the first film and as research subjects in the second. They are differentiated by their two different ways of imagining exploitation, generalized servitude or the exploitation of information. The latter seems more realistic, after all, medical testing on apes is a reality, but the former is ultimately more satisfying. Scenes in the original *Conquest* resemble a kind of simian *Fight Club*, with the apes acting out every day acts of refusal and sabotage, suggesting that the first film was trying to connect with the frustrations of waiters and shop clerks stuck at home watching "Ape week." The recent film offers no such identification with the day to day exploitation of the apes, unless you have been subject to medical trials. Despite the focus on science, and the generic "playing God" plot, the real incubator of revolutionary activity is the ape sanctuary, a prison of daily humiliations. It greatest success, however, is how much it vastly improves on the earlier film's scenes of apes in revolt. Caesar has often been referred to as a Che Guevera of the apes, but *Rise* really excels at its scenes of tactics; you get to watch as solidarity is developed across the species lines of gorilla, chimpanzee, and orangutan, and then see these alliances put to the test against humans. The final Golden Gate confrontation is a brilliant instance of tactics: if the cops control the streets, control the sky and the ground beneath them.

Finally, the turn towards comic books, old science fiction movies, and other elements of nerd culture as the basis for every summer blockbuster has created a kind of esoteric/exoteric divide in many films. Lines from old films, visual jokes, and other trivia become a kind of secret text, intended for the discriminating eyes and ears of those in the know, while the movie still delivers the explosions and romantic subplots for the masses. *Rise* is riddled with such moments, all of the iconic lines from the original are worked into the script ("bright eyes," "It's a mad house. A mad house," "Take your stinking paws off me, you damned dirty ape,"etc.) and if you look or listen closely you can find references to a missing Icarus spacecraft and a model Statue of Liberty. These are a little distracting, and the movie could have done without them. The movie does offer an interesting little scene during the closing credits (worth sticking around for). The scene is not a set up for a sequel, as we have seen in most summer movies, but a tiny bit of narrative closure, answering the question as to how revolt turns into revolution, how one ape saying "No" could lead to a global transformation. Unfortunately, it is more on the side of evolution than revolution, proving in this case that it is easier to imagine the end of the world than the end of specieism.

The myth of Casear, the ape who stood up to man and said "no," has been central to the Apes films since the beginning. At its best *Rise of the Planet of the Apes* makes that "no," that refusal, necessary and affirmative.

This is the only post on the Apes films reprinted in this book. However, posts on the subsequent films can be found on the Unemployed Negativity blog.

Man is a Wolf to Man: An Appreciation of Wolfen

Posted September 13, 2009.

One could argue that the three classic monsters of American culture are the vampire, zombie, and the werewolf, each handed down by folklore and solidified in popular culture. (I am leaving the Mummy out of this, as well as Frankenstein's monster which is not a generic type, but a specific monster) Of these three the first two are definitely dominant. They not only make up much of the films, comics, and TV shows, but they have proven themselves the most versatile in terms of both the kinds of stories they can tell and what they can symbolize. Vampires are truly polymorphous in their significations. They are situated everywhere that sex intersects with death and fear. Zombies have proven to be much more versatile, symbolizing everything from the drudgery of work to the insatiable desires of consumerism.

Werewolves have lagged behind their cinematic brethren for at least two reasons. The first is purely technical. The werewolf is difficult to pull off, it is hard to combine the figure of the wolf with that of a human in a way that looks both convincing and menacing. The new CGI technologies do not really help either, leaving us with oddly hairless werewolves in the case of the *Underworld* movies. More importantly the werewolf has not proven itself so adept at symbolization, at providing the subtext that makes a horror movie work. There is the general theme of the animal within, but this is almost too literal, too direct, in the case of the werewolf. When it comes to symbolizing unchecked desires, the id within, the vampire and zombie have the market cornered. Vampires have become such versatile symbols of sexuality that they can cover everything from queer identity (*True Blood*) to the fear and desire of a first sexual encounter (*Buffy*). Zombies cover a more inchoate desire or hunger, but one that has been linked to shopping ever since Romero's zombies went to the mall. With sex and consumption covered there is very little left of unchecked desire for the werewolf to symbolize.

However, it is possible to detect a bit of exhaustion with each of the two big figures. When vampires become part of a series of novels about teenage abstinence and when zombies are part of a Woody Harrelson comedy, one has to ask how many more movies can be churned out. It is at this point that our attention turns toward the werewolf as perhaps the next big thing in movies. In order for this to happen the werewolf will have to find its place in some kind of symbolic economy.

This idea, the idea of the monster as symbol, is not sophisticated at all; in fact, one could argue that it constitutes a kind of degree zero of film interpretation, cited by almost anyone who does not know the gaze from the look. That is precisely my interest in it, and in so-called genre films themselves, which demand at least a minimum of interpretation to be viewed at all.

All of this is really a preamble to writing a few words about *Wolfen*. Wolfen was released the year that the werewolf was very much in vogue: *An American Werewolf in London* and *The Howling* were also both released the same year, 1981. Of the three *Wolfen* is perhaps the strangest and most difficult to categorize, which is probably why it is the only narrative film released by its director, Michael Wadleigh (His only other film is a documentary on Woodstock).

The opening scene situates the film within the universe of the post-Watergate paranoid thrillers and the early films of Cronenberg. It is a world in which total and complete surveillance is emerging as a reality, carried out by a global corporation in a sterile and imposing office tower. This corporation, ESS, is responsible for protecting the elite against such forces as the Red Brigades, NAM, and Red Army Faction (all mentioned by name in the film). Caught between these two global forces are the police, city coroner, and a scientist at the city zoo, their dilapidated offices stand in sharp contrast to ultra-sleek interiors of the corporations and super rich. This is very much a film about urban space, about the layers of space as the new city is built over the old. The old city cannot be entirely effaced by the new—the ruins, Native Americans, and wolves remain. The different spaces also constitute a kind of shorthand for the dynamics of power: the powerful inhabit the skyscrapers and the powerless dwell in the derelict spaces of old buildings, the middle ground is made up of small shops and overburdened structures of civil society.

The plot of the movie begins when the wolves (or, as they inexplicably referred to in the film, wolfen) attack and kill a wealthy real estate developer, his wife, and driver. (As something of an aside I should point out that these are wolves, at least in appearance, and not awkward half-wolf/half human creatures that I wrote about above. Their human part comes in through their intelligence, and the suggestion that they were once part of an original tribe of man and wolf, a kind of cross-species primitive communism. In appearance they are indistinguishable from wolves, and are played by wolves in the film) The police and private corporation (ESS) each conduct their investigation of the murders, and from that point forward the film becomes explicitly about what is seen and unseen. This is highlighted in the films primary special effect, a kind of wolf-vision, in which the wolf's perspectives is shown in a kind of pseudo-infrared, seeing in the dark where humans cannot see. Less explicitly, the corporation turns its attention to the usual subjects, various international terrorist groups and even a disgruntled rich daughter, playing at being radical, subjecting them to the latest biometric techniques to distinguish truth from fiction. In contrast to this the cop, Dewey Wilson (played by Albert Finney) teams up with the city coroner (played by Gregory Hines) to investigate the margins of the city, derelict spaces and a Native American bar. All of the different actors of the film are distinguished as much by what they can see as what they look at.

The difference of vision is not just framed in terms of how the two investigation agencies look—the corporation rounding up subjects to place in their high tech monitoring lie detection equipment versus the street smart cop investigating leads—but ultimately in terms of what they see. Wilson's investigation leads to an encounter with a group of Native Americans who have relocated to New York City to work in the construction industry. One of these, Eddie Holt (played by Edward James Olmos), plays the role of informant, explaining to Wilson the origin of the wolves that live at the heart of New York City. As Holt and an elderly native American explain to Wilson.

> Eddie Holt: "It's not wolves, it's Wolfen. For 20,000 years Wilson—ten times your fucking Christian era—the 'skins and wolves, the great hunting nations, lived together, nature in balance. Then the slaughter came. The smartest ones, they went underground into a new wilderness, YOUR CITIES. You have your technology but you lost. You lost your senses."
>
> Elderly Native American: "In their world, there can be no lies, no crimes."
>
> Eddie Holt: No need for detectives.
>
> Elderly Native American: In their eyes, YOU ARE THE SAVAGE.

In the end this how Wilson does not so much solve the crime, but brings the narrative to a close, by recognizing that the savage and brutal attacks that he has been investigating are a kind of justice. He learns to see himself as savage, as outsider, to his own city. The wealthy real estate developer killed in the beginning was planning to convert the wolves' space, the abandoned buildings they live in, hunting the sick and forgotten of the human pack, into condos and commercial development. In the final scene, when Wilson is cornered and surrounded by the wolf pack, he destroys the model of the new real estate development that will replace the ruins where the wolfen live. This is an interesting reversal of the clichéd scene from horror and fantasy movies in which the protagonist has to destroy the magic amulet or some other cursed object in order to destroy the monster: the same magic which created the monster must be destroyed, restoring a natural balance. In this case the monster is us, and what has to be destroyed is not some primitive magic, but a symbol of urban gentrification. In the end what makes the movie interesting is how it solves the problem of the werewolf as symbol and subtext. The wolves are not symbols of some repressed animal nature, but are the return of the repressed, the vengeance of a population subject to genocidal slaughter.

This is the only werewolf film discussed in this book, but reviews of *An American Werewolf in London* and *The Howling* can be found on the blog Unemployed Negativity.

The Primitive Accumulation of Prehistory: On the Jurassic Park films

Originally posted in June of 2018.

As a kid I was obsessed with dinosaurs like a lot of kids. My obsession took place at a time before there was an adequate pop culture outlet for that obsession. It was before the *Jurassic Park* films before even *The Land Before Time* films. So I sought out every dinosaur film I could whenever they played on the afternoon or late night movie, *The Land that Time Forgot*, *The Last Dinosaur*, *Dinosaurus*, etc., These films were hard to come by, and many of them are not very good at all. There is a story told in my family, a legend of sorts, of the night we all ended up in a motel while taking the yearly pilgrimage to visit the grandparents, flipped through channels only to stumble upon a showing of *The Valley of the Gwangi*. Not a great dinosaur film but one that nonetheless benefitted from the work of Ray Harryhausen. It was a different time, one defined by the scarcity of cultural products rather than their proliferation. Dinosaur films were hard to come by, and good ones less so, so a dinosaur obsessed kid took what they could.

There was an interesting diversity of premises in the dinosaur films made during the fifties, sixties, and seventies. The problem of all dinosaur films is the same, how to get prehistoric creatures in the same place and time with humans (that is if one does not just fake prehistory, putting dinosaurs and cavemen in the same film as in the famous *One Million Years B.C.*). One could chart a crude history of solutions to this problem, a history that begins first with an undiscovered island or valley untouched by the progress of evolution, a premise that became increasingly untenable with the mapping of the entire world. Hence the creation of the dinosaur period film, combining dinosaurs and cowboys (*Gwangi* and the far inferior *Beast From Hollow Mountain*) or set during World War One (*The Land that Time Forgot* and *The People that Time Forgot*), all of which takes one back to a time in which one could still believe in an undiscovered island. Or if that did not work the lost world could be moved underground (*Voyage to the Center of the Earth*) or to another planet. (*Planet of Dinosaurs*). (I am working from memory here, but surprisingly time travel did not feature in many of these films at all. Although it did show up in fiction, most notably Ray Bradbury's great short story "The Sound of Thunder" which also functioned as its own argument against future time travel films.) The history of the dinosaur film largely follows the history of colonialism and resource extraction from the "new world" to the north pole and beyond. It is no wonder that Jefferson and the Koch brothers are such big fans of paleontology. W.J.T. Mitchell has written a whole book on the dinosaur as an icon of the modern state and corporation.[1]

The diversity of premises was undermined by a fairly limited, even repetitive cast of dinosaurs. Almost all of them featured a Tyrannosaurus Rex, or as it is known today T-Rex, as the star. With a triceratops, pterodactyl, and a few others rounding out the cast. Dinosaurs were an interesting cultural creation, caught someplace between real creatures and fantastic monsters. As cultural creations

---

[1] W.J.T. Mitchell, *The Last Dinosaur Book: The Life and Times of a Cultural Icon*, Chicago, University of Chicago, 1998.

they belonged to a kind of common culture, at least to children in the twentieth century. The T-Rex could show up anywhere from the museum to the movies; it was famous, but belonged to no one.

In thinking about *Jurassic Park* I found a passage from Michael Crichton on the film's IMDB page that explicitly cites the fame, or as the say nowadays, brand recognition of the dinosaur as part of the impetus for the original novel. As Crichton states

> "I went to a museum and they had this sideshow. There was a little boy who couldn't have been more than six. His feet didn't even touch the ground. Each time they showed a dinosaur he would shout, "Tyrannosaurus!" "Stegosaurus!". He did that for an hour and I thought, "What is it about dinosaurs that's so fascinating?" That's when I decided to write "Jurassic Park".

It is hard not to think of this as some kind of "eureka" moment, the discovery not of some fossil or oil reserve, but of a massive untapped cultural reserve.

Jurassic Park can first be understood as first and foremost an updating of the specific genre problem of the dinosaur film. Genetic manipulation becomes the new frontier to be explored and commodified. The mapping of the genome makes possible what the mapping of the earth precluded, the return of dinosaurs into our world. The diegetic technical innovation is coupled with the technical innovation that made the film possible. It would not be the last time that genetic manipulation and computer generated imagery would combine as two faces of the informatics of domination, one on the screen and the other behind the scenes. If the original *Jurassic Park* is notable for anything it is for its effects; situated between the fall of animatronic practical effects and the rise of the digital effects it hit a kind of sweet spot in which the two ways of producing effects were combined. The end result is more convincing than stop motion but without the video game feel of the modern digital effects.

I would also suggest that the original Jurassic Park film can be situated with the predominance of the "Set piece" filmmaking.

The term Spielbergian has been used to mean many things, the schmaltzy family connections, the commodification of a particular brand of childlike wonder, etc., but I would argue it is also the fragmentation of the film into a series of memorable set pieces held together by the thinnest of plots (themselves usually about family connections). Spielberg's films almost seem to be designed to be stumbled upon on cable, watched for the big exciting scenes, like the T-Rex escape, only to resume flipping channels once the scene has ended. There are only a few Spielberg films that I would even consider watching again from beginning to end, *Raiders of the Lost Ark*, *Jaws*, and *Close Encounters of the Third Kind*. The rest just seem like the whole is lesser than its parts. I barely remember his *War of the Worlds* remake, but I would watch that attack on the ferry again. I know that Michael Bay has been associated with fragmentation and chaos, but Spielberg is in some sense the prehistory of the destruction of attention. This maybe as much a reflection of the changing mediascape, which is defined less by scarcity than by an overabundance of options, as it is the films themselves.

Jurassic Park can also be understood as a kind of nostalgia film, one that mines the childhood fascination with dinosaurs in the same way other films extract value from the recognized figures of Transformers and the USS Enterprise. Unlike other nostalgia films which cash in on a particular cartoon, comic book, or toy line that belongs to a media conglomerate, *Jurassic Park* cashes in on something generic, earth's common natural history. I remember reading that this was a challenge for the inevitable marketing of toys and other tie-ins for the first film. Unlike Transformers or stormtroopers anyone can sell a toy T-Rex (the German company Schleich makes a great one that is sold at many museums). *Jurassic Park* countered this by placing a conspicuous JP brand on every toy, and ran commercials encouraging kids to look for the specific JP brand on their dinosaur toys. The films and their marketing campaign are an attempt to make natural history a specifically branded experience, part of a different sort of empire. To some extent this worked; despite its success there have been remarkably few dinosaur movies since the creation of *Jurassic Park*. What had limited success at the level of toys has succeeded at the level of films. If you want to see dinosaurs, even ones created by computers and rubber, you have to go to *Jurassic Park*.

With the later sequels this particular problem of branding moves from marketing to the interior of the film itself, becoming an integral part of the plot. Much of the plot of the recent films concerns the park creating its own dinosaurs. Something confusing at the level of narrative given the expanding number of dinosaurs to draw from. The created dinosaurs solve two problems, one external and one internal to the films. First, given that the creations are products of artistic directors, special effects artists, and toy marketers and not paleontologists and museums, I am sure that they are wholly owned intellectual properties of Universal and Amblin Entertainment. Anyone call sell a toy T-Rex but an Indominus Rex is always going to be Jurassic Park brand. The genetically modified dinosaurs, the Indominus Rex and Indoraptor, also solve another problem internal to the films, splitting the monster from the animal. Of course every film that tries to make an actual animal into a cinematic monster comes up against such difficulties. It is hard to explain why an animal would continue to pursue and kill humans with such dedication when there are other sources of food. Animals are not serial killers. This becomes even more difficult with the dinosaur, which unlike the shark is loved as much as it is feared. In the latter films the genetically modified monster becomes the villain and the actually existing dinosaurs become if not the hero then at least sympathetic. One recurring element of the films is to have the T-Rex save the day without necessarily intending to (or at the very least devour an unscrupulous executive on the way out). The dinosaur is both an object of fear and fascination.

If there is anything good to be said about the latest film, *Jurassic World: Fallen Kingdom* it is that it these two solutions turn against each other. While every *Jurassic Park* film is set up against a commons and the privation of that commons, dinosaurs as a part of cultural history and natural history on the one hand and the *Jurassic Park* branded dinosaur experience on the other, the most recent film makes this opposition explicit, becoming a kind of self-criticism. The dinosaurs just want to be left alone to return to some sort of natural world, and the villains want to weaponize and monetize them to make them something profitable. The film's villains are the ones who want to contain, brand, and market everything, and the human protagonists are the ones who ultimately want to smash the cages and let everything escape.

On this last point we can draw a parallel with the other Michael Crichton story being remade, *Westworld*. Both *Westworld* and *Jurassic Park* began with the (same) nightmare scenario of a theme park gone amok, with the robots and dinosaurs escaping, but both have ended on the same point with the creatures (artificial lifeforms) escaping the park altogether, now considered less a nightmare than a necessary, perhaps even utopian, salvation. The old adage that "we have met the enemy and it is us" has its necessary corollary the recognition that our monsters might just be our salvation.

Updated 6/9/2022

My tendency to click unto the latest news about dinosaurs eventually caught up with me to the point that I started to see ads for dinosaur toys from Schleich. The striking thing is that it seems that the company has responded to Jurassic Park's attempt to contain the paleontological commons. They have made a toy of every dinosaur featured in the recent films, Mosaurus, Pachycephalosaurus, and even the Gigantosaurus from the yet to be released new film. In this way they have turned the tables on the film's logic of commodification, using them for advertising of some new and unpopular dinosaurs. They have even created their own Dino Park set. To paraphrase the films, commodification finds a way. The tendency for one company to own collective imagination is countered by capitalist competition. Just as Jurassic Park cannot own the images of dinosaurs they cannot copyright the idea of a dinosaur theme park.

For more on animals in horror check out "Live Every Week Like it is Shark Week: Remarks on the Ecology of the Mediasphere."

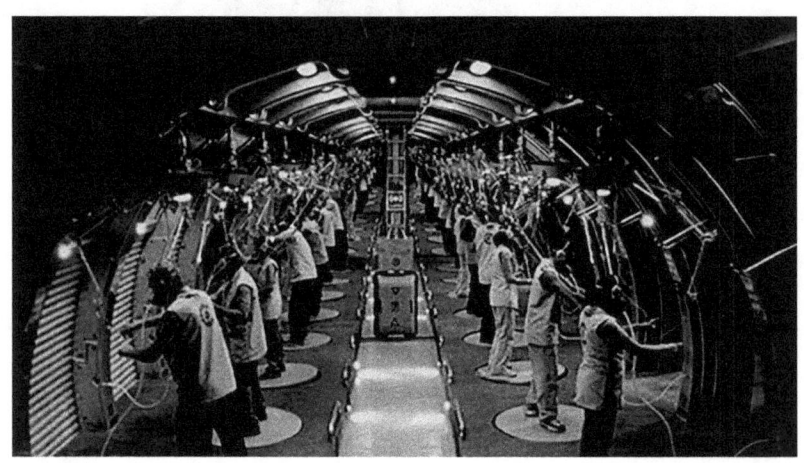

Violence and the Common: Truth is Structured Like a (Science) Fiction

First published October 1, 2009.

It has been said that every generation invents its own Marx: imperialism, alienation, commodity fetishism, and living labor have all at one time or another occupied center stage as different texts by are discovered and rediscovered against the vicissitudes of different struggles. If this is true, then it could be argued that the Marxist themes that define the present are violence and the common. The first, violence, is primarily examined through the concluding chapters of *Capital* on primitive accumulation. Although this is not the only point of reference, the overt violence of primitive accumulation has also made possible a renewed examination into the structural violence of capital, the anonymous violence of day-to-day exploitation. While the second, the common appears first and foremost as the commons, as the commonly held resources, such as land and woods, that primitive accumulation destroys. It is also not limited to that historical reference, however, there is also a reading of the common that works through the concept of species being and Marx's writing on cooperation in the factory to articulate a different sense of the common. Not the common as a thing, but potentialities and relations internal to subjectivity.

As it has been indicated above these two concepts often appear together: violence, the violence of primitive accumulation is aimed against the common, in the sense of the new enclosures. However, they do not always appear together. Althusser's aleatory materialism is in part based on a reading of the contingent (and overdetermined formation of capitalism in primitive accumulation), but does not develop an understanding of the common. Alternately, much of the writing on the common in the works of Paolo Virno and others, does not consider it in relation violence, at least the constitutive violence of primitive accumulation. Beyond this distinction, there is the difference of level of the specific philosophical engagement and conceptualization, what could be considered, for lack of a better word, abstraction. Sometimes these themes of primitive accumulation and the common are considered on a register that is primarily sociological or economic: this is the case in David Harvey's writing on "accumulation by dispossession" and De Angelis writing on the commons and "new enclosures." In other contexts, however, primitive accumulation is not so much the basis for theorizing neoliberalism, as it is the condition for a meditation on contingency, violence, and social relations. The same could be said about the common, which is sometimes used to refer to the environment or the knowledge commons of the internet, and is sometimes used to refer to subjective possibilities, the capacity to constitute relations through language, affects, and habits. The common is figured both as a way of thinking about resources, natural or artificial, or a way of thinking about the transindividual conditions of individuation. It is simultaneously concrete and abstract. I do not see this last point as a limitation, far from it. In fact, it seems that there is a constant movement within various Marxisms where concepts are constantly extended beyond their strictly socio-economic register to become general philosophical provocations: alienation, labor, reification, and commodity fetishism all have been extended or generalized in this way. This movement, from specificity to abstraction, duplicates Marx's own theoretical production, which Etienne Balibar has described as simultaneously going beyond and falling short of philosophy. Going beyond philosophy in subjecting philosophy itself to a criticism that historicizes its supposed eternal truths: falling short in that its must stunning philosophical pronouncements, about the nature of history, experience, and practice, are often asserted in the midst of social and historical analysis without context or clarification.[1]

The full ramifications of these concepts, as well as an explanation as to why they appear now (what is it about the present that makes the common and primitive accumulation appear as necessary points of reference?) will have to wait. I merely indicate this now as a provocation and reminder.

However, it struck me that the film *Sleep Dealer* serves as interesting illustration of at least some of these ideas, most specifically the relation between the two sense of the common, the commons as resource and the common as communicative relation. The film takes place in Mexico in the not too distant future. The first thing that we learn about this future is the water, the water that would irrigate crops, is no longer a free-flowing resource, part of the ecological commons, but a privately held and sold resource. In the beginning of the film we see Memo, the protagonist, and his father walk up a dry riverbed in order to purchase water. We learn that these privately owned water-reservoirs are protected by unmanned drones; these drones are controlled by high-tech workers in the US, who are hardwired into their machines. One of the movies best satirical moments has to do with the reality based TV show that follows these drones as they protect property. The show is modeled after such programs as America's Most Wanted, with an enthusiastic and smiling love of authority and violence. In the meantime Memo

---

[1] Etienne Balibar, *The Philosophy of Marx*, Translated by Chris Turner, New York: Verso, 2017, 4.

desires to be connected to the larger digital world, running a pirate connection to the global digital network in his garage.

It is a world of virtual connections and real borders: workers in the US send drones to police water and other properties, while workers in Mexico provide the intellectual and affective component to machines in the US. They are prevented from crossing into the US by a giant wall, the sort that now only exists in right wing fantasies. As one character in the film describes the situation, it is what the US always wanted "work without workers." The two sources of precarious labor, automation and global outsourcing coexist as mechanization makes it possible for workers across borders to provide the small bit of intelligence and care that cannot be automated.

What makes the film interesting is the way that it explores the relation between the physical borders, defending nation and property, and virtual connections. Memo meets a woman who considers herself a writer. A writer in this future is one who uploads their memories, thoughts, feelings, and desires, up onto a network where they can be purchased by anyone. They are not exactly common, since they are bought and sold, but they are not private either. I do not want to give too much of the film away, but ultimately the plot concerns the relation between these two senses of the common: the first, the commons of resources that are privately owned and the second, which despite being owned, still circulates and has effects.

If film is, as Fredric Jameson argued, a kind of cognitive mapping of the present, the *Sleep Dealer* does a good job of illustrating a world that is simultaneously more disconnected, divided by borders and divisions, and more connected than we often think.

For more on "Primitive Accumulation" see The Original Sin of Accumulation: Trying to Say Something Original About Ursprüngliche Akkumulation.

How Can It Not Know What It Is? On Blade Runner 2049

Originally posted in October of 2017.

I think that I may have grown up watching *Blade Runner*. I do not mean that I watched the film several times growing up, although that is probably the case, but something happened when I first watched it that was integral to growing up. All of this is because I grew up, in the first sense, watching Harrison Ford play a hero; *Star Wars* and *Raiders of the Lost Ark* were a big part of my childhood imagination. I had the toys and I am sure I went as Indiana Jones one Halloween. So when I saw *Blade Runner* for the first time, I think on VHS, I expected the same comic book morality of good versus evil and the same wisecracking character (Let's just be honest and admit that Han Solo and Indiana Jones are basically the same character). The movie both thwarted and ultimately exceeded my expectations: in its failure to live up to my genre expectations it helped redefined what made a good film. I do not think that I could watch films again in the same way; incidentally, I am fairly sure that it was my attempt to see the film on the big screen a few years later that drew me to my local art house theater, the Cleveland Cinematheque. It is not just that *Blade Runner* has a formal connection to film noir and larger film world, for me it had an anecdotal one as well.

I am not going to rehash all of the ways in which *Blade Runner* subverts the standards of the science fiction action film. They have been pointed out elsewhere, but suffice to say, when Deckard, the hard-boiled anti-hero, is not getting his ass kicked, he is shooting unarmed (android) women in the back as they run away. I am not going to rehash those points in part because I want to make a different point, a point that seems worth making in a series of movies about the manufacture of memories, and that has to do with this overlap between memory and history, between experience and pop culture. Far from a crude division between things we directly experience (or the primary and secondary retentions that make up memory) and things that we consume through the countless mediations of words, images, sounds, and screens (or tertiary retentions) it is perhaps more accurate to say that experience is the intersection of the two. It is not just childhood we experience or the *Star Wars* trilogy, but a childhood framed by *Star Wars* (the original trilogy or prequels). Generational difference that define our attachment to particular cultural commodities are in part effects of when and at what age we first encounter something. Or, to make a point derived in part from Bernard Stiegler, generations are defined less by some passage through the years as parents beget children than their place with respect to the periodization of different cultural products. How else could someone like the *Star Wars* prequels, or the original for that matter. I remember hearing someone say once with respect to Walter Benjamin, nostalgia is just memory of a prior stage of commodification. Part of what we like about these films from our childhood is not just that they remind us of our naive past, but of a simpler time of cultural production.

All of this might just be a preamble to say that any sequel would necessarily fail to meet my expectations: just as there is no *Star Wars* film that could possibly recreate seeing the first one at seven, there is no *Blade Runner* sequel that could recreate having my definitions of heroism and what a film could do challenged at thirteen.

There is sometimes a crude dialectic to sequels when they do not try to repeat the original; if the first one travels back in time, the second will travel into the future and so on, creating difference in the crudest possible terms. There is a little of that in *Blade Runner 2049*. Where the first film gave us what might be a human hunting replicants the second gives us a replicant searching for what might be a human. (This change further underscores the fact that blade runner is basically a slave hunter, "retiring" beings that are defined more as property than living things. As Grégoire Chamayou demonstrates, historically slave hunters were often drawn from the very population they were meant to patrol[1].) At a deeper level the first film presented us with a replicant that believed she was real because of fake memories, while the second gives us a replicant who believes he is fake because of real memories. Or, rather, he is aware that memories are implanted and thus understands his own memory, his subjectivity to be made rather than formed. Sticking with these crude reversals, and holding off on the spoilers for a bit, the most interesting reversal has to do with the Voight-Kampff test.

In the first film this was the machine that separated human from replicant, marking humanity through emotional intelligence. No such test exists thirty years later, as replicants have become more sophisticated, living long enough to develop their own emotional intelligence. This does not mean that the test, or a variant of it has disappeared, however, the replicant cop, K (Ryan Gosling) must regularly report to be tested by a kind of device that measures his emotional baseline. Emotional intelligence functions less as a law, drawing a divide between human and nonhuman, but as a norm, as something that must be continually reinforced. Whereas the first film presented a sharp division between human and replicant, the sequel is more complex. There are different generations of replicants, with different abilities to obey or disobey, and replicants are not the only artificial life.

---

1 Grégoire Chamayou, *Manhunts: A Philosophical History*, Translated by Steven Rendall, Princeton: Princeton University, 2012.

Perhaps the most interesting aspect of the film concerns the relationship between K, the replicant, and JOI his artificial companion. JOI appears as a hologram, first limited to K's apartment and later, through a portable projector, able to travel with K. She is advertised as "Everything You Want to Hear/Everything You Want to See," and provides the complete "girlfriend experience" performing both emotional labor and sex work. The question with her, as with the replicants, is how much of her is program and how much is her own initiative. She seems willing to risk her own well-being to assist K, but of course her constant devotion and care could be "everything you want to hear," exactly what she was designed to do, or it could be an autonomous action, a bond between AI and android.

This is a high tech version of the paradox of "emotional labor," the labor of bartenders, baristas, and exotic dancers: it is expected, demanded, and in some sense programmed, but must always appear as freely undertaken, as autonomous. We all know that the barista at our local coffee place must smile and laugh at everyone's dumb joke, but we delude ourselves into believing that he or she is laughing at our jokes, that we are truly "liked" by the people we pay to act friendly towards us. "More human than human" is not just the Tyrell company motto, but everyday life under the regime of affective and caring labor. We are constantly confronted with people who are friendlier to us than we deserve, greeting our gruff indifference with friendly smiles and courteous service, but these people are for the most part barely seen as people to us. More human than human is never far from than less than human. Perhaps we need a Voight-Kampff test for day to day life, to navigate the confusing world of emotional labor, and remind us that there are people underneath those smiles. Perhaps someone can design an app.

The relationship between an android, or replicant, and AI is perhaps the most interesting aspect of the film, suggesting a kind of solidarity amongst different exploited nonhumans, but unfortunately it is fairly marginal. All of the allegories about labor and exploitation, of nonhuman subjectivity, is dropped in favor of a religious metaphor and the reproduction of family bonds—the thermidor of contemporary film. This is perhaps what the sequel shares with the original. The truly interesting stuff is at the margins.

To return to the themes of memories, both manufactured and lived, that I started with, the second film picks up where much of the speculation about the first film, at least the director's cut leaves off, with a question of a memory: is it fabricated or real? As I suggested at the outset, I found myself asking the same questions about my memories of the first film. The answer is both, that all our most treasured memories are both invented and real, part of our experience and part of the cultural industry, but you really can't expect a film to breakdown that wall.

One last aside, the digital recreated Rachel that appears at the end, looking just like Sean Young in the original is not new, we have seen digital restored youth (and life) before, Carrie Fisher and Peter Cushing in *Rogue One*, but this is the first time form matched content.

For more on Grégoir Chamayou see "Put a Drone on it: Chamayou's Theory of a Drone".

Avenge Me: The Avengers and the Culture Industry

Originally posted May 12, 2012.

I did not think that I was going to write anything about *The Avengers*. This is partly because I am too busy writing, book writing, to really do much blogging, but also because I did not think anything of it. I enjoyed, but I did so in a kind of moment of absolute regression. The Hulk smashed things, Thor wielded his hammer, humorous quips were uttered, and things went boom. To quote Adorno, "It is no coincidence that cynical American film producers are heard to say that their pictures must take into consideration the level of eleven-year-olds. In doing so they would very much like to make adults into eleven-year-olds."[1] On that level the film succeeded, I felt exactly like I did leafing through marvel comics at Comics Closet or reading comics in the back of the bus with Chip Carter.

To continue this line of thought of Adorno's on the culture industry and regression a little more, one easy criticism of the film is to say that it is the culmination of the culture industry's tendency to

---

1 Theodor Adorno, "The Culture Industry Reconsidered," in *The Culture Industry*. Edited and Translated by J.M. Bernstein. (New York: Routledge, 1991) Pg.105.

turn everything into an advertisement of itself. Books become adds for movies, movies for soundtracks, soundtracks for videogames, etc. everything exists just to advertise something else. *The Avengers* takes this to a new level, starting with *Iron Man* in 2008 there have a series of films with cameos and post-credit scenes that have built up to this film. One is reminded of Jameson's remarks about the "becoming-film" of previews. As Jameson writes,

> "Now the preview is obliged, not merely to exhibit a few images of the stars and a few samples of the high points, but virtually to recapitulate all the plot's twists and turns, and to preview the entire plot in advance. At length, the inveterate viewer of these enforced coming attractions (five or six of them preceding every feature presentation and replacing the older kind of shorts) is led to make a momentous discovery: namely, that the preview is really all you need. You no longer need to see the 'full' two-hour version (unless the object is to kill time)."[2]

The films leading up to *The Avengers* are a kind of reversal of this, a becoming preview of film, as the films exist to promote the next film, all leading up to *The Avengers*. Although the crucial scenes are often after the credits, creating a kind of atmosphere of esoteric dedication. (As an aside, it is worth noting how much Jameson's remark could be "historicized." In the case of films like *The Avengers* we now have previews for previews. The preview as cultural form has only expanded since Jameson's remarks were written, a transformation that would have to be read against the changing dynamics of financial capital).

The Avengers can be viewed as the culmination of this tendency of cross platform marketing. However, there are two exceptions. First, since the Jameson quote comes from an essay on finance capital, the dominant trend in blockbuster filmmaking has been a kind of "pump and dump" strategy. A film is hyped through every possible

---

[2] Fredric Jameson, The Cultural Turn: Selected Writings on the Postmodern 1983-1998, (New York: Verso,) pg. 155

means, opens on several thousand screens, and makes big money before the critical response and word of mouth can sink it the next weekend after which it is replaced by a new film, and so on. It is a cycle of boom and bust. In contrast to this strategy, the whole idea of spending four years building up a film, a film that would them become the basis of future films is at least a "long con," if not a long term investment. Second, and perhaps more importantly, as much as it is possible to see this cross-branding as a culmination of movie advertising, it also reflects the medium of comics. Comics, especially Marvel comics, are as much about a "universe," to borrow Nick Fury's line, as they are about individual characters. *The Avengers* can thus be seen as comic book movie more than a superhero movie. It is less about a "hero's journey" and more about envisioning a world where Norse gods trade blows and insults with super soldiers. It translates the intertextual references long familiar to comic book readers onto the big screen. When the film references Hydra, the Tesseract, or the Hulk's adventures in New York, one can almost see the footnotes that dotted the pages of Marvel comics or hear Stan Lee's voice reminding us of the previous films. Of course this construction of a universe was always a marketing strategy as well, as anyone who got to their favorite issue of *X-Men*, *Daredevil*, or *Avengers* only to find out that story was continued in some other comic, can attest.

However, it still seems that *The Avengers* can be seen through this intersection of marketing form and pulp culture content. This can be seen in the selection of Joss Whedon as the director, a choice with little commercial viability (two canceled shows, a marginally successful movie) but a great deal of fan dedication (cult hits, blogs, and t-shirts). Much of the fan dedication is based on the fact that Whedon appears to be a fan himself, a comic book film director who reads comics. It makes sense that the general cultural reversal in which TV are the new movies would also include its own auteurs, television creators such as Joss Whedon, David Simon, Matt Weiner, etc. who are discussed and studied according to their styles.

What is interesting about the selection of Whedon, that this movie follows his much delayed *Cabin in the Woods*, which could be viewed as an allegory of filmmaking. In that film a group of men huddled over surveillance monitors, pressing buttons and twisting dials to construct scenes that would please unseen gods. It just so happened that what these gods wanted were the clichés of the horror film, nubile hypersexualized teens pursued by monsters. *The Avengers* also has its almost unseen rulers, "The Council" and a group of men huddled over monitors in a helicarrier. The exchanges between Nick Fury and the Council end up being about the structure of the film. The Council wants to deal with the alien threats through superior technology, while Fury prefers to assemble his team of Avengers. The exchange where the Council express concern about his group of isolated weirdos sounds like an investors meeting a Disney. "We're putting everything behind a movie about a Norse god, WWII hero, and robot man?" *The Avengers* often wears its construction on its sleeve. The big cathartic moment, the moment that gives the avengers something to avenge, turns out to be orchestrated onscreen as much as off. The same can be true for the big final showdown. These meta-moments often take the form of debates between Nick Fury, who discusses the ideals of heroism and the need for proper motivation, and the Council, which prefers the efficiency of technology. It is hard not to see these as externalizations of the film's pitch meetings. The film externalizes the conflict between comic book geek turned director and movie studio. The final post credit scene which includes an hidden Easter Egg about Thanos the comic book villain is in this case a kind of victory of the former over the latter.

Beyond this meta-angle, the film is mostly a comic book brought to the screen. There have been attempts to argue that it is the first post 9/11 movie.[3] I think it perhaps more interesting to look at the way it normalizes some of the trends of the post 9/11 era, namely torture and surveillance. The first doesn't take place in the film, even

---

3 J. Hoberman, "The Avengers: Why Hollywood is No Longer Afraid to Tackle 9/11," *The Guardian*, May 11, 2012. https://www.theguardian.com/film/2012/may/11/avengers-hollywood-afraid-tackle-9-11

though the whole film could be understood to be a ticking tesseract scenario, but it is constantly implied or assumed. There are several allusions to it, from the scene that introduces Black Widow, to Loki's time aboard the helicarrier. Although to be fair, Thor refuses to torture his brother (and ultimately returns him to Asgard to face some kind of intergalactic criminal court), suggesting that the basic structures of criminal justice have at least not eroded on Asgard. More interesting is the way the film deals with surveillance. *The Dark Knight* made total surveillance a central object of its plot, and ethical hand wringing: Batman only agreed to its use in a "state of exception" to stop the Joker, destroying the technology afterwards. *The Avengers* has a scene where a Shield agent matter of factly states that they are scanning every possible camera, cellphones, laptops, etc. to find the whereabouts of Loki. Total surveillance has become the backdrop. One could take this a bit further and argue that the film's central tactical political debate, should threats be dealt with by group of highly skilled individuals or by superior technology and firepower, can be understood as some afterimage of military strategy post 9/11. However, I was too distracted by the Hulk smashing things to really follow that logic.

For More on the Adorno's Theory of the Culture Industry see The Use and Abuse of Blockbusters for Life: Movies and Memes in the Age of Viral Collapse. For more on superhero films see Becoming Spider-Man: Deleuze and the Superhero Film.

The vibe at all the restaurants reopening

The Use and Abuse of Blockbusters for Life: Movies and Memes in the Age of Viral Collapse

Written in the summer of 2020 during the first year of Covid and the brief lockdowns.

Lately, I have been considering a hopelessly naive question, namely: What is popular culture for? Or, more to the point how does it function for us as culture, as a way to make sense of the world and express our desires. I have been prompted by this question by two unrelated events. First, I am currently preparing a Freshman Seminar on Politics and Culture which has me reviewing some of the classic arguments about the use and abuse of culture from Williams to Adorno and De Certeau. Second, and more immediately, when I am not working on this course or doing anything productive, I am doing what nearly everyone is doing and that is trying to figure out what movie or TV show might pass the time of lockdown.

Or, more to the point, I have tried to ask myself how to best past the time. Sometimes I just want to be distracted (I watched the entire run of *The Prisoner* and some old *Star Trek*), and sometimes I want to think a little about this current moment but a distance, through the safety of mediations (I guess *The Plot of Against America* counts as the latter, but I have avoided any attempt to really think about pandemics and apocalypses in the present moment. I can't bring myself to watch *Contagion* right now). It is hard enough to stumble into some plot line that brings me crashing into the present. The viral infection subplots of *The Host* and *Dawn of the Planet of the Apes* were a bit difficult to watch at this moment, especially the opening credits of the latter which depicts a virus leading to large scale social collapse. All of which is to say that I found myself asking a question that usually goes unasked when just watching a movie to pass time on a plane or to pass an evening; namely, what do I want from popular culture? Is it just a matter of distraction? Or should it be something more, something that helps us confront all of those things that are coming at us faster than ever—fear, anxiety, social upheaval, loss, and even death.

To put things rather simply, one aspect of Horkheimer and Adorno's critique of the "culture industry" is that the imperatives of mass production and profit produce a "culture" that is not one, does not offer us anything that would be meaningful or sustaining. As the following passages illustrate,

> The pre-digested quality of the product prevails, justifies itself and establishes itself all the more firmly in so far as it constantly refers to those who cannot digest anything not already pre-digested. It is baby-food: permanent self-reflection based upon the infantile compulsion towards the repetition of needs which it creates in the first place."[1]

> "Culture, in the true sense, did not simply accommodate itself to human beings; but it always simultaneously raised a protest against the petrified relations under which they lived, thereby honoring them. Insofar as culture becomes wholly assimilated to and integrated in those petrified relations, human beings

---

[1] Theodor Adorno, *The Culture Industry*, Edited and Translated by J.M. Bernstein, (New York: Routledge, 1991), pg. 67

are once more debased. Cultural entities typical of the culture industry are no longer also commodities, they are commodities through and through."[2]

"What might be called use value in the reception of cultural commodities is replaced by exchange value; in place of enjoyment there are gallery-visiting and factual knowledge: the prestige seeker replaces the connoisseur. The consumer becomes the ideology of the pleasure industry, whose institutions he cannot escape. One simply "has to" have seen Mrs. Miniver, just as one "has to" subscribe to Life and Time. Everything is looked at from only one aspect: that it can be used for something else, however vague the notion of this use may be. No object has an inherent value; it is valuable only to the extent that it can be exchanged."[3]

    If this seems too extreme, which is almost always the accusation when it comes to Horkheimer and Adorno, then think of the commonly used phrase "[Blank] holds up" when revisiting some old film or show, the surprise that there was something there, some use, long after a given film circulates as the "must see" event of the moment. Culture becomes not just a commodity, but a kind of currency something that is exchanged every time we make small talk, or log onto social media. We use it only in exchanging it, and if we lack currency, if we do not know the latest bit of culture, we are cast out of the marketplace, left for broke. This circulation, the exchange value, comes at the expense of any use value, any taste (to use the baby food analogy). It is in turning to social media that we see a different use, something other than just circulation or exchange. I am thinking specifically of the memes and other jokes that repurpose plot points from films in order to do something other than just circulate the currency, they debase it, or at the very least puts it to use with a different value.

---

2 Ibid., pg. 100.
3 Max Horkheimer and Theodor Adorno, *Dialectic of Enlightenment: Philosophical Fragments*. Translated by Edmund Jephcott. (Stanford: Stanford University, 2002) Pg. 128.

I am thinking specifically of memes that have used Hollywood blockbusters, specifically *Alien* and *Jaws* to make sense of, and comment on, the government response to the COVID-19 pandemic. With respect to *Alien* some of these memes, such as the one directly above, just cite original dialogue and plot points that take on new significance in an age of lockdowns and quarantine. While others, like the one at the top of the post, begin to suggest a different reading of the film, one that focuses less on the alien of the film's title as the villain than the corporation that sends the crew of the Nostromo after it. The assertion that the "crew is expendable" takes on new meaning and relevance at a time when people are returning to work in the midst of a pandemic. We are all onboard the Nostromo now, worried about the bonus situation and considered expendable in the eyes of our employers.

While Boris Johnson, in the most bizarrely on brand misreading of popular culture, labels Mayor Vaughn a hero, the rest of us see the Mayor as the embodiment of every politician that puts the maintenance of profits and capital above the preservation of life, which is to say every politician.[4] The focus on the mayor as the figure of evil in the film offers a different reading than the more ideological one that Fredric Jameson initially argued for in his interpretation. Jameson, reading the film against the novel, focuses on the way in which the survival of Brody and Hooper at the expense of Quint posits a changing version of America. As Jameson argues:

---

4 Stuart Heritage, "Boris Johnson's Hero is the Mayor Who Kept the Beaches Open. That's fine by Me." *The Guardian*, March 13, 2020. https://www.theguardian.com/film/2020/mar/13/boris-johnson-coronavirus-hero-mayor-larry-vaughn-jaws

"Now the content of the partnership between Hooper and Brody projected by the film may be specified socially and politically, as the allegory of an alliance between the forces of law-and order and the new technocracy of the multinational corporations: an alliance which must be cemented, not merely by its fantasized triumph over the ill-defined menace of the shark itself, but above all by the indispensable precondition of the effacement of that more traditional image of an older America which must be eliminated from historical consciousness and social memory before the new power system takes its place. This operation may continue to be read in terms of mythic archetypes, if one likes, but then in that case it is a Utopian and ritual vision which is also a whole—very alarming—political and social program. It touches on present-day social contradictions and anxieties only to use them for its new task of ideological resolution, symbolically urging us to bury the older populisms and to respond to an image of political partnership which projects a whole new strategy of legitimation; and it effectively displaces the class antagonisms between rich and poor which persist in consumer society (and in the novel from which the film was adapted) by substituting for them a new and spurious kind of fraternity in which the viewer rejoices without understanding that he or she is excluded from it."[5]

Jameson sees himself as offering a dialectical corrective to Horkheimer and Adorno's point. The culture industry has to have some use, offer us something useful other than the references we exchange in small talk. We would not eat even baby food unless it offered us something to taste or digest, some utopian content, in the form of a resolution of existing contradictions and conflicts. That utopian dimension is itself distorted and reified to the point where we find ourselves cheering for the sacrifice of Quint in the face of the new Hooper/Brody alliance, the technocratic and police order.

---

5 Fredric Jameson, *Signatures of the Visible*, (New York; Routledge, 1992) pg. 38.

The focus on the Mayor is a figure of the brutal insistence on the profit motive is a less sophisticated reading, but it is also one with a different political aspect. It is no longer about the alliance of technocracy and police becoming a new force of order, but the way in which the alliance of business and politics is the order that we all live under even in the good old days of small town America (something that becomes all the more clear as the film drops the book's subplot about mafia corruption).

These memes are less a detournement of these film's original meaning than a change of emphasis. *Jaws* and *Alien* were always as much defined by their conflicts between police chief and mayor, crew and corporation, as they were stories of man versus nature. The corporation or mayor's profit motive was necessary to sustain or provoke the conflict with the animal or alien that just wants to survive. One could also argue that both these films were at the cusp of a certain transformation into the contemporary blockbuster form, and are in some sense richer in narrative, character, and even subtext than the latest string of corporate tie ins, but it seems that part of the way that the contemporary culture industry functions is by constantly creating nostalgia for what seems like an earlier, better version of itself. This is perhaps something that not even Horkheimer and Adorno could have predicted. Despite all of these caveats I am more interested in the way in which the memes draws out the anti-capitalist content that was always there. In this context, I am interested in the way in which the meme produce and reflect a new sensibility one that is not so much pacified by the culture industry as it is able to poach it for its latent critical potential (to use De Certeau's terminology). (Of course this is not limited to these two films. *Jurassic Park* has also been joked about and memed in this context. One could imagine an entire rereading of Hollywood films for corporations that are more interested in profits than preserving lives. It wouldn't be hard. It even seems unavoidable.)

This does not seem like much of a point to make, but I guess the real point is that when I recently rewatched both *Alien* and *Jaws* inspired by their new viral life as memes critical of the response to the pandemic I thought for a second about writing a blogpost arguing for their anti-capitalist stance, but I did not need to do that. That was already done for me by the various memes and jokes. The films seemed to already have been rewritten by the new context and the new use they had been put to as commentary on this context. Our popular culture might not offer us much to work with, might be baby food after all, but even baby food can be flung against the wall in rage, and that rage is going to be necessary for us to not only get through the current political moment, but on building something new. As Mark Fisher argued about the anti-capitalism of the Hunger Games, it is sometimes useful to just remember who the enemy is, to take the anti-corporate nature of popular culture at face value. Even the products of the culture industry can be used to not just reinforce existing ideologies, build new myths. I know that I will never look at *Jaws* or *Alien* the same way again.

For more on Jaws "Live Every Week Like it is Shark Week: Remarks on the Ecology of the Mediasphere." For more on the Culture Industry "Avenge Me: Avengers and the Culture Industry." For more on *Jurassic Park* see The Primitive Accumulation of Prehistory: On the Jurassic Park Films.

Revenge of the Children of Marx and Coca-Cola: Remarks on Deleuze, Vertov, and Godard

First posted in the summer of 2010 after teaching *Philosophy of Film.*

I must admit that at first I did not much care for Deleuze's *Cinema* books. There are several reasons for this, first; I simply was not prepared by the sheer breadth of their cinematic references, everything from Vidor to Ozu; second, after *Capitalism and Schizophrenia*, in which the general problem of signification, of regimes of signs, was developed through an engagement with the problem of capitalism, the rarefied typology of images, movement images and time images, seemed too aesthetic for me, too much of a reflection on film for film's sake.

My opinion has changed considerably since then. First, I have finally caught up with at least some of Deleuze's references: Vidor's *The Crowd* is still difficult to track down as is *Europa 51*, and for some reason it took me forever to find a copy of even *Winchester '73*. However, the major points of reference, Eisenstein, Vertov, Welles, Godard, and Hitchcock are all films I am more than familiar with, and have come to appreciate thanks to Deleuze. This is not what I want to write about. It is the second reaction that has changed as well. I have begun to think that there is a somewhat subtle politics to Deleuze's film books. More specifically they concern the question as to what it means to act. I would even argue that they are concerned with what it means to act now, in an age dominated by images, what we could call, for lack of a better word, the spectacle. As Deleuze writes, in one of the few historical/social asides that dot the arid conceptual landscape of the book, explaining the breakdown between the opposition of movement and action: "There were social and scientific factors which placed more and more movement into conscious life, and more and more images in the material world."[1] Thus it is possible to triangulate Deleuze's writing between the work of Paolo Virno (who most succinctly posed the question of acting in the modern world) and Maurizio Lazzarato's remarks regarding control as power that does not so much act on actions, but on the very possibility of actions.

This shouldn't seem like such a stretch, after all, in the first book action pretty much defines the movement image. The three variants of the movement image perception image, affection image, and action image, are defined by their relation to the center of indetermination, to the body/or brain, which introduces the interval/the gap between action and reaction. Every action begins with a perception which first becomes an internal reaction, an affect, before becoming an action in the world: see, feel, act, is the basic schema of action. Film simultaneously underscores and displaces this schema.

It underscores it through the conventions of the shot/reverse shot, the shot of the thing reacted to and the reaction, add a close up of affect to this, a shot of fear or anger, and you have perception, affection, action. This is why Deleuze sees a sensory-motor schema underlying most films. The dominant Hollywood genres, western,

---

[1] Gilles Deleuze, *Cinema 1: The Movement Image*, Translated by Hugh Tomlinson and Barbara Habberjam, (Minneapolis: University of Minnesota, 1986) pg. 56.

detective, comedy, and their variants in the samurai film etc., follow the basic pattern of either S-A-S' (situation-action-situation) or A-S-A (action-situation-action): in the first, actions transform situations (the duel brings peace and justice to the town) and in the second, actions disclose situations (the search for clues reveals that the conspiracy is deeper than imagined). What links this two is a kind of a connection that links actions to their milieu, actions are entirely adequate to their situations.

At the same time, film has the capacity to completely de-center the coordinates of perception, introducing angles and shots that are inaccessible to our human all too human perception. Deleuze is very enthralled by Vertov's *Man With a Movie Camera*, a film which realizes this ideal. It is possible to say that Deleuze's approach to film is as much Vertovian as it is Bergsonian. The latter may provide a general ontology of images, but this increasingly understood in materialist terms, an immanent plane of images affecting other images. As Deleuze writes, in one of the few passages that cites the terminology of his co-authored books, "The material universe, the plane of immanence, is the machine assemblage of movement images."[2]

There is thus a tension between these two aspects of cinema: the sensory-motor schema that governs the relation of images and the materialist plane of images affecting other images. However, this tension is not irresolvable. It is possible to see film as revealing the genesis of subjectivity, as the plane of images is constantly folding and unfolding around particular contingent centers. Situations are constantly giving rise to actions and being transformed by them: the plane of immanence is constantly given rise to contingent centers. Which is why the "stylistics" that Deleuze refers to, the particular way of combining (perception, action, and affection) images that defines a director, could also be considered a particular way of resolving the relations between situation and action, a particular way of framing how one acts in a world. One acts differently in the

---

2 Ibid., pg. 59.

world of Griffiths, Eisenstein, Ford, Kurosawa, or Hitchcock.

What interests Deleuze, however, is the breakdown of this connection between situation and action. "We hardly believe any longer that a global situation can give rise to an action which is capable of modifying it—no more than we believe that an action can force a situation to disclose itself, even partially."³ The reasons for this remain both overdetermined (Deleuze refers to "social, economic, political, moral and other [factors], more internal to art, to literature, and to the cinema in particular") and off-screen, Deleuze does not so much represent this history as present its effects on the world of movies. Like a classic horror film, we get the reaction shot but never see the monster.

The two cinematic transformations that reflect this history are Italian neo-realism and the French new wave. The first gives us situations that cannot be reacted to, that remain too disparate, too excessive for any determinate action. (*Bicycle Thief* as a testament to the impossibility of action). While the second, the new wave, and specifically Godard, demonstrates what has come to fill this space, short circuiting the relationship between situation and action: clichés. "They are these floating images, these anonymous clichés, which circulate in the external world, but which also penetrate each one of us and constitutes this internal world, so that everyone possesses only psychic clichés by which he thinks and feels, is thought and is felt, being himself a cliché among the others in the world which surrounds him."⁴ These clichés are in the citations of other films and genres that lead to actions that are disconnected and disparate.

For Deleuze these two transformations in film represent a shift in film itself, from the movement image to the time image, but we could also see this as a continuation and exasperation of the question as to what it means to act in the modern world. There is no longer a situation, a "west" that can be defended or even a "city" whose story can be told, that can coordinate action. In its place we

---

3 Ibid., pg. 206.
4 Ibid., pg. 213.

have the clichés of film and popular culture. As Deleuze writes, "… it is a civilization of the cliché where all the powers have an interest in hiding images from us, not necessarily in hiding the same thing from us, but in hiding something in the image."[5] These clichés come from film, from precisely the films of the movement image (SAS' and ASA) that Deleuze argues the soul of cinema has passed by, to move into new directions. To act today means to not only reconnect action with the situation, which requires some kind of cognitive map of the situation, but to recognize that the clichés must be mapped as well, as the form part of both the world and any possible action on the world.

In *Cinema 2* Deleuze makes some interesting remarks about the colonization of life by film. However, a thorough account of the role of cinema must go beyond the cliché's of popular culture to a political economy of the image. As Jonathan Beller has argued cinema has to be placed within a general political economy of attention. The movies are nothing other than an apparatus of capture of attention, that has now passed through the multiplicity of screens that make up social life. "[Cinema] realizes capitalist tendencies toward the extension of the work day (via entertainment, email) the deterritorialization of the factory (through cottage industry, TV) the marketing of attention (to advertisers), the building of media pathways (formerly roads) and the retooling of subjects."[6]

I do not have a conclusion for this, but given the two figures I have focused on here, Vertov and Godard, it seems to me that the task for contemporary cinema would be to combine Vertov's project to map social relations with a post-Godardian awareness that such a map must included the clichés are internal to those relations. It is not enough to film the audience entering the theater, as Vertov did, but also the movie entering the audience, as the image enters thought and desire. Moreover, it seems to me that political action

---

5 Gilles Deleuze, *Cinema 2: The Time Image*, Translatd by Hugh Tomlinson and Robert Galeta, (Minneapolis: University of Minnesota, 1989) pg. 21.
6 Jonathan Beller, *The Cinematic Mode of Production: Attention Economy and the Society of the Spectacle*, (Hanover: Dartmouth College Press, 2006) pg. 13.

today will take place not in spite of the clichés of cinema, in some kind of attention to a real world existing outside of images, but through them.

For more on Deleuze's theory of cinema see "Becoming Spider-Man: Deleuze and the Superhero Film" and "Any Bird Whatsoever: On Fujita's Ciné-Capital."

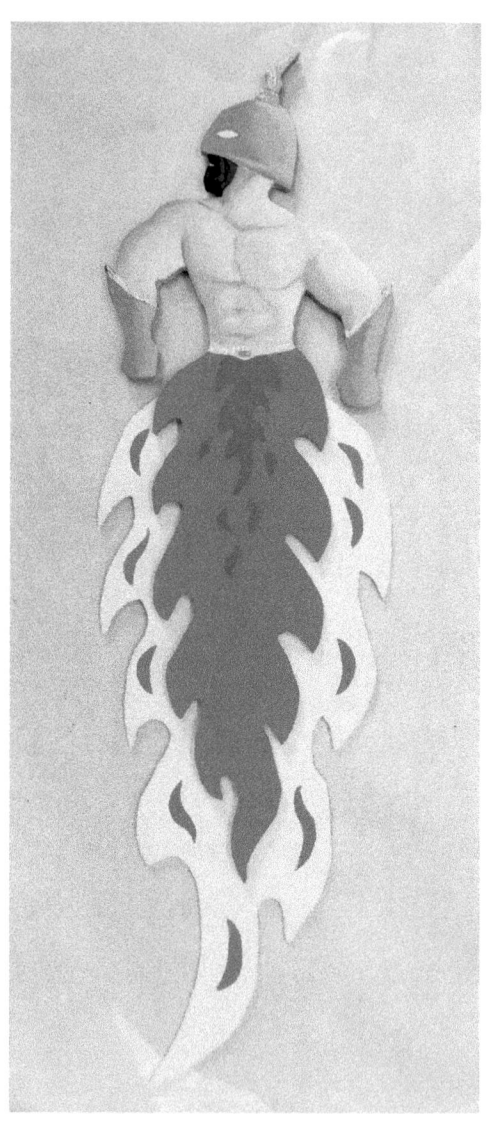

What Are Your Superpowers? By Jon Read

Becoming Spider-Man: Deleuze and the Superhero Film

Originally posted April 15, 2019.

In the end of *Cinema, Volume One: The Movement Image* writes the following about the demise of the movement image:

> "Certainly people continue to make [movement image] films: the greatest commercial successes always take that route, but the soul of cinema no longer does. The soul of the cinema demands increasing thought even if thought begins by undoing the systems of actions, perceptions, and affections on which the cinema had fed up to that point. We hardly believe any longer that a global situation can give rise to an action which is capable of modifying it—no more than we believe that an action can force a situation to disclose itself, even partially."[1]

It seems to me that Deleuze's picture of the movement image lingering on might be one way to make sense of the superhero film. In a certain sense the superhero film epitomizes one formulation

---

1 Gilles Deleuze, *Cinema 1: The Movement Image,* Translated by Hugh Tomlinson and Barbara Habberjam, (Minneapolis: University of Minnesota, 1986) pg. 206.

of the movement image, Situation–Action–Situation (SAS). In explaining this it is worth noting the central role of origin stories in the transition from film to comics. As someone who grew up reading comics the experience was less of origins and endings than an experience of beginning in the middle (as Deleuze would say). Origins were sometimes referred to by footnotes, sometimes available in reprints, and sometimes retconned, reexamined, or restarted, Peter Parker's parents, Miller's *Batman: Year One*, and Marvel's *Ultimates*. For the most part, however, one picked up the story whenever and wherever one started, and figured out what came before by reading the footnotes or finding back issues or reprints.

The transition to film has made the origin story central, if not the exclusive matter. It is the emphasis of origin that not only distinguishes the comic book film from their four color inspirations but also makes it fit so neatly into the structure of the action image. The origin is mirrored in the end that it sets up, the final confrontation. As Deleuze argues the classic films of the large form of the action image were the Westerns of Ford and others. One begins with a situation, to take *The Man Who Shot Liberty Valance* as an example, a young idealist arrives at a town under the grips of a ruthless outlaw. This situation sets up an action, a showdown between the idealist and outlaw, but it is one that the film will build to eventually. As Deleuze writes, "But, normally, the path from the milieu to the final duel is a long one. This is because the hero is not immediately ripe for action."[2] As Deleuze goes onto write "there must be a big gap between the situation and the action to come, but this gap only exists to be filled by a process marked by caesuras, as so many retrogressions and progressions." After the showdown, the defining action, we get a new situation, a new west of laws and states complete with a myth of its founding. To quote Deleuze again, "In *The Man Who Shot Liberty Valance* the bandit is killed and order re-established; but the cowboy who has killed him allows us to think it is the future senator, thus accepting the transformation of the law which ceases to be the tacit epic law of the West in order to become the written or novelistic law of industrial civilization."[3] The action image was the cinema of cowboys and samurai, of heroes who rise to the challenge and in doing so transform their world.

The superhero film, especially the early ones dedicated to origins, follows a restricted and predictable version of this formula. It generally runs as follows: Individual gains super powers; individual confronts villains and handily defeats them; individual has first encounter with empowered villain (who, in the early films was often a product of the same experiment/accident/discovery) and is defeated; individual reconsiders his or her task and responsibility (and possibly revisits some issues with a father figure or love interest); and then finally defeats the super villain. There is still a transformed

---

2 Ibid., pg. 154.
3 Ibid., pg. 147.

world, but the mythic transformation of violence into order but of a new order, a fiction of a more just and more exciting world. There are variations of this formula. Some superheroes begin with a purpose, a mission, and construct their powers or come into them because of their mission (Batman, Captain America) and some begin by gaining powers only to find their purpose and mission afterwards (Spider-Man, Iron Man). A recent variation of this has been the more self-critical superhero film in which the hero finds out that his or her purpose was itself a kind of lie, or deception, and thus must find a true purpose. I am thinking here of *Thor:Ragnorak*, *Black Panther*, and *Captain Marvel*.

It is possible to conclude that the superhero film is then just one way in which the action image has lingered on, continuing the idea of action transforming situations, even if cinema's soul is elsewhere. To make such an assertion is to overlook one of Deleuze's central ideas of the action image, that it is predicated on a sensory motor link, on a naturalism of behavior. "The action image inspires a cinema of behaviour (behaviourism) since behaviour is an action which passes from one situation to another, which responds to a situation in order to try and modify it or to set up a new situation."[4] It seems to me that the superhero film continues the link between action and situation at the point in which behavior is broken down.

There are three ways to think about this, the first, and most obvious, is that superhero films must necessarily break any sensory motor link, any naturalism of behavior, since their actions are not only superhuman, but are less a gradual development of new capacities than a sudden transformation. Moreover, in the gradual build up to the final confrontation, to the action that transforms the situation, it is less a matter of progressions of capacities (the superhero film has eliminated the training montage that dominated a previous decade's action film) than a renewed sense of purpose or meaning. Generally the hero has a conversation with some mentor, love interest, or recalls some absent father figure, and is reminded of

---

4 Ibid., pg. 155.

their purpose, mission, or responsibility: it is not a new behavior but a renewed sense of purpose or ideology that drives them to the final confrontation. The combination of the miraculous power and the mundane motivation gives us something we are meant to relate to, to aspire to, but in a way that we never will. Superhero films give us great slogans to repeat, "with great power comes great responsibility," but their greatness lies in being bumpersticker slogans, things that sound nice but are never put into practice. If the action image of the western and the samurai film was a story of how an ordinary person could become a myth or a legend, the superhero is a legend that an ordinary person can never become. One repeated theme of the superhero movie is the displacement of the rest of humanity, us mere mortals, from the center of action, all of us regular humans become just something to be rescued or, at worst, collateral damage.

One of the other mutations of the superhero from print to film is that for the most part the secret identity is downplayed to the point of being nonexistent (Spider-Man and Batman being obvious exceptions). The connection with normal mere mortals is entirely broken, which is perhaps why the superheroes always look so ridiculous when they disguise themselves to blend into crowds (with the same cap and aviator glasses).

(As something of an aside I will say that Spider-Man is an interesting example in terms of thinking through Deleuze's ideas of action and milieu. He is the only superhero with a determinant milieu. Webslinging and wallcrawling only work as powers amongst the skyscrapers of New York City. This is often coupled with the sense that he is a kid of the city, connected to its people. That is why they call him the friendly neighborhood Spider-Man. He is also the one superhero that maintains the connection with everyday reality. Yes, I have a fondness for Spider-Man and the recent *Homecoming* and *Into the Spider-Verse*).

However, I think that the breakdown of the link goes beyond the narrative of superhuman action. This break is triangulated between narrative, visual effects, and visual content. The rise of the superhero film runs parallel with the increasing dominance of computer generated effects. Entire sets, costumes, or characters are generated through digital images. As the effects dominate the final scenes of the film there is the increasing sense of watching a video game. This transformation of the visual effects is coupled with a transformation of the visual and auditory world of the superhero film. Form matches content as the digital manipulation of images is how the film is made, but it also permeate the world of the film. Superheroes increasingly interact with a world that is thoroughly mediated by images and sounds, by visual heads up displays, or accompanied with voices of artificial intelligence. This is most obviously the case in the *Iron Man* films, but has been extended through other franchises as characters spend as much time talking to projected voices as to other characters. As Deleuze writes, "The modern world is that in which information has replaced nature."[5] As Evan Calder Williams has argued about Iron Man:

> "...the capacity for Iron Man to save the day is not limited to his ability to fly faster...or carry a nuclear weapon through a portal. It depends instead on his capacity aided by an in-visor heads up display that highlights relevant dangers, to look at this total muddle of a collapsing city and decide what matters and what doesn't, what is an about-to-die love interest and what is just shards...Iron Man, conqueror of aesthetic experience."[6]

Or, to cite Deleuze one more time...

> "But when the frame or the screen functions as instrument panel, printing or computing table the image is constantly being cut into another image, being printed through a visible mesh, sliding over other images in 'incessant stream of messages,' and the shot itself is less like an eye than an overloaded brain

---

5 Gilles Deleuze, *Cinema 2: The Time Image*, Translatd by Hugh Tomlinson and Robert Galeta, (Minneapolis: University of Minnesota, 1989) pg.269.
6 Evan Calder Williams, "Shard Cinema," *Third Rail Quaterly*, http://thirdrailquarterly.org/evan-calder-williams-shard-cinema/

endlessly absorbing information: it is the brain-information, brain-city couple which replaces that of the eye of nature."[7]

One could say that there are three means by which the action situation link is severed in the superhero film: the mythic nature of the action, the artifice of its representation, and the nature of its mediation. To put it bluntly, and in Deleuze's terms, superhero films are action films for people who no longer believe in action, for whom the capacity to act has been overtaken by the spectacle.

Post-Script on the Becoming Fan of the Spectator (10/12/21)

It is possible to argue that Deleuze gives two different versions of the crisis of the action image, one exterior to film and the other interior to it. The first is not really given by Deleuze, just summed up by a series of factors, "the war...other factors that were social, economic, political, and moral." The list is less an exhaustive account of factors than a gesture towards what is not represented. If the two volumes of *Cinema* were a movie they would be something like a murder mystery in which the crime is never seen but we deal only with its effects or clues.

There is another crisis internal to the image that Deleuze gives and that is Hitchcock's attempt to create a mental image. A mental image is not an image of thinking or thought, but an attempt to make the thoughts of the character on the screen correspond with that of the spectator. The classic example of this for Deleuze is *Rear Window* in which the audience is largely given the same clues as Jeff (Jimmy Stewart) and tries to make the same connection. Putting thought on the screen entails making the characters themselves immobile "If one of Hitchcock's innovations was to implicate the spectator in the film, did not the characters themselves have to be capable—in a more or less obvious manner—of being assimilated to spectators?"[8]

---

7 Gilles Deleuze, *Cinema 2: The Time Image*, 267.
8 Gilles Deleuze, *Cinema 1: The Movement Image*, 205.

In the comic book movie the characters on the screen and the audience converge in a different manner, not through the intersection of the thought process of the character and the audience that defines suspense but through the way in which there is a becoming fan of the character. To give an example: In *Wandavision* two characters, Jimmy Woo (Randall Park) and Darcy Lewis (Kat Dennings) who are actual the products of prior franchises, *Ant-man* and *Thor*, discuss who is stronger the Scarlet Witch or Captain Marvel.

They are referencing a scene from *Avengers: Endgame* which is not only a film that not only neither character appeared in, but is also a scene that they would have no way of seeing. The final battle of that film does not take place in the middle of New York City where there could be thousands of cameras watching but in a digital any-place-whatsoever that is supposed to be someplace in upstate New York. Arguably no one saw this battle except the participants. We can only include that they are both in an MCU television program and have seen the movie. This transformation of the character into fan continues through the latter television series. In *Loki* the titular character who has been ripped from the timeline not only watches the rest of his arc culminating in his death, but he spends most of the film interacting with Mobius (Owen Wilson) who is his biggest fan. Much of the drama of that series has to do with Mobius "shipping" Loki, believing that Loki the villain can become a hero in the same way that the fans of a series could believe that two characters are destined to become a romantic couple. This becoming fan element has become integral to all the latest television productions. *Falcon and the Winter Soldier* is in part an argument about who is best suited to cosplay as Captain America.

Watching MCU movies has become internal to the movies, as the screens that display the world increasingly replay scenes from the movies we have seen, just as characters in the film reveal themselves to be fans of other characters. This is the culmination of decades of fan service, of including various easter eggs that only fans could recognize. Thus we see another end to the action image, not in terms of Hitchcock's mental image, but in terms of the fan image, or image as intellectual property. The image incorporates the spectator but as a fan rather than thinker. The point is not to make the connections between images, but to feel recognized by the image, to be acknowledged as a fan. The action image is not elevated to the mental image, as relations that are acted become relations to be thought, but is brought down to fan service as characters on the screen and in the audience rejoice at seeing the same callbacks. The spectacle becomes mirror.

For more on Deleuze's theory of film see "Revenge of the Children of Marx and Coca Cola: Remarks on Marx, Vertov, and Godard." For more on superhero movies see "Avenge Me: Avengers and the Culture Industry."

Danny Lloyd rocking the same haircut I had as a kid

Shine On: We Are All in Room 237 Now

Written in November of 2021.

Of all of the various concepts and neologisms that populate *A Thousand Plateaus* that of the "regime of signs" is one that never really caught on. It has not had the same effects as nomadology, rhizome, virtual, assemblage, body without organs, becoming etc., all of which have become the focus of articles, books, and even entire conferences. If I had to offer a quick explanation of this it is perhaps because the idea of the sign, and of a regime of signs, still seems like a remnant of an earlier period, more structuralist than post-structuralist. It is for that reason that it has remained something of a B-side or a deep cut, taking a clue from Deleuze and Guattari's assertion that the book is more like an album with different plateaus as songs than a linear progression of an argument.

It is perhaps worth revisiting the regime of signs now. I am thinking of the following passage from *A Thousand Plateaus*:

> "This is the situation Lévi-Strauss describes: the world begins to signify before anyone knows what it signifies; the signified is given without being known. Your wife looked at you with a funny expression. And this morning the mailman handed you a letter from the IRS and crossed his fingers. The you stepped in a pile of dogshit. You saw two sticks on the sidewalk positioned

like the hands of a watch. They were whispering behind your back when you arrived at the office. It does not matter what it means, it's still signifying. The sign refers to other signs in struck with a strange impotence and uncertainty, but might is the signifier that constitutes the chain. The paranoiac shares this impotence of the deterritorialized sign assailing him from every direction in the gliding atmosphere, but that only gives him better access to the superpower of the signifier, through the royal feeling of wrath, as master of the network spreading through the atmosphere. The paranoid despotic regime: they are attacking me and making me suffer, but I can guess what they're up to, I'm one step ahead of them, I've always known, I have power even in my impotence. "I'll get them."[1]

I was reminded of this passage for two reasons. First, after teaching Kubrick's *The Shining* in my philosophy of film course I decided to finally watch *Room 237*, the documentary/video essay on the different interpretations of *The Shining*.

It is hard to watch this film and feel that it does not in some sense illustrate the paranoiac regime of signs. Everything in the film, every flag on a desk, rocket ship on a sweater, and missing chair becomes a sign, an indicator of something else, something that needs to be decoded. Nothing is what it appears, and everything is something else, but everything can be decoded which is to say that it means something. Second, as much as it might be fun to engage with that kind of paranoid reading of films, declaring that this or that film is really about X, where X is some secret meaning available only to the right interpretation, it is hard to avoid the conclusion that these days the paranoid reading has left the movie theater and entered the world.

I am thinking here of Qanon, or, more specifically Wu Ming's understanding of Qanon as less a conspiracy theory than a kind of conspiracy game.[2] While the former would tell people what is

---

[1] Gilles Deleuze and Guattari, Félix *A Thousand Plateaus*, Translated by Brian Massumi, (Minneapolis: University of Minnesota Press, 1987) pg. 112.

[2] Wu Ming, "Blank Space QAnon. On the Success of a Conspiracy Fantasy as a Collective Text Interpretation Game," https://www.wumingfoundation.com/giap/blank-space-qanon/.

happening, often through a reference to a master text or narrative, the latter invites its followers to play, to interpret signs and clues. It has an active component.

To return then to the question, what has let the paranoid interpretation out of the multiplex, or videostore, and into the world? This question could be answered by looking to Deleuze and Guattari, I think that one of the things that is often overlooked about *A Thousand Plateaus* is the way that it puts forward its own theory of the relation between words and things, signs and pragmatics, or, to use their terms machinic assemblages of bodies and enunciation, one that is indebted to Marx, Foucault, and Spinoza. A regime of signs, an assemblage of enunciation, changes with a change of the machinic assemblage of bodies, with the technological and economic transformation of society. A full account of this transformation goes beyond a blogpost, however. So I would like to instead turn back to film, to *The Shining* specifically, and how films are viewed more generally to at least outline some of the shifts in bodies that have accompanied the shift in signs.

Machine in Deleuze and Guattari means more than technology, but it includes it as well. It is hard to overlook the technological changes which have altered our relationships to images and signs. The subjects interviewed in *Room 237* often mention that their theories really took off when they saw the movie on Blu-ray, the clarity of picture and the ability to pause and rewind repeatedly changed the film. Theories based on the minutiae of details in a film cannot come from one viewing in a theater, or, as more often the case, the lingering memories of a film. They demand repeat viewings and clear digital images. A similar technological change has migrated from movies to reality, not just in the internet that distributes conspiracy theories, but also in the generalized ability to pause the video of any press conference, all the better to find the clues, to freeze the video to see the lizard people. A regime of signs is in part a particular organization of the recording and dissemination of texts and images, as the technological conditions change so do the signs and how they are read (this is the connection between Deleuze and Guattari and Stiegler.)

A regime of signs is not just a technological condition, or rather, to put it in Deleuze and Guattari's terms the technological machine is itself determined by the social machine, and part of this social machine involves the production of subjectivity. Here, we can find an unlikely bedfellow for this idea of a different production of subjectivity in Fredric Jameson's reading of the film (which I taught in the class). Jameson argues that what he refers to as "the occult" aspect of the film, the shine, possession, ghosts of the past, is in some sense a distraction from its real core. As Jameson writes,

> "For one thing, the conventional motifs of the occult or supernatural thriller tends to distract us from the obvious fact that *The Shining*, whatever else it is, is also the story of a failed writer. Stephen King's original was far more openly and conventionally an artist's novel whose hero is already a writer of some minimal achievement and a classical American poète maudit whose talent is plagued and stimulated by alcoholism. Kubrick's hero, however, is already a reflexive commentary on this now conventional stereotype (Hemingway, O'Neill, Faulkner, the beats, etc.): his Jack Nicholson is not a writer, not someone who has something to say or likes doing things with words, but rather someone who would like to be a writer, who lives a fantasy about what the American writer is, along the lines of James Jones or Jack Kerouac. Yet even that fantasy is anachronistic and nostalgic; all those unexplored interstices of the system, which allowed the lumpens of the fifties to become, in their turn, figures of "the Great American Writer," have long since been absorbed into the sealed and achieved space of consumer society."[3]

For Jameson this interpretation is in part based on what is undoubtedly one of the most memorable scenes of the film,

---

3 Fredric Jameson, Signatures of the Visible, (New York; Routledge, 1992) pg. 127.

something everyone recalls whether or not they have watched it obsessively, the famous scene in which Wendy finds Jack's work, or absence of work.

As Jameson writes about Jack's writing, "The text in question is however very explicitly a text about work: it is a kind of zero point around which the film organizes itself, a kind of ultimate and empty auto-referential statement about the impossibility of cultural or literary production."[4] Less Jameson's interpretation focusing on writing and cultural production seems as outlandish as reading the film as a commentary on the Holocaust or the genocide of Native Americans (two interpretations in *Room 237*), it is worth remembering that scene in question resolves any ambiguity about the terms of conflict, from that moment forward Jack is clearly the villain, murderous axe in hand. (Although it is worth raising the question, albeit parenthetically, if at the end of the day one can ever draw a rigid division between the "readings" of the films offered by people like Jameson or Zizek and the work of "outsider" film theorists featured in the movie. I am fairly convinced that the students in my class have their doubts).

What does this reading, or interpretation of the film, have to do with the changing regime of signs, the expansion of the paranoid regime from a search to find the meaning of the text to discern the ultimate machinations of the world? In some sense Jack is the prototypical subject of conspiracy theories. One whose ultimate existential deadlock is to be found in the gap between his potential, his sense that he really could or should be something, and his reality, or his fears of what he will become. At one point in the film he tells Wendy that if he should leave the Overlook Hotel, give up his job in order to protect his family, he would be forced to resort to the only jobs available to the "lumpen," shoveling snow or working at a car wash. The novel goes in greater detail about how the job at the hotel and the chance that he could get some writing done is very much the last chance for a man whose life is falling apart due to addiction

---

4 Ibid., pg. 128.

and a cycle of abuse, but, as Jameson points out, the character in the novel is a writer, one who has been published, while the Jack of the film is a man who wants to be a writer. Jack is a man who is convinced that greatness is denied to him because of external forces, or as he says at one point in the film, "the white man's burden." This inability to confront his own limitations, the fact that he might not truly have any good ideas, or anything to say, by externalizing them into a world which has undermined him again and again is the subjective kernel of the paranoid view of the world. The typewriter has been replaced with the laptop and the memes no longer circulate endlessly on top of one another in different patterns typed onto the page as in the famous "All Work and No Play Make Jack a Dull Boy," but go out into the world.

For more on Conspiracy Theories see "Reduction to Ignorance: Spinoza in the Age of Conspiracy Theories," "The Dialectic of Conspiracy and Trust: Hegel on Conspiracy Theories" and "The Spontaneous Ideology of Conspiracy: This One on Marx."

TELEVISION/ STREAMING

"Look on my works, ye mighty, and despair!": Breaking Bad as Austerity Allegory

This piece was written over the course of watching the fifth and final season of *Breaking Bad* in the summer of 2013.

Before the much anticipated final season (or half season) of *Breaking Bad* aired at the end of this summer AMC ran a teaser of a trailer in which the words of Perce Bysse Shelley's poem "Ozymandias" are read by its star Bryan Cranston. One cannot help but here the final words of that poem, "My name is Ozymandias, King of Kings; Look on my Works, ye Mighty, and despair! Nothing beside remains. Round the decay Of that colossal Wreck, boundless and bare The lone and level sands stretch far away."

Aside from obeying the strict "no spoilers" rule that has become something of a mantra in the world of television, and highlighting the show's use of the colors and scenery of New Mexico, the use of Shelley's poem underscores the central theme of *Breaking Bad*, that of legacy. What remains of us after we die? The show began with Walt's worry that his cancer and meager salary as a public school teacher would leave his family destitute and drowning in debt. As the seasons progressed, however, legacy was defined less in terms of inheritance and more in terms of empire. One of the many questions that confronts *Breaking Bad* in the final episodes is what would remain of Walt's Heisenberg's empire after his (almost inevitable) demise.

Perhaps what is most striking about *Breaking Bad* is that for a show about the illicit drug trade, and the making of a drug kingpin (as well as the destruction of two other drug empires), it is relatively free of the conspicuous consumption, the bling, that we generally associate with the drug empire story. (Think of De Palma's *Scarface* which the show constantly references). Money is accumulated in massive amounts, piled, and even weighed, but it is rarely spent. The show dedicates a great deal of screen time to the physicality of money, the difficulty storing and concealing large amounts, but very little to what money is actually used for, buying commodities. Money is not spent, is not related to consumption, but is hoarded as part of a legacy. Hoarders by definition cannot spend and must ceaselessly accumulate.

I would like to suggest that this relation to money can be seen as part of the show's functioning as an austerity narrative. Initially the show's relationship to austerity was foregrounded in Walt's lack of adequate health insurance. While a certain version of austerity, or at least of public school budgets unable to care for their employees, set the plot in motion, the nature of austerity changed as the show progressed. Most notably, Walt's involvement with Gus' drug empire was framed through the intersection of layoffs and executions. The show used the drug world setting to put a dark spin on the struggle to remain valued and viable in one's job. As soon as one becomes redundant one is not so much handed a pink slip as given the red slash of a box cutter.

Walt's knowledge and skill, his particular ability "to cook" (not to mention his own violence) protects him from a lethal layoff. The tenor of his struggle as an employee changes with the different employers. The struggle with the drug kingpin Gus was primarily a struggle over the autonomy of the worker and knowledge. Gus sought to deskill the production of meth, replace Walt with his assistant, a fitting strategy for the owner of a fast food franchise; fast food is predicated on the deskilling of the preparation of food. After Gus's death, and Walt's brief stint as an independent businessman, he (also briefly) worked for Lydia. Lydia is an employee of the massive international Madrigal corporation who previously supplied the methylamine to Gus Fring. She briefly employs Walt to cook meth for export to the Czech Republic. Her attitude towards the production process is less about control over the production process than it is about maintenance of the brand identity. She understands the Heisenberg brand to be its signature blue color and purity. When Walt retires from the business, she is less interested in keeping him working than keeping the purity and identity of the brand. Much like her employer Madrigal, she is only interested in owning the brand, not controlling production. As long as the numbers are met, as long the product has its identifying blue color and 92% purity, she does not care who makes it or how it is produced.

The three bosses of *Breaking Bad*, Tuco, Gus, and Lydia, follow a trajectory from feudal control of territory, Tuco; to Fordist standardization of production, Gus; and finally to Lydia's control over brand identity. In this way the trajectory mirrors *The Wire's* trajectory from Avon to Stringer and Marlo. It is a trajectory from control of territory through control of product to control over brand. What is Gus but a successful Stringer Bell? It would take too long to go into this, but it is worth pointing out that in each case the last one, the one concerned with reputation (in the case of Marlo), or brand (in the case of Lydia), is also the one who is most brutal, most comfortable with killing off the competition (even if, in the case of Lydia, she closes her eyes while walking through the corpses).

In the final season the logic of austerity shifts from work, from keeping one's job or becoming one's own boss, to keeping control of one's savings. It becomes a question of retirement. The massive piles of money is both the possibility of a future and the greatest risk to the present. Following Frédéric Lordon we could say that this anxiety over money, combined with the absence of any conspicuous consumption follows an affective shift in the relation to money, money is not an object of hope, the possibility of desires realized, but the object of fear, the fears and threats that it staves off and the threat of its loss.[1]

What would become of Walt's empire is only one of the lingering questions that confronts the final season of the show. The second, which occupies much more of the final episodes, is which of Walt's many enemies would be his demise, Jesse, Hank, Skyler, or cancer. The different possibilities can all be read as different statements about the nature of Walt's fate and transgression.

Overall the final half of the final season of the show has turned inward, focusing on the question of family and loyalty. This is a marked shift from the first half of the fifth season, which expanded the show outward, connecting the drug trade with multinational corporations, railroad logistics, the countries of the former Soviet Union, and white power gangs in the US. The fifth season's foray into the expanded context of the meth trade is matched in the form of the show. *Breaking Bad's* artistic innovations are rarely to be found at the level of dialogue or narrative, it cannot compete with the expanding neo-realism of *The Wire*. What it excels at is the "cold open," the five to seven minutes shown before the opening credits and first commercial. These are generally used to draw the viewer in, a teaser. *Breaking Bad* increasing uses them to posit a kind of riddle, as images that are disconnected from the current narrative are often presented without dialogue. Sometimes these are flash forwards, the pink teddy bear of the second season or the events of Walter White's 52nd birthday which began the final season, but sometimes, as in the introduction of Madrigal Electromotive in season five, they are displaced miniature films, disconnected from what came before and what the audience expects to see. These brief vignettes suggest the expanding effects of the actions that make up the bulk of the series

---

1 Frédéric Lordon, *Willing Slaves of Capital: Spinoza and Marx on Desire*, Translated by Gabriel Ash, New York: Verso, 2014, 24.

narrative, as a German executive morosely samples new dipping sauces before killing himself, his life ruined by his connection to Los Pollos Hermanos. A similar vignette gives us a brief glimpse of a kid riding his dirt bike and catching spiders, introducing us to Drew Sharp before his untimely fate. The central story line focuses on Walt and the family, its larger effects are only given episodically in these series of mini-films.

The turn inward of the final episodes is not a huge shift. Unlike *The Wire*, *Breaking Bad* was never really interested in institutions, in the politics of the DEA or the politics of healthcare. It is more interested in individuals, even going so far as to unmoor individuals from their institutions, Walt has not been teaching since the third season and even Hank is fairly isolated from the DEA in the final seasons. The turn to the family, to the interior space, underscores an aspect of the show that is alternately criticized or celebrated, its whiteness. Some have argued that *Breaking Bad* has followed a familiar racist fantasy, at work in everything from *Tarzan* to *The Last Samurai*, in which a white man enters a field dominated by another ethnic group and immediately excels at it. Crazy Eight, Tuco Salamanca, and Gus Fring all go up against Walt and are in some way obliterated, his crystal meth is the best around, and so on. While others have argued that the show reflects the decline of white masculinity; Walt's anger and frustration at his station in life would not be out of place on Fox News. These different interpretations hinge on whether the interior spaces of white suburbia and the anger and frustration of a middle class and middle aged white man are understood to presented critically or uncritically. The introduction of Todd's Uncle Jake and the Neo-Nazis as both hired henchmen and eventual antagonists seem to reflect this ambiguity. Walt's attempt to use whiteness as a connection and advantage on furthers his self-destruction. One could draw a political parallel from this plot point to the fate of the ruling class in this country (as well as others) which tries to use white rage as a tactic to maintain power only to find that rage to be something uncontainable. Outsourcing muscle has its consequences.

Family is also presented ambiguously in these final episodes. It is both what Walt seeks to preserve, the purpose of his entire enterprise, and the source of conflicts. This is true of both Walt's actual family, as the lies fall apart one by one, and of his relation to Jesse, his meth family. With respect to the former, the season begins as Hank discovers Walt's identity as Heisenberg. He does so not as Heisenberg is continuing to expand his empire, but after he retires into a life of financial security and (relative) familial content. (The imperial ambitions of Walt/Heisenberg that have driven much of the show have subsided). Hank's discovery is framed against the backdrop of a utopian moment, the entire family gathered around the table next to the pool. The utopian ideal is given before its dissolution into a conflict, a conflict that always simmered beneath it. The rest of the final season follows a kind of dialectic of ideal and conflict in which the ideal of the family is in contradiction with its reality, the one undermining the other. Walt considers both Hank and Jesse to be family, and thus he cannot kill either of them (at least personally), never really considering that his ideal of family conflicts with the reality of a DEA agent for a brother in law and a "partner" he has manipulated and abused. He pursues a series of "half measures" with respect to both Hank and Jesse; these half measures prove disastrous for Walt as well as his "family members"/enemies. Walt persistently overestimates the importance of family connections, failing to see how these connections have been destroyed by his own actions.

Walt is not alone in having a distorted view of family. Even before Hank stumbled across a copy of *Leaves of Grass* on the toilet, the show has focused on the family as a locus of a kind of constitutive blindness. The only way that Hank could not see that Walt was Heisenberg despite the fact that he had the classic combination of opportunity, motive, and ability (plus the sudden windfall of cash) was that he had become accustomed to seeing Walt as his nebbish brother in-law. A similar constitutive blindness befalls Walt Jr./Flynn who is the last to know about Walt because he is so caught up in the image and ideal of the father that he cannot see the lies. This is demonstrated in one of the episodes in the final season when Walt's painfully strained lie to explain the saturation of the living room rug with gasoline falls apart. Flynn/Walt Jr sees through the lie, but what he sees is not the truth of the matter, that the gasoline is left over from Jesse's attempt to torch the house, but his own fantasy image of his father as a noble cancer patient, covering up the fact that he is too sickly to pump his own gas. It is unclear if this lie within a lie was Walt's intent all along, but there are suggestions that Walt's best lies are the ones that manipulate the image he has in the eyes of others. He is a fox in Machiavelli's sense, able to manipulate others because he is aware of how they see him.

If this season (or half season) began with an image of heaven, a family joyous gathered around a table with enough money to fill a self-storage unit, then its penultimate episode offers an image of austerity hell. Walt ends up in New Hampshire in a cabin. The details of life in this cabin read like a laundry list of modern conveniences cut from a shrinking budget. The cabin lacks cable and internet, only offering two copies of something called *Mr. Magorium's Wonder Emporium* for entertainment. Walt has the money, a big barrel of it, but what he cannot afford are even the minimal social connections that such conveniences necessitate, even cable television requires a visit from the cable man. Marx argued that in capitalism, "The individual carries his social power, as well as his bond with society, in his pocket."[2] Walt's situation reminds us that this power still requires a degree zero of sociality to function. No man is an island, even less one that has an industrial drum of money. Despite the unique situation of Walt's fate it also functions as an allegory of other, more common anxieties. It is the worst retirement ever, and I am fairly sure that if I drove from my home in Portland, Maine I could find someone who has just enough oil and firewood to get them through the winter and not much else. (Although they might own different movies). Jesse on the other hand is forced to work long past the point that he would like to retire. He is the very image of bare life stripped down to its capacity to work, to labor power. If, as I have argued earlier, the conflicts that animate this show are, at least in part, conflicts between workers and capitalist, management and labor, pitting Walt and Jesse against Tuco, Gus, and Lydia, then Uncle Jake discovers that the best management technique is the most brutal. Whereas Gus went to great pains to interpellate Jesse into his enterprise, even sending him on "a self-esteem workshop" with Mike, linking his fate to theirs through a shared sense of value and importance, Jake and Todd resort to much more literal chains and much more brutal methods. Retirement into poverty and work without end, these are the shows vision of hell. Needless to say these images of hell are closer to the anxiety of the show's viewers than jail. Pushed to their allegorical extreme, however, they become the image of bosses and workers in post austerity America. The first, the boss is isolated in his compound, unable to even walk the streets, the second, the worker is forced to live in order to work past the point of any enjoyment.

At its best *Breaking Bad* is a kind of melodrama of daily life, taking the mundane anxieties of health care costs, unemployment, work and retirement and infusing them with enough of the danger and excitement of the illicit drug trade to make them (just barely) watchable and enjoyable.

---

2 Karl Marx, *The Grundrisse*, Translated by Martin Nicolaus, New York: Penguin, 1973, 157.

For more on *Breaking Bad* see "Why Everybody Loves Kim: Breaking Bad on Better Call Saul."

Everybody Loves Kim: Breaking Bad on Better Call Saul

Written in May of 2020.

Breaking Bad and its spinoff/prequel *Better Call Saul* began with a premise that is familiar to nearly everyone. A mild mannered chemistry teacher moonlights as a producer of crystal meth in order to save his family from being bankrupted from his cancer diagnosis. However, as the title suggested it was initially a show about more than this, it is a show about crime as not just a way to make money but as a way to escape the rules and norms of modern life. This is particularly true of the first season in which Walter White is between two deaths, liberated from his life as a chemistry teacher, he not only cooks meth he also does all those things that we dream of but never do. He confronts someone who is bullying his son and blows up the car of an obnoxious lawyer.

As much as these moments of everyday rebellion form part of the cathartic identification with the show's everyman protagonist, which is to say one who is white, male, and middle class, they quickly dissipate after the first season. They are replaced by a different identification, one that is less cathartic and transgressive but also more familiar. As I have mentioned in the previous post, cooking meth ceases to be a rebellion for Walt and eventually becomes his new job. Much of the rest of the series is about struggles around work. The rebellion of breaking bad gives way to more mundane worries about whether or not your boss is going to replace you with a cheaper and more pliable worker. The only difference is being replaced in this case means being killed not just being fired. *Better Call Saul* continues this focus on work even as it flips the script from "breaking bad" to trying to make good, as Jimmy, a former conman, tries to go legit as an attorney.

Work is not just a focus of both the shows' plots it permeates the entire way of understanding the criminal underworld and its relation to the world of law and order. Gus Fring, Walt's boss, not only runs a fast food restaurant as a cover for his drug distribution empire, but actually seems to run it. He is more often than not at one of his franchises dressed in a shirt or tie and shows up for work in a Volvo like a responsible manager. This is a persistent theme throughout the shows in which the front of a running a business becomes a full time business. Ed Galbraith, "The disappearer" that Walt, Jesse, and Saul turn to create a new identity and a new life, does not just run his business from the front of a vacuum cleaner repair shop he actually runs a vacuum cleaner repair shop. He sells and repairs vacuums. Repeatedly throughout both shows the job that one takes as a cover becomes its own full time job. Walt and Skyler do not just launder their money through a car wash, but spend their days there greeting customers. Similarly, in *Better Call Saul*, the veterinarian that serves as a clearing house for various blackmarket jobs actually works as a vet, so much so that Mike gets a dog and Jimmy a goldfish so they have a reason to visit his office. When Mike's money is laundered through a fake job at the Madrigal Electronics firm he actually shows up to work, stealing a badge to become the security consultant his fake pay stub claims that he is. A life of crime does not free one from their day job because work is the ultimate alibi, the ultimate justification for existence. The only exception to this are the Mexican drug cartel, who lounge about by the pool all day, and this lounging proves to be their undoing.

This last bit is part of the racial politics of the show that has as its core the fundamental belief that a white person could do a better job than all of the "foreign" competition if he just had a fair chance. I think that the show tried to address this in the latter seasons in which Neo-Nazis replaced the cartels as the villains, but a show that is predicated so much on the anxieties and fantasies of the white middle class can never really dispense with its investment in masculinity and whiteness. It is the former rather than the latter that I am going to address here.

I think that this focus on work helps illustrate the popularity of Kim Wexler, Jimmy's friend, partner, and wife. In some sense it is hard not to view Kim as an anti-Skyler. Skyler, Walter's wife, was such an unpopular character that she received enough hate mail and online vitriol that Anna Gunn who played her wrote an editorial about it for the New York Times.[1] The source of Skyler's unpopularity was the fact that she was in some sense the stereotype of the nagging wife, worried about little things like the fact that Walter's drug business would get him and their kids killed. Kim is in some sense reverse engineered from Skyler. She is the ultimate "cool girl" game for a good con, and supporting Jimmy as he shifts and turns from an associate at a successful law firm to Saul Goodman the "criminal lawyer" we know from *Better Call Saul*.

The reduction of Kim to a "cool girl," to her status as girlfriend, however, overlooks her own relation to work. Like many of the characters on *Better Call Saul*, we know very little about her background, we know only that she came from Red Cloud Nebraska, and had a childhood spent under the constant threat of eviction. Like Jimmy she worked her way through law school. It is perhaps for this reason that Kim starts the series as a believer in the virtues of hard work. When confronted with adversity she works

---

1 Anna Gunn, "I have a Character Issue, " *New York Times*, August 23, 2013,
  https://www.nytimes.com/2013/08/24/opinion/i-have-a-character-issue.html

harder. Working harder, working better, working smarter is her solution to every problem and obstacle. In season four she nearly kills herself overworking. It is at this point that her relation to work begins to change. When given the choice to either return to work immediately or spend time recovering she hits up Blockbuster and takes a vacation she more than deserves. When she does return to work she has more or less split her world of work in two. She continues to work for Mesa Verde Bank, a job that pays the bills and seems relatively neutral. A sort of neither victim nor executioner for an attorney. As a lawyer there are worse things you can do than help a bank open new branches. To counter this she spends more of her time, and much of her passion working for pro bono clients, doing good as a lawyer. It is worth noting that lawyers use this little latin phrase to simultaneously acknowledge and deny the fact that if you want to do good you have to forget about getting paid.

This division works for Kim, until her work for Mesa Verde forces her to remove an unwilling tenant from his land. She can no longer claim neutrality in the conflicts that define society. This eventually causes her to leave the law firm, to give up her lucrative position filing permits for a bank. It is worth noting that when she leaves she takes only one thing with her, the cork from a high priced tequila bottle that she and Jimmy got one of their "marks" to pay for. It is then in the final episode of the penultimate season that Kim suggests a more radical break with the world of work than either Walt or Jimmy. She and Jimmy will scam their way into millions, destroying the career of one lawyer along the way, and that will make it possible for her to dedicate her life to her pro bono work, to doing good.

It is hard to say if Kim will break bad, or what the final season will entail, but she has broken something that the rest of the characters, and the rest of the show has held together, and that is work. Walter thought that he could do good for his family and make good money. Kim understands that making money is just a scam, a scam in which someone always gets hurt, and that if you want to do good then the first thing you have to do is free yourself from the demands of making a living.

For more on *Breaking Bad* see "Look on My Works, Ye Mighty and Despair: Breaking Bad as Austerity Allegory."

The Devil is in the Details: Twilight Zone's Demonology of Capital

Originally written in March of 2019.

It is impossible to overstate how much a fan I was of *The Twilight Zone*. I watched every episode of the old show, it was the reason that I had a small black and white TV in my bedroom growing up; I also subscribed to the magazine with the same name, which covered science fiction and published original short stories, and I also watched the movie that was released in the eighties and at least one of the reboots.

Perhaps the most iconic plot on the original run of *The Twilight Zone* is the deal with the devil. The story usually goes as follows, an individual makes a deal with the devil for some desired outcome, riches, power, or health, and finds himself suddenly faced with the unintended consequences of their wish. The devil is in the details and every attempt to orchestrate the perfect wish inevitably backfires. One can wish to be the ruler of a powerful country and find oneself Hitler, or wish to have piles of money only to have to deal with the taxes, and so on. (Those examples are from The Man in the Bottle, which in this case dealt with a genie and not the devil).

It is tempting to see the devil as just the characterization of the show's irony, and love of the twist ending. That a deal with the devil could go wrong is not something that the characters on the show are unaware of, however, everyone tries to outsmart the devil. Take the season one episode titled "Escape Clause" for example. A bitter and angry hypochondriac named Walter Bedecker makes a deal with the devil for eternal health and life. Walter Bedecker, doesn't seem to enjoy life, spending every hour convinced he is sick he miserably lashes out at the doctor and his wife. He exemplifies Aristotle's picture of the miser, he is not interested in the quality of life, in living well, but the endless accumulation of its quantity. As Aristotle puts it, "The reason they are so disposed, however, is that they are preoccupied with living, not with living well." He is not without his cunning however. From the outset the devil, a jolly rotund man named Cadawaller, seems to be outwitted; someone who never dies will never have a soul for the devil to own. Walter Bedecker takes on his newfound immortality with reckless abandon, throwing himself onto train tracks, drinking poison, etc. His wife finds him about to leap from a building and dies trying to stop him. Walter confesses to killing her with the idea that the electric chair would be a fun thing to try. Unfortunately his hardworking lawyer gets him a life sentence instead. Hell is a place on Earth. Luckily this particular deal with the devil has an escape clause. Walter can opt out of eternal life at any moment, quickly shedding his mortal coil, and then his soul belongs to the devil. The devil is in the details, or, in this case, the fine print.

The Twilight Zone's devils may prey on the sins of vanity and greed, but their methods are more bureaucratic than theocratic. The deal is exactly as it is presented; what is concealed is only what the seller failed to see, the unintended consequences of their decision. It seems fitting that a society that venerated the unintended consequences of human actions through a theology of the market would find its image of the devil in these same actions. While the theology of the market is the invisible hand transforming unintended consequences into social benefits—our earthly god—its demonology is the way in which a pursuit of individual self-interest necessarily comes up

against the limits of individual knowledge bringing unanticipated consequences on the individual. No one can anticipate all the possible ramifications of one action, even of one wish, even eternal life has its unforeseen downside. The god of the market reassures us that our self-interested actions benefit society, but the devil of responsibility reminds us that we will be held accountable for even those things we never could have predicted. I should mention at this point that I have been reading Adam Kotsko's *Neoliberalism's Demons*, but I probably should have read *The Prince of this World*.

The episode that goes the furthest in this theology of capital is from season four, "Of Late I think of Cliffordville." Incidentally the episode is perhaps the source of one of the most famous misquotations in contemporary popular culture. In *Die Hard* Hans Gruber famously states, "And when Alexander saw the breadth of his domain, he wept, for their were no more worlds to conquer." He credits this line to Plutarch and thus to the benefits of his classical education. However, no such line appears in Plutarch[1].

---

1 Anne Perry, "The Wit and Wisdom of Hans Gruber." https://hodderscape.co.uk/wit-wisdom-hans-gruber/

It does, however, show up in *The Twilight Zone*. Perhaps by classical education he meant classic television. A similar sentiment appears in yet another classic, Marx's *Capital*. As Marx writes describing the logic of accumulation, "This contradiction between the quantitative limitation and the qualitative lack of limitation of money keeps driving the hoarder back to his Sisyphean task: accumulation. He is in the same situation as a world conqueror, who discovers a new boundary with each country he annexes."[2] It is not Alexander who needs new territories to conquer, but the modern demand of capitalist accumulation. As we will see this is in line with the episode in question.

The episode opens on the office of William Feathersmith, an energy tycoon who is shown buying out his last competitor. The completion of his empire is also the exhaustion of his purpose. It is the building's janitor who makes the connection to Alexander the Great. Upon leaving his office Mr. Feathersmith finds himself in the office of the Devlin Travel Services. He meets the owner, Miss Devlin (played by Julie Newmar) who makes no attempt to conceal her demonic nature. Mr. Feathersmith expects that she is looking for him to sell his soul, but it turns out to already be in the devil's possession. There are almost no classic Faustian bargains on the Twilight Zone. Mr. Feathersmith's lifetime of accumulation has destroyed countless lives dooming him to eternal damnation. Miss Devlin deals in cash. In exchange for most of Mr. Feathersmith's wealth Miss Devlin is able to realize his dream. Mr. Feathersmith desires to travel back in time to the Cliffordsville of his youth, to 1910, so he can rebuild his empire. This is a repetition with a difference, however, Mr. Feathersmith knows now what he does not know then; he knows where untapped oil reserves are, the fate of several companies on the stock market, and every invention for the last fifty years. Mr. Feathersmith extols the virtues of competition yet wants to enter a game that is entirely rigged in his favor.

---

2 Karl Marx, *Capital: A Critique of Political Economy, Volume I*, Translated by Ben Fowkes, (New York: Penguin, 1977), 230.

Mr. Feathersmith's attempts to rig the game fail. The oil field that he knows about cannot be excavated for several decades. It is too deep under the ground to be tapped by the machinery of nineteen-ten. Moreover, his knowledge of such inventions as a self-starting motor, radio, and aluminum is not the knowledge of a worker or engineer but of an investor or consumer. He only knows the vague generalities of these devices, not the concrete specificity that would make it possible to invent them. He tries to talk to a few mechanics but knowing something will exist in the future tells them nothing of how to make it in the present. The entire episode seems like "Reification and the Consciousness of the Proletariat" as rewritten by Rod Serling. The bourgeoisie cannot comprehend history, the actual process of historical change, because he is necessarily absent from the site of its making, from the site of production. In its place there is only the mythology of great individuals, or Mr. Feathersmith's confidence that he, like Alexander, is one of those great individuals that make history and the confidence in the objectivity of historical progress. The oil was discovered outside of Cliffordsville in the thirties so it could just as easily be discovered in nineteen ten. History is not a process without a subject, but a story that is waiting for the right subject. As Lukács writes in the original, "As a result of its incapacity to understand history, the contemplative attitude of the bourgeoisie became polarized into two extremes: on the one hand, there were the 'great individuals' viewed as the autocratic makers of history, on the other hand, there were the 'natural laws' of the historical environment."[3] What is left out of these extremes is the real work of making history. Or as Miss Devlin puts it to Mr. Feathersmith,

> "Of course it didn't work. It could *never* work for *you*, Mr. Feathersmith; shall I tell you why? Because you are a wheeler and a dealer. A financier and a pusher. A brain, a manipulator, a raider. Because you are a taker instead of a builder. A conniver instead of a designer. An exploiter instead of an inventor. A user instead of a bringer."

In this case the struggle between man and devil is just a proxy war for the class struggle. Such as passage would not be out of place in Lukács critical discussion of bourgeois consciousness. In our world the unintended consequences of contractual obligations often plague the poor, who have no time to read the fine print of their credit cards or cellphone contracts, but in Serling's world it is the wealthy, the powerful, and cruel who are forces to confront the consequences of their actions by a devil that dwells in the details.

For more on Rod Serling as a social critic see "Ape Like Imitation: Repetition in Difference in the Planet of the Apes."

---

3 Georg Lukács, *History and Class Consciousness: Studies in Marxist Dialectics*, Translated by Rodney Livingstone, (Cambridge: MIT Press, 1971), 158.

"Live Every Week Like it is Shark Week": Remarks on the Ecology of the Mediasphere

First published August 7, 2011. Updated several times to follow the progress of the hurricane shark meme.

Friday morning, as the local and national media went on a feeding frenzy of sorts over Hurricane Irene, complete with radar maps and rain-soaked correspondents bracing themselves against the wind and rain, the following image, taken of a TV set in Miami made it onto Youtube and into my Facebook news feed.

I must confess that I posted it and shared it. And since one confession deserves another, I should say that I was obsessed with sharks as a kid. I would check out books on sharks from the library, and once even owned a book called *Shark* which was nothing more than a series of brief descriptions, like a police blotter only more gory, of every documented shark attack for the better part of a century. This book was sold as part of a school book fair, because nothing encourages young readers like death. My desire to post it was part of my lingering fascination and fear of sharks, which I would like to critically unpack here.

Initially, it occurred to me that this image, with its evocation of sharks riding storm surges into city streets and preying on beleaguered hurricane survivors, had already been done as film (albeit yet to be released) as an example of life imitating a bad movie. A film called *Bait* details what happens when sharks swim ashore after a hurricane and end up hunting in a big box store.

It turns out that there is a third act to the story, it was later revealed that the image that made it onto the news is a fake, a doctored image. It is a photoshop of perhaps one of the most famous shark images to be produced recently. The original photo was taken by Thomas P. Peschak of a great white shark curiously following a kayak.

There is nothing exceptional about this little story, it is in some sense mundane, there are countless youtube phenomena that turn out to be fakes and hoaxes, but it does illustrate several things that define our moment. First, we have the TV news, which has responded to the decline in audience share and the rise of digital image capturing devises (cameras, smart phones, etc.) by more or less outsourcing its news gathering. "Send us your pictures, video, comments, and tweets," is the demand made by every newspaper and television station. This might be a way to make up for the loss of reporters, or it might be a way to gain audience, perhaps the news editors figure that people will watch and read just to see if their images and comments have made it onto the air. We could celebrate this breakdown of the distinction between author and producer, see it as the democratization of the news: "You Report, You Decide," or something to that effect. However, doing so overlooks at least two things. First of all, there is the news media's imperative to capture attention, in this case, to ride the storm of attention by offering the most extreme photos and the satellite pictures with the most vivid colors. Immediacy and capturing attention take precedence over truth and verification. There is no time to fact check the shark when you have to get it on the air before the other network does. They might have the picture of the wind toppling a McDonald's sign but they do not have the blood thirsty shark cruising along the interstate. Second, and with all apologies to Walter Benjamin, any simple identification of the author as producer overlooks the way in which affects, such as fear, and imaginaries, such as the image of the shark, are disseminated just as fast as digital images. The audience that produces is itself a product of culture industry, to frame this whole issue in terms of the Benjamin/Adorno dialectic.

This brings us to sharks, my childhood object of fascination and fear. It will one day be necessary to write the history of the shark as image, as spectacle (perhaps this has already been done). This history, at least the history that I am thinking of, begins with *Jaws*, which we all know begins the history of that unique cultural form, the summer blockbuster. Despite this success at the level of form, *Jaws* has not really been duplicated at the level of content or genre. There have been a handful of sequels, a few lackluster shark movies, and the occasional piranha or killer bear. (One is reminded of Nobuhiko Obayashi's remarks about the limits of the culture industry, "A hit movie about shark attacks leads to a movie about bear attacks. That is the best they can do.")[1] What is more perplexing is that the shark movies that are made become more and more outlandish, with sharknados, octosharks, megalons, etc., moving

---

1 https://socialismandorbarbarism.blogspot.com/2011/02/nobuhiko-obayashi-explains-limitations.html

further and further from the fundamental fear of being in the water surrounded by unseen creatures. This failure at the level of fiction has been more than made up for at the level of fact, or pseudo-fact: we do not get a shark movie every year, or every few years, as we do slasher films, films about demonic possessions, or zombies, but we do get *Shark Week*. *Jaws* has permeated our consciousness in countless staged attacks by sharks on chunks of meat and dummies made up to look like surfers.

Sharks have permeated our imaginary, become objects of fear, despite the fact that shark attacks are still incredibly rare. After all, that book on shark attacks that I once owned was incredibly thin and small. A book of highway accidents or bathtub accidents, or just people killed in hurricanes, would be much thicker. At the same time sharks, actual sharks, are becoming increasingly vulnerable and threatened as a species, victims of the appetite for shark fin soup and the perils of being an alpha predator in a declining ecosphere. This is what it might mean to "live every week like it is shark week," to repeat the quote stolen from Tracy Jordan on *30 Rock*, it is to live in a world of imagined fears, of shark attacks and wars on terror, on a continued heightened state of alert, without seeing the real dangers, and, most importantly, the role we play in creating them. The really depressing part is that we create not only the real dangers, the dangers of oceans on the verge of dying, but we create the fake ones as well, submitting our images and tweets, and, if necessary, inventing them.

Updated 8/30/17:

The shark image resurfaced again after Hurricane Harvey and, like before, it made its way from the hoax infested waters of social media to the supposedly more serene and safer waters of journalism, proving once again that those borders are even less stable then they were six years ago. Or, to paraphrase a documentary about *Jaws*, the shark is still working. It still shows up, proving that people often believe what they want to believe.

It is possible to see the shark as the token image of the Anthropocene, of not only the destruction of the oceans and the environment, but our own self destruction as well, our inability to think through these dire times. Humanity jumping the shark.

Updated 3/24/18

It thus seems fitting that Donald Trump is obsessed with shark week not just because he is the presidency jumping the shark, a desperate attempt to revitalize a collapsing institution with every shameless trick, but because shark week is the logic of his politics. He lives off of invented threats from illegal immigration to the specter of transgender people in the military, a whole bestiary of imagined threats. As with the shark, real sharks, his imagined threats are often the most vulnerable and threatened people in society, people subject to discrimination and abuse. It is an inverted world in which the vulnerable become threatening and the threatening see themselves as vulnerable. The breakdown of the media ecology is also a breakdown in psychic ecology. To borrow a phrase from Félix Guattari, Shark Week is the collapse of three ecologies, natural, social, and psychic. No species can survive that.

Updated 8/22/21

Once again "the shark is still working," it is still out there, ready to be shared anew with every hurricane. Is it still being taken seriously, or is it is a joke now, has it jumped the shark becoming a knowing meme about online lies and our tendency to believe them? And what sort of difference would that make?

Updated 9/30/22

As with the wolf in the story of the boy who cried wolf, the hurricane shark appears to have become real this time. Video from Fort Myers seems to show a shark swimming in a park. The *New York Times* article on this charts the long history of the highway shark meme.[2] Of course in the story of the boy who cried wolf everything comes to an end when the real wolf appears. The real shark might have killed the meme, or it may have finally jumped the shark to another species. I also saw this picture from the aftermath of Hurricane Ian of an alligator inside a house. I am no expert, but the lack of any ripple or distortion around the alligator suggests photoshop to me. It appears that this photograph is not unlike its more famous relative, the highway shark, it is a picture that circulates again and again with different hurricanes, typhoons, and floods.[3]

More importantly, or more to the point, this particular image existed first as a movie before it became a meme, *Crawl* was released in 2019, suggesting that we are still dealing as much with a crisis of the media produced imagination as the fossil fuel produced ecosphere. Life may not imitate art, but our imagination imitates summer blockbusters.

---

2 https://www.nytimes.com/2022/09/30/us/hurricane-shark-ian-hoax.html
3 https://www.newsweek.com/did-alligator-break-house-hurricane-ian-1747775

These Hollywood images of sharks swimming down the highway or alligators cruising through living rooms are in some sense the screen memory of the anthropocene in two senses of the word, what screens us from confronting climate collapse and what comes to us through the screens that infuse our lives. <u>When faced with an actual apocalypse we prefer to rerun the one that is in our head.</u>

Old Time Religion: On American Gods the book and TV show

Originally written in June of 2017 after the first season of the television show, a show that I did not continue watching beyond that point.

The following passage from Marx's Grundrisse could serve as a fairly accurate pitch meeting for *American Gods*:

> "Let us take e.g. the relation of Greek art and then of Shakespeare to the present time. It is well known that Greek mythology is not only the arsenal of Greek art but also its foundation. Is the view of nature and of social relations on which the Greek imagination and hence Greek [mythology] is based possible with self-acting mule spindles and railways and locomotives and electrical telegraphs? What chance has Vulcan against Roberts and Co., Jupiter against the lightning-rod and Hermes against the Crédit Mobilier? All mythology overcomes and dominates and shapes the forces of nature in the imagination and by the imagination; it therefore vanishes with the advent of real mastery over them...

From another side: is Achilles possible with powder and lead? Or the Iliad with the printing press, not to mention the printing machine? Do not the song and the saga and the muse necessarily come to an end with the printer's bar, hence do not the necessary conditions of epic poetry vanish?"[1]

The show, which is based on Neil Gaiman's novel of the same name, concerns the conflict between the "old gods" and the "new gods." The old gods are the gods of gods of disparate pagan traditions from Odin to Anansi, all brought to this country on slave ships and with those who came to these shores as indentured servants and immigrants, all in decline, forgotten by the people who once brought them to these shores. The new gods, at least the ones we meet are Media, World (globalization), and Technology, the new forces that people look to in their despair and aspire to in their desires. As Odin, or Mr. Wednesday as more commonly known as, puts it in Neil Gaiman's novel, "There are new gods growing in America, clinging to growing knots of belief: gods of credit card and freeway, of Internet and telephone, of radio and hospital and television, gods of plastic and of beeper and of neon. Proud gods, fat and foolish creatures, puffed up with their own newness and importance."

The explanation of the existence of Gods and their conflict is more Feuerbach than Marx, as the novel makes clear. The gods' thrive on belief, on prayer, and sacrifice,

"People believe, thought Shadow. It's what people do. They believe, and then they do not take responsibility for their beliefs; they conjure things, and do not trust the conjuration. People populate the darkness; with ghosts, with gods, with electrons, with tales. People imagine, and people believe; and it is that rock solid belief, that makes things happen.

American Gods is a literary formulation of the paradox of alienation, to use the term familiar to both Marx and Feuerbach:

---

1 Karl Marx, *The Grundrisse*, Translated by Martin Nicolaus, New York: Penguin, 1973, 110.

what people create, what people believe, ends up controlling them. Or, to use a different name for this same process, one closer to the realm of narrative, it is what Yves Citton calls "Immanent transcendence," what is entirely immanent to human existence, desire, fear, and imagination, produces as an effect an image of transcendence, of some instance standing above society, God, the sovereign, the state. The effect then becomes a cause (or what Deleuze and Guattari call a quasi-cause) dictating actions, desires, and beliefs. It is not surprising that writers are drawn to the idea: the notion that stories have power but only if people believe in them has been going on long before Tinkerbell drank the potion. The idea of the power of stories is in some sense the founding myth of literature in the same way that philosophers believe in reason and economists put their faith in the market. Triangles imagine triangular gods and dogs dream of dog gods. This multiplicity, the presence of the immanence in the transcendence, is not something the novel is silent on.

"Have you thought about what it means to be a god? … It means you give up your mortal existence to become a meme: something that lives forever in people's minds, like the tune of a nursery rhyme. It means that everyone gets to re-create you in their own minds. You barely have your own identity any more. Instead, you're a thousand aspects of what people need you to be. And everyone wants something different from you. Nothing is fixed, nothing is stable."

It is at this point that the differences between the novel and the series become relevant. The series sticks to the first few plot points of the novel, the first two episodes are mapped neatly onto the first few chapters of the book. A few episodes in, however, the two diverge, the series is set in the world of the novel but is not an adaptation of its plot, at least word for word. There is an interesting formal question here: the adaptation of novel for film used to be a paring down of extraneous elements, as plots and characters are dropped to fit into a film, but, now with television displacing film, adapting a novel into a series becomes a matter of stretching out the premise into something that can sustain indefinite variations. Novels, films, and television series are predicated on different economies of desire and belief, doling out their satisfactions and frustrations differently. The change of form cannot but affect content.

The series greatest departure, at least so far, is how it presents the conflict between the old and the new. In the series the old gods are not just forgotten they are also transformed. As Mad Sweeney, the leprechaun puts it. "I was a king once. Then they made me a bird. Then mother church came along and turned us all into saints and trolls and fairies. General Mills did the rest." A history not so much of being forgotten but of being retrofitted and reinterpreted. "Whatever exists, having somehow come into being, is again and again reinterpreted to new ends, taken over, transformed and redirected by some power superior to it." Pop-Nietzscheanism rather than pop-Feuerbach. Ostara lives in a home with dozens of Jesuses (Jesi?) of multiple races and denominations, bunnies, and plates covered with plates and jelly beans.

Along these lines, the new gods do not just want to wipe the old ones out, they want to rebrand them, take some of their power, their name and put it onto new platforms. A goddess of desire is offered a second life on tindr. This is illustrated most clearly in the case of Vulcan, an old god who has sold out to the new gods. He has gone from the god of fire to firearms, ruling over a company town where cartridges are manufactured.

"You are what you worship. God of the volcano. Those who worship hold a volcano in the palm of their hand. It's filled with prayers in my name. The power of fire is fire power. Not god, but godlike. And they believe. It fills their spirits every time they pull the trigger. They feel my heat on their hip and it keeps them warm at night."

As a god of firearms Vulcan is well placed to understand the circularity of belief generating belief, of effects become causes and vice versa. As he explains, "Every bullet fired in a crowded movie theater is a prayer in my name. And that prayer makes them want to pray even harder." Worship of guns generates worship of guns. The worship and adoration of firearms is an unstable combination of fear and security that seems to partake of something very ancient, even old testament.

It is then appropriate that the title *American Gods* is indeterminate, suggesting both the melting pot of diverse deities and demigods and the slick new gods of fame and fortune. The novel and series also invoke the heteronomy of americana, of road side attractions and other wayward beliefs, but underneath this plurality there is still the struggle for dominance and hegemony.

I am not going to oversell *American Gods*, it is yet another entry in the increasing pantheon to which we sacrifice our time, but it does offer an interesting illustration of not so much the paradox of immanent transcendence, but of a temporality in which America appears as "a motley painting of everything that has ever been believed," to paraphrase Deleuze and Guattari. The pagan, the monotheistic, and the modern coexist and transform each other. It is not a matter of some metanarrative of progress or decline but temporal overdetermination, of constant reinvention and transformation with the added caveat that reinvention is sometimes just a way for the oldest superstitions to live on.

For more on "immanent transcendence" see "Let Me Tell You of the Time That Something Occurred: On Yves Citton's Mythocratie." For more on stories and their power see "Meta-Fiction: The Comic Book."

The Golden Pig: Okja and the limits of Satire

Originally written in July of 2017.

Critics of *Okja* have been quick to point out its jarring tonalities, one part satire of the world of corporations and branding events and one part touching story of a girl and her (giant mutant) pig. This seems to be off for at least two reasons. Tonal shifts seem to be something Bong Joon-Ho revels in. *The Host* also melded horror, a family drama, and a scathing account of the US involvement in South Korea, and *Snowpiercer reveled in shifting tones*, as every new railcar opened to a new scene and a new mood, from its own satire of the ideological state apparatus to the horrorific scene of black hooded executioners of the repressive state apparatus. A kind of jarring tonal shift is not new to this movie.

   The second reason is the more interesting one. I think on some level the reason *Okja* fails as satire is that satire demands on some level a minimum level of dissonance between ideals and actuality. One can satirize politics, revealing the petty squabbles behind the grand projects because there are supposed to be grand ideals. The same is true of education, the church, etc. Satire exploits the space between the state ideals of institutions and their actual functioning. This becomes harder to do with respect to contemporary capitalism. *Okja* opens with a massive rebranding of the Mirando corporation (basically Monsanto), which after years of negative press plans to feed the world with a new breed of superpig, pigs the size of hippos. Mirando's branding campaign has everything we would expect from modern PR, it is a little United Colors of Benneton and a little bit like the "micro-credit" that Whole Foods is always pitching. It is as transparent as it is obvious, none of these things are actually believed by anyone. I guess one could say, as Zizek might, that these things are not meant to be believed but are addressed to the subject supposed to believe. That might be the case, but the transparency of the illusion makes the satire difficult to sustain. This is most painfully obvious in the case of Jake Gyllenhaal's parody of an animal planet television host. The joke would seem to be that he is woefully out of place in nature, struggling to hike up a hill, but even that is punctured by the fact that he is aware of his failing ratings. If everyone knows that the illusion is an illusion then what is there left to satirize.

However, I would argue that *Okja* is aware of the limits of satire. Its most intense and resonate scene has nothing to do with aggressive re-brandings or reality tv charlatans but is simply a stockyard and slaughterhouse. The only thing fantastic about this slaughterhouse is the size of the pigs. Everything else plays out like a kind of CGI cinema verité: everything is true and mundane except the creatures. There is an interesting dimension to this ruse. *Okja's* turn to the brutality of the slaughterhouse is prefigured by the narrative of the film; before the film shocks us with the brutality of slaughter the Animal Liberation Front (ALF) depicted in the film hijacks a PR stunt with video of the brutal treatment of Okja. The film narrates its own strategy. The creature feature pretext is really just a lure to get an audience to watch the ALF documentary they would never consider watching. Okja is a fictional pig, and her bond with Mija is the stuff of fiction, but the images of pig corpses dangling from the ceiling is harder to dismiss. *Okja* at times seems like a vegan propaganda film. However, in order for that propaganda to work there must be some shock, some power of images. The slaughterhouse must be something unknown or at least actively repressed for its revelation to have effects.

In the final scenes of the film Mija has tracked her beloved pig to the slaughterhouse, following her to the killing floor. There she is confronted by the butcher, air gun pointed directly between Okja's eyes. Mija removes from her fanny pack an old photograph of a younger her clutching a smaller pig, hoping that this image will change the pig from meat to pet. The butcher hesitates, but does not stop. Then a few seconds later, Nancy Mirando the CEO of Mirando enters the room. It is worth noting that Tilda Swinton plays both Lucy and Nancy Mirando, twins. Lucy and Mirando are distinguished by their relationship to the brand and image of the company. Lucy wants Mirando to be loved, wants to change its image from its brutal past to becoming the company that solved world hunger. Nancy, however, just wants to make a profit; for her the ultimate selling point of the giant pigs is not the heartwarming story of how they brought prosperity to a small village but how cheap the meat will be. It is not a matter of branding but of cost benefit analysis for everyone involved. When Mija confronts Nancy Mirando she does not show her an image of a childhood pet, or attempt to threaten her brand image, she simply makes a deal. She offers the golden pig in exchange for Okja's life, or, more to the point, she buys the pig.

This is the limit of satire that the film stages. Lucy Mirando, the believer in brands and images, can be satirized and scandalized, but Nancy, the calculator cannot. Perhaps on this point it is worthwhile to remember Marx. In Capital Marx has the worker address the capitalist as follows:

> "You may be a model citizen, perhaps a member of the R.S.P.C.A. [Royal Society for the Prevention of Cruelty to Animals], and you may be in the odour of sanctity as well; but the thing you represent when you come face to face with me has no heart in its breast."[1]

It is always possible to satirize human, all too human intentions, indicating the pettiness and cruelty underlying ideals, but the heart of capital is something entirely inhuman, the shear calculation of profits, it cannot be scandalized, only forced to calculate costs. There are no more golden calves, false idols to be taken down, just golden pigs to be exchanged.

The most powerful moment of the film, and most heartbreaking, is watching Mija and Okja leave the slaughterhouse as the rest of the superpigs are marched to slaughter. It is the most heartbreaking, but also the most accurate. Bargaining with capital, contending on its terms can save some but not all, and those who escape the slaughterhouse will always shoulder that burden.

For more on satire see "Man is a Super Villain to Man: On The Boys and Satire".

---

[1] Karl Marx, *Capital: A Critique of Political Economy, Volume I*, Translated by Ben Fowkes, (New York: Penguin, 1977), 343.

Man is a Super-Villain to Man: The Boys and the limits of Satire

Originally written in October of 2020.

Horkheimer and Adorno had to invent the neologism the "culture industry" to criticize the subordination of culture to commerce, these days we can accomplish the same thing by just saying "comic book movies." The comic book movie, or, to be more specific, Marvel movie has become a kind of shorthand for the dominance of culture by industry, intellectual property over creativity. I would argue that this particular shorthand leaves too many terrible, cynical, and derivative products off of the hook, like the execrable *The Rise of Skywalker* and the latest sequels to Jurassic Park and Terminator, but that is not the point here. My point is the way that the Amazon series *The Boys* takes this idea of the superhero as a figure of cultural and commercial dominance and doubles down on it only to turn it entirely inside out.

In the world of *The Boys* superheroes are "real," part of the real world, but unlike Watchmen (Moore's original version) where the reality of superheroes changes the nature of their fiction (leading to the popularity of pirate comics in place of superheroes) in the world of the Boys superheroes are both real people and cultural icons. They save the world and star in movies saving the world, and they also sponsor energy drinks, theme parks, casual dining restaurants, and release hit singles. Superheroes are not just situated at the intersection of commerce and culture they are at the pinnacle of the entire entertainment-corporate security-evangelical state-casual dining apparatus. The show can be understood as a satire of superheroes, but more than that it uses superheroes as figures for various forms of power and authority. The superheroes are also celebrities and politicians. It merges fictions of powers with the reality of power, fusing the two with often repeated dictum that power corrupts, adding that if power corrupts then imagine what superpowers would do.

The show functions as a kind of blowup, imagine if all of the myriad powers of our world, corporate, cultural, economic, political, religious, etc., coalesced in one particular institution, that of corporate superheroes. It presents the ideological state apparatus singing one song, as Althusser put it, or, a kind of Christmas effect, as J.K. Gibson-Graham put it, that moment when all the world, every company, every institution seems to be perfectly aligned behind the same message and aesthetic[1]. I think that this might be part of the show's appeal. The show is less about power fantasies that the audience gets to indulge in than the way most people feel utterly powerless in the face of our dominant corporate culture. More specifically, the way anyone on the "left" feels today. I am using that term broadly for anyone who thinks that there is more to life, to human existence, than simply creating more wealth for billionaires. If you believe that then you are up against the dominant sensibilities of politics, culture, and entertainment, against forces so powerful that they might as well be bulletproof and able to fly.

---

1 J.K. Gibson-Graham, *The End of Capitalism (As We Knew It): A Feminist Critique of Political Economy*, Minneapolis: University of Minnesota, 1996, xxxviii

Proof that sometimes The Boys wears its anti-capitalist allegory on its sleeve

On the show, the pinnacle of power is The Seven. The Seven who are more or less modeled after the Justice League (or Superfriends if you are more familiar with the television version) are made up of Homelander, a Superman like figure who is also a completely amoral narcissist; Queen Maeve, a closeted Wonder Woman who is filled with self-loathing for what she has become; The Deep, an Aquaman who makes up for his status as punchline by being a sexual predator; A Train, a speedster like the Flash who is hooked on a drug called Compound V; Black Noir, a batman like ninja who is a murdering sociopath; and, as the one deviation from the Justice League model, Translucent, an invisible man who is, like all invisible men, is a voyeuristic creep. (I know that is only six, more on that in a moment) As much as we see their various flaws, this is not how the world sees them, to the world they are heroes. They keep their true nature hidden not by masks and mild-mannered alter egos but with a public relations team and the real world powers of non-disclosure agreements and generous settlement checks. One of the show's most creative ways of playing with the superhero is to replace all of the various weaknesses of superheroes, the proverbial kryptonite, with one singular weakness, bad publicity. The superheroes that can deflect bullets can be brought down by leaked video of any of their misdeeds.

Season one of the show is framed by two characters who function as audience surrogates, introducing us to this world. First we meet Hughie Campbell whose girlfriend is killed when A-Train runs through her at top speed. (It is worth noting that the show begins with collateral damage. If superhero movies are in some sense the cultural form of the 9/11 era, as Dan Hassler-Forest puts it, then collateral damage could be considered a kind of a return of the repressed—a recognition of the limits of the narrative of avenging justice.)[2] Hughie is offered the usual settlement and NDA but refuses to go along out of grief and a sense of injustice. He then gets more or less dragged into the anti-superhero vigilantes that I guess could be called The Boys of the show's title, but are never referred to as that in the show. Then we meet Annie January, also known as Starlight a young superhero who is called up to the big leagues to join the Seven, replacing a retired member. It is through their eyes that we learn that the world is not as it seems, or, in the words of the show's advertising, "Never meet your heroes." The show's focus on the dark underbelly of superheroes extends to other cultural institutions such as religious evangelicals, politicians, and the media, all of which are shown to be corrupt. Hughie and Annie both learn the world is not as it seems as their idealism is thrown against the cynical functioning of the world.

I mention Hughie and Annie because I think that they are a necessary counterpart to the show's celebration of violence, gore, and embrace of a kind of "everything sucks" mentality. They are idealistic, hopelessly so, and dorky, fans of Billy Joel. Their star-crossed romance of anti-superhero vigilante and superhero is the heart of the show's heartless world. I also mention Annie because despite the show's title, and advertising, it is not nearly as testosterone driven as it first appears. Hughie proves to be quite adept at becoming a vigilante, despite his modest milquetoast background, and Annie proves to be incapable of stomaching the

---

2 Dan Hassler Forest, *Capitalist Superheroes Caped Crusaders in the Neoliberal Age*, London: Zero Books, 2012.

hypocrisy of becoming a newly manufactured superhero, rejecting her corporate image and her role within evangelical Christianity.

The big reveal of the first season is that Vought, the company that sponsors the superheroes, also created them with a chemical known as Compound V. (In an odd mashup the superheroes from *The Boys* are modeled after DC comics but their real origin story is very Marvel, chemically created mutations). Not only did Vought create them, but it keeps creating new super-villains with this compound. The ultimate goal of this is to create enough fear that the US will authorize superheroes in the military in the same way that superhero movies seek military tie-in contracts. That is where the big money is. For the Vought corporation superheroes are simply the best way to make money.

The closer the characters on the show get to uncovering the big conspiracy, that Vought is primarily interested in money, the more the show touches upon the limitation of satire. I will admit that I was late to watch the show, but binge watched the first season in a few nights. I watched the second as well, but it was hard not to see some limits of its satire as the show progressed.

The second season had some moments. A new character, Stormfront is introduced as a member of the Seven. She replaces The Deep who is ousted after Starlight reveals his history of sexual harassment. As the name suggests Stormfront is a racist with ties back to Nazi Germany and a violent history in the Jim Crow South. She has concealed this with a bit of rebranding, although it is never really clear where she has been for fifty years. Perhaps the most interesting thing about Stormfront is the way that she engages in a different form of public relations. She does not have the expertly crafted look or scripted storylines of the rest of the Seven, but protects her image with any army of trolls and memes, which push some familiar sounding fears about super terrorists crossing our borders. At times the show can get very close to the way power, real power, the kind that flows through airwaves and mobilizes anger, actually works, as in the scene that shows the radicalization of a lone wolf shooter. (Sometimes *The Boys* seems to get at the heart of the real in a way that only a show about fantasy can).

After establishing that the Seven are constrained only by bad publicity, that a video of one of their murders or other crimes is their kryptonite, it would have been brilliant to introduce a character that is immune to bad publicity. Who can turn out a few memes and turn every bad publicity against her enemies. The show hints at that, but then returns to its theme of the Vought corporation's pursuit of profit. In the second season we learn that Vought is moving away from superheroes to directly selling the compound that makes superheroes, eliminating the middle man and selling the ultimate weapon of super soldiers. Stormfront's shittposting is just a means to this end, a way to make people angry and afraid, turning that anger and fear into profits.

All of this culminates in the scene in which Stan Edgar, the CEO of Vought reveals that everything, all of the politics and public relations comes down to one thing, making money. The thing about this scene is that there is not really any place to go with it, at least as far as satire goes, once you have revealed that everything, superheroes, super-villains, nations, and security, are just ways of making money, there is not much to satirize anymore. Satire demands ideals to satirize. There are only two directions to go in once you arrive at the idea that everything is all about money: you either make everything about mankind's greedy and corrupt nature, do a kind of pop-Hobbes, or you begin to ask questions of how it came to be that everything is about money, and what drives that, in other words, Marx. The first has been done to death, and the second is hard to do, at least in a show on Amazon about superheroes.

For More on superhero films see "Avenge Me: Avengers and the Culture Industr"y and "Becoming Spider-Man: Deleuze and the Superhero Film." For more on satire and its limits see "The Golden Pig: Okja and the limits of Satire."

In Space No One Can Hear You Struggle: On The Expanse

Originally posted June of 2017, updated in February of 2021.

As it has often been noted, Science fiction has been relatively absent from the so-called golden age of television, the kind of television that gets written about in blogs and websites. Sure, there have been shows such as *Battlestar Galactica*, *Black Mirror* and, recently, *Westworld*, but most prestige television has been dominated by a particular kind of melodrama set in either in the present or some nostalgic past. There is of course *Game of Thrones*, as one exception, which has brought fantasy to television. Science fiction has generally not broken through into prestige television.

Both *Game of Thrones* and *The Expanse* are developed from a series of novels, that is the most obvious point of comparison. Beyond they have a similarity in narrative device, as multiple threads across different locations occasionally intersect in a larger conflict. This is underscored in the opening credits of the second season of *The Expanse* which even borrows the images of tiny models depicting the different locations of Earth, Mars, and the belt. Beyond this similar narrative structure there is a similar narrative thematic to both shows. As it has often been noted, *Game of Thrones* is framed between a kind of Machiavellian realpolitik, in which different individuals and families vie for the throne with murder and deception, and a Manichaean opposition of light and dark, good and evil, in which all of humanity is pitted against the "white walkers." The latter is of course more familiar to fantasy fans ever since Frodo traveled to Mordor. Much of the supposed sophistication of *Game of Thrones* stems from the fact that it sprinkles its fantastic battle of light and dark with human conflicts. It is the television equivalent of the "salted caramel" flavor that has become so popular—salty nuance applied to children's candy.

If I was going to write more about *Game of Thrones* I would be tempted to write a dialectical critique that pointed out that its realism tends to become increasingly fantastic, as its plots about power struggles devolve into a kind of theater of cruelty, while its fantasy elements, zombies and dragons, point to the reality of a society oblivious to its own destruction. To put it bluntly, when your "realism" is dogs eating someone's face it has crossed the line into its own (darker) fantasy. Many critics have argued that the show's realpolitik realism is one in which rape and torture function as the ultimate evidence of reality. I suppose that this critique would only be remotely dialectical if I could point out that the other element, its fantasy is more realistic than the show claims, in that it is ultimately about the way a society confronts, or fails to confront, an existential threat such as global warming that makes all of the realpolitik struggles for power appear to be a kind of fantasy

The Expanse is not without its Machiavellian and Manichaean elements. Mars, Earth, and the various denizens of the cluster of space stations and mining colonies constantly struggle for power and domination. This is especially true of "the belt," the collection of mining colonies and space stations in the asteroid field between Mars and Jupiter and the locus of much of the show's action. The belt is divided between different factions all vying for control. The "Outer Planets Alliance" or OPA functions as the most militant, or from the perspective of Earth, radical dimension of this conflict. Earth and Mars are poised on the constant verge of a cold war turning hot, or as hot as things can get in the vacuum of space. This three way Machiavellian struggle begins to unearth a more manichaeanism opposition between the denizens of our solar system and some alien "protomolecule"—a weapon or form of life that could destroy or remake all of human life. (The name "protomolecule" comes from Protogen the corporation that initially begins experimenting with it. Its true name and function remains unclear.) The squabbles within the solar system take place against the backdrop of a larger alien threat.

Sticking with the letter "M," it is possible to argue that *The Expanse* adds Marx, or at least a certain aspect of Marx to the Machiavellian/Manichaean mix. Many commentators have made this connection with "the belters" who are the exploited working class of space. This is no doubt true, and the show does a better job of continuing the theme of workers in space than the recent Alien film. What I think makes for a more interesting Marxist dimension is the way in which the show restores a particular strong reading of Marx's concept of the mode of production. The different planets and outer planets are distinguished in terms of not just their place in a power struggle, but in terms of their different material conditions. Earth is defined by a relative abundance of water and air, an abundance which is squandered and destroyed by a population that takes it for granted; Mars by a common project of terraforming, by collective discipline and purpose, and the belt by scarcity and exploitation, by a kind of precarity one can only experience if food and water are constantly at risk.

Now of course it is possible to map Earth, Mars, and the belt, along the (dated) schema of first, second, and third worlds. You have the two superpowers, with their different attitudes towards wealth, production and consumption, and you have the exploited smaller countries between them. What is most interesting about *The Expanse* is the way this solar-political difference forms the basis of not only different cultures, but a division of humanity. Earth, Mars, and the belt are different versions of humanity. Belters look different than Earthers and Martians, they are taller and thinner due to the lack of gravity, and are often covered with tattoos. Even those from Mars can barely tolerate the high gravity, bright sun, and open horizons of Earth.

The show then expands the mode of production in two ways. First, it incorporates nature, the conditions of production, into the concept. Mars, Earth, and the belt differ not just in terms of how they produce and who they produce for, but also in terms of what they produce from. Earth is post-scarcity because the basic conditions of survival are given rather than produced, Mars is defined by a collective project to make a planet livable, a project and a telos, while the belt is defined by an absolutely hostile life against a harsh vacuum. It is a depiction of the mode of production fitting for the anthropocene in which nature and culture are thoroughly intertwined. However, it is as much interested in anthropos as the environment. The second change of the concept, or at least its pop figuration, is that the different productive conditions, or modes of production, have anthropological effects. As much as *The Expanse* has aliens of a more conventional variety, beings from outside the solar system, it is also a story of the becoming alien of humanity, of differences of production being somatized in differences of body. Of course, one could argue that this has always been the case, this anthropological division appears in Marx's earliest texts on alienation. As Marx writes,

> "It is true that labour produces marvels for the rich, but it produces privation for the worker. It produces palaces, but hovels for the worker. It produces beauty, but deformity for the worker. It replaces labour by machines, but it casts some of the workers back into barbarous forms of labour and turns others into machines. It produces intelligence, but it produces idiocy and cretinism for the worker."[1]

Or to cite a passage from Balibar that I returned to more than once on this blog:

---

1 Karl Marx, *Early Writings*, trans, Rodney Livingstone and Gregor Benton, (New York: Penguin, 1975) 326.

> "This process modifies the status of the human body (the human status of the body): it creates body-men, men whose body is a machine-body, that is fragmented and dominated, and used to perform one isolated function or gesture, being both destroyed in its integrity and fetishized, atrophied and hypertrophied in its 'useful' organs. Like all violence, this is inseparable from a resistance and also a sense of guilt...This is an unbearable process for the worker, but one which is no more 'acceptable,' without ideological and phantasmic elaboration, for the worker's masters: the fact that there are body-men, mean that there are also men without bodies."[2]

The two expansions, pardon the pun, of the mode of production, its incorporation into nature and its extension into the body suggest what is most necessary to reviving the concept today. The mode of production must make sense of a world in which nature can longer function as a simple outside, as raw material, but must be understood to be both a condition and effect of transformations of production, of the search for cheap nature and the metabolic rift that undermines the very reproduction of our life. It must also be brought to bear on a world which, to cite Balibar once again, in "which humankind becomes economically and, to some extent, culturally "united," it is violently divided "biopolitically." To which I would add, divided anthropologically, as the common notion of humanity is split into multiple divisions that seem to have less and less in common.

Lest I go too far, it should be noted that *The Expanse* is a science fiction television show, and thus it requires, as such things often do, a ragtag group of individuals in a spaceship having adventures. However, what is interesting is that the crew of the Rocinante (pictured above) is made up of two former Earthers, one Martian, and one Belter (at least in the first five seasons). Their uneasy alliance suggests a kind of solidarity. Workers of the solar system unite, you have nothing to lose but your chains."

---

2 Etienne Balibar, "Class Racism" Translated by Chris Turner in Etienne Balibar and Immanuel Wallerstein *Race, Nation, Class: Ambiguous Identities*, Verso, 1991, 211.

Update 2/3/2021

After reading the fifth book, *Nemesis Games* and watching season five of the show, it strikes me that the "belters" as a representation of the working class are thoroughly ambivalent. On the one hand they are hyper-exploited, so much so that even those the most basic needs, fresh air, clean water, and basic food are constantly at risk. Here once again the young Marx is useful.

> "This estrangement partly manifests itself in the fact that the refinement of needs and of the means of fulfilling them gives rise to a bestial degeneration and a complete, crude and abstract simplicity of need; or rather, that it merely reproduces itself in its opposite sense. Even the need for fresh air ceases to be a need for the worker. Man reverts once more to living in a cave, but the cave is now polluted by the mephitic and pestilential breath of civilization. Moreover, the worker has no more than a precarious right to live in it, for it is for him an alien power that can be daily withdrawn and from which, should he fail to pay, he can be evicted at any time. He actually has to pay for this mortuary. A dwelling in the light, which Prometheus describes in Aeschylus as one of the great gifts through which he transformed savages into men, ceases to exist for the worker. Light, air, etc.—the simplest animal cleanliness—ceases to be a need for man. Dirt—this pollution and putrefaction of man, the sewage (this word is to be understood in its literal sense) of civilization—becomes an element of life for him. Universal unnatural neglect, putrefied nature, becomes an element of life for him."[3]

As the show progresses, or, to be more precise, as "the ring" opens up progress for the colonization of multiple habitable worlds beyond the solar system, the belters biopolitical status takes on a different meaning. The belters have lived their entire lives in the low gravity of space. This has shaped their bodies, they are supposed to be skinny

---

3 Karl Marx, *Early Writings*, trans, Rodney Livingstone and Gregor Benton, (New York: Penguin, 1975) 360.

and taller than Earthers or Martians. "Skinnies" is even quasi racist epithet This is something that the show can only gesture towards within its limited budget by casting tall and skinny actors to play belters. This means that they cannot progress, cannot move into the new worlds of the future. They are stuck in space, unable to move forward into a new frontier. This inability to move forward, to change, is one of the central motivations of Marco Inaros' Free Navy attack on Earth. He understands that with the opening of the "ring" the belters won't even be exploited, their work, their resources, will be bypassed by the ability to exploit other planets. The belters struggle against being obsolete as much as they struggle against their exploitation. Obsolescence is a fate even worse than exploitation, a fate of being utterly disposable and forgotten. The belt becomes the rust belt.

Science fiction offers an allegory for the ambiguity of what the term "working class" means in contemporary culture, situated someplace between exploitation and obsolescence. As much as their hard work is acknowledged they are seen as a relic, as something from a past, a past that should either be brought back (Make the Belt Great Again) or bypassed in some new, more automated and diverse future. Entering the ring is *The Expanse's* equivalent of learning to code, or embracing some new future.

It is hard not to think of that last aspect, working class as remnant and refusal to embrace the future, especially after learning that Jeff Bezos is a fan of the show (and was instrumental in bringing them to Amazon). The fifth season of the show even ends with a different image of workers coming together, it is the same crew, plus Bobbie as the new martian, but now they are under the auspices of the UN, celebrated by overcoming their different ethnicities. It is not so much a matter of the working class coming together to overcome exploitation, but a managed image of diversity. "This is how we win," Avasarala says.

For more on science fiction see "Violence and the Common: Truth is Structured Like a Science Fiction."

Gonna Leave You All Severed: Initial Reflections on Severance

Originally posted in April of 2022.

I was slow to get to *Severance*. Partly this has to do with conditions of contemporary cultural consumption. The shift from movies to television and from television to streaming, accelerated by the pandemic, has raised particular hurdles to watching new television shows even as everything can be viewed from one's home. Every new show comes with the subscription to a new service (or a way to work around it) and the proliferation of these services with their own branding and marketing enough to make me miss the catholic nature of movie theaters and video stores. Of the different services I had particular disdain for Apple TV, mostly due to the cross brand marketing and the lingering aftertaste of itunes as an app. Anything that could immediately disseminate a U2 album should not only be shunned but the people who made it should be banished.

People kept telling me to watch *Severance*, but it was not until Leigh Johnson referred to it as a follow up to *Black Mirror* that I became curious. No one knows and appreciates *Black Mirror* more than her. Now that I have seen the show I would go further back and say that it can be understood as a contemporary *Twilight Zone* in that at its core it is about a wish and its unintended consequences. What is the wish, though? For those of you still reluctant to join a new streaming service, I will sum up the basic premise of the show. It deals with a group of employees for the company Lumon who have volunteered to be "severed," the work life and memories separated from their home life. When they are at work they remember only work, and at home they remember only their home life. The popular response to this is that the fantasy underlying such a technology is that it is an attempt to find the much sought after "work/life balance:" no more anxieties about work deadlines keeping one up late at night and no more personal problems interfering with work. Everything is back in its proper place, the worker is at work when he or she is working and at home when they are home. This fantasy is reflected in the show's aesthetic, which suggests a nostalgia for the cubicle and the central office in the age of the cellphone, laptop, and the disseminated office.

This very much reflects current anxieties, but it seems to me that the show deals with a division that precedes the contemporary concern of time spent in the office. As Marx argues, wage labor, the selling of one's time and labor power, presupposes a division between the worker as both owner and seller of this commodity. As owner he or she is, like any other owner, seeking the best possible price, the best possible deal, for their time and effort; as seller the worker loses control over not only this commodity, but their time and activity belongs to someone else, and they are all the more alienated because they cannot alienate themselves, which is to say remove themselves from its use. They have to live out their day as their time, activity, thoughts and passions are controlled by another. As Pierre Macherey writes, "The condition for the wage system to produce all its effects is therefore that the worker has been put in the position of a divided subject, remaining entirely master of his labor power, has alienated only its use, which supposes that this force can be materially separated from its use."[1] The wish, the fundamental dream

---

1 Pierre Macherey *Le Sujet Productif*, Éditions Amsterdam, 2014, 159. My translation.

underlying *Severance*, is the fantasy that one could only occupy one side of this exchange, to sell labor power and never endure its use. To leave your body and mind at work and come back and pick them up at the end of the day. This would be the dream, a life of consumption without production, of free time without having to work, but *Severance* shows how that dream once realized, made literal, becomes a nightmare.

In *Severance* this split in the subject becomes a split between two subjects. One, the "innie," only knows about work, and is, at least in his or her perspective, is always at work; the other, the outie, is never at work and knows nothing about it. That this is an asymmetrical deal is illustrated by the character of Hellie (Britt Lower), who is severed at the beginning of the first episode, waking up at work, unable to remember anything about the outside world and beginning her life as an innie. She recognizes that she has the short end of the stick and wants out as soon as possible—literally running for the exits, but it turns out that her real jailer is not the corporation or her boss but herself, her "outie" who considers herself to be "the real person," leaving her work self to pay for her existence. One Hellie, the "outie," lives in the heaven of the sphere of exchange, free to spend her time and money as she pleases, while the other, "the innie," is stuck in the hell of the hidden abode of production. (This is an interesting twist on the idea of a doppelgänger.)

As much as *Severance* can be understood as picture of a kind of cubicle hell, focusing for the most part on the workday of those who will never know anything else, part of its genius is that it is attentive to all of the little strategies that make the workday not only livable, but actively desired. One of the central characters, Mark (Adam Scott), who we see as both an innie and outie, as both worker and person at home, is grieving the loss of his wife. Work is a respite from the pain of his home life. This is something that most critics of work overlook that in an increasingly atomized and mobile society work is for many people their social life. Work is portrayed as a place of friendships and frustrations, an entire world of social relations that is often desirable because, for all of its pains and boredom, there are at least other people, and, if you meet the right productivity goals, there are finger traps and waffle parties. (As Frédéric Lordon argues, part of what sustains the control that work has over our imagination and lives is our ability to adjust, to make the small pleasures of work fill the void left by the inability to struggle for greater ones.)

The rest of the members of the Macro Data Department, the department where Hellie and Mark work, make up the basis of a community of sorts complete with its little frustrations and pleasures. We have Irving (John Turturro) who has memorized the handbook, chapter and verse, and idealizes Lumon's founder and CEO, and Dylan (Zach Cherry) a man who has never passed up a chance to earn a waffle party. In the midst of all of *Severance* mysteries and satire there is a the basis for a pretty good workplace sitcom. This genre mashup, the moments of levity among the horror, only serve to punctuate the nightmare. It is because work is not a total hell in some theological sense, a place of total and complete horror, that it becomes our living hell.

So in the end, and I must admit that I have not finished the show yet (I am about halfway through), I am tempted to read its science fiction device as less a future possibility and more of a way of getting at a current reality. It is not a matter of asking, as in the case of *Black Mirror*, what would happen if we had this technology, if we could split ourselves into two selves, but that we already do. All of our dreams in capitalist society, of vacations, of things to buy, even of retirement, to the extent that it exists, are constituted in actively forgetting that they are paid for by our nightmares, of endless hours under neon doing pointless and meaningless tasks. We are always already severed and constantly subjecting our own "innie," to more and more work, so that we can live our lives as the "outie" that we take ourselves to be. The question that the show provokes in me is not what would it be like to be severed, or would you agree to be severed, but what would be like to live an integrated life, to live not as two sides of a commodity, owner and user, always at odds with oneself, but a life not subject to such divisions.

For more on the Twilight Zone see "The Devil is in the Details: The Twilight Zone's Demonology of Capital" For more on Frédéric Lordon see "Immanent Cause: Between Reproduction and Nonreproduction."

POLITICS

The Methlab of Democracy: More on the Micropolitics of Neoliberalism

Originally posted in June of 2010.

In a recent episode of the *The Daily Show* Jon Stewart, in a quip that is smarter than he knows, referred to Arizona as "the methlab of democracy." His reference is primarily to the recently passed immigration law. Stewart probably just meant that Arizona's law is crazy, hence methlab. (Crazy and racist, he actually gets in some good points about the latter as well, comparing the law to slavery era legislation). However, I think that there is a good reason that "meth" is the drug of our era, in the same way that pot, crack, and coke, all seemed to metonymically stand in for their respective eras, expressing the "tune out" rebellion of the sixties, urban poverty of the post-civil rights era, and "irrational exuberance" of the nineties. The major ingredient of meth is synthesized in corporate labs, but it is "cooked" in trailer parks. Meth stands in for the short circuit between corporate power and rural anger that seems to define contemporary US politics. (This is something that the TV series *Breaking Bad* has picked up on: the show not only deals with meth, but is set in the strip malls and housing developments of New Mexico, reflecting America's new spiritual home.)

The most recent Harper's also offers an examination of Arizona as the laboratory of America politics, as a place in which the "tea party" has already taken power. Perhaps the most interesting part of the article is the following quote by an unnamed government worker:

> "People who have swimming pools don't need state parks. If you buy your books at Borders you don't need libraries. If your kids are in private school, you don't need K-12. The people here, or at least those who vote, don't see the need for government. Since a lot of the population are not citizens, the message is that government exists to help the undeserving, so we shouldn't have it at all. People think it's OK to cut spending because ESL is about people who refuse to assimilate and health care pays for illegals."[1]

Putting aside for a moment the odd racist conflation of non-citizens and the undeserving at the end of the passage, the first part is strikingly similar to a passage in Wendy Brown's analysis of neoliberalism:

> "As neoliberalism converts every political or social problem into market terms, it converts them to individual problems with market solutions. Examples in the United States are legion: bottled water as a response to contamination of the water table; private schools, charter schools, and voucher systems as a response to the collapse of quality public education; anti-theft devices, private security guards, and gated communities (and nations) as a response to the production of a throwaway class and intensifying economic inequality; boutique medicine as a response to crumbling health care provision; "V-chips" as a response to the explosion of violent and pornographic material on every type of household screen; ergonomic tools and technologies as a response to the work conditions of

---

[1] Ken Silverstein, "Tea Party in the Sonora," *Harper's Magazine*, July, 2010. https://harpers.org/archive/2010/07/tea-party-in-the-sonora/

information capitalism; and, of course, finely differentiated and titrated pharmaceutical antidepressants as a response to lives of meaninglessness or despair amidst wealth and freedom. This conversion of socially, economically, and politically produced problems into consumer items depoliticizes what has been historically produced, and it especially depoliticizes capitalism itself. Moreover, as neoliberal political rationality devolves both political problems and solutions from public to private, it further dissipates political or public life: the project of navigating the social becomes entirely one of discerning, affording, and procuring a personal solution to every socially produced problem. This is depoliticization on an unprecedented level: the economy is tailored to it, citizenship is organized by it, the media are dominated by it, and the political rationality of neoliberalism frames and endorses it."[2]

Brown's passage, and the remarks from Arizona, demonstrate a kind of micropolitics of neoliberalism. The way in which neoliberalism does not just operate at the level of state policy, but at the level of quotidian practices and daily transactions. These practices and transactions produce a subject that sees him or herself as isolated and autonomous, producing disconnection that alternates between absolute freedom and total alienation.

All of this is offered as something of a rejoinder to J.M. Bernstein's recent piece for The New York Times philosophy column. Bernstein writes the following:

> "My hypothesis is that what all the events precipitating the Tea Party movement share is that they demonstrated, emphatically and unconditionally, the depths of the absolute dependence of us all on government action, and in so doing they undermined the deeply held fiction of individual autonomy and self-sufficiency that are intrinsic parts of Americans' collective self-understanding.

---

2 Wendy Brown, "American Nightmare: Neo-liberalism, Neo-Conservatism, and De-Democratization, *Political Theory*, Volume 34, Number 6, 2006, 704.

The implicit bargain that many Americans struck with the state institutions supporting modern life is that they would be politically acceptable only to the degree to which they remained invisible, and that for all intents and purposes each citizen could continue to believe that she was sovereign over her life; she would, of course, pay taxes, use the roads and schools, receive Medicare and Social Security, but only so long as these could be perceived not as radical dependencies, but simply as the conditions for leading an autonomous and self-sufficient life. Recent events have left that bargain in tatters."[3]

Bernstein primarily sees the Tea Party as a conflict between two views of freedom: one liberal, in which freedom is naturally given and must be realized, and the other Hegelian, in which freedom is a historical product, made possible by institutions. This is all well and good, but Bernstein then argues that the Tea Party is ultimately a metaphysical rather than political rebellion: they have no concrete proposals and are primarily reacting to a loss of a metaphysical ideal, that of the individual. The opposition between the metaphysical and the political overlooks the dimension of political economy entirely, or what I would prefer to call, following the remarks of Brown and the anonymous citizen from Arizona, the micro-politics of political economy, the point where political economy intersects with and transforms subjectivity. An adequate response to the current conjuncture cannot simply return to the opposition of Locke and Hegel, or politics versus metaphysics, but must take seriously the transversal intersections of politics, economics, and metaphysics.

For More on Individuality see "The Means of Individuation: Castel on Dialectics of Individuality" for the collapse of solidarity see "Negative Solidarity: Towards the Definition of a Concept."

---

3 J.M. Berstein, "The Very Angry Tea Party," *New York Times*, June 13, 2010. https://archive.nytimes.com/opinionator.blogs.nytimes.com/2010/06/13/the-very-angry-tea-party/

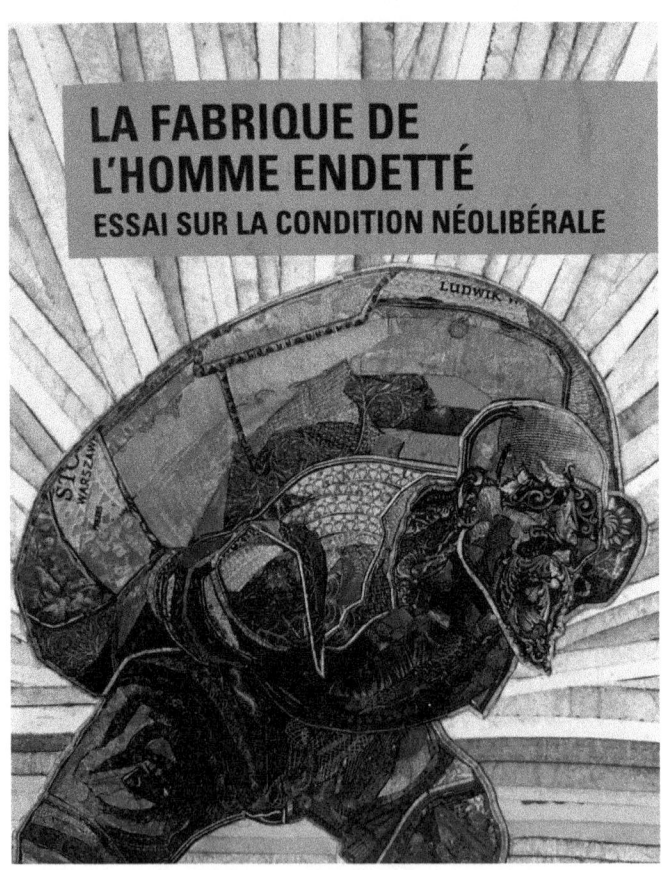

Debt Collectors: The Economics, Politics, and Morality of Debt

Originally posted in November of 2011.

Any philosophical consideration of the politics of debt must perhaps begin with the fact that the entire rhetoric of debt, owing and paying one's debts, is at once a moral and an economic vocabulary. This point is related to, but opposed to, Nietzsche's well-known argument in the *Genealogy of Morals*. Whereas Nietzsche argued that morality, or, more specifically, guilt, was simply debt, a payment in suffering for those who could not pay the price, an examination of debt reveals how much paying one's debts, paying one's bills, is a moral imperative as much as an economic relation.

As David Graeber argues, even from the standpoint of standard economic theory the positing of debt as some kind of moral duty, as something which can never be dispensed with, runs counter to not only the justification of interest, which is supposedly a compensation based on risk, but the immense apparatus dedicated to the assessment of risk, discerning good and bad risk. The moral imperative to pay one's debt contradicts the economic idea of debt as the other side of an investment, and a risk. The idea of paying one's debts is nothing other than a moral idea, and idea of an absolute moral obligation transposed into the realm of economy. One could consider this morality to be a slavish one, in that it keeps everyone paying their mortgage for a house that is underwater, and paying their student loans without ever getting the job promised by such an education. It would seem then that the political task is a matter of simply separating the morality of obligation from the economy of debt. The knot is a little more tangled than just tossing aside the language of debt entirely, since debt, is the predominant way of expressing social obligations. Graeber has argued that the prehistory of debt, the prehistory that explains the etymology of economics and morality, is based on the obligations that sustain society, between parents and children, husbands and wives, etc. However, these obligations were not monetized. To take a contemporary example, we owe a debt to our parents, but could never pay this back with a check, or doing so would be an insult. These debts exist in the form of obligations that are all the more binding in that they can never be calculated or paid. For a long time these non-monetized debts sustained social relations and individuals. The recent history of debt is one in which this dependency, at least partially recognized in terms of social rights, rights to education, care, etc., have become social debts, entitlements, which are in turn privatized and individualized. The primary sources of debt, especially in the US, are education, housing, and healthcare, are expressions of need, our radical lack of self-sufficiency as human beings. Untying the knot of economics and morality is not a matter of just throwing out the language of debt, but of subtracting dependency from the economy of debt, or in Graeber's terms, the human economy from the economy.

How is this to be done? How is it possible to draw a line between economics and morality? This is a question not just of words, of the same words for debt and obligation but of the interrelation of different practices and comportments, of the mode of production and the mode of subjection. Marx's commentary on James Mill offers an interesting examination of these questions. As Marx writes with respect to credit,

> "…a rich man gives credit to a poor man whom he considers industrious and decent. This kind of credit belongs to the

romantic, sentimental part of political economy, to its aberrations, excesses, *exceptions*, not to the *rule*. But even assuming this exception and granting this romantic possibility, the life of the poor man and his talents and labours serve the rich man as a *guarantee* that the money he has lent will be returned. That means, therefore, that the totality of the poor man's social virtues, the content of his life activity, his very existence, represent for the rich man the repayment of his capital with the customary interest."[1]

What Marx dismisses here as the "romantic" and "sentimental" aspect of political economy, is the personal relation of individual to individual. It is perhaps striking to juxtapose this text, written in eighteen forty four, with another passage from the same period, "The Power of Money in Bourgeois Society." In this text, Marx holds out the possibility of a relation between individuals unmediated by money. In such a society, Marx writes, "Each one of your relations to man—and to nature—must be a particular expression, corresponding to the object of your will, of your real individual life."[2] In that text the abstraction of money, its power to dissolve all social qualities displacing them with its social power, is opposed to a human relation, a relation of individual to individual. In contrast to this argument, the passage on credit suggests that such human evaluations, the estimation of a man's worth that form the basis of Horatio Alger myths and rags to riches fantasies, are not an exception to the rule of money but its realization. The credit relation is not a moment of unmediated relation and evaluation in a world dominated by the abstractions of money, but only the complete penetration of money into all of life. As Marx writes,

> "In the credit system man replaces metal or paper as the mediator of exchange. However, he does this not as a man but as the incarnation of capital and interest. Thus although

---

[1] Karl Marx, *Early Writings*, Translated by Rodney Livingstone and Gregor Benton, New York: Penguin, 1975, 263.
[2] Karl Marx, *Early Writings*, 379.

it is true that the medium of exchange has migrated from its material form and returned to man it has done so only because man has been exiled from himself and transformed into material form. Money has not been transcended in man within the credit system, but man is himself transformed into money, or, in other words, money is incarnate in him. Human individuality, human morality, have become both articles of commerce and the material which money inhabits. The substance, the body clothing the spirit of money is not money, paper, but instead it is my personal existence, my flesh and blood, my social worth and status. Credit no longer actualizes money-values in actual money but in human flesh and human hearts. Thus all the advances and illogicalities within a false system turn out to be the greatest imaginable regression and at the same time they can be seen as perfidy taken to its logical conclusion."[3]

Credit and debt is not some moment of personal evaluation outside of the economy, some moment of values in the calculation of value, but the complete penetration of calculation of value into all of life. There is no longer an opposition between money as an abstract and quantifiable power that renders everything interchangeable and human relations which are always relations of particulars, of particular qualities. Credit and debt are completely particular, complete individuated, but this individuation is not outside of the abstraction of money, but its complete subsumption of the most intimate area of subjectivity. The human economy, the economy of obligations and actions, does not exist as something underneath or beyond the economy of debt, but is thoroughly subsumed by it.

As much we could read Marx's text as a yet another prophetic text by Marx, one that appears to have foretold the era of credit agencies scanning social media sites and Wal-Mart taking out insurance policies on its employees, the important difference is that the penetration of such estimations into the inner details of credit and existence does not take place by an personal evaluation, by a

---

3 Karl Marx, *Early Writings*, 264.

creditor evaluating the cut of a debtor's jib, but through impersonal and unseen calculations. Do you know your credit score? Or whether your employer has taken out an insurance policy on your life? As much as credit and debt renders everything calculable, converting subjectivity into a nothing other than a series of assets and risks, it does so behind one's back (to echo Marx's formulation about the constitution of abstract value).

This suggests another division, another duality, not between the economics of debt and the ethics of obligation, or between the abstraction of money and the direct personal relations, but between two different relations to money. As owners, possessors, and exchangers of money it appears as something that we use, something subject to our own choices, ideals, and values, as much as those ideals and values are restricted by the quantity of money available and the money form itself. At the same time, however, as debtors, we have a different relation with money, one that passes through us without us knowing it. In *The Making of Indebted Man: An Essay on the Neoliberal Condition*, Maurizio Lazzarato describes these two aspects as follows:

> "Debt/money implicates subjectivity in two different but complementary ways: "social subjection" operates molar control on the subject through the mobilization of his conscience, memory, and representations, whereas "machinic subjugation" has a molecular, infrapersonal, and preindividual hold on subjectivity that does not pass through reflexive consciousness and its representations, nor through the "self."[4]

When it comes to our wages, to the money in our pocket, we are interpellated as individuals, as consumers who can spend and realize our buying potential, but when it comes to debt, to the money that we are rather than possess, we are not individuals, but dividuals,

---

4 Maurizio Lazzarato, *The Making of Indebted Man: An Essay on the Neoliberal Condition*, Translated by Joshua David Jordan, New York: Semiotexte, 2011, 146.

divided and dissembled into constitutive acts and qualities, acts and qualities which are in turn grouped into larger aggregates and collections. The individual makes use of money, but at the preindividual level, the level of the dividual, the same person, or its component parts, is used by money.

Despite the fact that debt is more or less deterritorialized, broken down in relation to abstract actions, qualities, and projections, and then assembled in collections, or securitized, does not mean that it does not reterritorialize itself in terms of concrete effects and relations. These effects are located most directly at the level of actions and choices, what Lazzarato refers to as the specific labor on the self that the regime of debt requires. To take one example: student loans are relatively indifferent to the particular major or course of study one takes, an indifference made possible by the force of the state, but this does not keep the abstract quantity of debt having an effect on the individuals concerned. Anyone who teaches at a University is perhaps aware of the chilling effect that student debt has an intellectual inquiry and education. Students do not ask themselves the questions: what interests me? And what discipline or field do I show talent for? But ask instead: what will get me a job? What will the market demand? Debt is the future acting on the present. Debts might be calculated at the level of preindividual actions, and transindividual collections, but it is internalized at the level of individual actions and decisions.

As forgiving student debt, or the idea of an organized mass default of student debt circulates amongst members of the Occupy Wall Street movement, there are the seemingly inevitable invocations of responsibility. It is argued that those who took out student loans took their risks, decided to major in art history or philosophy, or, whenever offering relief to mortgage debt is proposed, it is argued that those who took out mortgages on houses they could not afford should not be rewarded. Debt is reterritorialized on the objects of nation and community, and subject to a hierarchy of acceptable objects and goals. The morality of debt is fundamentally anti-egalitarian: it is not just that there are debtors and creditors, but everyone has taken their chances, equality contradicts the morality of risk and reward. Debt is a mutation of homo economicus: it is no longer, as Marx argued, the subject of "freedom, equality, and Bentham," but the subject of obligation, inequality, and Becker. As Lazzarto argues, the entire economy of debt is implicated within a work on the self, in which the individual is governed by the idea of maximizing value and managing risks in a series of choices that are radically individuated, but what he does not mention is that the perception of these risks crosses the terrain of thoroughly moralized ideas of hard work, national, and communal belonging.

It is precisely this moralization that any politics of debt, of debt refusal and debt, must actively refuse and combat. It must refuse it not simply as an ideology, as a set of ideas and representations that can be dispensed with, but as what Lazzarato refers to as a production of subjectivity. Debt and the calculation of life and activity in terms of risks and benefits are not just a set of ideas, they are a way in which subjectivity is produced and governed. Debt is not just a set of ideas one has about obligations, but an experience, a suffocating experience of what is possible or desirable. It "is a collective phenomenon suffered individually."[5] To say that it is a collective phenomenon does not mean that it constitutes a collectivity. It is difficult and tenuous to say "we debtors." This is not just because of the moralizing divisions between homeowners, citizens, and students, but because the collective phenomenon is constituted more at the level of the preindividual dimensions of existence, patterns of risk, consumption, and other factors that do not constitute an individual. Debt is individualized at the level of guilt, but its collective conditions remain dispersed and disparate. Collective action requires a minimum of social solidarity, which is perhaps provided by the occupations of campuses and public spaces. As much as we might be critical of the spurious divisions between

---

5 https://libcom.org/article/generation-debt-university-default-undoing-campus-life

"Wall Street" and "Main Street," financial capital and middle class, the very constitution of this movement suggests an inchoate awareness of a new antagonistic collectivity. Moving beyond the immediate connections formed by these actions, connections that still risk dividing debtors into good or bad debtors, will require a critical constitution of this collectivity.

The starting point for the politics of debt is the current crisis, a crisis which undermines much of the conventional wisdom of the twentieth century, wisdom which claimed that consumer society would forestall any revolution in the developed capitalist countries. Debt, specifically housing debt, was initially, at least in the US constructed around an ideal of a nation of homeowners and college graduates, individuals who would be invested, both psychically and economically in the existing order. Debt works to conceal the shrinking wages and declining support of private education by postponing the due date to the future. Now, it has begun to create its opposite, a mass condition far more precarious than wage labor. Debt affects not just working conditions, or the possibility of finding work, but living, shelter, and ultimately, especially in the case of the student loans, the possibility of any future.

In this uncertain future it is possible to glimpse two other things, which function as the basis for a politics of debt. First, is that debt is not just some way of affording a home, an education, a car, without cash, but it is the exploitation of these various needs, a way to make profit off all spheres of life and all relations. Second, debt exposes the idea of a neutral state, dealing with competing interests: it is not just that the state is on the side of the creditors, guaranteeing loans and garnishing wages, it makes their very existence possible. Thus it is possible to argue that as much as debt cuts transversally across the various transindividuations of citizen, student, and worker, it undermines two of the individuations that have forestalled political action: the consumer, too placated by mass marketed desires to act politically, and the citizen, caught up in the fictions of neutrality and equality before the law. Thus, while it is true that it is difficult to articulate the collectivity of debt, a difficulty made possible by its abstraction, it has perhaps cleared away the residue of the past. All that remains is the most persistent and difficult residue to dispense with, that of the responsible and isolated subject. The task of constituting collective refusal will be difficult, crossing the line between the abstractions of debt and concrete repression of the state, but one thing is clear, the morality of debt, with its ideas of individual responsibility for a collective condition, must be refused at all cost.

For more on the politics of debt see Starting from Year Zero: Occupy Wall Street and the Transformation of the Socio-Political.

Day and Night, by Occuprint

Starting from Year Zero: Occupy Wall Street and the Transformations of the Socio-Political

Presented at Occupy Philosophy Conference Michigan State University in February of 2012.

To consider what Occupy Wall Street has to do with philosophy, to Occupy Philosophy, is already to depart from one of the longstanding dictums of the relationship between philosophy and political invents. I am thinking of Hegel, who as much as he argued that philosophy is its own time comprehended in thought, also famously argued that philosophy can only comprehend its own time retrospectively, can only paint grey on grey once the ink has dried. Occupy, or OWS to use a preferred moniker, preferred not because it ties the movement to the hashtag, making it one of the many instances of the supposed twitter revolutions, but because it abstracts the movement from a specific place making it a general political transformation and not a specific occupation, is very much an active movement. Any statement about it, about its ultimate meaning, possibility, or limitations, must confront the fact that it is still in the process of shaping and forming.

This difficulty, the difficulty of saying something about a movement in process, is complicated by at least three other factors. First, there is the complexity of the movement itself. The fact that there are one, two, many occupations means that any one of the occupations may have very different characteristics, characteristics determined by local histories and reactions. Occupy Oakland with its militant "general strike" against the ports and its refusal of police cooperation is very different from the Occupations elsewhere, such as Maine or Cleveland, that have actively courted support from the local police. Second, any description of what Occupy means must confront not only this geographical complexity, but the complexity of orientations and interpretations that defines and divides each occupation. The political goals of occupation are diverse, from a destruction of capitalism itself and the creation of a new political and economic order through the general assemblies and commons of the occupation to political and economic reforms brought about through a left counterweight to the "Tea Parties." The tactics are no less diverse, from direct attempts at the communization of existing private property to organized exodus of money from large international banks to local banks and credit unions. This strategic and tactical diversity can be seen as a symptom of a certain void a lack of dominant intellectual and political voice or organization to address the fundamental issues at the heart of occupy. Every issue addressed by Occupy, from the most reformist, the dominance of lobbying and big money in politics, to the most radical, the dominance of capital itself over all elements of life, is outside of the range of the dominant parties, unions, and mainstream political organizations in the US. Of course this void can be space of possibility, a space that has been kept open by the sustained attempt on the part of the occupations to not be coopted by a party or organization. However, this void is also a gap between the critiques of capital that have at the very least persevered (if not flourished) in various sections of Anglo-American academia and anything like a movement or political party. Just as the dominant political parties were caught off guard by people suddenly wanting to discuss the very issues that the immense political spectacle is meant to conceal, academics and intellectuals have been caught off guard by the idea that someone outside of a lecture hall or hotel conference room might actually want to hear and discuss what they want to talk about. So is not only Occupy difficult to discuss because of its active transformations and contradictions, talking about it involves speaking to new audiences, creating new vocabularies and new modes of transmission.

The difficulties and contradictions could be enumerated ad nauseam, but it might be possible to work through them, rather than use them as an excuse or statement of (false) academic modesty. What I propose here is to work through some of the tensions and contradictions. To begin with, and at the most basic level, it might be worth starting with a few of the things that differentiates Occupy from a long history of protests against wars and other government actions and policies, that have vanished from memory almost as soon as they begin. First, we have the location itself, the occupation of Wall Street rather than another march on Washington, DC. This entails a shift of focus, and a shift of an awareness of the locus of power, from the Capitol to the symbolic center of capital. As much as the focus is on Wall Street, on the center of financial capital, many of the signs and slogans refer to the decision of Citizen's United, to the idea of corporations as personhood, not to the economic power of corporations, power over work and consumption, but to the political power of corporations, the power that corporations wield in the writing of laws, policy, and the election of candidates. The very slogan, "We are the 99%" is situated in the space between economics and politics. Statistically it refers to the 99% of the population that controls a dwindling percentage of wealth in this country, in contrast to the immense wealth of the 1%. However, it gets much of its rhetorical force from its appeal to majority rule, to the populist idea of 99% of the population excluded from political power. Thus, despite the focus on Wall Street, on inequality and wealth, the focus of Occupy Wall Street is on the political effects of the economy, not the economy itself. Hence the often repeated slogan of getting the money out of Washington and the goal of destroying corporate personhood, all of which are about the idea of not so much changing the economy, of contesting capitalism, but limiting its influence on the political process.

Another way to sum up these aspects of Occupy Wall Street would be to say that they are gatherings of citizens rather than workers. Their goal has been to reclaim a public space, a public space that is increasingly disappearing, rather than to politicize the factories, workplaces, and offices. Following Étienne Balibar and Bernard Stiegler's work on Gilbert Simondon, we can define a citizen as a particular kind of transindividual individuation, a particular formation of collectivity, a "we," and individuality, an "I." The citizen is a transindividual individuation in which the collective and the individual reinforce each other, in which every claim for rights, even the rights to be left alone, unaffected by others, is dependent upon its recognition by others. The citizen is neither exclusively collective nor individual, neither simply equal or free, but the intersection between equality and liberty, what Balibar calls "equaliberty." This transindividual relation is thus always in flux, not just between the individual and the collective, but between its role as constituted power, function as the basis for state authority, and its constituent, or insurrectionist dimension, claiming the right to contest power and legitimate new structures. In the case of Occupy, we see a claim for the citizen as not only an insurrection, as a right to revolt, but one that claims the will of the people as the source of authority, against representatives and the perversion of the political process by corporations and money, the citizen against Citizen's United. This is what differentiates the Occupy Movement, even in its most populist dimensions, from the Tea Party; the latter fetishized a founding moment, a founding document, as the source of authority, a source that we could only be viewed as having fallen from, while the former claims the right to revolt, to invent new structures and new relations in the present. Moreover, the spaces that are occupied are what remains of public space, parks, town commons, etc., which initially had a political as well as a recreational function. The conflicts over these occupations, conflicts over the right to occupy, have pitted first amendment principles against a series of laws against public loitering, public sleeping, and public urination aimed at the homeless and guaranteeing "quality of life." Thus in this sense to, in the control of space, they could be understood as claims by citizens against the reconstruction of urban space around a public that is only a docile consumer.

Focusing on the claims for citizenship, for the restoration of democracy, or even the invention of new forms of democracy, risk concealing the manner in which the economy, capitalism, figures in a more direct way in the politics of Occupy even if it does not take the recognizable form of past demands against capitalism, demands for increased wages and benefits, demands structured around the transindividual individuation of the worker. A quick purview of the "We are the 99%" tumblr site which emerged in the opening days of the Occupation, sees debt, housing debt, student debt, and the debt incurred through medical costs, appearing again and again as a central complaint. The centrality of debt begins to foreground a different relation between politics and money than the demand to simply remove the former from the influence of the latter. This is still not exploitation in its Marxist definition; the economic equation at the center of these protests is not framed between wages and profit, the exploitation that defines surplus value, but between wages and debt. This difference is immense, as students, unemployed individuals, and others burdened with massive debt calculate the gap that separates debt and earnings. These debts are not just quantitatively huge, qualitatively they are unpayable; houses are underwater, caught between a high mortgage and current devaluations, and students who took on massive debt to finance their education find that there are no jobs waiting for them when they graduate. Or, to quote, After the Fall, a document produced by the wave of Occupations in the University of California, "We work and we borrow in order to work and to borrow. And the jobs we work toward are the jobs we already have."[1] Or, to put it more succinctly,

---

[1] After the Fall: Communique from an Absent Future, https://illwill.com/print/communique-from-an-absent-future

"No future." Future is what debt, especially the debt of student loans, counts on, the promise of future earnings, and it is precisely this promise that appears radically foreclosed. The future appears to be sold off in advance.

Starting from debt, from the economics and politics of debt, offers another understanding of the intersection of politics and economics than the populist idea of democracy without capitalism, even if this idea is not articulated. In both cases it is a matter of a fundamental blurring of the divides between economics and politics, private and public, but in the first case, that of the citizen against Citizen's United, there is the idea of a possible reform, a restoration of politics without money, however flawed it may be. The focus on debt, however, changes the focus on both economics and politics. Economics is no longer restricted to the power of big business, of corporations, to lobby and influence politics, but is the exploitation of day-to-day life; in a similar fashion, politics is no longer democracy, either in its representative form, or in the invention of new direct forms, but is the control over life. As Gilles Deleuze states in his text on control, "A Man is no longer a man confined, but a man in debt."[2] Which is to say that debt, student debt, housing, and the debts of health care is as much about control over life as it is an extraction of wealth. As Maurizio Lazzarato argues, debt "functions equally as an apparatus of production and a way to govern individual and collective subjects."[3]

On the economic side, debt is situated in the transformations of neoliberalism. With respect to the debtor, debt was able to augment the declining real wages of the last forty years, making it possible for people to still make the same purchases and maintain the same status as past generations, and it provided access to things such as higher education, even as state spending on higher education declined. With respect to the creditor, we have an increase of the

---

2 Gilles Deleuze, *"Postscript on Control Societies,"* in *Negotiations*, Translated by Martin Joughlin, New York: Columbia, 1995, 181.
3 Maurizio Lazzarato, *The Making of Indebted Man: An Essay on the Neoliberal Condition*, Translated by Joshua David Jordan, New York: Semiotexte, 2011, 29.

power of money, and the possibility to extract money from activities that were once expenditures. Declining wages and declining state services not only tip the balance from expenses to profits, as labor becomes cheaper and payments to the state are reduced, but become themselves a source of wealth. We can already begin to see the "subjective" dimension of this accumulation by debt as well. First, at the most basic level debt, in the form of second mortgages and credit card debt, makes it possible for people whose wages are declining to see themselves as being able to purchase the necessary components of middle class identity. Middle class being defined less on a particular economic status, let alone a relation to the means of production, than on the capacity to purchase certain goods, such as homes and cars, and an ability to afford higher education. In the US much of the legitimacy of the political and economic order rests on the ability of the majority to identify with this class.

The subjective dimension of debt is not limited to the way in which it extends class belonging, patching over a decline of wages. There is a dark side as well; debt infuses this belonging with insecurity, and isolation. There is a qualitative difference in going to college because it has been made affordable by public funding and financing an education through loans. The first is won and maintained collectively as a social good, the second is not only maintained individually, but individuates, subjecting people to their debt. This individuation takes many levels, some of it takes place beyond one's back, in the form of a credit score and the multiple ways one's activity can be tracked online. In other ways it is directly manifest in actions and relations. This can be seen in student loan debt. As students take on more and more loans to fund their education, their education changes form. Anyone who teaches at a university is perhaps aware of the chilling effect that student debt has an intellectual inquiry and education. Students do not ask themselves the questions: what interests me? And what discipline or field do I show talent for? But ask instead: what will get me a job? What will the market demand? Debt is the future acting on the present. The idea of future debt, of the cost of student loans, acts on the present, determining choices and limiting possibilities. Debt is mode of governmentality, a way to restrict and curtail actions; a mode that is all the more effective in being internalized.

Student debt can be understood as a transformation of the educational experience and the university, one that uses the power of the state, taxation and the allocation of funds, to restructure the university from below.[4] Indebted students, students desperately seeking wages adequate to their debt, are less likely to demand courses and programs engaging in critical thinking, let alone engage in the political activism that made the "student" a political transindividual individuation, defined by its liminal position between home and work. Debt produces students who desperately try to match their actions to the mercurial job market, rather than rethink society and their place within it. The politics of debt are produced from above, but the effects are felt from below in the daily actions of not only students, who ask only "how can this course get me a job," but also an increasingly precarious adjunct teaching faculty forced to tailor their teaching to whatever can get them work.

In an early text by Marx this internalization of credit is described as transformation of morality and human relationships. With debt, everything that was outside of the monetary relation, particular skills, talents, desires, and aptitudes, becomes part of it. As Marx writes,

> "In the credit system man replaces metal or paper as the mediator of exchange. However, he does this not as a man but as the incarnation of capital and interest. Thus although it is true that the medium of exchange has migrated from its material form and returned to man it has done so only because man has been exiled from himself and transformed into material form. Money has not been transcended in man within the credit system, but man is himself transformed into money, or, in

---

[4] Wacquant describes neoliberalism as "an articulation of the state, market, and citizenship that harnesses the first to impose the stamp of the second onto the third." [Loic Wacquant, "A Historical Anthropology of Actually Existing Neoliberalism," pg. 71] To which I would add that it is not just the citizen is restructured, becoming a consumer of state services, but other identities such as the students.

other words, money is incarnate in him. Human individuality, human morality, have become both articles of commerce and the material which money inhabits. The substance, the body clothing the spirit of money is not money, paper, but instead it is my personal existence, my flesh and blood, my social worth and status. Credit no longer actualizes money-values in actual money but in human flesh and human hearts. Thus all the advances and illogicalities within a false system turn out to be the greatest imaginable regression and at the same time they can be seen as perfidy taken to its logical conclusion."[5]

As Lazzarto argues, the entire economy of debt is implicated within a work on the self, in which the individual is governed by the idea of maximizing value and managing risks in a series of choices that are not only radically individuated but moralized. Morality is not the subordination of economic concerns to moral criteria, to some concern with the individual person, but the reverse, the subordination of morality to the economy, the subsumption of morality to the economy. Trust, responsibility, and obligation become concepts of the moralization of the economy, the point where economic relations become moralized.

The subject of debt is isolated, separated from others, who are no longer seen as part of a collective condition. With debt there is only one's responsibility, one's isolation, one's fears up against an economic situation of abstract calculation. It is very difficult to say "we" debtors, in the way one could say "we" citizens or "we" workers. Part of debt passes beneath us, in the calculations, quantifications, and aggregations that make up our digital self, our virtual identity, and is this respect we cannot even say "I." But even that part that individuates us, the part that we carry with us as a burden, does not allow for the creation of a "We." This is because debt is seen less as a collective condition, as part of a new regime of accumulation and a new governmentality, than as an individual fate. Debt splinters into its myriad kinds, student debt, mortgage debt, and consumer

---

5 Karl Marx, *Early Writings*, 264.

debt, and the various individual relations to it, the choices made and risks taken. Viewed in this way debt, or financialization, is perhaps only an extreme point in the neo-liberal economy. Its general characteristics are, as we have seen, an extraction of wealth from relations outside of the worker-capital relationship, as not just production but reproduction become the basis for debt and wealth, and a production of subjectivity, that is oriented towards isolation, fragmentation, and inequality. In this manner debt is consistent with transformations of labor in the thirty years, which have lead to short term contracts, temp work, limited union membership and collective bargaining. It is also consistent with the rise of digital technologies that create new possibilities of individuation in consumer profiles, tailored advertisements, etc. all of which transform consumption and leisure into ways of capturing attention and generating profits.

If one looks beyond the focus on lobbyists, on the claims for citizenship, to the anxiety about debt and precarious labor, then it is possible to begin to understand a different relationship with the economy and politics. Yes, it is true that people are not organizing as workers, in terms of the identities, tactics, and spaces occupied, and this has led some to dismiss the occupations as simply populist movements with no real critique of capital. We should not rush to conclude that the lack of the worker as transindividual individuation to be a negative thing, there is, after all, a long tradition of writing in the Marxist tradition, which has argued against the ideal of critique capital from the perspective of workers. This tradition, beginning with Mario Tronti and the autonomist tradition and continuing through the idea communization, has stressed that the politics of such a critique can only be a politics of reform, a struggle for better wages and benefits. "To abolish capital is at the same time to negate oneself as a worker and not to self-organize as such: it's a movement of the abolition of enterprises, of factories, of the product, of exchange (whatever its form)."[6] From this perspective we should not

---

6 Communization and its Discontents: Contestation, Critique, and Contemporary Struggles, Edited by Benjamin Noys, New York: Minor Compositions, 2011, 43.

spend too much time mourning the lack of the worker as an identity organizing Occupy Wall Street, or hold out hopes for unions to be revitalized. Such actions can only lead to reforms, to better wages and more work, and would return us to the division of worker and student, waged work and unpaid reproductive work. There is a positivity to this absence, a positivity that only takes an inchoate form in not just the politicization of debt, but also in the global nature of the protests, a positivity that recognizes the full spectrum of exploitation.

The question remains, however, as to how to articulate this nascent critique of capital that is framed in terms of debt and insecurity and how to organize this mass of debtors, the unemployed, and precariously employed. Some writers, such as David Graeber, have turned to the long history of debt to see the current situation as yet another chapter in a long history of debt revolts. In this five thousand year history, the struggle over wages and exploitation, appears only as a brief chapter in a long durée of struggle of debtors against creditors. The present is the time of jubilees. Opposed to this return of the past there are those who argue that we find in the contemporary production process an entirely new subjectivity, that of a multitude or precariat, and thus a new kind of politics. As work becomes increasingly oriented towards the reproduction of social relations, knowledge and affects, it also becomes increasingly vulnerable as the boundaries between waged and unwaged become even more permeable. The present is understood as either the reflection of the oldest inequalities, or to be made up of new exploitations. This same contradiction between the new and the old can be found at the level of liberation, at the level of the possibilities for organizing: some point to the resilience of the oldest tactics, direct democracy, direct action, and even espouse an ideal of locality as a goal, as the general assembly becomes the new democratic model; on the opposite side there are those who point to the role of facebook, twitter, and social networking as the central organizing tools, placing these actions, like the revolts in the Arab world, under the rubric of twitter revolutions, as new political possibilities opened up by networks of communication. Exploitation and liberation are both caught between the old and the new. Rather than reconcile these two points of view in a sort of on the one hand and then the other, or attempt to find some kind of dialectical sublimation of the two, it is necessary to examine the contradictions and limitations of the Occupy Wall Street movement through an examination of its composition.

Composition in this sense follows the work of the Italian autonomists who emphasized the examination of class composition. This work, which began with the early autonomists such as Mario Tronti, was intended to move away from taking class as a given, as a subject forever poised between the in-itself and the for-itself of the "now hidden, now open" class struggle. In its place there is an examination of both the way in which class is constituted, according to its technological and political components, the division of labor and the level of organization, and constitutive, reshaping capitalist accumulation through its struggles. I would add to this, following the worker of Franco Berardi, Stephven Shukatis and Maurizio Lazzarato, that this composition the subjective composition, the affects (hope, fear) ideas and images that motivate and drive individuals and collectives. We have already seen how these three elements combine in the case of debt: debt is dependent upon a new technological regime of surveillance and data sharing, is part of a political strategy of neoliberal governmentality, and perpetuates a subjectivity of isolation and anxiety. A fleshed out compositional analysis would examine this not just in terms of debt, but also work, consumption, and the relation to the state. I can only provide a few notes in that direction here.

The various relations to the kinds of debt, housing, student, and consumer, is one of the constituent dimensions of the occupations. As such it defines both a commonality, a common grievance against Wall Street, against the power of finance, while at the same time being a point of contradiction and division. As I have already stated this division concerns the various types of debt, student, housing, and consumer, all of which are endlessly individuated according to risks and choices, responsibility as fragmentation. It constitutes an economic and affective commonality, but one that is experienced in terms of individuation. The fragmentation and isolation of debt, with its individualization through surveillance and anxiety, is mirrored in the sphere of production. Work has been restructured through temporary contracts, loss of collective bargaining, and generalized insecurity all of which lead to similar isolation and individuation. Work, even the work at a given office, call center, or distribution site, is no longer that of a "we," of a collective identity, but is individualized into temporary contracts, continual performance reviews, and a dispersed workplace. To call this an "I" with all of its connotation of independence and autonomy, is not entirely accurate. As with debt the balance sheet of any one's particular performance and hard work remains completely outside of their efforts. People are hired and fired not because of their efforts, but because of the balance of profits and losses, and the cost of wages halfway around the globe. Despite this the "work ethic" remains, or it is perhaps all that remains. Work ceases to be the predominant productive force, displaced by the general knowledge of society externalized in various machines, what Marx called the "general intellect" but it remains the enforced measure. All that remains of work as it loses its central economic function and its transindividual dimension, constituting the basis for collective belonging and individual identity, is its disciplinary function, the demand to "be professional." Thus to some extent work goes full circle: it began with the protestant ethic, with a discipline without guarantee, a work on oneself to remind oneself of one's chose status, and it ends that way as well. All one is left with is a dogged determination to keep working, to take out another loan to learn a new skill, to maximize one's potential.

The transformation of work from an economic necessity to an ethical or disciplinary imperative is reflected in some of the opposition to Occupy Wall Street. The first real reaction to Occupy

Wall Street, the "We are the 53%" tumblr site not only shifted the entire idea from exploitation to taxes, but the various testimonies stressed the idea of hard work, often including testimonies of people who worked multiple jobs. That these individuals had to work multiple jobs, or worked long hours, was not presented as a critique of the economic system but a testament to their individual worth and virtue. This idea, or at least an inclination of it can be found in all of the counter-protesters who some up their opposition by yelling, "Get a job!" As much as this critique carries with all of the old ideological ghosts of welfare queens, of people living off of the public, it also expresses a kind of disciplinary injunction. The "job" is not so much an economic imperative, but a moral and political one, a job is understood as precisely what keeps people off the street, keeps people from protesting, keeping them too busy or too tired to do anything but work. The idea of everyone doing their job and nothing but their job, the fantasy of Plato's *Republic* returns as work is shrinking. What we are dealing with is not the work ethic living on long past its economic usefulness, an imperative to work haunting an economy that automates and out sources jobs, but an intensification of it. As work disappears especially in the face of a mounting recession, it becomes all the more imperative at the level of ethics and morality. The unemployed are told to blame themselves, for some failure in their attitude, rather than look to the economic and social conditions of their situation. This insistence of the moral over and above the economic can also be seen in terms of debt as well. As much as it might make political and economic sense to offer some kind of debt forgiveness to those burdened with mortgages or students facing loans that they cannot pay, it is argued that the moral risk is too great, forgiveness would corrupt the foundations of the republic. The moral imperative to pay one's debts and to work hard outlasts the economic imperative and possibility. If the obligation to pay one's debts and the work ethic are ghosts, remnants of another economic era, then they are angry and vengeful ghosts, becoming more intense as they become more impossible.

To complete the picture of the current historical moment, one would have to add punishment and the penal regime to debt and work. Punishment and law have also combined the individualizing techniques of surveillance and the moralizing rhetoric of individual responsibility to impose a new authoritarian regime. Individual responsibility has become the lynchpin linking debt, work, and law. Any discussion of social conditions, especially the social conditions that have driven people into debt, left them without work, makes the drug trade the only possible economic activity for some, is excluded in advance, all that remains is individual responsibility. Collective action to remedy these conditions is thus also excluded, and when government acts it can only act to further discipline individual responsibility. This moralizing lynchpin is absent when it comes to discussing the collapse of the economy, all accountability disappears in the supposed complexity of the economy itself. It is for this reason that Loïc Wacquant describes the contemporary state as a Centaur, with fundamentally different rules for those who find themselves at the top or bottom. "Actually existing neoliberalism extolls 'laissez faire et lasser passer' for the dominant, but it turns out to be paternalist and intrusive for the subaltern, and especially for the urban precariat whose life parameters it restricts through the combined mesh of supervisory workfare and judicial oversight."[7]

The common denominator of debt, work, and punishment in the current conjuncture is not only that of their ethical dimension, their existence as individual imperatives rather than collective economic condition, but of insecurity and precariousness. This precariousness is often branded, which is to say marketed, as autonomy and freedom. The lack of collective bargaining contracts, of stable commitments, and of social provisions that pass through the state, is presented as a kind of freedom and liberation. The subject of contemporary society, of neoliberal society, is one who is free to maximize his or her human capital, as well as other resources such

---

[7] Loic Wacquant, "Three Steps Towards a Historical Anthropology of Actually Existing Neoliberalism," Social Anthropology/Anthropologie Sociale (2012) 20, 1 66–79. pg. 74.

as a home, benefiting from the lack of constraints and connections to maximize profit. This is a situation in which any lateral connection, any connection with other workers, students, or even other customers of insurance, that is not networking, not oriented towards maximizing one's potential is unnecessary or avoided. It is perhaps more accurately described as class decomposition than composition, as students and workers are isolated and fragmented into individuals and aggregates of fragmented bits of intelligence and knowledge. The identification is not between other individuals, any collective, but with capital itself, with the enterprise. The worker becomes an entrepreneur of the self, and the student an investor in one's own human capital. It is perhaps in this sense that "corporate personhood" should be taken as issue: it is not that capitalism would be better if we could somehow just return it to individuals exploiting individuals, but capitalism functions by modeling a person that aligns his or her striving, with its functioning.

The identity of individual striving with the functioning of capital has its limits, however, and these limits came to the front as the economy collapsed. One could possibly say that just as there was a housing bubble, and we are in the midst of a higher education bubble, there is also a subjectivity bubble. As long as housing prices increased, as long as it seemed possible to continue to maximize one's potential, one's profit, then this identification of individual striving with the economy as a whole persisted. As the economy collapsed so too did this ideal of subjectivity, this way of relating to others and the world. The turnout, the popularity of the occupations around the country, is itself a symptom of a breakdown of the identification of individuals and the interest of capital. The occupations are a cause as well as an effect of this rupture, the presence of occupations all over the country makes it easier for people to identify, to act. The action and presence of others becomes a catalyst. It is precisely this spiral of cause and effect that has intensified the Occupy Wall Street movement in the last few months. However, the collapse of the asocial sociality of debt and precarity does not in itself constitute a new collectivity, a new transindividual individuation. Instead, as we have seen, there is a return to all the old ideologies and histories of the past, such as the ideal of the citizen and the populist ideal of a 99%. While this language of citizenship and a republic sold out makes for snazzy placards and effective slogans, something different takes place in the actual occupations, as people from different economic strata, differently situated with respect to risk and uncertainty, to exploitation, come together. The problem is immense as a society lacking class composition, or even any identification across class is suddenly confronted with forming relations and solidarity across divisions of class, race, and other inequalities.

The occupations have become not just symbols, protests against inequality, but symptoms as well, as the collapsing "safety net" of a society of debt and inequality dumps people into one place. As much as there is a unification, albeit an inchoate one, of a central message, there is also a division across the degrees of precarity, the difference that divides a student facing immense debt and an uncertain job situation from an unemployed person who has lost her home As George Caffentzis has argued, unemployment and homelessness has been one of the major divisions within the occupy camps. The media has presented this as a division between the dedicated, principled occupiers and the dangerous and unstable freeloaders that have come to the occupations. That dichotomy has not been confirmed by my experience, or much of what I have read of Occupy. However, it has forced the occupations to deal in a concrete way with the very effects of the policies and politics they are protesting. It is one thing to be opposed to the wars in Afghanistan and Iraq, against the cutting of mental health programs, and the defunding of homeless shelters, but it is another to be in a sleeping bag woken up by someone suffering post-traumatic stress order. To suggest that the homeless are a burden to the camps is incredibly unfair. In my experience many homeless have embraced the camps, sometimes even leaving the disciplinary confines of shelters that police their comings and goings to enter into a space where they are not only fed and sheltered but where they can act and speak, changing the world around them. It is in this aspect that the occupations deserve the name communes, in place of a system that can only deal with collective conditions individually, moralizing and disciplining dependence, the occupations suggest another possibility based on solidarity and commonality. They are factories for generating solidarity.

This does not mean that there are not divisions within the occupations. The division might best be described as a division between different stakes in the occupation themselves. For some they are homes, providing necessary food and shelter, while for others they are symbols, actions, even if they suggest the possibility of another economy. It might be useful to think of the compositions of the occupations as crisscrossed with different relations to not only the contemporary situation of exploitation, debt and work, but investment in the existing system, the capacity or desire to identify with it. There are those that believe that the existing economic system can be reformed, that its failures can be traced to recent transformations, and those who understand, sometimes at the core of their being, that it cannot. Which is not to see that these two axes are coordinated, not all of those who are most exploited are most radical in their demands and comfortably employed activists and tenured radicals can be seen in the occupations. There is, however, a heterogeneity of concrete needs and abstract desires, of economic and affective composition.

Any discussion of the composition of the occupations must also include the transformative effect of the occupation themselves. The four months of occupation have provided lessons for those inside and outside the occupations about the functioning of power. First, and foremost the very existence of the Occupy Wall Street has proven that what we speak of in monolithic terms as "the media" or the spectacle, that distracts people from the economic and political realities of the world, is not as monolithic as it appears. It can be punctured by actions, coopted by memes, and gradually infiltrated by narratives that outside of its purview. Second, the occupations have exposed the brutality and corruption of the police. The police have shown themselves again and again to be protectors not of "the peace" but of existing property relations, of exploitation. The entire history of occupy is punctuated by images from the pepper-spray in New York, to Scott Olsen, and the cop at UC Davis, which have exposed the violence of our own social order. Of course many of these images have been circulated through the internet, drawing these two points together: the images of police violence and the protests against inequality combine in a corrosive mixture that eats away at the dominant image of a benevolent and just order. This is not news to everyone, but the occupation has become an education to many, as videos of a very different America than the one broadcast on television is shown on Youtube. However, as much as these two lessons have transformed the movement, and have shifted the very contours of political action, the central point of Occupy, the economy, inequality, or capitalism, has not emerged with any clarity. This is not a matter of demands, demands are always addressed to some power, rather it is a matter of internal theoretical understanding and clarity. For Occupy to last, for it to truly become a transformative moment in national and global politics, it must counter the tendencies of isolation and fragmentation with shared concepts and shared debates, with an intellectual project that can outlast the shared campsites and cooking pots. This is difficult given the long history of not only anti-intellectualism, but of the intellectual hegemony of the spontaneous philosophies of fragmentation and isolation. As I have already suggested, this lack can be seen in the gulf that separates the stories that the 99% tells about itself—stories of debt and economic insecurity—which indicate a fundamental intensification of exploitation, and the slogans it carries—which suggest an ideal of a kinder and gentler capitalism.

As much as Occupy signals a change in the relation between economics and politics, a relation that still needs to be thought out, still needs to be theorized. It also involves a fundamental transformation of the relationship between theory, between intellectual production, and political action. For decades, at least in the US, this relation was primarily a non-relation: academics talked of critiques of capital, of exploitation, of the new power relations, knowing full well that only other academics were listening. Occupy Wall Street has changed this, as inequality, class, debt, and even the nature of capitalism itself suddenly emerges on the national and global discourse, like the return of the repressed. This represents a challenge and an opportunity for renewal and transformation of thinking, for political thought that is not just a reflection on something called politics, but thought that actively engages with the conditions and limits of its transmission, articulation, and reception (conditions that are primarily economic). It is a matter of not just a thought of politics, but a politics and economics of thought. The challenge then is that this is happening at the very moment where the institution that has historically supported such political reflection, the university, is being undermined from within by debt and the economic insecurity of casualization. The opportunity is that suddenly all these questions and intellectual traditions that have remained sequester in graduate seminars, like so many terrariums for endangered species, have the chance to not only be heard but critically examined and transformed. How and why the current economic order can be transformed is appearing to be less and less of an academic question. Working through these limitations and opportunities is what it might mean to occupy philosophy. As I have suggested here, the starting point that I would suggest for such an occupation, is first and foremost the intersection of politics and economics, an intersection that goes beyond the influence of lobbyists to encompass the transformation of daily life according to new economic structures, and secondly it involves the articulation of individuation and collectivity.

For more on Debt see Debt Collectors: The Economics, Political, and Morality of Debt.

Image courtesy of Mitch O'Connell

Trumped: The Ecology of Attention and Affects

Originally posted in February of 2016.

Pitch for a sequel to *They Live*. The "ghouls" (as they are referred to in the script), or aliens, have been unmasked by Nada's (Roddy Piper) destruction of the signal in the first film. Some are hunted down, while it is rumored that others have gone into hiding, finding new ways to disguise their horrifying appearance and devious plans. The destruction of the ghouls does very little to change things, the wealthy still dominate and the poor still suffer. Then one day a ghoul emerges that does not conceal his appearance, or his intentions. He makes it clear that he plans to continue accumulating massive wealth. When people point out that his kind exploited and depleted the planet he freely admits it, pointing out that running an interdimensional conglomerate is no small task. It was a huge and impressive endeavor. As much as one might be critical of the ghoul's exploitation of the planet, no one can doubt that they got things done. This ghoul then states that he is running for president. Critics declare that he is a ghoul, but he makes no secret of it. No one can unmask him, for he is already unmasked; attempts to reveal his sinister motives are belied by his willingness to state them clearly. The ghoul eventually wins, and once again the country is under their thrall, only now openly so.

My sequel pitch is meant as both an attempt to convey something of the weirdness of the phenomena of Trump, who seems like something from an early Carpenter or Cronenberg film (the hair has something of Cronenberg body horror to it) and of the limits of ideology critique in grasping this particular phenomena. *If They Live* can be seen as "Ideology Critique 101" then Trump reveals how inadequate ideology critique is to the present.

Trump has dispensed with every dog whistle, with every coded reference to racism, class domination, and misogyny, preferring instead to openly declare racist, sexist, and jingoistic statements. I will spare you the litany; everyone remembers "the Mexican rapist," the comments about Megyn Kelly, the promise to exclude all Muslims, etc. With each statement pundits declared that Trump's career was over. This, after all, was the logic of past elections. This did not happen, and might never happen, suggesting that something else is happening—some mutation of the mediasphere.

Two steps towards a theory of Trump.

I do not think that it is possible to overstate the role of celebrity in Trump's case. It is, however, a particular kind of celebrity. Trump is not a rich person, well not that rich by the standards of the US oligarchy, he just plays one on TV. He has converted his wealth and economic value into "sign value." He understands that universal concepts need their particular instantiation in order to be comprehended or imagined. They need a figure, a face, something to give the abstract idea of wealth and success a definite shape. Trump has been all too willing to play the figure of the wealthy businessman so much so that his movie and television appearances are inseparable from his name. For decades he has become the symbol of wealth and power. His oddly coiffed hair replacing the figure of the monocle and top hat of Mr. Moneybags. He is the spectacle of wealth not its reality.

Trump belongs to a particular subset of celebrities, mainly reality TV stars, heirs and heiresses, and other minor celebrities, that have managed to squeek out far more than they should from their fifteen minutes of fame. These celebrities disappear from the public's eye momentarily only to return with a "controversial tweet," "scandalous instagram pic, or other nonevent. In doing so they show that they perhaps understand the "ecology of attention" better than we give them credit for.[1] They tap into the short term distractions of "trending topics" all the while building name brand recognition. This is a different kind of reputation, a different kind of value, than the sort built up by a career in politics (or film or music). Its brilliance is that unlike other forms of reputation or authority it appears not to be imposed but consented to. It stems not from education or talent, but from the faux-democracy of retweets and late night television jokes. Trump's genius is in convincing us that we made him, that he is the product of our clicks, conversations, etc. That is how an oligarch, even the image of one, becomes a populist.

It is impossible to talk about Trump without talking about affects, and the politics of affects. Much has been made of his rage, his anger, and his ability to tap into the rage of a white working class. He has gone further than any candidate in mobilizing a racist anger and fantasies. However, he also understands the importance of joyful affects. His "Make America Great Again," and references to "winning," even his claim that he would make it so people said Merry Christmas again, are pure assertions of a kind of joy tinged with sadness—in other words nostalgia. They are not meant to have content or clarity. Specific proposals and goals would only dampen the feeling. They tap into a general sense that things were better once. Trump is a remake of Reagan.

These aspects of Trump's candidacy are not going away, no matter what becomes of him. They are elements of the current state of the spectacle. As Angela Mitropoulis has stated, the question is not whether or not Trump is a fascism but what fascism becomes in a media driven economy.

---

[1] Jason Read, Distracted by Attention, *New Inquiry*, December 18, 2014. https://thenewinquiry.com/distracted-by-attention/

Updated 6/21/18

If you have ever watched reality TV. You know two things define programs like *The Bachelor*. First, they are constantly advertising themselves as you are watching them. Every commercial break is bookmarked by a promise of what is "coming up" with clips of drama and heartbreak. All television shows advertise but reality TV never stops advertising—even when you are already watching the show. Second, these clips are often fabrications. The actual events are never nearly as dramatic as they are promised. Clips promising a dramatic confrontation turn out to be edited together from disparate events; the blood spilled on the floor is not from a violent confrontation but from someone slipping by the pool. The lie is no sooner revealed than the next dramatic event is promised. I am not going to connect all of the dots here, but in the end I think reality TV is a more instructive manual for understanding Trump's presidency than any work of political theory.

For more on Trump see Must Love Dogs: Animals and Racism in the Age of Trump.

Must Love Dogs: Animals and Racism in the Age of Trump

Originally posted in November of 2019.

Trump is not a dog person, or, for that matter, a cat person. He is supposedly the first president in a century to not have a pet. Past presidents have had dogs, cats, horses, even alligators. While many animal lovers breathe a sigh of relief at such news it has recently taken a strange turn. After a long history of resorting to calling people dogs as his favorite phrase of contempt, he tweeted praise of a Belgian Malinois named Conan used in the raid on Abu Bakr al-Baghdadi. Even going so far as to retweet a doctored picture of him giving the medal of honor to the animal, adding that the real dog will be visiting the White House soon.

As if this shift from dog hater to dog lover was not stunning enough, Trump claimed that al-Baghdadi spent his last moments "whimpering and crying like a dog," a story that seems to be as much as a fabrication as the photographic of Trump pinning a medal on the "good boy." We could decry both of these as fake news, but they demonstrate how much Trump understands the affective logic of fake news. Stories work if they invoke existing scripts of good dogs and cowardly villains. Trump's new found love of dogs could in some way be an attempt to drum up support after being booed at the World Series. What does America love more than baseball? More than the fabricated nature of both of these stories and their emotional appeal it is this simultaneous veneration of a dog as a hero and the denigration of a human as a dog that provokes thought. How can the dog be both an object of praise and a term of abuse? Such a question returns us to the center of contemporary reflections on philosophical anthropology, of the distinction between human and animal, but also the divisions within and among humans.

To cite Etienne Balibar:

> "no definition of the human as such, or the "position of man in the universe could ever be attempted which did not include the infinite process of demarcation between the human, the more-than-human, and the less than human, and the reflection of these two limits within the imaginary boundaries of the human "species."[1]

Or, to put it differently, some dogs are seen as more than human and some humans are seen as less than dogs. Grégoire Chamayou offers a historical explanation for this anthropological problem. As Chamayou argues, maintaining a racial order is often outsourced to either outsiders, the use of former slaves as slave hunters, this outsourcing of domination continues through the dog, and ultimately the drone. The use of a non-human hunter short circuits any master-slave dialectic, and its eventual overcoming. As he does.

> "If the master is recognized as an autonomous self-consciousness, that is precisely because he does not have to expose himself to death. In order to be the master, he has not risked his life, he has not scorned life in himself as he does in others, but only in others. His consciousness as dominator is

---

1 Etienne Balibar, *Masses, Classes, Ideas: Studies on Politics and Philosophy Before and After Marx*, Translated by James Swenson, New York: Verso, 1994, 197.

manifested in this exclusive play with others' lives: it is in the eyes of the prey caught by dogs that he sees that he is master, because what he sees is that for the prey, he is death, that is the absolute master...The genealogy of modern slavery is not that of a duel but that of a hunt."[2]

To refer back to Trump's new love of dogs, this may in part explain why he celebrates the dog and not the soldiers that carried out the raid. To do the latter would be to acknowledge the minimal equality that war or conflict entails—recognition in the struggle to risk one's life, as Hegel would put it. You cannot engage an enemy in battle if you are unable to acknowledge their intelligence and strength—to in some sense see them as human. To be killed, or caught by a dog, is to whimper like a dog, to be beneath the realm of human struggle. The contradiction is not a contradiction at all. In order for some people to be seen as less than human some animals need to be elevated to the status of human, or even more than human. Twitter in all of its pithiness has a different version of all of this in the often quoted phrase "White people love dogs more than they love black people."

saira rao
@sairasameerarao

White America cares a billion times more about dogs than they do about Black and brown people. That's a fact.

1:43 PM · Aug 24, 2019 · Twitter for iPhone

2.4K Retweets   10.2K Likes

I have to admit that as a dog lover, nominal "white person," and anti-racist that when I first read that tweet I was prompted to the usual reactions of defensiveness that is endemic to social media. Luckily I stopped myself before tweeting "Not all white people." Upon further reflection, and returning to the anthropological distinctions above, it is possible to say that division of man from

---

2 Grégoire Chamayou, *Manhunts: A Philosophical History*, Princeton: Princeton, 2012, 67.

animal intersect with, and reproduce, divisions within humanity. Anyone attempting to address either, to confront racism or speciesism, without examining their intersection risks reproducing one aspect of this order while confronting the other. Case in point PETA's (always an easy target on how not to do things) infamous "Animal Cruelty is Slavery" campaign.³

Two conclusions. First, I intend to think more about this issue, and for this reason I recently ordered Bénédict Boisseron's *Afro-Dog: Blackness and the Animal Question*; a book I only know about from Lewis Gordon's column on it.⁴ There is obviously more work to be done to untangle the knot of intertwined racism, imperialism, and speciesism. I think that every white person, and every white person who loves dogs, must necessarily do this in order to avoid playing a horrible part in a script that is written for us.

---

3 https://www.peta.org/blog/meat-equals-slavery/
4 Lewis Gordon, Benedict Boisson's Afro Dog, https://blog.apaonline.org/2019/10/01/benedicte-boisserons-afro-dog/

Second, just to get the image of Trump and the dog out of my head, and to make the point that there is more to dog loving than supporting the racist order, I would argue that what some people love in and through dogs is something even utopian, the care, generosity, play, and devotion of dogs is a glimpse of another relation to species and perhaps even different relations amongst humans. Dogs are not just parts in the script of denigrating the humanity of others, they can also help us write a different story, one based more on empathy than conflict. Or, to end what is nothing more than a reflection on a series of tweets with a tweet. I will end with Eve Ewing's tweet about Hatty the emotional support dog.[5]

For more on Grégoire Chamayou see "Put a Drone on it: Chamayou's Theory of a Drone" for more on Trump see "Trumped: The Ecology of Attention and Affects".

---

5 https://blockclubchicago.org/2019/10/29/hatty-the-support-dog-will-soon-help-children-survivors-of-sex-abuse-as-they-navigate-criminal-justice-system/

Reduction to Ignorance: Spinoza in the Age of Conspiracy Theories

This is the first in a series of posts which attempt to think through the contemporary rise of conspiracy theories through the philosophers, Spinoza, Hegel, and Marx. It could be considered an attempt to think through contemporary superstition with the earlier critiques of superstition, faith, and fetishism.

At some point in my adolescence I was obsessed with conspiracy theories. I listened to late night radio shows dedicated to alien abductions, satanic messages on records, and a more local phenomena known as the melonheads. These were jokes to me, or at least half jokes, I never took any of them seriously. However, they did contribute to growing sense that there was more to the world than what I was told. Adolescence and conspiracy theories go well together.[1] In recent years, however, it increasingly seems like conspiracy theories have moved from the periphery of cultural life to the mainstream, from late night radio to prime time news, and from entertainment to politics. It is hard to avoid the fact that we are

---

1 https://www.theatlantic.com/ideas/archive/2020/05/i-was-a-teenage-conspiracist/610975/

living through a profound transformation of knowledge, authority, and politics, and a revival of mystical and mythic forms of knowledge that goes beyond any dialectic of enlightenment. It may then turn out that the old arguments regarding superstition have taken on a new relevance. As is often the case on this blog, I am starting here with Spinoza, to be followed with a post on Hegel and then Marx.

Perhaps the best way to approach Spinoza on this point is through a joke, "Conspiracy theories are what happens when the attempt to understand the world through final causes reaches its culmination." In other words, conspiracies often begin with the effect of an action or an event, what could be called the final cause, and then retroactively construct the cause and the intent from that effect. To take two examples, the 9/11 terrorist attacks made possible both the massive expansion of government powers domestically as well as an expansion of empire globally. Or, a little closer to home, the COVID-19 pandemic undermined Trump's presidency, presenting what had up until then been a four year victory lap for winning the election with an actual problem for the government to address—ruining all the fun. Thus, it must be a conspiracy. In the mind of a conspiracy theorist the effect becomes a cause, the reason why the event happened in the first place. Since they had these effects that must have been the reason that they happened. 9/11 was an inside job and COVID was an attempt to undermine Trump. To cite Spinoza "For what is really a cause, it considers a an effect, and conversely what is an effect it considers as a cause."

Conspiracy theories are in some sense the secularization of final causes. It is no longer the intentions of god that we see behind the world, but darker forces orchestrating devious plans. Everything is interpreted according to intentions and plans. What remains the same is not just the final cause as the interpretive principle, understanding things through their effects, but also that the world then becomes a series of signs, things to be decoded in order to see intentions. While truth for Spinoza might be "the standard of itself and the false," making the light and darkness plain, signs need an interpretation, which in turn needs an interpretation. This instability is both their limitation and possibility. Interpreting signs is a kind of joy, a mastery of the world, and imposing your interpretation on others is a way to dominate and control others. As Wu-Ming argue, contemporary conspiracies are much more interactive than the old fears of secret societies, making it possible for everyone to find their own signs and figures.[2] Once everything becomes a sign of something else then it becomes possible to see even more nefarious intentions. Everything is interpreted and everything means something. The more we see dark forces, the more we see dark forces.

Superstition on this interpretation is less a matter of a specific content, such as scripture, the anthropomorphic idea of god, etc., than it is a form, or what Althusser called a matrix, a grid of intelligibility. This matrix is dominated by final causes, by the notion that everything that has an effect must have been done for such an effect, and signs, by the notion that everything that is perceived has to interpreted as an indication of something else. This brings me to what I think might be the most provocative and useful passage from Spinoza with respect to conspiracy theories as the new superstition. In the Appendix of Part One of the *Ethics* Spinoza writes,

> "Nor ought we here to pass over the fact that the followers of this doctrine, who have wanted to show off their cleverness in assigning the ends of things, have introduced—to prove this doctrine of theirs—a new way of arguing; by reducing things, not to the impossible, but to ignorance. This shows that no other way of defending their doctrine was open to them. For example, if a stone has fallen from a roof onto someone's head and killed him, they will show, in the following way, that the stone fell in order to kill the man. For if it did not fall to that end, God willing it, how could so many circumstances have concurred by chance (for often many circumstances do concur at once)? Perhaps you will answer that it happened because the wind was blowing and the man was walking that way. But they

---

2 https://www.wumingfoundation.com/giap/blank-space-qanon/

will persist: why was the wind blowing hard at that time? Why was the man walking that way at the same time? If you answer again that the wind arose then because on the preceding day, while the weather was still calm, the sea began to toss, and that the man had been invited by a friend, they will press on--for there is no end to the questions which can be asked...And so they will not stop asking for the causes of causes until you take refuge in the will of god, that is, the sanctuary of ignorance."

Spinoza could be understood to describing a particular kind of trolling that is often described as "sea lioning" thanks to <u>the comic by David Malki</u>. A persistent attempt to ask "why" behind every claim until one reaches exasperation or ignorance. However, beyond the persistent questions there is a second point from Spinoza that is no less important. Despite the fact that there are, as the passage suggests, causal conditions for everything, these causes and their connections often exceed our (largely inadequate) knowledge of the world. An ignorance of how the world works, how weather patterns emerge and why people do what they do, is in some sense irreducible as we will never grasp all of the causes. In its place conspiracy theories seem to offer at least an answer to the question. Beyond the specifics of Spinoza's example it is worth noting that most of us, even the well informed and philosophically inclined, float upon a sea of ignorance. We might know a little about the science behind climate change, a little about what is happening in this or that part of the world, but all in all our ignorance exceeds our knowledge. We often then defer to others, the meteorologist explains weather to us, and so on. Conspiracy theorists have a name for those that have implicit trust in others' knowledge and expertise, and that word is "sheeple." We might say that the reduction to ignorance becomes often a reduction to an appeal to authority; at some point, when confronted with questions about how we know climate change is a reality that we must face or how we know that there is not an evil cabal of satanic pedophiles running the country at some point we have to defer to some sort of authority, to some source other than our own experience. Thus, in some sense authority is unavoidable fact of human existence, even if it constantly overstepping its boundaries and claiming more than it rightfully demands, and thus eliciting contestation and rebellion. Authority is both useful, and excessive, contesting authority is also both useful and excessive.³

Of course one could argue that all immediate knowledge is a combination of experience and authority, of what Spinoza calls things directly experienced and knowledge gathered from signs. Follwing Deleuze and Guattari we could call this an assemblage, a combination of affects, experiences, and signs. It is from this assemblage that we construct knowledge of the world. From this angle we could argue that a conspiracy theory is a particular way of combining experience and signs, of knowledge and interpretation. The central aspect of this sign, that which is in need of interpretation, but no less central is the privilege such knowledge attaches to the immediacy of experience. As Jodi Dean argues,

---

3 On this point I am indebted to Dimitris Vardoulakis, Spinoza, The Epicurean: Authority and Utility in Materialism, Edinburgh: Edinburgh University, 2020.

Reduction to Ignorance **243**

the antechamber of the modern conspiracy theory is the UFO encounter or alien abduction story, which privileges the testimony and authenticity of experience, of witness accounts. Neglected or recovered experience has played a role in a whole history of conspiracies from alien abductions to satanic panics. The subject of contemporary conspiracy is less someone who directly experienced things kept secret from the rest of us, but has decoded or discovered a secret closed to most of us. They have not been onboard the space ship, but they can pinpoint the exact moment in the video that the lizard person reveals his or her true nature. The central claim of every contemporary conspiracy theory is less "this happened to me" than "I did my own research." The first person is the privileged mode of this research. It is not what "they" say, but what "I" have come to know. As much as this "I" is constructed in opposition to "they" to what it perceives as conformity to authority, as we have seen it is also framed in terms of another "they," that of the conspirators it imagines. One could add here Spinoza's remark that we imagine the other's temperament, their constitution, through our own, projecting our strivings and struggles onto them. The "them" in most conspiracy theories are a reflection of the "us," a mirror image of our intentions and goals. They are just like us and that is why they cannot be trusted.

What is the experience behind the conspiracy theorist's claim to knowledge? For Spinoza the first kind of knowledge, that which is drawn from experience and signs, is what he terms inadequate knowledge. Inadequate knowledge involves an encounter between our body and another body, between us and something in the world, but it tells us little of either. What we get is a mix of our own desires, fears, and hopes and some qualities of the object, of what we encounter, but these appear jumbled, as our perceptions and projections shape and distort the object while the object only reveals part of who we are. It is from this perspective that we can grasp contemporary conspiracy theories which often begin from certain kind of empiricism, not the empiricism of experiments and labs, but of immediate everyday experience and desires. It is this experience, the experience of the world as one sees it, an experience that seems increasingly insignificant in the face of contemporary society, that conspiracies bestow with a new importance and dignity. Anything that does not conform to this immediate experience, Helen Keller's remarkable life[4], or even the way that the snow in Texas melts[5], is discounted because it does not conform to this experience. The last example is particularly instructive, the videos of people melting snowballs demonstrates that sometimes empirical evidence is just another word for inadequate ideas.

Flat earthers, people who believe Covid is a hoax, and even those (mainly white people) who claim that racism does not exist base their claims on what they have directly experienced without examining the limits or conditions of that experience. This then is combined with a particular desire, whether it is a desire to believe that one is the center of the universe, as in the case of flat earthers; that we are not in the midst of a pandemic, in the case of Covid deniers; or that we are absolved of history, in the case of people who refuse to believe that racism continues to be a reality. The final ingredient is then research; this research is, as has often been remarked, a particular kind of confirmation bias, people find sources which confirm what they think, a tendency that is increased by the algorithms of Youtube and facebook, which are increasingly engineered to confirm our biases and desires. Spinoza wrote that we are conscious of desires and ignorant of the causes of things; to which we could add that the contemporary individual is born conscious of their desires but ignorant of the algorithms that show them what they see, that structure their experience.

To return to a theme that I have been thinking about a lot recently, it is not just that contemporary subjection is treated as salvation, as Spinoza argued, but it increasingly appears as rebellion.

---

[4] https://www.theguardian.com/books/2021/jan/07/helen-keller-why-is-a-tiktok-conspiracy-theory-undermining-her-story
[5] https://www.distractify.com/p/texas-fake-snow-conspiracy-tiktok

Those who seem themselves as rebelling against the mandates of mask orders, of belief in global warming, and other conspiracies, are in and through their rebellion conforming more than they know to a society that has no real ability or desire to address a pandemic, not if it will threaten corporate profits, or avert a global catastrophe at the expense of profits.

Conspiracy theories are a particular assemblage, a particular combination of experience and signs, affect and desire, technology and subjectivity. A particular way of combining what is experienced, what we want or fear, and the technology mediations that make up much of life. Viewing it this way, as an assemblage, makes it possible to think about how the same elements, how experience, desire, and technology could be used to construct a different assemblage a different kind of knowledge, one that is not suspended between two subjects, the one who is supposed to know and the other who is supposed to conspire, but sees the world defined not just in terms of intentions, but structures and relations, and because of this such a world cannot simply be grasped by the immediacy of experience.

This piece has two direct sequels, The Dialectic of Conspiracy and Trust: Hegel on Conspiracy Theories and The Spontaneous Ideology of Conspiracy: This One on Marx. More on conspiracy theories as an assemblage can be found in "Shine On: We are all in Room 237 Now."

> SCIENCE IS REAL
> BLACK LIVES MATTER
> NO HUMAN IS ILLEGAL
> LOVE IS LOVE
> WOMEN'S RIGHTS ARE HUMAN RIGHTS
> KINDNESS IS EVERYTHING

Don't worry I will explain why I picked this image

The Dialectic of Conspiracy and Trust: Hegel and Conspiracy Theories

Originally posted in October of 2021.

This post is an immediate follow up or even sequel to an earlier post on Spinoza and conspiracy theories. In a more oblique way it is also a follow up to something that I have said repeatedly, not only is there more to Hegel's *Phenomenology of Spirit* than the master and slave, but that the other dialectical scenes or figures can be wrestled from the linear progression of Hegel's thought to become the basis of social and political criticism. Kojeve can't have all of the fun.

One such section is the dialectic of enlightenment and superstition. In some sense this is a dialectic of a fundamental misrecognition. As Hegel argues superstition and enlightenment, or faith and pure insight, are, as pure consciousness, more identical than they would admit. They are differentiated only in terms of their form, in the former it is thought without concept, religion remaining only a picture thinking of the absolute, while in the latter it is pure consciousness of the self.

In some sense the enlightenment begins from the perspective that superstition is fundamentally deceived about the object of its faith, stressing the non-identity of what it claims to believe and the truth of this belief. Religion is something other than what faith claims, having a different history and politics, The Enlightenment sees the distortions and deceptions of priests and despots beneath its proclamations of faith. It understands its proclamations and rituals to be nothing other than fallacious statements about the nature of things. "Accordingly, it says of faith that its absolute essence is a piece of stone, a block of wood with eyes that do not see, or else that it is something made of bread-dough obtained from the field, which, when transformed by men, is then returned there."[1] The enlightenment turns the customs and habits of faith into erroneous matters of fact, reminding it that bread is just bread, not the body of Christ, and the cross is just wood.

The Enlightenment makes faith into its own image, makes its actions, actions of belief, into statements, statements about the actual world that can be disproven. This is the criticism of every atheist who states the impossibility of a global flood, of fitting all the animals onto an ark, and so on seeing in religion nothing other than bad science and poor history. For Hegel faith should refuse such claims,

The Creation Museum

---

1 G.W.F Hegel, *The Phenomenology of Spirit*, Translated by Terry Pinkard, Oxford: Oxford University, 2018. pg. 321.

recognizing that its true object, its true insight, is something more than facts of astronomy and zoology. It is tempting to argue part of our contemporary dialectic of the enlightenment is that modern faith has taken this misrecognition as a challenge, and has tried to prove, if not the authenticity of the body and the reality of the cross, then at least the reality of the bible's story of creation.

It is worth pausing for a minute and asking what drives this particular dialectic, this particular identity and difference, as faith and enlightenment become their opposites, or see themselves as identical even as they are opposed. Etienne Balibar offers the following explanation in his book on universals, possibly his most Hegelian book: first, as Balibar describes the general structure of the *Phenomenology*, "*The enunciation of the universal* (and, as a consequence, its *inscription*, its *institution*, its historical *realization*) immediately entails its transformation into its opposite (the particular, the contingent) or the production of its negation."[2] (I should add that it seems to me that this is a very Spinozist way of framing things, the universal is always tainted by the particular.) As Balibar describes the particular trajectory of the enlightenment in the passage in question, "The more it turns the universal into a pure rational form (a form of "pure reason"), the more it relies in reality on anthropological postulates, on an image of man and the human that suppresses a whole unconscious portion of itself and, as a consequence, the more it relies on the presence of an unsaid within itself."[3]

The universal reveals the particular within itself the more it totalizes, the more it tries to present everything according to its logic. The contemporary version of this, the modern "dialectic of enlightenment" that could be suggested here, one that is not without its relation to the book of the same name, is one of two competing totalizations. In the first, faith remakes itself in the model of the enlightenment's critique, turning biblical narratives into the

---

2 Etienne Balibar, *On Universals: Constructing and Deconstructing Community*, Translated by Joshua David Jordan, New York: Fordham, 2020, 47.
3 Etienne Balibar, *Citizen Subject: Foundations for a Philosophical Anthropology*, Translated by Stephen Miller, New York: Fordham, 2017, pg. 163.

basis for "intelligent design" and theories of "young Earth." Faith becomes science. The reverse would seem to be equally true, science increasingly turns itself into a faith of sorts. One counters the ichthys, the "Jesus Fish" with their own Darwin Fish complete with little evolutionary legs. On the one hand there is a faith that recognizes that faith is not enough, that in in order to vanquish its enemy, the secular world view, it must beat it at its own game becoming science. On the other there is a science that strives to have the same relation to identity as faith does, to become a world view and not just knowledge. Each tries to win by playing by the other's rules.

I want to be careful about this point, because accusation that a given group treats something, some idea, as an object of faith, or religion, is one of those crude sorts of criticism that one hears all the more in that it is so imprecise. Not only does it not clarify how, and in what way, something is being treated as religion, often making that word synonymous with dogma and authority, it too has its own odd dialectic in that it seems to imply that treating something as religion is bad so long as what is being treated this way is not religion proper. It is also worth pointing out that this criticism, which is really the criticism of fanaticism, has as assumed norm the idea that one should not take things too seriously or with too much conviction. Ours is an age of flexibility and opportunism.

Nonetheless, it still seems possible to say that science, an idea of science, has become something like an object of faith. When people say that "Science is Real" or that they "Fuckin' Love Science" they are expressing not so much a specific point about this or that scientific discovery or the scientific method, but a kind of faith in science. What they like could be referred to, following Althusser, as the spontaneous philosophy of science, the amalgamation of "neato facts," secularized wonder, and vague confidence in progress that makes up a certain image of science. We could say, following Althusser that science cannot become an identity, cannot become a subject, or if we wanted to be Badiouian about it, we would say that such fidelity is only possible with respect to a specific scientific discovery not science as such, which at the level of generality can only be an ideology.

In this rough updating of the *Phenomenology* I am turning to the two things that we return to Hegel for again and again; namely, the identity and difference of contradiction. The way that ways of thinking not only define themselves by opposition but in doing so begin to take on characteristics of their opposition. Faith becomes science and science becomes a kind of faith. It seems that the worst thing that one could do in this age of anti-enlightenment, an age defined by conspiracy theories and pseudo-science, would be to turn to science as an object of faith. One of the risks of the proliferation of such theories is that it would seem to make an uncritical turn to the authority of science tempting. The misguided skepticism of conspiracy theories creates the oddest dogmas of traditions and institutions. One counters the faith in conspiracy theories with a faith in not only science in the abstract, but the existing institutions of expertise.

The very worst version of this is to be found in the celebration of Pfizer and Moderna as if they were dueling houses from Harry Potter and not multibillion companies who have not only benefited immensely from the pandemic but have in some sense perpetuated it in maintaining profits over distributing vaccines. I know that this is not really a conclusion, and there is a lot of dots left to connect between "Science is Real" and "Team Pfizer," the celebration of science is not the same as the brand identification with a pharmaceutical company. However, they have the same cause, in that both are a reaction to an identity, and as a reaction they are too similar, too identical, to that which they are opposed to.

For more on conspiracy theories see "The Dialectic of Conspiracy and Trust: Hegel on Conspiracy Theories" and The Spontaneous Ideology of Conspiracy: This One on Marx.

The Spontaneous Ideology of Conspiracy: This One on Marx

Originally posted in December of 2022.

Sometime ago I came up with the idea of doing a trilogy of posts on conspiracy theory, or modern conspiracy thought, read through Spinoza, Hegel and Marx. I am not exactly sure why the idea appealed to me, in part because I increasingly increasingly consider Spinoza, Hegel, and Marx to be the cornerstone of my philosophical thought, even if these cornerstones come through the mediations of Tosel, Jameson, and Althusser (to name a few), but in this case, more specifically it seemed worth asking what would three critics of the mystifications of their day make of our modern mystifications.

After writing the pieces on Spinoza and Hegel it took me a long time to even consider writing a piece on Marx. The intersection of Marx and conspiracy theory just seems too big to take on in a blogpost. This is in part because for many in the US, Marxism is both the name of a supposed conspiracy and a conspiracy theory. It has become increasingly the former as the right has dealt with end of the Soviet Union not by giving up on red scares, but by making the threat of Marxism to be more diffuse and conspiratorial.[1] Marxism, or communism, are not to just to be found in open appeals to revolution, or organizing workers; instead everything from Critical Race Theory to the casting of a Disney film can now be seen to be the work of Marxism in its more diffuse cultural form, a plot that becomes more insidious the more indirect its connection discernible political goals become.

At the same time that Marxism is seen as conspiracy it is argued that its understanding of history and politics, which sees the interest of the ruling class behind everything, is fundamentally a conspiracy theory, if not the fundamental conspiracy theory. As is often the case, I would argue that this idea that Marxism is a conspiracy theory gets things wrong and upside down. To gesture to a much larger argument, I would argue that Marx's fundamental theoretical innovation is to present an understanding of economic, social, and political relations that breaks with every conspiracy theory in that its primary mode of explanation is not individual intentions, or collective strategies, but the economic and social conditions that exceed any intention or strategy. The actions of capitalist with respect to wages and working conditions are, to use the parlance of our times, dictated by the demands of the market, by the demand to be competitive, etc., what Marx would perhaps more simply call the extraction of surplus value. Marx stresses that this structure is absolutely indifferent to the conscious intentions of not only the workers, who must conform to it in selling their labor power or risk starving, but to the capitalist as well, who must conform to the demands of competition. As Marx puts it, in the mouth of the worker addressing the capitalist, "You may be a model citizen, perhaps a member of the R.S.P.C.A. [Royal Society for the Prevention of Cruelty to Animals], and you may be in the odour of sanctity as well; but the thing you represent when you come face to face

---

1 Richard Seymour has referred to this as "anti-communism without communism."
Richard Seymour, "Why is the Nationalist Right Hallucinating a "Communist Enemy?" *The Guardian*, September 26, 2020. https://www.theguardian.com/commentisfree/2020/sep/26/communist-enemy-nationalist-right-trump-us-bolsonaro-brazil

with me has no heart in its breast."² As I argued with respect to Spinoza, if the defining characteristic of most conspiracy theories is understanding the world in terms of ends, of deducing the conspiracy from effects (if talking about race makes white people feel bad that must be the reason behind such teaching, and so on), Marx's fundamental argument is how little ends and intentions mean in understanding social and political life. Marx's criticism is not one of "capitalist greed" as a moral failing, but of the structural conditions that cause capitalists to seek cheaper workers, to demand more of workers, and so on regardless of their moral character. This is the real meaning of Marx's invocation of vampires and werewolves, not to call the capitalist a monster, but to claim that there is something monstrous in capital that exceeds intensions and is found not in the hearts of human beings but in the social relations that produce and reproduce them.

---

2 Karl Marx, *Capital: A Critique of Political Economy, Volume I*, Translated by Ben Fowkes, (New York: Penguin, 1977), 343.

The Spontaneous Ideology of Conspiracy   **257**

As something of an aside, I will suggest that part of Marx's legacy on critical theory, for lack of a better term, is this demand to think in terms of structures that exceed and situate consciousness, this is partly what is at stake in the concept of the mode of production. This legacy goes beyond those who are explicitly Marxist. What Foucault called a dispositif, or apparatus, what Deleuze and Guattari referred to as assemblages or machines, were also an attempt to think the structural over and above the intentional. They are in some sense an attempt to articulate a concept that could displace the mode of production understood as the articulation of material practices and ideas, what Marx called base and superstructure. In Foucault this becomes the relation of power to knowledge (or apparatuses and discourses), while in Deleuze and Guattari it becomes that of machinic assemblages of bodies to collective assemblages of enunciation. Both of which could be understood as an attempt to expand the explanatory framework beyond the putatively economic to encompass the production of knowledge and desire.

Closer to home, the insistence on the term "structural" in "structural racism," as well as similar attempts to think patriarchy as a social and political structure, are all attempts to theorize racism, sexism, or misogyny without reducing it to individual prejudices, biases, or psychological attitudes. I would then say, summing this up all too quickly, not only is Marx's thought not a conspiracy theory, Marx's fundamental move of thinking relations, structures, and institution in excess of intentions and understandings is the antechamber or all theories that want to be more than conspiracy theories that want to understand structural conditions rather than individual attitudes as the basis for exploitation, marginalization, and domination.

Such a point is beyond the focus of a blogpost, and, moreover, it was not what I intend to get at here. My question is what does Marx offer for thinking the conspiratorial turn in contemporary politics? The first point, which I have already more or less uttered, is that a great deal of what we call conspiracy theories are really just anti-communism, and that these theories have become more

baroque and oblique as communism as a political force retreats into historical memory. They are in some sense a kind of anti-communism without communism, as Richard Seymour argues. It is the decline of Marxism as a political force that leads to the demand to find it everywhere; everything that challenges the existing order, not just the economic order but its racial and gender aspects as well, from teaching about the history of slavery to non-binary gender identity can be labelled "Marxist." (The irony of this is that actually existing Marxism, especially in its more official state varieties, has had a spotty at best record when it comes to understanding race and gender as sites of domination and exploitation. Many Marxists of an old school variety would perhaps be surprised to learn that anti-racist education is secretly Marxist and that Marxists are behind the demand to respect individual's choice of pronouns). Second, Marxism is integral to understanding the real conditions of social and political life which are in some sense experienced as a vast conspiracy. As I have alluded to above, Marx explains, better than any conspiracy theory the way in which prevailing economic and political relations produce the feeling of helplessness and lack of control that is, as Marcus Gilroy-Ware argues, the raw material for most conspiracy theories.[3]

Of course the fundamental question is if it is in some sense the relations of capitalism that create the conditions of alienation and powerlessness which are the conditions for conspiracy theorizing, why do such theories name everything but capital, or the ruling class, as the agent of this conspiracy. This is part because the demands of capital are too out in the open to be the object of a conspiracy theory. There is no riddle to solve in saying that capital is driven by the extraction of surplus value, or, as they say, the pursuit of profit. The latter is openly declared in every newspaper, website, and news broadcast. Without a secret, without the ability to be in the know, there is no affective appeal to a conspiracy theory. We are stuck in a kind of perpetual purloined letter situation in which it is because the existing goals of the ruling class are so out in the open that there is a need to create a kind of bizarro world inversion of this world in order to believe in the conspiracy that would explain it. While it is fairly clear to anyone paying attention that the established position on COVID for example is to declare it over again and again in order to be able to get people back to work and to end any state spending on aid, testing, or vaccines, such a goal is too open to muster any theorizing, too public to generate any critique, so we get a bizarro inversion where the powers that be want lockdowns, mask mandates, and vaccines to perpetuate some vague idea of control. At the same time, it could be argued that the fact that conspiracy theories generally leave capitalism untouched, approaching it only obliquely through the antisemitic fear of global elites, demonstrates to what extent the demands of capitalism have become, as Marx writes, "self-evident natural laws," wage labor as a mode of existence and commodification as the realization of pleasures remain unexamined by conspiracy theories.[4] Thus to butcher a phrase,

---

3 Marcus Gilroy-Ware, *After the Fact? The Truth about Fake News*, London: Repeater, 2020.
4 Karl Marx, *Capital: A Critique of Political Economy, Volume I*, Translated by Ben Fowkes, (New York: Penguin, 1977), 799.

it is easier to imagine the world controlled by lizard people than it is to question the existence of wage labor and the commodity form.

For more on conspiracy theories see "Reduction to Ignorance: Spinoza in the Age of Conspiracy Theories" and The Dialectic of Conspiracy and Trust: Hegel on Conspiracy Theories." For more on Covid see "Despair and Indignation: The Inevitable Reflection on Covid (with Marx and Spinoza).

Woke Capital and Twilight of the Bourgeoisie (How is that for a title?)

Originally posted in April of 2021.

For anyone who has any historical memory whatsoever the controversies around woke seem like just a remake, or possible a reboot, of the panic around political correctness a generation prior. It is a matter of the same fears, the same threats, and the same bad guys and good guys. College campuses and postmodernism are once again to blame, and the same hallowed traditions are threatened. On one reading, and it is a fairly plausible one, is that this is just a repetition. The only reason that the names have been changed, the only reason terms like "woke" have replaced "political correctness" is that repeating the old name would be admitting that this new threat is quite old. Political correctness came and went, but the skies did not darken and the rivers did not run red with blood. New logo, same package. There are, however, some differences and these differences have something to say about the changing nature of culture and power.

The first thing that comes to mind, illustrated stunningly by an unintentionally hilarious editorial on how "wokeness" is ruining Disney World published in *The Orlando Sentinel*, is that there is a fundamental shift in what is under assault.¹ It is no longer the hallowed classics of Shakespeare, Dickens, and Milton that are under attack but Mr. Potato Head, "Trader Sam," and some of Dr. Seuss' forgotten books. Woke is what happens when the canon wars go low, threatening the detritus of junk culture. This also changes the nature of the defense from this assault. Whereas the defenders of the classics could write *The Closing of the American Mind* and make a claim for the universality of western culture, the contemporary defenders of toys and theme parks have to embrace the irreducible particularity of their claim. Jokes about headhunters, "eskimos," and African savages only seem fun and harmless if you are not affected by them. What is being defended in many of these cases are the pleasures of casual racism.

The second difference is that while college professors and their duped students are still the primary purveyors of woke culture, the list of villains now includes corporations. All of the decisions referred to above were made by the corporations themselves. In fact what is often bemoaned as a "woke" decision is really just marketing. What the ardent Disney fan above seems to miss is that Disney is in the process of making a film based on its ride, and the retooling of the ride will eventually match the film. Disney seems to excel at this particular kind of cultural recycling, making live action films that are adaptations of its animated films and making films based on its rides that then become the basis for retooling the rides to match the films and so on, becoming a kind of cultural perpetual motion machine.

Often what is bemoaned as the excess of woke capitalism is nothing more than an attempt to expand markets. This is the universalizing aspect of capital that Marx recognized as revolutionary. To cite Marx,

> "The bourgeoisie, wherever it has got the upper hand, has put an end to all feudal, patriarchal, idyllic relations. It has pitilessly torn asunder the motley feudal ties that bound man to his "natural superiors", and has left remaining no other nexus between man and man than naked self-interest, than callous

---

1 Unfortunately the article in question is now behind a paywall. https://www.orlandosentinel.com/2021/04/23/i-love-disney-world-but-wokeness-is-ruining-the-experience-commentary/

"cash payment". It has drowned the most heavenly ecstasies of religious fervour, of chivalrous enthusiasm, of philistine sentimentalism, in the icy water of egotistical calculation. It has resolved personal worth into exchange value, and in place of the numberless indefeasible chartered freedoms, has set up that single, unconscionable freedom — Free Trade. In one word, for exploitation, veiled by religious and political illusions, it has substituted naked, shameless, direct, brutal exploitation."[2]

Moving beyond the passionate defenders of junk culture, and turning our attention to more important matters, the recent limitations to voting passed in Georgia: restrictions that disproportionately affect urban, working, and minority voters, have been met with boycotts and condemnations by corporations from Major League Baseball to Delta airlines. This has led to politicians, the very same politicians who take millions from corporate lobbyists and donors, chastising corporate America for its influence in politics.[3]

Taken together these two aspects of the current battle against the "outrage industrial complex" to use McConnell's term, which I must admit I kind of like, are part of the twilight of the bourgeoisie. By decline of the bourgeoisie I do not mean the decline of the power of capital, of those who own the means of production, nor do I necessarily mean, as some have argued, that we are entering into some new post-capitalist and neo-feudalist age in which the ruling class are no longer the bourgeoisie but some new form of digital overlord. Rather following Balibar, I mean the creation of a "class of the super-rich which no longer have pretension of distinction other than that of consumption."[4] To which I would add that the decline of pretension of distinction is also a decline of universalism. Part of

---

2 Karl Marx and Friedrich Engels, *Manifesto of the Communist Party*, in *The Marx/Engels Reader*, ed. Robert Tucker, Norton, 1978.
3 Bess Levin, "Mitch McConnell Doesn't Have a Problem With Corporations Getting Involved in Politics When He's Suckling at the Corporate Teat," *Vanity Fair*, April 6, 2021. https://www.vanityfair.com/news/2021/04/mitch-mcconnell-corporate-donors
4 Etienne Balibar, "Sur les interpretations de Mai 68" in *Histoire Interminable: D'un siècle l'autre, Écrits I*, Paris: La Découverte, 2020, 109.

what sustained the bourgeoisie as a class, and as form of rule, was not only its distinction, the culture and norms which supposedly made it better, but its universalism, that anyone could acquire this culture and norms. Hence the importance of education and the ideology of meritocracy during the heyday of its rule. The contemporary ruling class claims no such basis for its dominance and rule. As much as I hate to bring him up, Trump was perhaps the first post-bourgeois president, or at the very least the presidency in the decline of the symbolic efficacy of the bourgeois.

Trump eschewed the norms and conventions of bourgeois taste at every possible turn. This was a sharp distinction with Obama who openly embraced bourgeois conventions as precisely those things which everyone regardless of race or background could acquire. Obama was both the first black president and the last gasp of the bourgeoisie, and the latter because of the former. This contrast led some to see Trump as in some odd sense working class, but there is a big difference between the decline of symbolic efficacy of the bourgeois markers of distinction (to use a term from Jodi Dean) and an actual class transformation. More importantly, Trump of course never made any pretension of being anything other than rich, but his capital never passed through the mediation of cultural capital. His wealth was tacky and without the slightest hint of distinction.

One could argue that this carried a more universalizing message, one that did not pass through cultural institutions, through education, but through the more base, and more general, aspiration to simply be rich. That Trump displayed his wealth through a quantitative accumulation of what is qualitatively indistinguishable from most day to day commodities made it all the more approachable. A table covered with fast food combines opulence and accessibility: it is both a symbol of unimagined wealth and approachability, or, to use the parlance of our times, it is "relatable." However, to identify Trump, and, more importantly, the current ruling class, with the ersatz universality of the Big Mac is to overlook the point that I began with. The critics of "woke capital," or to use a more absurd term, "corporate communism," are not espousing the universality of brands like Disney and plastic potato heads, but are clamoring for their right to enjoy these things in the irreducible racial and gendered particularity.

This seems to be the moment we are living in, a moment in which corporations have more stock in universality and equality, even if it is only the universality of exploitation and equality to consume the same products, than the state and its politicians, which openly embrace racial hierarchy and patriarchal gender norms. It is a moment of reaction and regression to hierarchies and exclusions that we believed to be left in the past. The task, it seems to me is to not only avoid the market revivals of "freedom, equality, and Bentham," to embrace our new corporate sponsors of human rights, but also to construct an actual universalism from below, opposed to both that of the market, which is only the equality to be exploited, and the bourgeois state, which is increasingly surrendering equality to maintain the power of a select elite.

For more on Trump see Trumped: The Ecology of Attention and Affects.

Despair and Indignation: The Inevitable Reflection on Covid (with Marx and Spinoza)

Originally posted in January of 2022.

The last thing anyone needs is another hot take on Covid. In the early months of the pandemic there were a series of reflections that came too soon and undercooked, as everyone reached into familiar concepts such as "biopower" or "totalitarianism" to make sense of what was happening. It seemed to be in good taste to not say anything, to go on as if things would return to normal, but now, two years in, not saying anything about COVID feels a little like watching one of the films or television shows that have gone in production since the pandemic started, in which the actors inhabit a pre-COVID world while the masks and precautions stay off of camera. The reality of these images of a life without COVID has begun to appear as fantastic as any CGI trip to a far off planet or the distant past. All television and film, not just those set in the Marvel Cinematic Universe or the Star Wars Universe, begin to appear as a depiction of an alternate timeline, one in which the COVID pandemic did not take place.

In other words making sense of the COVID world feels less and less like an attempt to cash in on the latest trend than a necessary way to make sense of the world. Talking about anything, politics, economy, and society without talking about COVID is a little like talking about politics without talking about the internet—it can be done, but I am not sure such a discussion would be connected to the actual reality of the world. The unavoidable reality of COVID comes with its affective tenor, it is hard to think of the pandemic without also processing the anger, sadness, and despair. This was not always true. There were two moments of hope that I can recall. First, there was the optimism connecting with the moment of shutdowns and solidarity, however fleeting, that marked the first few months of the pandemic. Some of this solidarity was symbolic, the banging of pots and pans in appreciation of "essential workers," and some was real, the emergence of mutual aid, but all of it suggested a transformed world. I vividly remember walking my dog on a Friday night down a quiet street that ordinarily would be packed with cars driving to and from the restaurants and bars downtown and finding some comfort in the quiet. It seemed like a moment of collective action if not solidarity. Such lockdowns and shutdowns were incomplete and thus ineffective and the virus raged on. A second figure of hope arrived soon after and that was the vaccines. Technology seemed to be able to save us when we could not save ourselves. Now, with the omicron variant vaccines have proven less effective than we hoped, and, we have given up on most preventive measures—hope has given way to despair.

If writing this means anything it is an attempt to avoid despair, not with a new figure of hope, but, as Spinoza puts it, to replace it with understanding. What I would like to understand most of all is not just why all efforts to do anything to stop the spread of the virus have collapsed, folded into an entirely individualized and thus unequal imperative to get vaccinated, get a good mask, and stock up on testing kits—if you can find or afford them, but why this abandonment has produced little indignation or anger. In fact, it would seem that most of the anger, the indignation, is not on

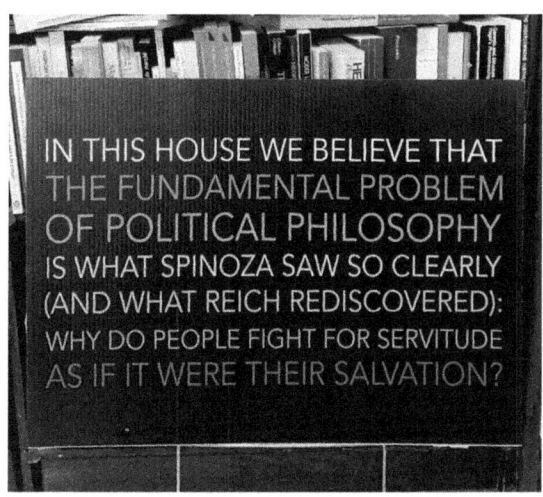

This was a limited edition product of Crit-drip

the failure to do anything, to give up and hope that the omicron variant truly is milder and that there will be no future mutations, but directed at the few attempts to do anything. Attempts to impose mask restrictions or proof of vaccines are met with hostility and even death threats. To twist a formulation from Spinoza again, we fight for our infection as if it was our liberation.

In order to understand it is necessary to first dispense with the fantasies of power that cloud our judgment. The specter of biopower is one such fantasy. Early on it was possible to imagine vaccine mandates, contact tracing, and quarantines becoming a new expansion of power, a new digital bio-panopticon that would monitor and control our every move. But to twist a quote from Michel Foucault, "We must conceptualize the deployment of biopower on the basis of techniques of power that are contemporary with it."[1] We have to base our analysis on the way that power functions now not how it has functioned in the past. In other words, we have to stop looking for the figure of the gestapo behind

---

[1] Michel Foucault, *The History of Sexuality: Volume 1: An Introduction*. Translated by Robert Hurley. New York: Vintage, 1978, 149.

the demand for vaccination cards, for the specter of the state, and recognize that the person asking for our card is the hostess at the Cheesecake Factory, or that the person requiring us to wear our mask is not a cop (who rarely wear masks anyway) but our boss. With a few exceptions it has been the corporation, not the state, that has required proof of vaccination or imposed mask mandates.

We have an entire vocabulary, almost an entire discipline, dedicated to the excesses of state power from the ancient warnings about tyrants to the modern era's concern with totalitarianism. This language becomes our default for understanding the control of capital over our lives. This is true not only of pundits who write without irony about corporate communism, but also of political theorists that refer to the power of corporations over the employees as communist dictatorships. This lacunae is no accident. Referring back to Foucault again it is worth remembering his argument that "power is tolerable only on condition that it mask a substantial part of itself."[2] For Foucault this could be seen in the way in which the liberties, the rights of man, had as their dark underside disciplinary power and the norms, a division that more or less maps unto the divide between the state and the economy. The factory was the primary site of discipline while the liberties reigned outside of its walls.

Of course such a reading makes Foucault a crypto-Marxist, (and to be honest that is always for me the best Foucault), especially since the idea of such a divide between two scenes, base and superstructure runs throughout Marx's thought. It also defines the division between the market, as the realm of freedom, equality, and Bentham, and the hidden abode of production defined by inequality and exploitation. I would like to discuss a third way that this division is formulated, not in terms of base and superstructure, exchange and production, but in terms of two different divisions of labor, the social division of labor and the division of labor in production, which correspond to two different types of authority. To illustrate what

---

2 Michel Foucault, *The History of Sexuality*, 86.

I am saying I would like to turn to two passages, the first is from *The Poverty of Philosophy* in which Marx writes,

> "It can even be laid down as a general rule that the less authority presides over the division of labor inside society, the more the division of labor develops inside the workshop, and the more it is subjected there to the authority of a single person. Thus authority in society, in relation to the division of labor, are in inverse ratio to each other."[3]

And then, perhaps more well known, in *Volume One* of *Capital*:

> "The same bourgeois consciousness which celebrates the division of labour in the workshop, the lifelong annexation of the worker to partial operation, and his complete subjection to capital, as an organization of labour that increases its productive power, denounces with equal vigour every conscious attempt to control and regulate the process of production socially as an inroad upon such sacred things as the rights of property, freedom and the self-determining 'genius' of the individual capitalist."[4]

What writers like Elizabeth Anderson see as a bug, that people put up with authority in the workplace that they would not tolerate outside of it, in politics, turns out to be a feature, an integral aspect of capitalist society. Our freedom as consumers, or more to the point, the freedom of capital to move from industry to industry, has as its necessary condition the subjection of workers. This can be seen in the way two things invite derision and scorn, freedom in the workplace and control over the market, both are seen as antithetical to the economy as such, to be recipes for social disaster.

Much more can be said about this, but to tie it back to our central concern, that of COVID, we at least have an answer of sorts to the question "Why is nothing being done?" Why are there no new relief

---

[3] Karl Marx, *The Poverty of Philosophy*, International, 1963, 136.
[4] Karl Marx, *Capital: A Critique of Political Economy, Volume I*, Translated by Ben Fowkes, New York: Penguin, 1977, 477.

checks, no new mandates (at least above the city level), and now, thanks to the Supreme Court, no attempt to impose vaccinations? It is because, as the first passage from Marx argues, authority in the workplace and authority in society are in inverse relation to each other. The more society acts to mitigate the pandemic by providing aid and access to food and shelter the more it loosens the control of employers, and capital in general, and that is something that, in our society, must not happen. This is the lesson that the government has taken from the "great resignation," that any interruption, even a temporary one, of the connection between working and living undermines the working conditions necessary to capitalism. In other words, and to put it bluntly, why is the government powerless to do anything but say "get vaccinated and good luck"? It is because powerlessness at the level of the state is necessary to sustain the power of capital over our lives. (One could argue that the pandemic is being used to increase the power of capital, as the frustration and exhaustion of parents is being leveraged to mobilize anger against teachers unions, but that is another matter.)

Hot Girl Winter 🤍🥀🤍
@Vicky_ACAB

Biden admin and politico inability to understand the Great Refusal of 2021 as a continuation and expansion of the 2020 uprising means they think the repression/recuperation worked, and that therefore they should not repeat the mistakes of pandemic support that led to 2020

3:19 PM · Jan 13, 2022 · Twitter Web App

45 Retweets   4 Quote Tweets   223 Likes

What we are confronted with now, however, is not the ghoulish insistence that people should be willing to sacrifice their lives in order to keep the economy going, as in the summer of 2020, but a quieter acquiescence to the rule of capital as simply the way things are, we have to get back to work, keep schools open, and so on, just because it is the way things have to be, the way of the world.

It is at this point, that Marx's distinction between the two different attitudes towards authority can be supplemented by a Spinozist distinction regarding the affects. In the *Ethics* Spinoza argues, we love or hate something more if we imagine it to free than if we imagine it to be necessary. To which Spinoza adds, that since we consider ourselves and other humans to be free we feel love or hatred stronger. As Spinoza writes, "love toward a thing will be greater if we imagine it to be free than if we imagine it to be necessary, And similarly for hate."[5] We largely consider the human world, the world of other people and their actions, to be more worthy of hatred and love than the natural world in part because the former is seen as contingent, as free, while the latter is understood to be necessary. It is foolish to get angry at the weather. To which we could add the following assertion from Marx, that the more the economy is perceived as itself a kind of nature, or second nature, obeying its laws which are outside of human action or intervention, the less it is subject to the same affects, the same love or hatred. As Marx writes, "The advance of capitalist production develops a working class which by education, tradition, and habit looks upon the requirements of that mode of production as self-evident natural laws."[6] This perspective, seeing the requirements as self-evident natural laws, does not just efface history and change, as Marx stressed, but also, as Spinoza would emphasize, includes an affective dimension as well. The more the capitalist mode of production is seen as necessary, as functioning according to the mute compulsion of its own economic laws, the less it makes sense to become angry or indignant at its actions. It is just the way things are, not an institution, a product of human actions, that benefits some and not others. There is a second dimension, a second intersection of affect and modality. As Spinoza writes, "An affect toward a thing we imagine as necessary is more intense, other things being equal, than one toward a thing we imagine as possible

---

5 Benedict de Spinoza, *Ethics*, Translated by Edwin Curley, New York, Penguin, 1994, EIIIP49.
6 Karl Marx, *Capital: A Critique of Political Economy, Volume I*, Translated by Ben Fowkes, (New York: Penguin, 1977), 799.

or contingent, or not necessary."[7] The contradiction here is only an apparent one, anger and joy are stronger given the idea of freedom, the idea that things could be done otherwise, but overall the more necessary something is seen, the stronger the affect will be because it is seen as inevitable. Those things that are perceived as immanent and unavoidable generate more fear than anything perceived to be contingent or possible. The perception, or imagination, of necessity or freedom each have their different affective dimensions; the former are more intense because they are seen as certain, while the contingency of the latter elicits more love or anger because it could have been otherwise.

Secretary Marcia L. Fudge ✓
@SecFudge

The United States is the only major economy in the world where the economy as a whole is stronger now than before the pandemic.

2:17 PM · Jan 8, 2022 · TweetDeck

3,225 Retweets **4,468** Quote Tweets **13.4K** Likes

It is hard not to feel despair now as the hope in collective action, the symbols of solidarity that marked the first wave of the pandemic, or belief in technological innovation, the hope attached to vaccines that followed, have given way to the fear that nothing will change, that we will have to accept the idea that we can get sick at work, perhaps even die, the same way that we have accepted longer hours and less power over our lives. Against this despair we have to hold onto, and perhaps even cultivate, indignation, an indignation grounded on the fact that things could be otherwise. I do not think, as some moralists claim, that "the great resignation" is driven by the aid checks that were distributed way back in March of 2020, or by the hold on student loans, at least materially (those checks were spent a long time ago) but perhaps at the level of affects or imagination what they did reveal, ever so slightly, was that

---

7 Benedict de Spinoza, *Ethics*, Translated by Edwin Curley, New York, Penguin, 1994, EIVP11.

things could be otherwise, that the connection between work and life, needing to work in order to survive, is less a fact of nature than a product of our society. The great resignation must become the great indignation.

For more on Spinoza and Marx see "Nexus Rerum: (Spinoza and Marx, again)" and "Economies of Affect/Affective Economies: Towards a Spinozist Critique of Political Economy."

BOOKS

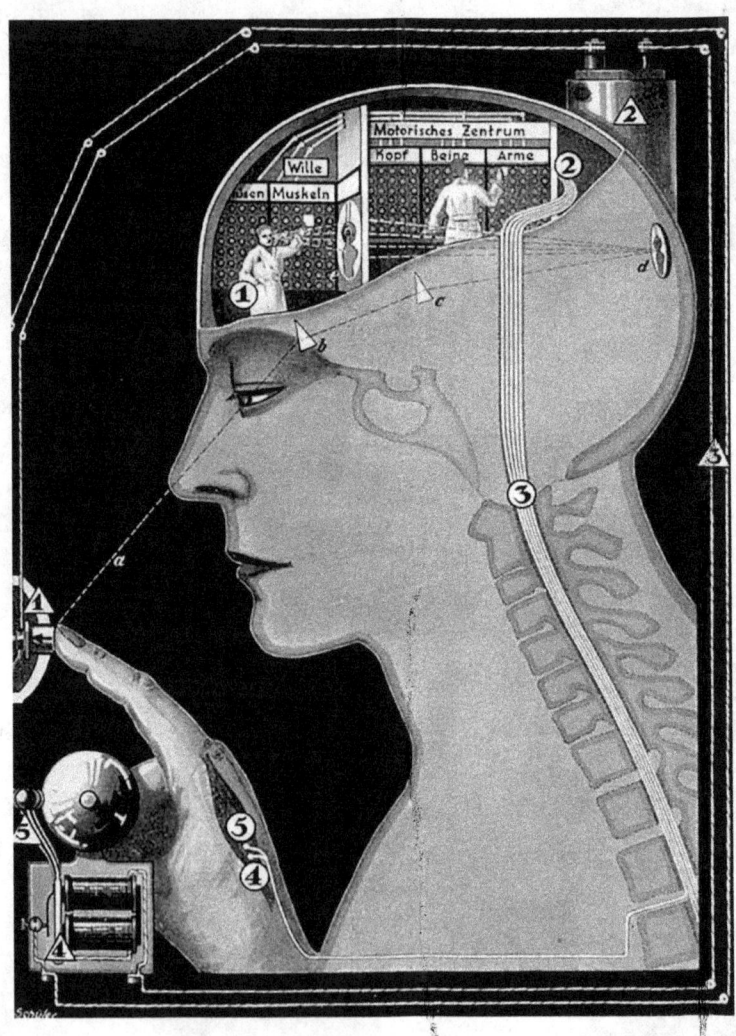

Personalized Ideology (or Ideology Personified): Silva's Mood Economy

Originally posted in December of 2013.

Do not demand of politics that it restore the "rights" of the individual, as philosophy has defined them. The individual is the product of power. What is needed is to "de-individualize" by means of multiplication and displacement, diverse combinations. The group must not be the organic bond uniting hierarchized individuals, but a constant generation of de-individualization.

– Michel Foucault, Preface to Anti-Oedipus.[1]

In the past few weeks I have returned again and again to the idea of "negative solidarity" that I previously commented on in this blog. I found myself mentally bookmarking news reports and articles that seem to be evidence of hostility to any collective organization for wages or benefits. The affect of ressentiment, the distinct sense that someone somewhere was benefiting at your expense, seemed prevalent. What makes this solidarity negative is that the "someones"

---

1 Michel Foucault, Preface to *Anti-Oedipus: Capitalism and Schizophrenia*, University of Minnesota, 1983, xiv.

in question are never the wealthy or the powerful, the ruling class, but either other workers who fare slightly better, often because of collective bargaining, or, more often, an entirely imagined figment of welfare queens or immigrants benefiting from government largess. In pursuing such examples negative solidarity risks having all of the characteristics of what Louis Althusser called a "descriptive theory," a sophisticated sounding recasting of what one already knows and thinks. The dangers of descriptive theories is that they provide a moment of recognition, ("That is it, dude; totally,") but no way to move forward. So the question which I returned to again, is how to account for the genesis and constitution of negative solidarity, how to move beyond description. This is a question of socio-political theory, but it is a necessary precondition of political action as well. Negative Solidarity is also another name to the barrier of any politics whatsoever. It prevents the formation of any real solidarity.

It is perhaps for this reason that I only had to read a few sentences describing Jennifer Silva's *Coming Up Short: Working Class Adulthood in an Age of Uncertainty* before I decided to buy it. I read it eagerly, starting it on the plane over Thanksgiving and finishing it during the brief break between the end of classes and the onslaught of grading.

Silva's certain concern, her central thesis, is that the current economic transformations, which could be broadly described as a combination of neoliberalism and austerity, have produced a new adulthood, a new subjectivity, that is individualized, psychologized, and therapeutic. As Silva writes,

> "At its core, this emerging working-class adult self is characterized by low expectations of work, wariness toward romantic commitment widespread of social institutions, profound isolation from others, and an overriding focus on their emotions and psychic health. Rather than turn to politics to address the obstacles standing in the way of a secure adult life, the majority of the men and women I interview crafted deeply *personal* coming of age stories, grounding their adult identities in recovering from their painful pasts—whether addition

childhood abuse, family trauma, or abandonment and forging an emancipated, transformed and adult self."[2]

Drawing from a series of interviews of young working class individuals in Richmond, Virginia and Lowell, Massachusetts, Silva paints a familiar picture of lives that go from school, to military, to community college, and sometimes back home, passing in and through these institutions without every constituting the traditional linear arrow of familial home, school, work, marriage. etc. As Silva argues the linear narrative of life is then constructed not in terms of career, marriage, and family, but in terms of past trauma and present victory. As Silva argues,

> "I make sense of the phenomenon of therapeutic adulthood through the concept of the mood economy. I argue that working-class men and women inhabit a social world in which the legitimacy and dignity due adults are purchased not with traditional currencies such as work or marriage but instead through the ability to organize their difficult emotions into a narrative of self-transformation."[3]

On this reading a mood economy would offer a different sense of validation and compensation, one that fills the void that is left not only from the markers of progress on the standard middle class biography ("time's arrow" in Sennett's sense) but from monetary compensation in general. In place of the standard biography of job, marriage, and children, or even the quantitative accumulation of wealth, there is a biography which charts its victories and defeats on a much more intimate scale, on overcoming addiction, abuse, or simply the ever important "taking responsibility" for oneself and one's actions. What is interesting about Silva's book is that she presents this narrative less as some kind of new found concern with

---

[2] Jennifer Silva, *Coming Up Short: Working Age Adulthood in an Age of Uncertainty*, Oxford University Press, 2015, 11.
[3] Ibid., 73.

inner life, with all of its positive valuations, than as an isolation, people turning away from politics, community, and love, turning into the infinite morass of their feelings and history.

In this way Silva's "mood economy" is similar to a particular articulation of what I have called, following Frédéric Lordon an "Affective economy." As Lordon argues one of the primary goals of the organization of affect and the imagination, these two things never being too far apart for a Spinozist, at least in a hierarchal society, is the simultaneous "elevation" of the puny objects and goals left to the majority, the workers in capitalism, and the denigration of any systemic change as impossible. As Lordon argues in *Willing Slaves of Capital: Marx and Spinoza on Desire*:

> "Symbolic violence consists then properly speaking in the production of a double imaginary, the imaginary of fulfillment, which makes the humble joys to which the dominated are assigned appear sufficient, and the imaginary of powerlessness, which convince them to renounce any greater ones to which they might aspire. 'For whatever man imagines he cannot do, he necessarily imagines; and he is so disposed by this imagination that he really cannot do what he imagines he cannot do' (EIIIDXXVIII) Here is the passionate mechanism for converting designation into self-designation put to work by the (social) imaginary of powerlessness."[4]

Read along these lines Silva's "mood economy" offers an even more meager reward than even the consumer society. No longer is the promise one of buying things the ultimate capture of desire, compensating for a life sold away in labor, but the promise of "self-help, of organizing one's hopes and desires. In austerity there is no longer the promise of endless accumulation, but endless introspection—which comes much cheaper. An insipid spiritualism supplants a decadent materialism. It just so happens that the central watchword of this spiritualism is responsibility, the subject

---

4 Frédéric Lordon, *Willing Slaves of Capital: Marx and Spinoza on Desire*, Verso, 2010, 144.

it produces is infinitely responsible for every lost job, for debt, for a tattered world of community and relations. The self-help subject is the perfect subject of a contemporary labor situation we demands responsibility and flexibility.

In this way Silva's conception of a "mood economy" is in some sense similar to Rob Horning's analysis of the virtual compensations of social media, the retweets, likes and reblogs that give us a sense of validation.[5] In each case "economy" or "compensation" functions as a kind of consolation prize, these economies function to paper over the decline of real wages and actual connections with others. Our rewards get smaller, and with each spiral inward the idea of changing the system becomes harder and harder to imagine.

As much as Silva's book could be used to chart a kind of psychic economy of the tendency of the rate of profit to fall, a kind of diminishing returns of psychic investments, its focus on interviews, on the narratives individuals construct of their own lives, also sheds light on contemporary politics. The idea that social welfare damages responsibility, that it encourages the laziness of the unemployed,

---

5 Rob Horning, "Social Media, Social Factory," *New Inquiry*, July 29. 2011, https://thenewinquiry.com/social-media-social-factory/.

has been around at least since Reagan's "welfare queen" and shows no sign of waning as a powerful political image or ideology.[6] The idea that one should be held responsible and accountable for the loss of their job would seem to be absurd, especially after the current recession. However, Silva's analysis suggests that the calls for "personal responsibility" from elected leaders resonate with the personal narratives of responsibility being constructed in front of television sets and in the pages of the latest self-help bestseller. As Yves Citton argues in his book *Mediarchy*, political myths, the narratives of nation and party, can only function, can only take hold, if they in some sense capture and resonate with the narratives through which individuals make sense of their own lives (and vice versa)[7]. A population turned inward, turned towards the narratives of past trauma and present responsibility, will thus be more receptive to a politics and economics of personal responsibility, no matter how economically incoherent it is.

Thus, to conclude by invoking the epigraph above, over thirty years ago Deleuze and Guattari wrote *Anti-Oedipus*, critiquing the conservative individualism at the heart of psychoanalysis, perhaps it is now necessary to write the necessary follow-up, *Anti-Oprah*. Of course the point is not Oprah, or any specific guru, but the entire tendency to turn ever inwards in moments of crisis, constructing our defeats and victories in the interior space of feelings and narrative. That space is a cage.

For more on Yves Citton's concept of Myth see "Let Me Tell You of the Time That Something Occurred: On Yves Citton's *Mythocratie*." For More on Negative Solidarity see Negative Solidarity: Towards the Definition of a Concept.

---

6 Beth Reinhard and the National Journal, "The Return of the Welfare Queen," *The Atlantic*, December 13, 2013. https://www.theatlantic.com/politics/archive/2013/12/the-return-of-the-welfare-queen/282337/

7 Yves Citton, *Mediarchy*, Translated by Andrew Brown, Polity, 2019, 98.

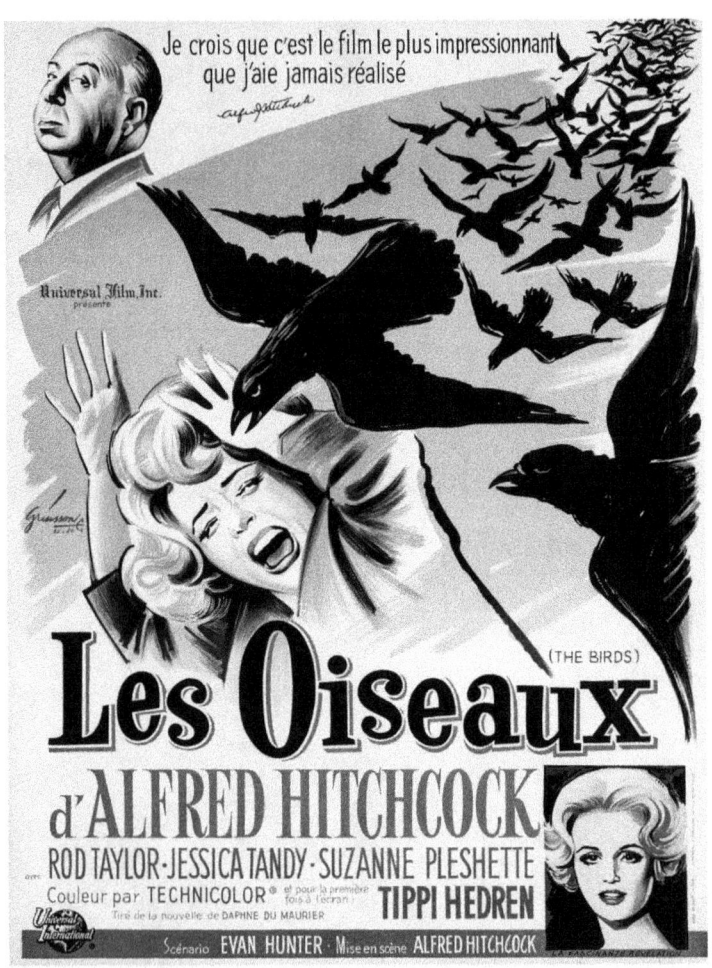

Any Bird Whatsoever: on Fujita's Le Ciné-Capital: D'Hitchcock à Ozu

Originally posted in February of 2022.

In his conversations with François Truffaut Alfred Hitchcock insisted that the birds in his film *The Birds* had to be ordinary birds, seagulls, ravens, sparrows, and not the more spectacular, and arguably more frightening hawks and eagles. This particular anecdote is relayed in Jun Fujita's *Le Ciné-Capital: D'Hitchcock à Ozu* and in some sense it functions as the lynchpin that connects Deleuze's understanding of film, Marx's understanding of *Capital*, and revolutionary politics.

With respect to the former as Deleuze argues in *Cinema 1: The Movement Image*, cinema represents a fundamental transformation of the way movement is depicted. In the ancient world, movement could only be depicted by extracting immobile poses that paradoxically conveyed movement through their own static nature by selecting an image that functioned as an icon: the lifted leg and arm for running, the drawn bow for shooting an arrow, the cocked arm for punching, or, in the pictures below, the sword frozen at the end of its arc for cutting. These immobile sections continue to live on to this day, forming the basis of everything from the crude stick figures representing activities available at a city park (fishing, archery, swimming, etc.) to the panels of comic books. They are in some sense a Platonism of movement, representing movement by finding its ideal immobile image.

Image from Lone Wolf and Cub by Kazuo Koike and Goseki Kojima

Cinema effectively overturns this Platonism, not just in that it is able to depict movement without freezing it, but because this movement is not made out of iconic poses but out of an assemblage of unexceptional moments, of stills made up of any image whatsoever. It is these images, sped up and moved, that create movement not by an ideal form but through an apparent flow of images that are a far cry from icons. The clearest example of the latter is to take a section of film or video of an action sequence and randomly hit pause or freeze it: nine times out of ten the image that one ends up with will not be an iconic still of the action in question but something awkward and hard to understand; for example, a fistfight looks like an odd dance or running looks like falling. This is another way to think about Muybridge's famous sequence of a horse trotting: actual movement does not resemble our idealized iconic image of it. This is in some sense the scientific or industrial aspect of film, the transformation of movement from an idealized form to a constant process of modification, but this is not the entirety. Anyone who watches films is aware that there are breathtaking moments, truly amazing sequences, and images, but these qualitative moments of transformation are themselves made from the quantitative reduction of movement to a series of still images. As Deleuze writes, "Now the production of singularities (the qualitative leap) is achieved by the accumulation of banalities (quantitative process), so that the singular is taken from the any-whatever, and is itself any whatever which is simply non-ordinary and non-regular."[1]

So here is our first point about any bird whatsoever, Hitchcock's film, which uses regular birds to create its moments of terror is in some sense a depiction of this production of the qualitative transformation from the quantitative reduction, of the exceptional from the mundane. One crow, even a few crows, on a jungle gym are not even worth mentioning, but at some point that it is hard to place the quantitative accumulation of ordinary birds becomes an uncanny and frightening image of attacking birds. As Fujita writes, "Cinema produces the surplus value of images: the extraordinary is produced from the collective work of ordinary images, in the same way that the color green is produced as the surplus value in the cooperation of yellow and blue, but in a differential relation."[2]

This brings us to the second transformation of the ordinary into the extraordinary, and that is Marx's theory of surplus value. Just as film is made from the assembly of multiple interchangeable and ordinary images, capital itself is the accumulation of a surplus from ordinary everyday labor. Fujita is not the first to consider film production to be an allegory or even a homology of capitalist production: others such as Jonathan Beller have considered film, with its montage of scenes assembled from disparate locations, to be in some sense the image of capital. Fujita draws on Simondon and Marx's writings on cooperation to argue that capital has to be understood as an exploitation of not individual labor power, but

---

[1] Gilles Deleuze, *Cinema 1: The Movement Image*, trans. Hugh Tomlinson and Barbara Habberjam, University of Minnesota, 1986, 6.
[2] Jun Fujita, *Le Ciné-capital: d'Hitchcock à Ozu, Une lecture marxiste de Cinema de Gilles Deleuze*, Hermann, 2018, 15.

the collective power of production. As Fujita writes, "the capitalist pays each worker for its individual act of work, but it does not pay for its preindividual labor power, that it consumes in combination with other workers in their transindividual cooperation. Under an apparent exchange of equivalent values operates an exchange that is unequal, asymmetrical, and exploitative."[3] Or, put differently, capital can be understood as the commodification of the individual and the exploitation of the transindividual.

To relate this back to film, or specifically the film in question, *The Birds*, it is worth noting that Deleuze cites *The Birds* very early in *Cinema 1: The Movement Image*. The first bird attack, on Melanie Daniels (Tippi Hedren) as she crosses Bodega Bay is used to illustrate the relationship between the shot, what we see, and the whole, that which is unseen but implied in the shot. As Deleuze writes,

> "But the sole cinematographic consciousness is not us, the spectator, nor the hero: it is the camera—sometimes human, sometimes inhuman, or superhuman. Take, for example, the movement of water, that of a bird in the distance, and that of a person on a boat: they are blended into a single perception, a peaceful whole of humanized nature. But then the bird, an ordinary seagull, swoops down and wounds the person: the three fluxes are divided and become external to each other. The whole will be reformed, but it will have changed: it will have become the single consciousness or the perception of a whole of birds, testifying to an entirely bird-centered Nature...The shot, that is to say consciousness, traces a movement which means that the things between which it arises are continuously reuniting into a whole, and the whole is continuously dividing between things."[4]

---

3 Jun Fujita, *Le Ciné-capital: d'Hitchcock à Ozu, Une lecture marxiste de Cinema de Gilles Deleuze*, Hermann, 2018, 18.
4 Gilles Deleuze, *Cinema 1: The Movement Image*, trans. Hugh Tomlinson and Barbara Habberjam, University of Minnesota, 1986, 20.

In Deleuze's account of cinema the shot is a more or less bounded assemblage of elements, a bird, a boat, a person, but the relations between its elements is constantly interacting with a whole that exceeds them. Fujita makes the connection between this ontology (which I would argue is as much Spinozist as it is Simondonian) and that of labor under capital, every individual labor is simultaneously a part, a component, and a presentation of the whole. It is part of the latter because it exceeds the former, because there is an irreducible pre-individual (or virtual) element to each part. In the world of film each shot always contains more than the elements that are first recognized, the bird is just initially part of the background, and it is this excess that makes possible the transformation of the whole.

Any image whatsoever can be combined to create a qualitative transformation in the whole, creating a remarkable point of transformation out of instances that are not in themselves remarkable. Any labor whatsoever, labor indifferent to and an excess of the subject performing it, what Marx called 'the capability of the species' (Gattungsvermögen), is assembled to create a quantitative and qualitative transformation in capital. There is a third possible synthesis and that is in the way in which elements combine in a revolutionary transformation.

This in part explains Fujita's interest in *The Birds*; it is in some sense a film about revolution, "birds of the world, unite!" as Fujita puts it. The ordinary everyday birds come together not just to produce a new image, but to change and invert the world. For Fujita the crucial image of this reversal is the shift from the caged birds that open the film to Melanie Daniels caged in a phone booth in the attack on Bodega Bay, the world turned upside down. This transformed an inverted world is produced by nothing other than the combination and synthesis of a bunch of smaller actions: it is the force of collectivity.

I must admit that I have always considered *The Birds* to be lesser Hitchcock. Fujita makes a claim for its importance based in part on Hitchcock's remarks but also on its constitutive omission:

we never learn the cause of the birds' attack. The attack has no cause behind or beyond it, and exists solely on the surface as an accumulation of actions, sounds, and images. Fujita follows Deleuze's understanding of sense from *Logic of Sense* to insist on the superficiality of the attacks, resisting the temptation to posit some kind of cause, or to make the cause itself symbolic of the family plot, as in psychoanalytic readings of the film. In doing so he draws out the third sense, or meaning, of the ordinary images of ordinary birds, not the accumulation of ordinary images into a transformed scene, or the accumulation of abstract labor into surplus value, but the accumulation of little acts of resistance into revolution. The connection of film with revolutionary politics is not that of history, of the causes of the events depicted but of becoming, of a change in the sense or meaning of action.

Of the three synthesis outlined by Fujita, the first two are most often aligned as the accumulation of images into spectacles reinforces and underlines the accumulation of labor into capital, the spectacles of the movies keep us coming back to work, but perhaps what keeps us coming back to the movies are those moments when that accumulation is interrupted, when we can glimpse a different sensibility, a different way that the pre-individual can become transindividual, can produce a collective. For Fujita the politics of film is less Leninist, organizing the masses, than Guevarist, proliferating the crisis of the cliches, one, two, many, bird revolutions.

For More on Deleuze's theory of Cinema see Revenge of the Children of Marx and Coca Cola: Remarks on Marx, Vertov, and Godard.

It's Competition All the Way Down: On the Spontaneous Anthropology of Contemporary Capitalism

Originally posted in December of 2018.

As much as people love to cite that ubiquitous remark by Fredric Jameson about the end of the world and the end of capitalism—the one how it is easier to imagine the former than the latter—there is another, less discussed line, that covers the same terrain of ideological struggle and limits of the imagination which I prefer. It is, "The market is in human nature' is the proposition that cannot be allowed to stand unchallenged; in my opinion, it is the most crucial terrain of ideological struggle in our time."[1]

I have heard some version of this claim nearly every time I have discussed Marx or capitalism in a philosophy course. The argument, to the extent that it can be called that, takes two forms. The first

---

1 Fredric Jameson, *Postmodernism: Or, The Cultural Logic of Late Capitalism*, Durham: Duke, 1991, 263.

version goes something like this, we are competitive by nature thus any political or economic system not driven by competition will be necessarily a repression of our fundamental nature and doomed to fail. While the second version argues that everything that makes our life livable, every discovery, every scientific breakthrough, and all productivity stems from competition. Life without competition would be nasty, brutish, and short. A world without competition is a choice between two different versions of the gulag.

In *Contre-Courants Politiques* Yves Citton offers an interesting characterization of this spontaneous anthropology of competition. As Citton argues most people who believe in this ideal do not exactly live accordingly, are not throwing themselves into activities that risk life and well-being. As Citton states, "They are content to believe. They believe that they believe, and believe that it is either competition or the end of the world."[2] What strikes me is Citton's formulation "they believe that they believe." As Citton argues, competition is often less something that one actually engages in then a justification of the way things are. It allows those in power to reassure themselves that they played fairly and won. Competition is a veneer applied to existing hierarchies and inequalities giving them the shine of a contest. All complaints or criticism are relegated to sore losers.

Perhaps a few more words about Citton's book are necessary. Citton takes as his starting point the often uttered assertion that the old polarities of left and right no longer apply. Citton's response is not to accept uncritically this assertion, or to argue once again for the relevance of the old definitions of left and right but to critically take stock of the new divisions. The book is organized in nine dualities, mapping different points of tension. Some of them are familiar, taking up existing political divisions, like the Accelerationists and the various "slow" movements, food, thought, etc. others are attempts to name points of tension that are more inchoate, and do not as of yet have a name.

---

2 Yves Citton, Contre-Courants Politiques, Fayard, 2018, 164.

"Competitivists" is one pole in such a tension. As much as there are official and explicit ideologies of competition such as neoliberalism, there is also the more inchoate sense that capitalism is competition and competition is human nature. Underlying this belief in competition, or the belief in the belief, is the assertion that collectivity, the collective intelligence of human beings, manifests itself only by negating itself. The only collectivity capable of directing social life is the negation of collectivity, it is the invisible hand. Very often this ideal of competition does not end at the economy or the social world, throw in some evolutionary psychology or at least a few references to Darwin and it is competition all the way down. Every action, every living thing, is locked in a battle of all versus all.

This brings us to the opposite pole. Citton names this opposed pole "pollenists." Pollenists begin with the image of the bee, but a different fable than Mandeville's "public use of private vices." The bees in this case are the pollinators who are indispensable to agriculture, and thus our survival, while being overlooked by most of the tactics used to increase that productivity. Pollination is not in the bees self-interest, it is an unintended consequence of their activity of gathering pollen. Pollination exceeds any attempt to calculate based on competition. As Citton writes,

> "Pollenists see in pollination the image of a more general truth, which goes far beyond the world of insects to give the key to our inscription in our world. What is education, if not something that pollinates our knowledge and our human relationships? How to measure (compartmentalize, individualize, digitize, calculate) what our societies gain with the production, the diffusion, the circulation of a knowledge, an idea, a gesture, an image, a melody, of a play on words."[3]

The new fable of the bees is one about the externalities necessary to biological and social existence. In place of isolated individuals locked

---

3 Ibid., 176.

in competition there are relations of influence, dependence, and mutual transformation that exceed calculation and individuation. Citton sees these as two different polarities in political opposition. However, it is also possible to see them as two different aspects of capital itself. Marx famously argued that the sphere of exchange was one of "freedom, equality, and Bentham," that competition, individuation, were necessarily after-images of market relations. To this he juxtaposed the sphere of production, which was necessarily a sphere of cooperation, of collective work. More to the point, Marx sees this division in two different ways. Sometimes he posits cooperative production against individual exchange, including the exchange of one's labor, but in other instances the salient opposition is between the freedom of the market and the coercion of labor. As Marx writes,

> "The same bourgeois consciousness which celebrates the division of labour in the workshop, the lifelong annexation of the worker to partial operation, and his complete subjection to capital, as an organization of labour that increases its productive power, denounces with equal vigour every conscious attempt to control and regulate the process of production socially as an inroad upon such sacred things as the rights of property, freedom and the self-determining 'genius' of the individual capitalist."[4]

As something of an aside we could say that Marx's vacillation, seeing the site of production as both cooperation and coercion, is one of those divisions that continues to animate Marxism, caught between prefigurative workerism and the workerist "refusal of work." Work is something other than individual isolated self-interest, but what it is is split between social cooperation and imposed discipline. It is most likely a little from column A and a little from column B, a combination of cooperation and the coercion that transforms cooperation into something useable and sellable.

---

4 Karl Marx, *Capital: A Critique of Political Economy, Volume I*, Translated by Ben Fowkes, New York: Penguin, 1977, 477.

Competition is not just a belief, something one pays lip service to, it is also irreducibly limited perspective on the very economic world it attempts to encapsulate. In his own way David Graeber has argued against this anthropology of self-interest by stating that most of our actions are governed by a kind of everyday communism (or anarchism, he has used both terms). In most of our day to day interactions we help and assist others when we can with all sorts of little gestures of sociality, never thinking of anything like a cost benefit analysis. If someone asks me what time it is or asks for directions, I do not try to negotiate a price but answer if I can. "From each according to their ability to each according to their needs" is the governing principle of much of our interactions. It is worth noting that Graeber's two examples, asking directions and asking the time, are themselves being phased out by the ubiquitous smart phone which makes us more isolated and independent by placing social dependence, and social relations, in the black box of the machine. Turning back to Citton's book, there is a chapter dedicated to what he calls the ideology of "automobilists." The automobile is a machine that generates its own spontaneous ideology, one of independence and competition. Driving down the highway is the material condition of asocial sociality, everyone is looking out for number one, viewing others as at best an indifferent backdrop and at worst hostile enemies. Material transformations of technology and the built world produce and reproduce their own spontaneous ideologies.

The cooperative dimension of our social life is constantly faced with its own disappearance. It is eclipsed by the ideologies that tell us that we live brutal lives of competition and self-interest, and by the technologies that make it so. Social media has made friendship itself quantitative and competitive. However, it does not totally go away, and it cannot. As Peter Fleming has argued, it is precisely this incalculable sociality that is at the basis of contemporary work.[5]

---

[5] "The social commons stands in to cushion the blow caused by the subsidization economy, which today often takes the form of a massive reservoir of personal debt. "Peter Fleming, *The Mythology of Work: How Capitalism Persists Despite Itself,* Polity, 2015, 5.

Social relations not only sustain the workplace, as our attempts to assist and amuse each other do more for morale than any imposed "team building workshop," but are also essential outside of it as well, networks of care from carpooling to grandparents babysitting kids make possible the world of isolated and competitive workers. Every squeeze, every reduction of wages or increase in working times, may be addressed to us as competitive individuals, compelling us to increase our competitive leverage, but it materially affects us as parts of networks of relations that exceed it. Every cut to social services, every reduction in wages, is very often absorbed by increased pressure on relations of cooperation that are invisible to a society that tells itself it functions in and through competition. Cooperation functions as the concealed support and buttress for an ideology of competition. Cooperation is the obscured basis of competition just as social reproduction is the concealed backdrop of production.

It is not a matter of not only refusing to believe in competition, but to turn the networks of pollination into something other than support for our continued exploitation. Viewed from the outside and fairly superficially, the "gilet jaunes" in France would seem to be an example of what can happen when social relations contest capital rather than simply absorb its costs. It is necessary to go from worker bees to a swarm.

For more on David Graeber and "everyday communism" see "I Owe You an Explanation: Graeber and Marx on Origin Stories." For more on Yves Citton see Let Me Tell You of the Time That Something Occurred: On Yves Citton's Mythocratie.

Every Day I Write the Book: Macherey on the Quotidian

Originally posted in September of 2010.

Of the five who participated in the original edition of *Lire le Capital*, Louis Althusser, Etienne Balibar, Jacques Rancière, Pierre Macherey, and Roger Establet, Machery is not very well known in the US. While Rancière has become one of the French thinkers of the moment and Balibar is regularly translated, only the sociologist Roger Establet is less well known. This is unfortunate because it might be possible to argue that of the four, not counting Althusser, Macherey has been concerned with philosophy most explicitly. This might sound strange to those in the Anglo-American world who primarily know of Macherey from his translated works on literature, *For a Theory of Literary of Production* and *The Object of Literature*. However, this focus on philosophy can be seen in his published monographs, *Hegel ou Spinoza*, the five volume study of Spinoza's *Ethics*, and the short books on *The Theses on Feuerbach*, as well as the essays in *Histoires du dinosaur*, which continue Althusser's theses regarding philosophy as a practice and class struggle.

Since the publications of those books, and during it, Macherey has been teaching a seminar titled *Philosophe au sens large* ("Philosophy in the large sense"), which is dedicated to various themes that traverse philosophy, literature, sociology, history, and political economy.[1] This is in sharp contrast to the Anglo-American practice which could be described "philosophy in the smallest possible sense," reducing philosophy to a set of limited normative and logical questions until it could be safely drowned in the bathtub. The courses, which include lectures by Macherey as well as guest lectures by other philosophers on everything from Einstein to Judith Butler are a great resource for anyone who reads French.

A selection of Macherey's lectures from the year (2004-05) devoted to the concept of the "everyday" (quotidian) has been developed into a book, *Petits Riens: Ornières et derives du quotidien*. The lectures cover the usual suspects associated with the concept of "everyday life" such as Lefebvre, Debord, de Certeau, and Freud; as well as Pascal, Hegel, and Marx; and such literary figures as Joyce and Leiris. The book is structured around a series of lectures, and I must admit that I have not read all of them. I started the book to read the lecture on Hegel, since I am curious about Macherey's recent turn to Hegel, but I found it difficult to put down.

What follows are a series of observations/provocations from this book:

— First, Macherey frames the problem of the "everyday" or "everyday life" through two dialectics. The first could be called the "Thales/Heraclitus dialectic" drawn from the two classical figures named. Thales, as the story goes, was so preoccupied with looking towards the heavens that he fell into a well. The philosopher as so removed from worldly concerns that he risks his own survival. In contradiction to this there is the story of Heraclitus, who declared, when a group of visitors were surprised to see the philosopher warming himself by the fire, "The Gods dwell here also." Philosophy sees the most profound mysteries in the most mundane activities of life.

---

[1] https://philolarge.hypotheses.org/

Philosophy distances itself from the everyday, or attempts to discern the hidden logic of the most mundane activities. There is thus a fundamental ambiguity to this attempt. As Macherey writes:

> "There is an equivocal dimension of the reality of lived daily life that is impossible to eradicate, which condemns the quotidian to the status of a quasi-object, not susceptible to being examined directly: the consequence of this is that if one engages in a philosophy of everyday, there is the risk of thinking instability, movement, flow, where only partial synthesis operate, immediately placed in question, and where the results cannot easily be made the object of a global synthesis."[2]

— The second dialectic has to do with how the "everyday" is conceived: either as passivity, as pure repetition of customs, habits, and patterns; or as pure activity, as a thousand tiny inventions. This dialectic, also ambiguous, of activity and passivity can be seen in the political philosophies of the everyday, namely Lefebvre, Debord, and de Certeau.

As I have noted, the first lecture/essay, after the brief thematic introduction, is on Pascal. This might seem strange given that "everyday life" is often understood to be a concept of modernity, an experience that takes place against the backdrop of abstract labor and standardized commodities. This is explicitly the case in Lefebvre and Debord, but is even implied in Heidegger, mentioned only in the introduction, whose "Das Man" and circumspect comportment always read like a critique of modernity smuggled into the ontological investigation. Pascal then would seem to be out of place historically. However, Macherey locates in Pascal an essential aspect of the thought of the everyday: diversion. Diversion is the simple fact that mankind is occupied, distracted even, by a variety of interests

---

2 Pierre Macherey, *Petits Riens: Ornières et derives du quotidien*, Le Bord de L'Eau, 2009, 17.

and tasks. This is mankind's fallen nature, but this capacity to be preoccupied in this or that amusement is mankind's transcendence of any specific given nature. This inessential essentially, the absence of any determined task, defines humanity, Macherey refers to it as "anthropo-theological," the proximity of being fallen and saved. In the first case we are dealing with a theme that runs throughout the history of philosophy, in which mankind is defined by a certain indetermination, a deficiency of environmental stimuli. As Macherey latter argues, returning to Pascal in some of the subsequent lectures/essays, the everyday shares some of these same qualities with this definition of the human, especially in the work of Lefebvre for whom the everyday is untotalizable totality. It is what remains after the specific activities and objects of human life have been abstracted, art, science, etc., but this remainder is essential.

Macherey's reading of Hegel focuses on the ruse of reason, which is not what I expected. One would expect any discussion of Hegel and the everyday to focus on Hegel's discussion of the quotidian dimensions of the family and civil society in the *Philosophy of Right*. This is especially true of Macherey, who coauthored a slim volume on Civil Society with Jean-Pierre Lèfebvre. Macherey argues that the "ruse of reason" is Hegel's philosophy of the everyday; it is precisely the process by which a limited action, focused on its specific means and ends, brings into existence something other than itself. The passage that Macherey turns to is §209 from The Encyclopedia Logic:

> "Reason is as cunning as it is mighty. Its cunning generally consists in the mediating activity which, while it lets objects act upon one another according to their own nature, and wear each other out, executes only its purpose without itself mingling in the process."[3]

This teleological logic, as Lukacs has argued, is the logic of labor itself, which must surrender itself to the limits of the tools and

---

3 G. W. F. Hegel, *The Encyclopedia Logic*, trans. T. F. Geraets et al., Hackett, 284.a

material to produce anything. Labor does not so much master the world, as mastering it by surrendering to it, transforming the world by learning its principles and causality. This makes possible a specific staging of the Marx/Hegel encounter. For Macherey, Marx's objection to Hegel has little to do with "rational kernels and mystical shells," rather it has to do with the transition from Chapter Seven of *Capital: Volume One* between the "labor process" and the "valorization process." In the first case we are dealing with a teleological logic between a subject, instrument, and object: the subject transforming the object, and ultimately the self, through the intermediary of the instrument. The valorization process, which is to say capitalism, decenters this intentionality, fragmenting work to the point where the worker becomes a "conscious organ." There is no longer a telos of intentionality, at least one that rests in the mind and hands of a worker. Thus, we can ask with Macherey, if labor is our model of rationality, of the ruse of reason and historical process, what has the transformation of labor done to the very idea of rationality.

Macherey doesn't directly ask this question, moving onto other figures of the everyday. However, the ruse of reason does return in the later lectures; in fact, it is possible to read Macherey's lectures on the critical turn towards everyday life in the works of Barthes, Lefebvre, Debord, and de Certeau, which make up the final section of this book, as one long meditation on this ruse. Which is to say that all the thinkers consider the everyday to be the point where daily struggles confront the larger rationales and structures of social existence. This confrontation is riddled with ambiguity of activity and passivity referred to above. As Lefebvre writes of his project, "Our particular concern will be to extract what is living, new, positive—the worthwhile needs and fulfillments—from the negative: the alienations." What emerges in these critical works, and this has everything to do with their historical moment after the second war, is everyday life as a sphere of life characterized by a sharper duality than the ambiguity of passivity and activity, it is colonization versus rebellion. It is Debord that pushes this tension the furthest, the spectacle is nothing but the colonization of daily life. I am not going to go into all of Macherey's reading of Debord, but there are some interesting remarks regarding Debord and Feuerbach as well as Sartre. What is most striking, given the earlier section on Hegel's ruse of reason as a logic of everyday life, is the manner in which the situationist strategy of détournemount, altering the texts and images of the various commodities of the spectacle, returns as a kind or ruse of reason, a negation of negation, but an incomplete one. With détournemount one works with definite materials, with the inherent limitations, but what emerges is not a realization of reason. At best the "detouring," the shift, opens the gap between the spectacle and everyday life, between the passivity of everyday life and its constant reinvention.

For more on Macherey see Reworking Hegel: Philosophy of Work in Macherey's Petit Riens.

Images from Property is No Longer Theft

Reworking Hegel: Philosophies of Work in Macherey's Petit Riens

Originally posted in September of 2021.

There is a line that I used to attribute to Roland Barthes, "those who do not reread are doomed to read the same book over and over again." I liked the riddle like nature of the phrase, and the way it seemed to posit a first read which is often a restating of one's already existing preconceptions, hence the rereading of the same book under different covers, against a rereading that discovers difference in repetition.

It turns out my memory was false terms of the letter, but perhaps not in terms of the spirit, even though Barthes original passage was less about rereading philosophy than literature. Here is what Barthes writes in S/Z:

> "Rereading, an operation contrary to the commercial and ideological habits of our society, which would have us "throw away" the story once it has been consumed ("devoured"), so that we can then move on to another story, buy another book, and which is tolerated only in certain marginal categories of readers (children, old people, and professors), rereading

is here suggested at the outset, for it alone saves the text from repetition (those who fail to reread are obliged to read the same story everywhere), multiplies it in its variety and its plurality: rereading draws the text out of its internal chronology ("this happens before or after that") and recaptures a mythic time (without before or after); it contests the claim which would have us believe that the first reading is a primary, naïve, phenomenal reading which we will only, afterwards, have to "explicate," to intellectualize (as if there were a beginning of reading, as if everything were not already read: there is no first reading, even if the text is concerned to give us that illusion by several operations of suspense, artifices more spectacular than persuasive); rereading is no longer consumption, but play (that play which is the return of the different)."[1]

To put myself in the three categories above, that of the professor, I reread a great deal for teaching. I generally reread all of my assigned readings. Sometimes I am grateful for this, as I get to return to some of the texts that continue to provoke and inspire, returning to Marx, Hegel, Spinoza, Deleuze, etc., again and again. I also reread a great deal when writing. There are books outside of these two categories, books that I never get to teach because of either their difficulty or because they have not been translated that unfortunately are books I have not written on beyond a blogpost, which is nothing more than a document of that first reading. These books are definitely worth rereading, it is just hard to find the time and space for it.

For various reasons I decided to reread Macherey's *Petits Riens: Ornières et derives du quotidien*. That Macherey's book rewarded rereading goes without saying, but what I would like to write about here is the way that Macherey rereads one of the most reread philosophical relations, that of Hegel and Marx. Macherey's rereading begins from the place of labor in Hegel, focusing neither on the master/slave dialectic nor the discussion of the ethical role of labor in civil society in the *Philosophy of Right*. Macherey turns to a more

---

[1] Roland Barthes, *S/Z*, Translated by Richard Miller, Farrar, Straus, and Giroux, 1974, 15.

general discussion of a logic of work in the encyclopedia logic. Work is illustrative of the very cunning of reason in that in work in order to realize my ends, produce something, I must necessarily surrender my mastery and control by subordinating my action to mechanical and chemical processes that exceed my intentions. I must use mechanical properties, blades and weights, as well as chemical processes such as fire. It is these processes, and not my mastery, that actually do my work for me, realizing my goals by acting entirely outside of them. Macherey cites the Encyclopedia Logic on this point).

> "Reason is as cunning as it is powerful. Cunning may be said to lie in the intermediative action which, while it permits the objects to follow their own bent and act upon one another till they waste away, and does not itself directly interfere in the process, is nevertheless only working out its own aims. With this explanation, Divine Providence may be said to stand to the world and its process in the capacity of absolute cunning. God lets men do as they please with their particular passions and interests; but the result is the accomplishment of-not their plans, but his, and these differ decidedly from the ends primarily sought by those whom he employs."[2]

Macherey is not alone in reading Hegel on this point. Marx cites the same passage from Hegel in the chapter of *Capital* dedicated to the labor process. As Marx describes this process, [The worker] makes use of the mechanical, physical and chemical properties of some substances in order to set them to work on other substances as instruments of his power, and accordance with his purposes."

As Macherey describes this ruse, or detournement, at the heart of the labor process:

> "In the world, reason, in the strong sense of the word, works by insinuating itself through a ruse: all work in fact takes, as we have seen, the form of a ruse or a process of detouring

---

2 G. W. F. Hegel, *The Encyclopedia Logic*, trans. T. F. Geraets et al., Hackett, 284.

[détournement] by which the subject achieves his freedom by exploiting the forms of necessity which determine the objective world."[3]

If work remains the figure the general cunning of reason, the realization of ends by its subordination to means, as well as the figure of God's work in the world, then what does this mean for actual work, for the practice rather than the concept. In the *Economic and Philosophical Manuscripts of Eighteen Forty-Four*, in the section titled "Critique of the Hegelian Philosophy and the Dialectic of a Whole" Marx writes "The only labor which Hegel knows and recognizes is abstract mental labor."[4] I think that this remark reveals an interesting tension in Hegel's thought, who constantly tries to recognize the reality of work, or labor, placing it at the center of his thought, but subordinates that recognition to an abstract and idealized form of labor. I am thinking not just of the work of the bondsman in the *Phenomenology of Spirit* which becomes the basis for ethical recognition, but also Hegel's remarks about the limits of mechanization of agricultural work, and, most importantly, his concept of the rabble. As Hegel argues, the rabble are not just excluded from the material benefits of work, in other words poor, but also impoverished ethically because they are unable to benefit from the ethical dimension of work, work as the foundation of social respect and belonging. Whenever Hegel thinks of work, he thinks of in terms of the cunning of reason, of teleology realizing itself through necessity, failing to recognize other causal relations, and ultimately the overdetermination of work. Work is physical, anthropological, social, and economic, but not in such a way that lends itself to an easy contradiction between one and the other.

If we move from the general figure of the cunning of reason to the more specific figure of the proletariat, of the wage earner, the very logic of realizing one's ends by subordinating them to necessity

---

3 Pierre Macherey, *Petits Riens: Ornières et derives du quotidien*, Le Bord de L'Eau, 2009, 69.
4 Karl Marx, *Early Writings*, Translated by Rodney Livingston and Gregor Benton, Penguin, 1974, 386.

takes on a very different meaning. The idea of realizing your goals, your intentions, by subordinating them to not just mechanical and chemical processes, but social processes as well, by subordinating yourself to the realities of the world, becomes no longer a figure of reason, of God's march in the world, but ideology, a justification of the world as it is. As Macherey writes:

> "The wage earner is often subject to a cruel reality, most of all in periods of crises, and capable in all cases to be seen as an injustice, such that we do not see how we could reduce it to a form of exercising the power of reason, and this becomes a completely different interpretation, which radically shifts its content, as liberal ideology does by giving this fait accompli a legal sanction, insofar as it supposed to express the very law of history."[5]

To frame this in terms of Marx it is worth noting that Marx cites Hegel's statement about work being the cunning of reason in Chapter Seven of *Capital* on the labor process. The first part of that chapter is dedicated to considering the "labor process independently of any specific social formation." It is in this section that we get not only the schema of labor as the transformation of an object by a subject with an instrument (as schema that will be important of Althusser among others) but also the entire anthropological distinction separating the worst of architects from the best of bees (because there is an irreducible mental component to the former's work). However, this section is only a precursor to Marx's consideration of the valorization process, to the transformation that work undergoes when it becomes part of the capitalist search for surplus value. This tendency culminates in the utter transformation of worker, from the worker annexing nature as an organ, "adding stature to himself in spite of the Bible" to the worker being reduced to the conscious organ of the machine. What begins with

---

5 Pierre Macherey, *Petits Riens: Ornières et derives du quotidien*, Le Bord de L'Eau, 2009, 84.

promethean overtones ends in purgatory, as the valorization reduces the labor process to a means of the valorization process.

Macherey's book is on the problem of daily life, of how philosophy can comprehend the world in its actuality. The attempt to make daily life an object for philosophy risks idealizing that life not because it is disconnected from it, as in the standard criticism of idealism, but by rationalizing it. As Macherey writes:

> "This is another way of saying that everyday life [vie quotidienne] poses a problem for philosophy, not just because it reveals the impossibility of comprehending the totality, but also because it puts in question the fundamental enterprise of a philosophy of reality, by placing itself at a distance from reality is this not denying daily life its own quality of reality, by bringing it down to a level where it reveals itself to be in conformity with the requirements of reason?"[6]

In other words, any discussion of the labor process of work as an anthropological process of transformation of the world and self-transformation without a consideration of the valorization process, of the reality of work in capital becomes nothing other than an ideological justification of the latter. Work considered as an abstract mental activity becomes the alibi and justification for its existence as a material practice. This is another way to make sense of the famous eleventh thesis. It is not just that philosophers have only interpreted the world, failing to act, but that any interpretation that does not grasp the way that the world is already being transformed, in the process of transforming, becomes nothing other than ideology.

Rereading Macherey reading Hegel and Marx thus poses a different way of understanding the whole division of idealism and materialism. Hegel's idealism is not to be found in some supposed detachment from the world, from dwelling with spirit and the idea, but from precisely the way in which he interpreted reality, including

---

6 Ibid., 85.

political economy and labor, to be realization of ideas. Posed this way the break with Hegel is nothing less than a break with philosophy, a transformation of philosophy, as Althusser wrote.

For more on Macherey's book on everyday life see "Every day I write the Book: Macherey on the Quotidian".

Chantal Jaquet
Transclasses
A Theory of Social Non-reproduction

The Class Struggle at Home: Jaquet's Transclasses

Originally posted in January of 2015.

Perhaps the best way to approach Chantal Jaquet's *Transclasses: A Theory of Social Non-Reproduction* is by situating it between caricatures of two intellectual positions. On the one hand, the left one, we have studies of the "reproduction of the relations of production," the work of Bourdieu most importantly, but also that of Althusser, that stresses how the classes endlessly reproduce themselves, or are reproduced by the institutions of schools, media, and so on. On this reading the institutions of capitalist society, from the school to the family, reproduce the conditions of production, making it so working class kids get working class jobs. On the other hand, the right one, we have various "pulled up by one's bootstraps" narratives, all of which stress that individual will and fortitude can overcome all social or economic barriers. One offers a theory of the necessary reproduction of the relations of production, while on the other puts forward is the entire anecdotal history of exceptions to prove that this is not always the case.

Jaquet's goal is to theorize non-reproduction, to theorize the exceptions to reproduction. This must be done without recourse to free will, ambition, or any other notion which is nothing other than a thinly veiled conceptual stand in for an ideology of individual achievement and individual blame. It is necessary to conceptualize non-reproduction, the trajectory of individuals who traverse the barriers of class, race, or gender, without recourse to a concept of the will, or lapsing into a Horatio Alger story. As Jaquet writes, "In the absence of change on a collective scale, questions of the causes, means, and limits of individual non-reproduction are crucial."[1] I will return to this absence of change on a collective scale below, but it is important to note that Jaquet's project is to conceptualize this non-reproduction, to treat it as something other as an exception to the rule without, at the same time lapsing into conceptual alibis for the current economic order. It is a matter of understanding that non-reproduction, like reproduction, has causes as well, causes which exceed the individual.

Jaquet is a scholar of Spinoza and thus her theory of non-reproduction passes through Spinoza's theory of the affects. This connection proves to be fortuitous. Spinoza's affects provide two fundamental conditions for theorizing non-reproduction. First, there is the imitation of affects, the transindividual and social basis of individual strivings and desires. Reproduction and non-reproduction both involve an imitation of the affects, the tastes and proclivities, of another. The only difference is who is being imitated. Reproduction is an imitation of the immediate tastes and desires of one's family and class, non-reproduction, or what Jaquet calls transclass, often involves an imitation at a distance of the tastes and desires of others, a teacher, a friend from a different class, or the mediated images of a different life. "The existence of transclasses is in fact subject not so much to a logic of exception as one of divergence."[2] Important here is the Spinoza's notion of the ambivalence of the affects. As Jaquet argues every non-reproduction is fundamentally ambivalent; it is both a movement away from something, from the shame of one's

---

[1] Chantal Jaquet, *Transclasses: A Theory of Social Non-Reproduction*, Translated by Gregory Elliot, Verso, 2023, 6.
[2] Chantal Jaquet, *Transclasses*, 174.

class position, and towards something, the desired new class position. However, this ambivalence is often doubled. The shame of one's humble class origins are often the source of a new shame. Shame becomes internally ambivalent, divided between shame and shame of shame. Non-reproduction is a complex intersection of hopes and fears, shame and pride (as is reproduction).

As Jaquet writes, "The transclass is the bearer of two worlds, and is haunted by a dialectic of opposites without any guarantee that they might be harmonized and that the oscillations might resolve into some kind of equilibrium...Condemned to the big gap between often incompatible worlds, a transclass is necessarily worked on by open or subterranean contradictions."[3]

Jaquet's method offers two important theoretical transformations to the general problem of reproduction. First, she suggests that the Spinozist term ingenium or complexion, replace the term habitus. This is not a difference of words but a difference of logic. Complexion is less the intimate reproduction of the existing class order at the level of the individual than it is the intersection of class, familial, media, and other affects and desires in a complex, and even metastable, conjunction. The corollary of this is that class is not an identity, it is not something one is, but is situated at the intersection of striving, tastes, desires, and shames. Classes do not describe individuals, or families, but traverse both, defining both their aspirations and their fears. Class is a relation, but this relation is not just the grand battle between two classes on the field of history; it is an intimate relation that encompasses the conflicts within an institution, a family, and an individual. Class is transindividual.

Jaquet's immediate target includes such thinkers of reproduction as Bourdieu, but it could also be seen as a critique of Frédéric Lordon whose concept of affective reproduction falls into the trap of seeing individual striving as nothing other than the reproduction of the social order. As we strive to realize our desires via wage labor we reproduce a system founded on wage labor. For Jaquet, Individuals

---

3 Chantal Jaquet, *Transclasses*, 122.

do not simply reproduce the affective composition of their social relations as the part of a larger whole, or, more to the point, individuals are caught in the tension of simultaneously reproducing different relations, different affects at the same time, caught between the affective attachments to origins and the emulation of aspirations. This tension of multiple causes, multiple affects, and multiple desires, determines, in a singular way, both reproduction and non-reproduction. It is thus no accident that Jaquet draws most of her examples from novels and memoirs, including Stendhal, Wright, Baldwin, Larsen, and Eribon drawing from different forms of non-reproduction from passing to becoming part of the nouveau rich. The trajectory of non-reproduction can only be recounted in a singular case, a concrete situation. This is perhaps her strength, but her analysis lacks sufficient attentiveness to precisely what Frédéric Lordon underscores, the meta-structuring dimensions of wage labor and commodity production that underly all striving in capital.

It is at this point where it is possible to draw out the instructive tensions between Lordon and Jaquet's particular use of Spinoza to conceptualize reproduction and non-reproduction in contemporary capitalism. This difference touches on the role of singularity, of individual difference, in how capitalism reproduces itself. In *La Société des Affects*, Lordon augments the broad schematic differences of Fordism and neoliberalism of *Willing Slaves of Capital* by turning to two of the final propositions of Part Three of Ethics. Spinoza argues that there are as many loves and hates 'as there are species of objects by which we are affected' and 'each affect of each individual differs from the affect of another as much as the essence of one from the essence of the other.'[4] The multiple objects, and multiple strivings, constitute the basis for multiple affective compositions, each shifting and ambivalent as the same object is both the object of love and hate, and the same individual comes to hate what they once loved. Rereading these propositions back into the schematic

---

4 Benedict de Spinoza, *Ethics*, Translated by Edwin Curley, New York, Penguin, 1994 EIIIP56 and EIIIP57.

history of different affective modes of production does not dispense with the latter, shattering it into a pure multiplicity where a thousand flowers bloom. Rather, these differences, variations of love and hate, must be understood as variations on a dominant theme, a dominant structure. As Lordon argues there will always be bosses who are kind and generous, work situations that engage a broader range of activity, but these differences and deviations are ultimately just different expressions of the same fundamental relation. The nicest boss in the world cannot fundamentally alter the fundamental structure of the Fordist or neoliberal labor conditions, the affective engagement at the level of individual intention does nothing to alter the basic relation with the activity and object. This affective veneer, the work of human relations, is not inconsequential: more than the role it plays in motivating individual workers, the real work it does it producing the appearance of difference, a society of individual actions rather the persistent structures. As Spinoza argues, we are more likely to hate or love an act that we consider to be free than one which is considered necessary (EIIIP49). On this last point Spinoza's affective economy intersects with one of the central points of Marx's critique of political economy, that of fetishism, which could in part be summed up as perceiving the capitalist mode of production as necessary and natural rather than the product of social relations. The affective economy of capitalism is one in which it is easier to become angry and grateful at the deviations, the cruel bosses and the benevolent philanthropists, while the structure itself, the fundamental relations of exploitation, are deemed too necessary, too natural, to merit indignation.

This returns us to precisely what is analytically excluded from Jaquet's theory, "profound revolution." It is a matter of trying to think the conditions of a non-reproduction that would not simply be that of worker's daughter becoming an academic, but of a general refusal of society to reproduce itself. Non reproduction on an individual scale risks always risks being the means of reproduction on a social scale. As Jaquet argues, "non-reproduction is simply the continuation of reproduction by other means," distributing individuals amongst different classes, and, more importantly, functioning as the ultimate alibi for a class based society by offering individual stories of transformation.⁵ The question remains what are the affective and imaginary conditions for collective non-reproduction? How would the desires and aspirations currently attached to escaping one's class become the conditions for general transformation?

For more on transclass see Translating Transclass: Or Teaching Eribon in America.

---

5 Chantal Jaquet, *Transclasses*, 78.

Since this is a post about class, family, and returns – I thought that I would illustrate it with pictures illustrating the fact that I now live in the same neighborhood my mother lived in, but the neighborhood has changed except this old fishing/gun store.

Translating Transclass: Or Teaching Eribon in America

Originally posted in February of 2023.

I have often considered teaching to be a kind of translation and not just because much of the history of philosophy is written in different languages. Part of what one does in teaching is try to take the questions and concerns of a different time and figure out some way to bridge the gap between then and now, while at the same time being faithful to its original sense and meaning (just like translation). These thoughts occurred to me again when I decided to teach Didier Eribon's *Returning to Reims*.

I first heard about Eribon's book when I read Chantal Jaquet's *Transclasses: A Theory of Social Non-Reproduction* and was happy to learn that it was translated by Semiotext(e). After reading it I gave a copy to my father, and he loved it; as a first generation college student from a small mill town in Maine he could really relate to it. It was for that reason that I was excited to teach it in my seminar on *Race, Class, and Gender*. Many of the University of Southern Maine's students are first generation and higher education in part justifies itself by its ability to supposedly transform class belonging, so it seemed worthwhile to teach the book.

With the first discussion it became immediately clear how much work would need to be done to translate the book to a different time and place. Eribon's trajectory, is one in which the transformation of his class position was made both possible and desirable by a transformation of his cultural coordinates, a transformation made possible by reading Proust, Sartre, and Marx. Such a trajectory seemed difficult to understand in the American context where class was not only disconnected from such cultural markers, but actively repudiates them. This might be what it means to be transclass in the post-bourgeois age; the accumulation of capital has become divorced from cultural capital. As one student put it, her uncles had all changed their financial situation, but rather than cast off the culture that they grew up with they had made that transformation maintaining their connection with NASCAR and pick-up trucks.

However, it is possible to make these awkward elements of translation the basis for an engagement rather than a rejection of Eribon's book. It is through the difficulties of translation that it becomes possible to rethink the nature of class and its relation to individual and national identity. It is possible to delineate three levels of class in Eribon's analysis. The first is the one that describes one's position in the economic system. As Eribon writes, "In my case, I can say that I have always deeply had the feeling of belonging to a class, which does not mean that the class that I belonged to was conscious of itself as such. One can have the sense of belonging to a class without the class being aware of itself as such or being "a clearly defined group."[1] This could be called the class in itself, if one wanted to use that language. It is the aspect of class that is written on the body, on the exhaustion of work and the effects of poverty. In contrast to this is Eribon's memories of what class meant for his family when they were members of the communist party. As Eribon writes describing this dimension of class for itself, or for itself through the party, "You became a political subject by putting yourself into the hands of the party spokespersons, through whom

---

1 Didier Eribon, *Returning to Reims*, Translated by Michael Lucey, Semiotexte, 2013, 108.

the workers, the 'working class,' came to exist as an organized group, as a class that was aware of itself as such."² In between these two there is what could be called the class of itself, the way that class constitutes not just an economic position or a political subject, but a way of life or a habitus of a sort. As Eribon writes of these divisions of class, "These boundaries that divide these worlds help define within each of them radically different ways of perceiving what it is possible to be or become, of perceiving what it is possible to aspire to or not."³ This is class as it was lived in terms of the things one does and does not do, in terms of tastes, habits, and dress.

Eribon's story is one of both his own personal transformation, his own non-reproduction, to use Jaquet's term in which the son of a factory worker becomes a journalist and then a famous academic. It is also a story of the larger disarticulation of class composition, of how the working class in the economic sense, shifted from being a class organized by and through the communist party, to a bastion of nationalist and racist sentiment. This disarticulation has two aspects, first there is the transformation of the communist and socialist parties after 1981. As Eribon writes,

> "What actually occurred was a general and quite thoroughgoing metamorphosis of the ethos of the party as well as of its intellectual references. Gone was any talk of exploitation and resistance, replaced by talk of "necessary modernization" and of "radical social reform"; gone the references to relations between classes, replaced by talk of a "life in common": gone any mention of unequal social opportunities replaced by an emphasis on individual responsibility."⁴

At the same time that the party moved away from the class struggle, the terms of that struggle were changing for the workers, defined less in terms of revolution and more in terms of the hopes

---

2 Didier Eribon, *Returning to Reims*, 43.
3 Didier Eribon, *Returning to Reims*, 52.
4 Didier Eribon, *Returning to Reims*, 128.

and dreams of a consumer society. The rhetoric of class struggle, of nothing to lose but chains, begins to sound hollow to a class that aspires to buy a car or a vacation. As Eribon writes,

> "But what is the point of a political story that doesn't take into account what people are really like as it interprets their lives, a story whose result is that one ends up blaming the individuals in question for not conforming to the fiction one has constructed? It is clearly a story that needs to be rewritten in order to make it less unified and less simple, to build in more complexity and more contradictions. And to reintroduce historical time. The working class changes. It doesn't stay identical to itself. And clearly the working class of the 1960s and 1970s was no longer the same as that of the 1930s or the 1950s. The same position in the social field does not correspond to exactly the same realities, nor to the same aspirations."[5]

This disarticulation, the party moving away from class struggle, and the working class defining its struggle differently made possible a new articulation, not in terms of class but of nation. As Eribon writes,

> "Whose fault if the meaning of a "we" sustained or reconstituted in this way undergoes a transformation such that it comes to mean the "French" as opposed to "foreigners," whereas it had used to mean "workers" as opposed to the "bourgeoisie"? Or, to put it more precisely, whose fault is it if the opposition between "worker" and "bourgeois," even if it continues to exist in the form of an opposition between the "have nots" and the "haves" (which is not exactly the same opposition—it carries different political consequences), takes on a national and racial dimension, with the "haves" being perceived as favorably inclined to immigration and the "have nots" as suffering on a daily basis because of this same immigration, one that is held to be responsible for all their difficulties?"[6]

---

5 Didier Eribon, *Returning to Reims*, 89.
6 Didier Eribon, *Returning to Reims*, 133.

This story, which I have given here in terms of just a few key moments, is one of the disarticulation of class and revolution, class and party, and the rearticulation of class and reaction, class and nation. As we discussed in class, this story, the story of the disarticulation of the workers' party and the aspiration of workers' cannot be simply transposed onto the US, even if the ending is the same in terms of the similarity of the National Front and MAGA parties. It would be a massive mistranslation to simply replace the Communist Party with the Democratic Party. There is a much longer story to be told about the disarticulation and the disarray of class and party in the US, and it is told in W.E.B. Du Bois' *Black Reconstruction* and Mike Davis' *Prisoners of the American Dream* (So basically if you want the TL:DR version it is the wages of whiteness and Ronald Reagan). However, it might be possible to use Eribon's categories to make a different disarticulation or rearticulation, not that of the class in itself becoming another for itself, the for itself of the French, of the nation, but the way in which what could be called the class of itself, the habitus of class, the taste, habits and customs have shifted from one class to another. The lack of an articulation between economic position of class and political party has made way for a different articulation in which class is defined in terms of the cultural signifiers of guns, trucks, and Carhart. It is a brand and not a politics. This is the way our modern politicians appear to be "of the people" in Machiavelli's sense. This in part accounts for the bizarro world version of class in the US.

This difficulty in translation, the impossibility of neatly mapping Eribon's French story onto an American one made for interesting discussions, but I wonder if we were talking about something that went beyond the classroom. The devaluation of a certain kind of symbolic capital, that one no longer has to read a certain set of books or listen to the right kind of music, is part of the story of the decline of the university, or at least the humanities. The university, at least a state university, is no longer the same institution of transclass transformation. I think that things might be different at elite private colleges, but even there it is more about who one knows than what one knows, connections rather than cultural capital. At small state colleges people still seek to change their class status, but do so through trying to figure out how to accumulate capital in its more material and less symbolic form, they major in business or finance.

Where does this leave Eribon's own story of transclass transformation, his desire to become someone different, to leave Reims, to leave a culture dominated by sports, restricted gender roles, and fishing, to go to Paris, to a culture dominated by books and ideas, where it is possible to become someone else, something else? I still think people come to the university to do that, to transform themselves, and become something different, but that transformation has been disarticulated from class transformation. It has become an individual matter of discovery, and it located more in the arts and creative forms of study than in the canons of literature and philosophy.

For More on Transclass see The Class Struggle at Home: On Jaquet's Transclasses.

SPINOZA AFTER MARX

This conference will explore the encounter between the thought of Spinoza and Marx, posing the question of how to conceive the two bodies of thought as a joint project. We seek to trace the traditions this encounter has given rise to, internationally and across the disciplines. What about Spinoza's thought lends itself to revival of Marxism? Is Marx's thought necessary for reevaluation of Spinoza? What is the Marx-Spinoza encounter today?

MAY 27-29, 11:30-2:30 EDT

5/27 **Panels**
Mariana Gainza and Gil Morejón
Vittorio Morfino and Alejo Stark

5/28 **Roundtable**
Bernardo Bianchi
Cesare Casarino
Katja Diefenbach
Sandra Leonie Field
Eleanor Kaufman
Jacques Lezra
Tracie Matysik
Warren Montag
Siarhei Biareishyk

5/29 **Keynote**
A. Kiarina Kordela
Jason Read

What Does it Mean to be a Materialist: Thoughts After Spinoza after Marx

Originally posted in July of 2021.

Of all of the zoom events, conferences, and presentations that I have attended (zoomed?) this year the one dedicated to Spinoza after Marx was the most engaging, the one most capable of breaking through the zoom screen that makes everything feel further away even as it is so close, inches away even. This is in part because of the participants, but it was also due to the work of the organizers who, in an interesting variation on organizing around a common theme, presented a common set of theses that were discussed and debated over the course of the three days. Of course as great as this was as an online event it is hard not to think about how those conversations would have continued over dinner, at bars, and coffee shops. The event did create a collective act of thought, of thinking in common, but as Spinoza and Marx both know there is no thinking together, thinking in common, without acting and feeling in common.

This idea of bodies affecting minds, or, what could be understood as "materialism" turned out to be one of the debated points of the conference. Materialism was not named directly in the circulated set of theses, although there were a few that touched on it, remarking on Marx and Spinoza's commitment to immanence and the primacy of practice to consciousness. Important questions were raised as to whether or not Spinoza could even be considered a materialist, after all the separation of thought and extension as two different attributes is in some sense axiomatic to his thought.

I am not going to respond directly to the questions from the conference. Instead I would like to begin with Pascal Sévérac's answer to the question of what Materialism might mean with respect to Spinoza in a short book titled *Qu'y a-t-il de matérialiste chez Spinoza?* Sévérac is the author of one of the most influential books on Spinoza in recent years, *Le Devenir Actif Chez Spinoza*, as well as the author and editor of other books dedicated to Spinoza. However this recent book is part of HDiffusion's Permanent University series, a series dedicated to popular education aimed at political action and social transformation. That Spinoza appears in such a series along with Lenin and a book on the French Revolution (to name a few of the titles that have appeared so far) shows to what extent the radical Spinoza has taken hold in at least certain sectors of French intellectual life.

Sévérac begins with the question, that many in the Anglo-American philosophical world would dismiss out of hand: is Spinoza a materialist? It is difficult to simply answer this question in the affirmative, to reconcile a philosophy that starts from contemplating God sub specie aeternitas with the idea of materialism as it is generally conceived. Sévérac responds to this difficulty by changing the question, asking what does Spinoza's philosophy offer in terms of a reconsideration of materialism, or, how does it break with what has generally been considered materialism in order to redefine it?

Sévérac answers this question by looking at three senses in which Spinoza's thought could be considered materialist: empirical, ontological, and methodological. In answering the first Sévérac turns to Spinoza's own account of his experience of coming to philosophy in the *Treatise on the Emendation of the Intellect*. In that text Spinoza famously opens with the assertion that "After experience had taught me that all the things which regularly occur in ordinary life are empty and futile…" Philosophy emerges from experience, it is a search for a "greatest good…capable of communicating itself" brought about by the failures of the goods conventionally pursued in individual and collective life. Sévérac argues that this search makes it clear that philosophy is not only grounded on experience, on a search for truth that is also grounded in desire, but that it is ultimately a process of individual and collective transformation in a search for a different way of living. As Sévérac writes, "It is necessary to understand that for Spinoza the individual is a being collectively constituted, both from the organic and social point of view, from the the affective and cognitive point of view—and these two dimensions, affective and cognitive are indissociable."[1] Sévérac does not see the turn away from such goods as pleasure, money, and status and towards philosophy as a turn away from the worldly material things, but rather a transformation of material life, of desire itself. Philosophy is not an attempt to get outside of the world, but a different way of living in the world.

This empirical materialism is followed by a consideration of an ontological materialism grounded on the refusal of any such division between this world and its beyond. *Deus sive Natura* as Spinoza writes, there is only one reality, a reality that we comprehend in terms of ideas and things. As Sévérac writes, "Nature is not therefore entirely material, but could only be apprehended in part through its material dimension."[2] It is at this point where Spinoza most definitely breaks with a reduction of the ideal to the material, in which there are only bodies, or, to take on a different materialism, only material conditions, ideas are also another, ultimately different way of not only grasping this reality but part of reality as well. Spinoza works against two reductions. Against the idealist reduction of the body, of matter, to something fallen or just passive, Spinoza insists on its power and causality: against the materialist reduction of ideas to epiphenomenon

---

1 Pascal Sévérac, *Qu'y a-t-il de matérialiste chez Spinoza?* HD Philosophie, 2019, 27.
2 Pascal Sévérac, *Qu'y a-t-il de matérialiste chez Spinoza?* 37.

of material forces Spinoza insists on the their causality and efficacy. This intervention cuts against both positions, at least in their crude variant. Ontologically things and ideas are equal, but our perspective on this reality is shaped more by bodies than minds. Our ideas, our primarily formed through our bodily encounters and relations. There is no possible understanding of thought, of the activity of the mind without understanding the imagination and the affects, which is to say the encounters of the body.

As Sévérac writes, "If Spinoza is not therefore a reductive materialist in the sense that he reduces thought to an emanation of matter, and the mind to a function of the body, he nevertheless proposes a consistent materialism in the sense that for him one must always take consideration of bodies and its powers in order to know what the mind is capable of, to grasp the cognitive and affective capabilities."[3] This consistency can be found in the third aspect of materialism that Sévérac identifies, that of method, Spinoza refuses to treat, ideas, or the mental life, as anything other than another thing, with its own causal relations in the world. As Sévérac argues "Spinoza's grand idea is that psychic interiority does not any less than material exteriority obey the necessity of precise laws understood as causal relations."[4]

Does this make Spinoza a materialist? or more to the point how does this transform materialism? Here it might be useful to return to EIIP7, which in its own dialectical manner is both the strongest testament of Spinoza's materialism and its internal limitation. It is materialist in that it asserts the fundamental identity of things and ideas, extension and thought, as not only two different ways of grasping the same thing, the same reality, but as subject to the same order and connection, the same causal relations. At the same time, however, it is anti-materialist in that it posits these causal orders as separate, as Spinoza goes onto argue, only bodies can affect bodies and ideas can only affect ideas. To refer back to the discussion at the conference, the often asserted idea that material conditions shape

---

3 Pascal Sévérac, *Qu'y a-t-il de matérialiste chez Spinoza?* 50.
4 Pascal Sévérac, *Qu'y a-t-il de matérialiste chez Spinoza?* 56.

and determine ideas, that "life determines consciousness," an idea that is central to materialism of a Marxist variety, would be seem to be an impossibility for Spinoza. The emphasis would have to be on seem since Spinoza's entire ethical project is in part dependent on the premise that there must be some way that minds and bodies act on, or at least influence each other, some way that our thinking is shaped by how we live, and, conversely, some way that thinking can alter how we live. As Spinoza asserts, "we have the power of ordering and connecting the affections of the body according to the order of the intellect."[5] However, Spinoza tends to consider this "logic of alternation" (to use Chantal Jaquet's term,) working primarily in one direction, it is primarily a matter of organizing our thoughts in such a way to reorganize our affects. To the extent that Spinoza thinks in terms of the other direction, bodies, shaping ideas and influencing ideas, it is primarily in his political writings, most notably in the *Tractatus Theologico-Politicus*, where he discusses how habits and rituals shape thought to the point that for "men so habituated to it obedience must have appeared no longer as bondage, but freedom."[6]

One could restore the primacy of matter, of bodies, of material conditions through such an emphasis on bodies, habits, and powers, but that seems to overlook Spinoza's peculiar expansive materialism. It is one in which we are determined not just as a body, not just in terms of material conditions, but also as mind, as a spiritual automaton. Or, maybe, materialism is not the right word. Perhaps it is more a matter of naturalism or even determinism. With respect to the former I am influenced by Fischbach's *Marx With Spinoza*: where he writes:

> What exactly does this affirmation of man as a being of nature, as a part of nature, mean for Marx? After all, he did not, or could not give these formulations a literal spinozist sense. It means first of all that man is "an objective being, natural, and sensous" that is to say a finite mode amongst an infinity

---

5 Benedict de Spinoza, *Ethics*, Translated by Edwin Curley, New York, Penguin, 1994 EVP10.
6 Baruch Spinoza, *The Theological-Political Treatise*, Translated by Samuel Shirley, Hackett, 2001, 199.

of other such modes. The determination of humanity as an objective being would be returned to by Marx again and again up to *Capital*, where he writes that, "the human being itself, considered as a pure existence of labor power, is a natural object, a thing, certainly living and conscious of itself, but a thing—and work properly speaking is a reification of this force." Adopting the point of view according to which the human being is first of all a being in nature, a thing in the world, is exactly to adopt the spinozist point of view according to which humans must first be grasped as a finite mode: to start, as does Spinoza, from the double fact, to know that on one hand that "man thinks" and, on the other, that "we feel that a certain body is affected in many ways," it being understood that these two traits are at the same level and of equal importance, the fact that we find ourselves to be thinking our thoughts accompanies the fact that we are aware of our body being affected by other things since "the object of the idea constituting a human mind is body, nothing can happen in that body which is not perceived by the mind." In the same way that the affection of the body, thought is a fact of nature, it is part of the natural being of humanity: thought does not found the exceptional character of humanity in the sense of being something outside of nature.[7]

In other words, as finite beings that are both minds and bodies, feeling and thinking, we are doubly determined, inserted in relation to practices, bodies, and relations, but also ideas, concepts, and imagination. I am not sure if we could call this materialism, at least in the conventional sense, but I am sure that it is not idealism. In fact it is further from conventional idealism than what is generally understood to be materialism. The idea that ideas have causes, are determined, that thought is not a free faculty, is more opposed to idealism than the conventional materialism, the assertion of the priority of bodies. The latter can always be reincorporated into idealism, no pun intended, through the primacy of representation.

---

7 Franck Fischbach, *Marx With Spinoza: Production, Alienation, History*, Translated by Jason Read, Edinburgh, 2023, 23.

As long as matter is an object of thought, something contemplated or represented, we are closer to idealism than we think. The object may be material, but that it is an object for thought, to be contemplated and known, means that the method is idealist. Or, more to the point, the idea that we are determined by both material conditions and the conditions of thought, by the order and connection of ideas and bodies, might be a Spinoza that is closer to Marx, than any putative materialism that is restricted to the primacy of the body. Not to be too reductive but in some sense the most important concepts of Marx's thought from ideology to fetishism to even the emphasis on form in the sense of value form are in some sense concepts of the materiality of the ideal, or, if that is too much, do not fit in materialism conventionally understood as the primacy of bodies to minds, matter to ideas. In the end, and to conclude, perhaps the relation between Marx and Spinoza is not a matter of their shared materialism, but of their intersecting challenges to materialism—the way they expand materialism to go beyond the thing, the body, to encompass ideas and social relations.

For more on Marx and Spinoza see Nexus Rerum: (Spinoza and Marx, again) and Economies of Affect/Affective Economies: Towards a Spinozist Critique of Political Economy.

"Let Me Tell You of the Time that Something Occurred": On Yves Citton's Mythocratie

Originally posted in December of 2011.

Before approaching the idea of "storytelling" that is at the center of Yves Citton's book *Mythocratie: Storytelling et Imaginaire de Gauche* it is important to situate his position with respect to some of the dominant strands of Spinozism.

The works of contemporary interpreters of Spinoza, especially those translated into English, can be roughly divided into two perspectives. First, there is Althusser, who wrote little on Spinoza, but whose "Ideology and Ideological State Apparatuses" used the Appendix to Part One of *Ethics* as the "matrix of every possible theory of ideology." As Spinoza argues in the Appendix we begin conscious of our desires and ignorant of the causes of things, and from this ignorance we arrive at the idea that we are a subject, but this idea this image of our agency and capacity only deepens our subjection. Althusser's Spinoza is first and foremost a theory of human bondage, of subjection. In contrast to this, the Spinoza of Antonio Negri and Gilles Deleuze is a theorist of immanence, of potentia, in which the imagination is not ideology, but part of the creative powers of the multitude. The imagination is not subjection but subversion: it is how we create the world through our strivings and actions. The imagination is understood to be entirely subordinated to transcendent Power (potestas) or entirely created by immanent power (potentia).

Yves Citton offers a reconciliation of these opposed projects, seeing both subjection and subversion in the imagination. To think the way in which the immanent powers of desire create and maintain their own subjection and liberation. It is not enough to simply assert, as many readers of Spinoza (and Foucault and Deleuze have) that everything is immanent, that power flows horizontally. The immanent forces are not individuals, but are the transindividual affects and ideas that constitute both individuals and collectives. The real task is to understand how these horizontal flows create and sustain their own "transcendent effects," their own images of verticality, images that have very real effects. The predominance of what Citton calls "soft power," mass media and public relations make this problem even more pressing. Power is sustained by the control of attention and affects more than anything else.

An interest in narrative and Spinoza might surprise Anglo-American readers who think primarily of the geometric method, or of Spinoza's critique of scripture. Citton cites Proposition 10 of Part Five of *Ethics*, which refers to the minds power of ordering the "affections of the body according to the power of the intellect." This reordering of affections and ideas is the power of narrative. Or, as Citton writes, paraphrasing another idea from Spinoza, we still do not know what stories are capable of.

Combining Spinoza with such diverse sources as Lazarrato's idea of noopolitics, work on mirror neurons, Stiegler, Diderot, Sun Ra, Wu Ming, and traditional theorists of narrative such as Riceour, Citton argues that attention and affects are shaped, channeled by stories, which in turn attune us to be receptive to the same stories. There is a certain plasticity to consciousness, to the conatus, that makes us receptive to the same narrative elements. This is one way of looking at the intersection of the transcendent and immanent, of the meta-conduct and conducts: we often shape our stories and narratives according to dominant frames. The contemporary media provides us multiple examples where the immanent horizontal powers (potentia) are actually structured by (potestas), from the crude, the editing of "man on the street" interviews; the crass, reality television; to the difficult to perceive, Wikipedia. What interests Citton about the latter, Wikipedia and Google, is their ability to render the filters and frames invisible. In Google "we produce knowledge in searching for knowledge" and channel attention through our attention. This makes the production of attention, of the stories that seem important, all the more important.

As the title suggests, Citton is primarily interested in storytelling from the left, from a politics committed to equality. He argues that the right has been quite good at constructing such stories, stories which structure political and personal narratives, such as Reagan's "Welfare Queen" which dominates narratives in politics for thirty years. That Citton cites this, a thirty-year old narrative from the US in a book written in France, is testament to its power. Power which stems from its ability to channel feelings of frustration at an inchoate sense of powerlessness, corruption, and, racism. The Welfare Queen takes a feeling, that others are benefiting at one's expense, and makes into into a narrative that is all the more accessible in that it taps into already existing racism. The story functions by channeling frustrations, fears, and fantasies, but once it is written it becomes the focus for future fears and fantasies, becoming a script that aims those frustrations at particular people, the poor, and away from others. The "welfare queen" demonstrates the intersection of the interests of the dominant powers and the affects and desires of the dominated. As Citton writes,

> "For reasons that we must comprehend, the "right" (security, neoliberal, xenophobic) has become a widespread, open, but relatively coherent story of images, various facts, information, statistics, slogans, fears, and reflexes and objects of debate that

mutually reinforce the heart of one and the same "imaginary of the right." The (soft) force of this imaginary has been its ability to rapidly colonize the discourse of number of leaders of parties that are supposedly officially left. How has this "imaginary of the right" been able script large sections of our political life. On what bases is it possible to reinvigorate an imaginary of the left capable of taking charge of the powers of scripting."[1]

It is because the narratives of the right are so dominant that Citton argues that the task of any narrative politics is "disqualification of the given," the naturalness and unquestioned nature of the given political and economic order. Spinoza's task may have been the "disqualification of sovereignty" and Marx may have had his task the "disqualification of appropriation," but the contemporary task is that of the disqualification of the given itself. Citton argues that this can be seen throughout contemporary thought, from Badiou's idea of the event, Deleuze's idea of the virtual, and Rancière's distribution of the sensible. All attempts to break with the self-evident nature of what is given and assumed as natural by exposing the relations and powers that constitute it. For Citton this strategy of transforming the given by writing a new story is not limited to philosophy, it can be found in various artistic movements. The most important one is Sun Ra. As Citton writes,

> "The title of this book is written under the influence of the African American musician Sun Ra (1914-1993), who invented at the same time musical oeuvre of premier importance, that remains well know (from the post-bop compositions to collective improvisations relevant to experimental music), and a common creative mode of life, that he and his Arkestra maintained for almost a half, and a myth, such that he claimed to be originally from the planet Saturn. In the USA during the second half of the twentieth century Sun Ra, lived, embodied,

---

1 Yves Citton, *Mythocratie: Storytelling et Imaginaire de Gauche*, Paris: Éditions Amsterdam, 2010, 15.

and illustrated the emancipatory force of myth: changing his name, investing in an extraterrestrial identity, regarding Earth societies from an interplanetary point of view, all of which participated in an effort of counter scripting and resistance to racist oppression, classism, conformity, and anti-intellectualism that structured US society.

The term mythocracy does not refer solely to the political regime in which fairy tales are used to lull infantilized citizens to sleep. It designates also the capacity of myth—which acts as a simple enunciation (according to Greek etymology) or as a foundational story (according to its modern usage)—to give rise to new becomings, individual and collective. To try mythocracy, to respond to the citation of Sun Ra, "I'm telling people that they've tried everything, and now they have to try mythocracy. They've got a democracy, theocracy. The mythocracy is what you never came to be that you should be," which this book is an exegesis of, is precisely to confront the ambivalence that permits myth (speech, history) to at one and the same time to be our sleep and that which wakes us from our sleep, we push from our premier place in the imaginary to "what you never came to be that you should be".[2]

Myth is the current state of our subjection. We live under the dominance of myths that stress the individual responsibility against the collective power, racial ressentiment against social solidarity, and fear of others against confidence in our own abilities. However, these are not the only possible stories, the only possible ways to make sense of our fears and desires. It is possible to invent new stories, which could in turn make possible new ways of thinking and living.

For more on Mythocracy see "Meta-Fiction: The Comic Book" and "Old Time Religion: On American Gods the Book and the TV Show."

---

2 Yves Citton, *Mythocratie: Storytelling et Imaginaire de Gauche*, Paris: Éditions Amsterdam, 2010, 16.

Meta-Fiction: The Comic Book (Politics and Narrative, Part Two)

Originally posted in March of 2012.

Let's begin with a story, I decided to read Yves Citton's because I was interested in his reading of Spinoza that I encountered in other contexts. It just so happened that soon after I wrote the blog post on that book I also received a copy of Christian Salmon's *Storytelling: Bewitching the Modern Mind* which Citton cites. As the title suggests, Salmon's book is also about narrative as a tool for marketing, management, and politics. At this time I also started reading Mike Carey and Peter Gross' series *The Unwritten* based on a recommendation from my local comics shop, which also deals with the stories and their power. Narrative is not something that I am "working on," Spinoza, or post-Spinozist understandings of transindividuality are, but one thread led to another, and ended up intersecting with my reading of comics, something I rarely blog about (no one can confess everything). These two errant threads began to connect in something that suggested more than serendipity when the latest collected volume of *The Unwritten* was titled "On to Genesis," a pun that would seem to invoke Simondon's ontogenesis. So as my work and entertainment intersected I decided to make a "busman's holiday" of it and write about *The Unwritten*.

The convergence of theory and comics dealing with narrative might seem like Zizek's example of the "parallax view," in which the same phenomena is viewed from "high" and "low" culture. However, identifying the contemporary comic, or graphic novel to use the parlance of the times, as necessarily lowbrow or populist is an incredibly dated view, almost like calling them funny pages. Graphic novels have become very literary, or high culture, and theory has become very pop (something Zizek knows very well). *The Unwritten* follows a kind of meta-fiction, the closest precursor of which (at least that I can think of) is Alan Moore's *The League of Extraordinary Gentlemen*, but whereas Moore's comic was interested in transposing the narrative conventions of the comic book superhero team unto past generations of speculative fiction, making a superhero team of the invisible man, Mr. Hyde, Captain Nemo, etc., Carey and Gross make narrative the subject of their work.

The story of *The Unwritten* is still unfolding at thirty plus issues, and is difficult to entirely recount. It begins with Tom (or Tommy) Taylor who is both the son of Wilson Taylor, an author of an incredibly popular series of young adult books about wizards (and vampires), and the namesake of the central protagonist of these stories. It would be as if J.K Rowling had a son named Harry Potter, and he made a living appearing at fan conventions. Oh, and Wilson the author has disappeared, which begins to suggest that things are not as they seem. The overlap of reality and fiction, the reality of fictions, their particular power and force, and the fictions of reality, the stories we are told, and tell ourselves just to get by, are the central concerns of *The Unwritten*.

As the stories progress we learn of a secret and ancient dark cabal that is very concerned with what stories get told and how, they are "the unwritten" of the books title and they control the world by control of its stories. The story of the unwritten is fleshed by a series of literary allusions and references that become increasingly dense, spanning everything from the Epic of Gilgamesh to Mary Shelley's

Frankenstein. These references become increasingly important as the story progresses so much so that the comic alternates between stories having to do with Tommy and his friends as they uncover the actions of the unwritten and stories about the long history of the politics of narrative, covering everything from ancient myths to the invention of the printing press. The political dimensions are still a little unclear, although an early literary aside suggests that Rudyard Kipling is being controlled by the cabal and Mark Twain and Oscar Wilde are not. The opposition of Kipling, the literary colonialist, and Twain, one time member of the American Anti-Imperialist League (not to mention Wilde, author of *The Soul of Man Under Socialism*) suggests that the politics of this cabal are imperialist. Carey and Gross are not interested in such a direct allegory, but use Kipling to introduce one of the comic's central images, the whale. Kipling's "How the Whale Got his Throat" is introduced as a literary response to hidden and immense power of this cabal.

Whales become central to an entire storyline taking up several issues, as it is revealed that Tommy, as a person/character, is able to travel through different stories, and travels through the figure of the whale, a dense point of intersection between different stories. No sooner is Tommy swallowed by the whale than he finds himself encountering others who have been swallowed by whales, Baron Munchausen, Pinocchio, Sinbad, and Kipling's shipwrecked mariner. The whale turns out to be a dense metaphor. The terms of this metaphor are established by both Kipling's tale, in which the whale is cursed to eat only the smallest of fish, and Hobbes' *Leviathan*, in which the great beast is made up of individuals. As Carey and Gross write, "And Hobbes whale was just a symbol. It stood for the power of the masses. A billion living things making up one huge entity."

Carey and Gross' reading of Hobbes is somewhat Spinozist in that it suggests that the leviathan, the sovereign is nothing other the desires, dreams, and imagination of the multitude. More importantly, the leviathan becomes a symbol of the power of stories themselves, of the collective unconscious, of massive power which

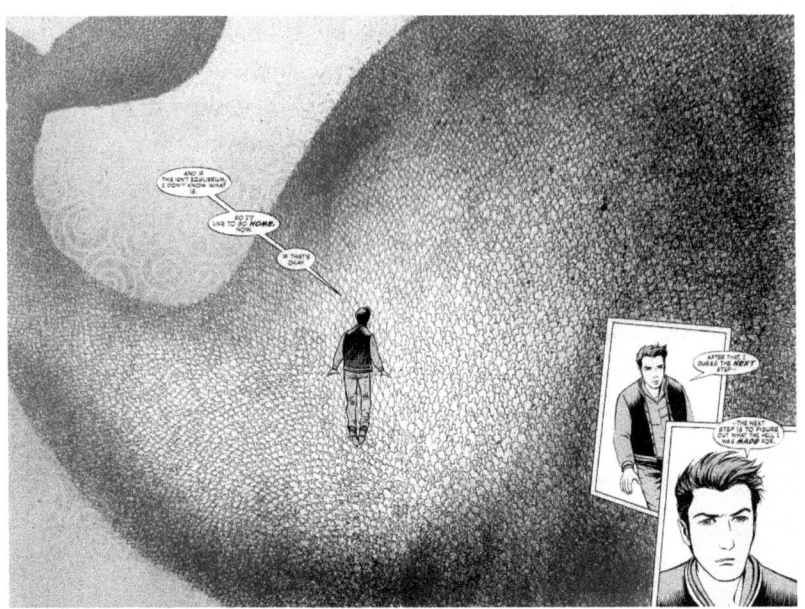

is nothing other than the power of the smallest and seemingly most ephemeral things, stories dreams and imagination.

This dialectic of the smallest and the largest underlies Salmon's book as well. Salmon begins by recounting how stories seem very slight, but goes onto to describe their centrality in marketing, as the age of the logo is replaced by the narrative; management, in which narratives become the new motiving force, the new spirit of capital; and politics, which can be seen as the battle over narratives. Salmon, like Citton, cites Reagan's story about "the welfare queen who'd purchased a Cadillac with government largesse," a story which continues to dominate contemporary politics. As Salmon argues, a direct line can be drawn from this story to Suskind's often quoted passage about the creation of reality. That is what stories do. Political power, economic power, and military power all rests on who tells a better story. As Salmon cites James Carville responding to Bush's commercial, dubbed "Ashley's Story." "A narrative is the key to everything. They produce a narrative, we [democrats] produce a litany." Salmon's book charts the rise of spin and storytelling in all forms of power, as not only electoral politics but market share increasingly belongs to the one who has constructed the best story.

If Salmon's book and Carey and Gross comic series are not to be juxtaposed as high to low, then how are they to be related. At first glance it would seem that Salmon is talking about something new, image consultants as a new job description, while Carey and Gross are talking about something very old, literature and myth. This is not entirely true, Carey and Gross have more illustrations of the internet, of webpages, news sites, and discussions, than any comic I have read. As much as it invokes the history of narrative it is fundamentally attuned to how that narrative is rewritten by modern forces. Its central story, that of a modern young adult book series, is thoroughly mediated by fan fiction and fan speculation. However, I do think that the tension between these two readings does suggest a problem: how to think through the intersection of the various technologies of narrative, from books to webpages. As Salmon suggests, part of the power of narrative comes from a kind of excess of information: it is because we are overwhelmed by so much information that narratives and stories hold so much power in sorting information. More to the point, I think that reading Carey and Gross' comic with Salmon (and Citton) helps underscore a central problem. We know that narratives are the point where the small become large, where the smallest fantasies and imaginations shape the world, and the stories only take hold, become big, by motivating these desires, but what remains obscure is how this happens. The history of fiction illustrates this, as books and films which were rejected and maligned eventually become blockbusters, taking hold of the imagination of millions. The opposite is sometimes also the case as films that were engineered to be massive successes fail to find an audience. Cult films and bombs illustrate the gap between scripts and desires. Politics has its unscripted moments as well, its rupture of existing narratives. Occupy Wall Street ruptured the existing narratives of politics and economics introducing a new language of inequality; Black Lives

Matter disrupted the narratives of racial progress and police power. Every rupture is brought back into the dominant narratives and established powers: politicians claim to represent the 99% and Black Lives Matter yard signs become a symbol of social conscience, but no script can completely cover these ruptures. What is lacking in every theory of the spectacle, of manufactured life is an account of these ruptures.

All images by Mike Carey and Peter Gross, covers by Yuko Shimizu, Vertigo comics.

For more on myth see Let Me Tell You of the Time That Something Occurred: On Yves Citton's Mythocratie.

I Owe You an Explanation: Graeber and Marx on Origin Stories

Originally posted in September of 2011.

The story of so-called primitive accumulation is well known to readers of Marx. This story was political economy's way of understanding the origins of capitalism, explaining how the world was divided into workers and capitalists. The story is a kind of grasshopper and ant tale, of those who save and those who squander, although Marx gives it a different literary spin. As Marx writes:

> "This primitive accumulation plays approximately the same role in political economy as original sin does in theology. Adam bit the apple, and thereupon sin fell on the human race. Its origin is supposed to be explained when it is told as an anecdote about the past. Long, long ago there were two sorts of people; one the diligent, intelligent, and above all frugal elite; the other lazy rascals, spending their substance, and more, in riotous living. The legend of theological original sin tells us certainly how man came to be condemned to eat his bread by the sweat of his brow; but the history of economic original sin reveals to us that there are people to whom this is by no means essential. Never mind! Thus it came to pass that the former sort accumulated

wealth, and the latter sort finally had nothing to sell except their own skins."[1]

Marx argues that this story is inadequate to account for the origin of capital. It is not enough to simply save money, because the accumulation of money does nothing to produce those with nothing to sell but their labor power. In order to get workers a huge population must be separated from the means of production, cast off the land and out of the commons. The origin of capitalism is not a moral story of thrift, but a bloody story of expropriation; a story which eventually encompasses the whole history of slavery, colonialism, and even the reformation.

Marx ended Volume One of *Capital* with this critique, David Graeber opens his book, *Debt: The First 5,000 Years* with a critique of another contemporary fable. This fable concerns the origin of money. This story, which can be traced back at least as far as Aristotle, begins with an economy based on barter, but, as anyone who has brought their cow to the market and came back with magic beans can tell you, barter is incredibly inconvenient. Money, the story claims, then comes into existence to solve the shortcomings of barter, the difficulty of bringing objects to the market, and the time spent waiting for someone who had what you wanted and wanted what you had. Most importantly, money is an affair of equals, grounded only on convenience and interest. This is why this story is so popular with Adam Smith and contemporary economic textbooks.

Graeber argues that there is one thing wrong with this story: it never happened. He uses a great deal of archeological and anthropological evidence to argue that this smooth transition from barter to money never took place. All of this historical evidence is based on one simple problem: barter presupposes a kind of sociality of people who are entirely disconnected, without bonds, but not engaged in direct conflict. Marx would say that it presuppose bourgeois

---

[1] Karl Marx, *Capital: A Critique of Political Economy*, Volume I, trans. Ben Fowkes, Penguin, 1977, 873.

subjects, subjects connected only by self-interest. What Graeber argues is that history, or rather anthropology, has documented all sorts of ways in which goods circulate, but this circulation is usually one in which bonds of all sorts, friendships and debts, circulate as well.

Graeber gives more credit (I actually don't know if I intended that pun or not) to a different account of money, primordial debt theory, which argues that money emerged from the taxes, from the state's need to generate money. This theory begins with a fundamental asymmetry, not an equivalence, an asymmetry that is often founded on religion, on the sense of debt owed to the world. (Readers of Deleuze and Guattari will recognize a great deal of this emphasis on the primordial debt running through *Anti-Oedipus and A Thousand Plateaus*).

As Graeber summarizes this dichotomy of these two viewpoints as follows:

> "This is a great trap of the twentieth century: on one side is the logic of the market, where we like to imagine that we all start out as individuals who don't owe each other anything. On the other is the logic of the state, where we all begin with a debt we can never truly pay. We are constantly told that they are opposites, and that between them they contain the only real human possibilities. But it's a false dichotomy. States created markets. Markets require states. Neither could continue to exist without the other, at least, in anything like the forms we would recognize today."[2]

What these two accounts illustrate is that debt is always a combination of equality and hierarchy. The false dichotomy of the account of the origins of money presents them as alternatives, but that misses the fact that they are always intertwined in debt. To quote Graeber again:

> "Debt is a very specific thing, and it arises from very specific situations. It first requires a relationship between two people who do not consider each other fundamentally different sorts of being,

---

2 David Graeber, *Debt: The First 5,000 Years*, Melville House, 2011, 71.

who at least potential equals, who are equals in those ways that are really important, and who are not currently in a state of equality—but for whom there is some way to set matters straight."[3]

Graeber spends much of the book analyzing the history of this particular logic of hierarchy and equality, hierarchies that determine who is expected to pay their debts and who can hold onto them. This hierarchy continues up to the present, to the current moment of bailouts for some and austerity for others. However, Graeber's book is not a history; yes, it covers the five thousand years of debt, slavery, the gold standard, and the fiat system are all discussed, but primary as different transformations of this logic. Graeber is primarily interested in the way in which monetized debt intersects with, and separates itself from, social bonds and obligations.

At the core of this anthropology is the following axiom about human society:

> "In fact, communism is the foundation of all human sociability. It is what makes society possible. There is always an assumption that anyone who is not actually an enemy can be expected on the principle of "from each according to their abilities," at least to an extent: for example, if one needs to figure out how to get somewhere, and the other knows the way."[4]

Graeber's point is well taken, there is much to be said for this communism of everyday life, the way in which cooperative relations permeate our daily actions. It is important to contest the anthropology of neoliberalism, the claim that we are always and naturally engaged in cutthroat competition, seeking maximum gain for minimum expenditure. Such an anthropology simply does not account for all of our tendencies to offer aid in all sorts of ways. It fails to describe actual daily life, even in capitalism.

As a somewhat abrupt conclusion let me say that I paired Graeber

---

3 Ibid., 120.
4 Ibid., 196.

with Marx for two reasons, two reasons that have nothing to do reviving some anarchism versus communism debate. First, I think that the fantasy of barter, of money arising from barter, is just as a false and pernicious ideology as the moral story of so-called primitive accumulation. These stories are pernicious not because of what they say about the past, even though they both are distortions of history, but what they do in the present. The moral idea of the thrifty capitalist and shifty worker continues into our contemporary discussions of "job creators" and lazy unemployment recipients, just as the idea of money as an egalitarian means of exchange underwrites the ideal of the free market as a social relation without subordination. Graeber's critique of barter needs to be placed alongside Marx's account of primitive accumulation. However, and this is the second reason, I read Marx's critique of so-called primitive accumulation to also be a critique of an explanation of history based entirely on human motives and intentions. In this view it is the moral difference of thrift and waste that produces the class difference of capitalist and worker. To which Marx responds, capitalism is not a matter of thrift, waste, or greed, or other human intentions, it is a matter of the destruction of the commons, of the accumulation of wealth made possible by colonialism workers on the one hand, and capitalists on the other. Thus, communism may be the foundation of all sociability, but capitalism is often indifferent to this sociability, or, worse still, exploits it.

As a topic of inquiry debt crosses back and forth from the economic to the moral, and thus it is tempting to locate its history in attitudes and ideas, but a true history of debt needs to also examine the structure that are indifferent to those ideas.

For more on Primitive Accumulation see The Original Sin of Accumulation: Trying to Say Something Original About Ursprüngliche Akkumulation for more on everyday communism see It is Competition all the Way Down: On the Spontaneous Anthropology of Contemporary Capitalism.

Waiting for the Robots: Benanav and Smith on the Illusions of Automation and Realities of Exploitation

Originally posted in December of 2020.

In the last month or so two remarkably similar books appeared, Aaron Benanav's *Automation and the Future of Work* and Jason E. Smith's *Smart Machines and Service Work: Automation in an Age of Stagnation*. The books are similar without being redundant. They are too similar to construct anything like a provocative debate between them. They are perhaps best viewed not just in terms of their polemics against certain fantasies or fears of automation but the way in which they constitute an emergent, or even dominant, sensibility and orientation of Marxist thought, one that makes sense of the present through the infamous tendency of the rate of profit to fall.

First, a personal aside, and this is just something that I have been thinking as of late, as I try to keep up with some of the latest writings, podcasts, and websites on Marxist thought, when I first began to study Marx in the nineties there was perhaps no aspect of Marx's thought in more disrepute than the tendency of the rate of profit to fall. It was considered part of the bad teleological aspect of Marx, best approached through a litany of counter-tendencies. Predictions of any future where considered part of some Hegelian residue. That was the philosophical criticism. The tendency of the rate of profit to fall also did not *seem* to correspond to the world we were living in, the Soviet Union had collapsed and capitalism seemed to be fueled by the dotcom boom. It is possible to argue that there was an entire wave of post-autonomist Marxism, at least in its American revival that was an attempt to image a transition to communism predicated not on capitalism's contradictions but its strengths, to image a post-capitalism and a transition that is predicated on abundance rather than immiseration, on activity rather than exclusion. The same could be said for accelarationism, which attempted to think post-capitalism from capital's ability to create technological progress (even if that progress was largely squandered or wasted).

Benanav and Smith's books can be read together as a not so much the emergence of a prominent counter-tendency to both of these orientations, it has been brewing for a long time in journals such as Endnotes and related projects. The publication of these two books marks the emergence of this orientation in a more public form, contending not just with other strains of readings of Marx but with the general and prevailing sense that technology and automation is the central driving force of capitalism, what could be considered the spontaneous ideology of the era of Uber and iphones.

Benanav argues that the spontaneous image we have of the current state of the economy, of technology and automation displacing jobs, and leading to precarious labor and unemployment is perhaps the wrong way of understanding what we are seeing. The precarious status of labor is not a product of the coming revolution of machines, but rather a byproduct of the stagnation and decline of capital. Benanav describes this particular illusion as follows:

> "Our collective sense that the pace of labor saving technological change is accelerating is an illusion. It is like the feeling you get when looking out of the window of a train car as it slows down at a station: passing cars on the other side of the tracks appear to speed up. Labor-saving technical change appears to be happening at a faster pace than before only when viewed from across the tracks—that is, from the standpoint of our ever more slow-growing economies."[1]

It is not automation that is driving unemployment and underemployment, but a general decline in profits. The train we are on is not moving towards some post-work future. The speed and instability we see is really the train on the other track, the track of profitability, slowing down, casting off workers, or more often than not, underemploying them. It is for this reason that the biggest technological changes affecting production in the last twenty years have neither been in production nor services but surveillance and tracking. The latter are less about increasing productivity overall, but of hyper-exploiting workers, getting more work out of less workers.

Why has the idea of automation, of a technological revolution, continued to be so persistent, returning time and time again in an almost cyclical prediction of the rise of robots and the end of work? Perhaps because so many of the technological changes of the past twenty years have not been in the factories or even in the restaurants

---

[1] Aaron Benanav, 'Automation isn't wiping out jobs. It's that our engine of growth is winding down', *The Guardian*, January 23, 2020, https://www.theguardian.com/commentisfree/2020/jan/23/robots-economy-growth-wages-jobs

but have been aimed at consumption and entertainment. Have ended up in our hand As Smith states in a recent interview in the *Brooklyn Rail* (recapping an argument he makes in the book).

> "The "smartphone" stands in as the signal innovation, or contrivance, of the age, its "star commodity." Its sheer pervasiveness, its presence on sidewalks, in boardrooms, classrooms, or at the dinner table, confirms its status as an epochal emblem. For the most part, it simply brings together older devices (the mobile phone, the personal computer). Providing access to a panoply of diversions—shopping, streaming music and video, interpersonal communication—by means of a single, interactive screen, these apparatuses complete a confluence underway for decades now: the fusion of commerce and news, entertainment and sociality, self-stylization and civic life on a one-size-fits-all, touch-sensitive LCD (or OLED) screen. Its user is torn between these registers, while performing them all at once; at a loss for bearings, their mood flickers between harmless diversion and inarticulate rage. Yet the heavy hand the largest technology companies have had in equities markets, combined with the concussive force they have unleashed on leisure, consumption, personal identity, and public discourse—all already in the throes of erosion and decomposition for decades—gave rise to claims for this core technology that far exceed its impact on how we shop, consume media, or interact with friends, family, and strangers. In the workplace these innovations promised to lead to what Paul Mason heralded as an "exponential takeoff in productivity." That's precisely what has not happened. What we got instead are increasingly tight webs of surveillance and tracing, on the streets and in workplaces."[2]

---

2 Jason E. Smith with Tony Smith, "The Upstarts and the Mandarins: Reflections on the Illusions of a Class," *Brooklyn Rail*, November 2020, https://brooklynrail.org/2020/11/field-notes/The-Upstarts-and-the-Mandarins-Reflections-of-the-Illusions-of-a-Class.

I should say that these two books complement each other nicely. Benanav spends more time working out the economics of stagnation, but Smith offers a little more of a sketch of why the spontaneous ideology of automation is so persistent; how our daily experience of technology, constantly checking our phones, makes us believe in a revolutionary transformation of production that has not only yet to manifest but is not coming under existing economic and social conditions. Consumption appears more revolutionary than production, and that is precisely because of the declining profits from production. The iphone is less a revolutionary force of production than it is a kind of profit squeeze, seeking get more consumption and work out of existing conditions of production. It is also a kind of dead end for gains of productivity, even if it becomes cheaper to produce iphones most people still need only one; Steve Jobs will never be another Henry Ford, the large scale effects of the automobile are just not possible for the cellphone despite its cultural ubiquity. As Smith points out, no one knows this better than Apple which spends most of its profits on stock buybacks rather than developing the next generation of iphones.

On this last point is worth focusing briefly on Uber and Proposition 22 in California, which classified drivers for Uber and other companies as independent contractors rather than workers. While the spectacle of Uber, and what Uber very much wants us to see is the app on the phone immediately showing us tiny maps and cars catering to our needs, what we really drives the company (which incidentally is yet to turn a profit) is its ability to circumvent the minimal requirements of labor laws. On standards of productivity Uber changes very little, it might get more cars on the road at peak hours but it is still using the same private automobiles and the same roads to transport people. It is basically a cab hailing software where the real innovation has to do with how it reclassifies workers and takes advantage of underemployed workers looking for extra hours or more work. It is hyper-exploitation masquerading as technological innovation.

The same could be said for the other supposedly cutting edge companies of the digital economy, when they are not using the wealth they accumulate to buy back stocks, they are investing not in ways of increasing productivity but ways of delivering advertisements (as in the case of Facebook) or improving forms of surveillance (as in the case of Google). Even the ATM machine is less a robot teller than it is a way to outsource much of the work of banking to customers. Technological innovations have not increased productivity. Where they have not been aimed at consumers, trying to target attention for advertising, they have been primarily focused at scheduling and surveilling workers, trying to squeeze more profits out of existing labor, and creating a constant sense of anxiety.

Where does this leave us? Both Benanav and Smith follow James Boggs in seeing that the revolutionary question has less to do with the working class than those who are displaced from work, or perpetually underemployed. The workers of a stagnating economy are increasingly isolated and divided, often split between the hyper-exploited and those that desperate for the chance to even be exploited. They are more in contact with their employers, who watch over them endlessly, and advertisers, who seek to exploit every remaining moment, than they are in touch with each other. As Smith argues the contemporary working class is one that is thoroughly infused with management, surveilling each other in positions that blur management and work. This presents monumental barriers to organization, which is perhaps why we live in an age of sporadic contestations that never become movements. Lastly, as Benanav argues, letting go of the fears of automation, of workers replaced by machines, also means letting go of the corresponding fantasies, of fully automated luxury communism. Capital is not building its own automated gravediggers; it is just driving its diggers to quicker graves. There is no post-work future to come, but there is a chance to struggle or a world where work, as well as creativity and research, is oriented more towards human needs and less to the declining standards of productivity.

For More on Technology and Capitalism see The General Intellect Personified: More on Capitalism as a Social Relation.

Image from Sleep Dealer

Put a Drone on It: Chamayou's A Theory of the Drone

Originally posted in February of 2015.

Drones are having their cultural moment right now. They have appeared in such films from *Interstellar* to *Captain America: Winter Soldier*. While in the first film the drone's cameo appearance was used to shuffle in some post-Empire concerns (the drone was an Indian Surveillance drone), in the latter film drones do not directly appear but the film deals with "drone anxiety." Drone anxiety is the fear that the very things that make drones strategically desirable— "precision targeting," low risk combat, and increased surveillance, will make possible a massive centralization and automation of state power. (*Sleep Dealer*, pictured above, was ahead of the curve on this point). The unmanned ariel vehicle becomes synonymous with a breakdown of individual responsibility and centralization of control. In many cases the fear of the drone then merges with the fear of robots, of automation. In any case drones are hot, and the war on terror is not (or at least less so).

Beyond popular culture drones have become what I consider "transdisciplinary theoretical objects." Transdisciplinary theoretical objects are things that nearly everyone writes about or reads about regardless of their specialization. Drones, financialization, social media, and climate change are such objects currently. Neoliberalism is fifteen minutes ago. Such objects not only reflect the cultural, economic, and technological transformations that define anything like a "conjuncture" but raise the question as to how the different disciplinary perspectives of philosophy, history, and media studies, the different tools of ontological speculation, textual analysis, historical reflection, and visual examination, can combine and augment each other. That would be the ideal, but all too often these shared objects of concern simply become the terrain upon which the narcissism of minor theoretical differences play themselves out.

Image from Captain America: The Winter Soldier

It is for all of these reasons that I was excited to read Grégoire Chamayou's *A Theory of the Drone*. It seemed like the logical continuation of his book on manhunts, not exactly a hot topic. After reading the earlier book I proposed that perhaps the two could be read together as a kind of outsourcing of risk and violence (the drone is the new slave hunter). My prediction was correct, Chamayou places the drone in a trajectory that is more of the manhunt than of combat. The drone sees, locates, and eliminates a target, it does not battle an enemy.

This one sided hunting relates to the first question Chamayou takes up, the much discussed figure of the drone operator. At one time or another it seemed that every major periodical from *The Atlantic* to *The New York Times* (not exactly a huge spread, I know) ran a profile of the drone operator. We could ask the question as to why the drone operator came to be such a figure of fascination, but that is not the question that Chamayou asks. Chamayou contests the attempts to attribute to drone operators the same post-traumatic stress found in the battlefield. Drone operators are subject to stress, to long hours, but their stress is to be subject to a kind of cognitive dissonance of living at home but working in a global battle zone. As Chamayou writes,

> "...relocating agents of armed violence to a domestic zone of peace places them in a social environment that may well not be able to understand them and which may actively, before their very eyes, contest the violence of which they are the agents."[1]

And latter...

> "And what if drone psychopathology lay not where it is believed to be, in the possible traumas of the drone operators, but in the industrial production of compartmentalized psyches, immunized against any possibility of reflecting upon their own violence, just as their bodies are already immunized against any possibility of being exposed to the enemy?"[2]

Image from Arrested Development

---

[1] Gregoire Chamayou, *A Theory of the Drone*, Translated by Janet Loyd, The New Press, 2015, 121

[2] Gregoire Chamayou, *A Theory of the Drone*, 123.

More important than the psychological or moral economy of the drone is where it fits in the politics and economy of war. If the drone's moral or psychic lineage includes the slave hunter then its political genealogy is much closer to home. It starts with Vietnam, with the US military's attempt to avoid another Vietnam not in the anti-imperialist or anti-war sense of the term, but in the sense that Vietnam exposed the US and the military to its dependence on popular opinion, on the draft, on the people. As Chamayou writes,

> "The Vietnam crisis made crystal clear all the latent political dangers associated with such a dependent relationship. The American ruling classes came to recognize the full scope of the powerful dynamics of social radicalization that could be engendered by an unpopular imperialistic war. They could also see to what extent the explosive synergies activated by the antiwar movement resonated with all the social movements agitating American society."[3]

Image from Captain America: The Winter Soldier

Drone warfare does not just shift the moral economy of war, the risk and bravery that makes killing justifiable, or the psychic economy, the dangers and damage of war, but is a shift in the political

---

3 Gregoire Chamayou, *A Theory of the Drone*, 191.

economy of war. Or, more to the point, is a shift in the moral, technical, and psychic economy of war as a response to the political economy of war. It is war divorced from the mass mobilizations that have largely defined conflict. The drone is not just some technological transformation of the means of war, but a fundamental transformation of its logic, limitations, and rationale. Its conditions and effects exceed the boundaries of war theory, political theory, political economy, or ethical philosophy. Chamayou's book offers a provocative introduction to drone theory, and an argument as to why we all need to think about drones. After all, they are everywhere.

For More on Drones and Movies see "Violence and the Common: Truth is Structured Like a Science Fiction".

Images by Jacques Villeglé

The Means of Individuation: Castel on the Dialectics of Individuality

Originally posted in March of 2018.

In the essay published as the conclusion to *La Montée des Incertitudes: Travail, Protections, Statut de L'individu* Robert Castel gives a genealogy of the contemporary individual. First, in a line of thinking that would seem to parallel Etienne Balibar because it is one of his sources, Castel argues that the modern individual is founded upon property. As Locke argued, "Though the earth, and all inferior creatures, be common to all men, yet every man has a property in his own person: this nobody has any right to but himself." As Castel stresses this connection between property and individuation is not a theoretical assertion but a practice as well. Bourgeois modernity is founded upon the reciprocal connection of the individual and property. Those who have property are recognized as individuals.

This first modernity is followed by the second in which the stark opposition between those with property and propertyless is mediated by the increasing political and social recognition of labor as not just a condition of property but a possession in itself. Labor is no longer the only property possessed by those who have nothing else to sell, the necessary precondition for future property, but becomes itself a kind of property, or status. Workers become employees, and are recognized as such through institutions of unemployment insurance, social security, disability, etc. As Castel writes, "It is the collective which protects the individual who is no longer protected by property."[1] The bourgeois subject of property is not only generalized and democratized by the figure of the (salaried) worker, but the worker is potentially more explicitly transindividual: property could always be naturalized, seen as something that stemmed from a pre-political state of nature as in Locke's account, but the rights to recognition as a worker necessarily stem from social institutions.

Although one could argue as much as this is true historically, describing the long battle for the recognition of the social status of the worker, a battle that had as one of its fronts the racial, national, and sexual exclusion of those who were deemed non-workers, as certain tasks, such as domestic service, and activities, such as agricultural work, were subject to their own rules and norms. In this battle to be considered a worker is to be recognized as performing a social function. Against this struggle for recognition through work there has been a counter-tendency to "naturalize" work and conceal its historical and social mediations. Or, more to the point, if the first tendency is institutionalized in the legal recognition of the individual as worker rather than just as property owner then the second is institutionalized in all of the myriad ways in which work appears as an isolated and individual activity rather than a social relation. Unemployment benefits and social security may recognize the worker as a social status, as something collectively won and organized, but against this the paycheck recognizes as the worker as individually responsible for his or her work. As Marx writes:

---

1 Robert Castel, *La Montée des Incertitudes: Travail, Protections, Statut de L'individu*, Éditions du Seuil, 2009, 417.

"In contrast to the slave, this labour becomes more productive because more intensive, since the slave works only under the spur of external fear but not for his existence which is guaranteed even if it does not belong to him. The free worker, however, is impelled by his wants. The consciousness (or better: the idea) of free self-determination, of liberty, makes a much better worker of one than of the other, as does the related feeling (sense) of responsibility; since he, like any seller of wares, is responsible for the goods he delivers and for the quality which he must provide, he must strive to ensure that he is not driven from the field by other sellers of same time as himself."[2]

"I pay my own bills" is our modern Robinsonade, a modern account of the independent individual that eclipses and conceals its historical and social relations.

All of this is really preamble to Castel's consideration of the two figures of contemporary, or what he calls "hypermodern" individuality. The first, what he calls individuality by excess. The excess in this context refers to an access to an excess of the conditions of individuation, access to the material, social, and symbolic capital

---

2 Karl Marx, *Capital: A Critique of Political Economy, Volume I*, Translated by Ben Fowkes, (New York: Penguin, 1977), 1031.

which makes individuation possible to the point that it has the paradoxical effect of a disaffiliation with any existing material, social, or symbolic collective. As Castel writes, "The individual in excess seems to me to perform a form of disaffiliation from the top through which the individual is detached/detaches himself from his collective affiliations because they are somehow saturated."³ It is an extreme version of Marx's claim that "the epoch which produces...the isolated individual, is also precisely that of the hitherto most developed social relations." it is an individual that denies its connection to any social, economic, or political condition of its individuation, of its very capacity to act, because these have been so thoroughly incorporated into its existence. This is partially what is meant by "privilege" to use the parlance of our time: the inability to see one's material, social, and cultural advantages because they have been so thoroughly intertwined in one's existence that it would be like fish seeing the water they swim in. The other form of individuality, individuality by default is the inverse of this. It is an individual that lacks access to even the fundamental conditions necessary to assume their individual liberty, to use Castel's terms. They are the disposable individuals of the contemporary society, outside of work and shuttled between various institutions designed more to manage them as an excess population than to bring them into any collective.

It is possible to see contemporary politics as defined by this opposition. On one side we have the individuals of excess, the ruling class, unable or unwilling to comprehend how others cannot "pull themselves up by their bootstraps" because they inherited self-pulling boots. As one resident from Arizona describes this retreat from the social by individuals of excess.

> "People who have swimming pools don't need state parks. If you buy your books at Borders you don't need libraries. If your kids are in private school, you don't need K-12. The people here, or at least those who vote, don't see the need for government.

---

3 Robert Castel, *La Montée des Incertitudes*, 433.

> Since a lot of the population are not citizens, the message is that government exists to help the undeserving, so we shouldn't have it at all. People think it's OK to cut spending because ESL is about people who refuse to assimilate and health care pays for illegals."[4]

On the other side we have the individuals by default, individuated not by their access to various conditions of social belonging, but by various layers of exclusion, control, and subjection. Loïc Wacquant distinguishes between two sides of the state, one ideological and the other repressive, corresponding to these two individuations. As Wacquant writes, "Actually existing neoliberalism extolls 'laissez faire et lasser passer' for the dominant, but it turns out to be paternalist and intrusive for the subaltern, and especially for the urban precariat whose life parameters it restricts through the combined mesh of supervisory workfare and judicial oversight."[5] The state is a centaur: addressing individuals of excess with a humanistic ideology of entrepreneurship while confronting individuals of default with a brutal logic of discipline.

There is another way to see this intersection of excess and default, however, one less oriented towards identifying two distinct classes than in grasping a dialectic of contemporary experience across various classes. I am thinking of social media, or social life as it is increasingly mediated by various forms of technological mediation. It opens up the possibility of a kind of excess for nearly everyone as suddenly something one did, wrote, or thought has gone viral. Fame is no longer just for the famous. This excess is predicated on a kind of default, not just the narcissistic emptiness that needs constant validation by "likes" and "retweets," but the more significant lack of any collective or community worthy of the name. Online fame and reputation is not built over time with others, but recreated each day anew in a field of others that are more of

---

4 Ken Silverstein, "Tea Party in the Sonora: For the Future of G.O.P. Governance, Look to Arizona," *Harper's Magazine*, July 2010.
5 Loic Wacquant, "Three Steps Towards a Historical Anthropology of Actually Existing Neoliberalism," *Social Anthropology/Anthropologie Sociale* (2012) 20, 1 66–79. pg. 74.

an audience than a community. There is no communication, no solidarity, just isolated individuals performing their relation to some purported communal norms in the name of trolling or virtue signaling. Negative individuality and negative solidarity are the transindividual conditions of each other. Thus, the same collective conditions that extend one's reach can drastically undermine one's life, and much of life on social media is the intertwining of this increase and decrease of one's power to act. The conditions of fame are the conditions of shame.

To take a less spectacular example, and to return to the connection between individuation and property we just need to look to Facebook and Cambridge Analytica. Once again we can see an intersection between excess and default, as the very thing which extends and supplements individuality, developing all of its aspects and nuance, is that which undermines self-possession. The means of individuation are at the same time the means of dispossession. We no longer have any illusions about possessing, as some kind of private property, the conditions of our individuation. Inchoate demands to "nationalize Facebook (or google)" reflect in their own way a recognition of the transindividual as a condition of individuation. As Balibar argues, ownership of the means of individuation, especially as they affect the "postulate of the individuality of the thought process" brings together politics and economics in a novel way. It is no longer the topography of base and superstructure but the identity of ownership and control.

> "It then becomes impossible in practice, and more and more difficult even to conceive of in theory, to pose on one side a right of property that would deal only with things, or with the individual concerned with the "administration of things" (with the societas rerum of the jurists of antiquity), and on the other side a sphere of the _vita activa_ (Hannah Arendt) that would be the sphere of "man's power over man" and man's obligations toward man, of the formation of "public opinion," and of the conflict of ideologies. Property (dominium) reenters

domination (imperium). The administration of things re-enters the government of men (if it had ever left it)."⁶

By way of a conclusion I am reminded of a remark in *The German Ideology* in which Marx states, "Thus things have now come to such a pass that the individuals must appropriate the existing totality of productive forces, not only to achieve self-activity, but, also, merely to safeguard their very existence."⁷ This remark seems to have taken on increased importance today as it is not just the means of production, but the means of individuation that have been expropriated.

For More on Negative Solidarity see Negative Solidarity: Towards the Definition of a Concept

---

6 Étienne Balibar, "Rights of Man and Rights of the Citizen: The Modern Dialectic of Equality and Freedom, in *Masses, Classes, Ideas: Studies on Politics and Philosophy before and after Marx*, Translated by James Swenson, Routledge, 222.
7 Karl Marx and Friedrich Engels, *The German Ideology*, Prometheus Books, 1998, 96.

PHILOSOPHY

I have more copies of Reading Capital than any other book

Althusser Effects: Philosophical Practices

Originally posted in March of 2021.

One of the most damning things anyone has ever said to me, at least about academic philosophy, was something to the effect of, "philosophy at universities today is to doing philosophy what art history is to making art." The implication being that emphasis of philosophy in the modern university is on following different philosophers; tracing their influences and transformations the way that a historian my trace the different periods of an artist or the different movements. It seemed damning, but not inaccurate, especially with respect to the way that there seems to be a trajectory, at least in continental programs of setting oneself up as [blank] guy, following a philosopher, interpreting, commenting and translating. There are a lot of questions that can be posed about this model, especially now, as philosophy continues to be pushed outside of the university, and forced to reinvent itself in new spaces and publications.

  I have never been comfortable with this way of working, even if I must admit that it does sometimes take a lot of work to even comprehend a philosopher, and that there are people who do amazing work this way. I find it more useful to try and situate myself between a few different philosophers and work on the places of contact and tension. This does not mean that I do not have my masters, as Badiou would say, and anyone who reads this blog can probably have a sense of who those are. Or you could just look at the list of names that come up again and again on this blog. Althusser is one of those names, as is are those in his circle.

All of which is a long preamble to set up what I consider to a few thoughts about Althusser. Althusser is probably someone whose thought has shaped my thinking in more ways than I am willing to admit, shaping even the way that I think about doing philosophy, even though I have not directly worked on him in a few years, and yet I rarely get a chance to teach him. That does not mean that Althusser does not affect how I teach, however.

One text that I do sometimes teach, for better or worse, is the famous, or infamous, *Ideology and Ideological State Apparatuses: Notes Towards an Investigation*. It is a text that I am increasingly convinced can only be thought of in its provisional and fragmentary status, a status which the publication and translation of *Sur la Reproduction* does not resolve or restore. It just adds more fragments and gaps. I am not sure if there is any way to restore it to any theoretical unity. The various commentaries that have accumulated in recent years tear it further asunder, stressing its Spinozist, Lacanian, or Gramscian dimensions. Then of course there are the scenes of interpellation and hailings that can be read in different ways turning the text into something to be interpreted, even deciphered. The quasi-literary dimension of these scenes makes the text both a theory for interpretation and a text to be interpreted. I do not have anything to add to all that, in fact what I have to add has less to do with teaching ideology (or its critique) and more about ideology in the classroom.

> Ideology, n. An imaginary relationship to a real situation.
> In common usage, what the other person has, especially when systematically distorting the facts.

From Kim Stanley Robinson's The Ministry of the Future

I have come to reflect that Althusser's famous statement, "Ideology interpellates individuals as subjects," can be understood something so basic and fundamental to the functioning of ideology, and that is quite simply that when you present people with the constitutive elements of their ideology, of the ideology that defines their age and era they will see themselves as exceptions, as outside of it. Ideology is thinking that one is not shaped by ideology, that one is a kingdom within a kingdom, unaffected by the economic, and social, forces of the world. To give one example, I used to co-teach a course on American Consumerism with faculty from English and Economics, and students were often more than willing to discuss consumerism in general but unwilling to admit that it had affected them at all. Everyone new someone who was caught up in the world of brands and products, but claimed that they themselves were unaffected by advertisements. I had a similar experience when I recently tried to teach about social media. Everyone knew someone who was on their iPhone all the time, or fit the definition of a consumer. Ideology was always for other people.

This is in some sense an unteachable moment, I think people can learn how to criticize ideology in a classroom but not why. I think most of people's political sensibilities are shaped by things that happen outside of the classroom. My second little lesson from Althusser reflects how I teach philosophy. I often find the idea of a symptomatic reading to be an interesting way of presenting texts from the history of philosophy. In other words it is sometimes useful and necessary to read texts for "problems without solutions" and "answers without questions." Although I must admit that my use of this practice is less in line with the rigor that Althusser defines it in *Lire Le Capital*, and closer to what he writes in the essay on Rousseau's *Social Contract*. In that essay the symptom is a matter of certain discrepancies which exist between the theoretical object and its historical, which is to say economic and social, situation.

To take one example, in Locke's *Second Treatise of Government* Locke, as it is well known makes the fundamental claim that labor, the mixing of one's body with something outside of it, is the natural basis for the accumulation of property. "The labor of his body, and the work of his hands, we may say are properly his,"[1] Locke goes onto include "grass my horse has bit" and, more importantly, "turfs my servant has cut" as examples of this principle. Including disappropriation as an example of appropriation, and doing so before anything like money or the conditions of wage labor have been introduced. It is an answer without a question, a conclusion without a premise. In some sense Locke is rushing ahead of himself to reassure his readers that the connection he has made between labor and property, between the work of the body and ownership exists to be severed by the institution of money.

To take another example from the same class, in Adam Smith's *Wealth of Nations* we get the following story of technological progress and change made possible by the division of labor:

> In the first fire-engines, a boy was constantly employed to open and shut alternately the communication between the boiler and the cylinder, according as the piston either ascended or descended. One of those boys, who loved to play with his companions, observed that, by tying a string from the handle of the valve which opened this communication to another part of the machine, the valve would open and shut without his assistance, and leave him at liberty to divert himself with his playfellows. One of the greatest improvements that has been made upon this machine, since it was first invented, was in this manner the discovery of a boy who wanted to save his own labour.[2]

Smith's story is not only an interesting reversal of where technological change comes from, it is also its own little "autonomist hypothesis," making resistance and the refusal of work the engine of technological change. More importantly, its idyllic scene of little

---

1 John Locke, *The Second Treatise on Government*, Indianapolis: Hackett, 1980, 9.
2 Adam Smith, *The Wealth of Nations*, Book One Chapter One, https://www.marxists.org/reference/archive/smith-adam/works/wealth-of-nations/book01/ch01.htm

boys rushing to join their friends omits an important fact: if this kid was working on a fire engine it was probably because he, or his family, needed the money. Smith does not mention that this kid has invented himself out of a job (as well as others). Whereas Locke rushed ahead, providing a conclusion without premises, or an answer before the question was asked, Smith's is more of an omission, a cause without an effect. In each case the symptom exists in the gap between the idea and its reality.

I do not think that it is an accident that both of these texts are part of the philosophical justification of capitalism. Capitalism perhaps more than any other mode of production is caught between its ideals, such as "freedom, equality, and Bentham," and its reality, exploitation. Any attempt to identify it with an ideal, whether it be an egalitarian ideal of property in the case of Locke or a universality of entrepreneurial creativity and invention in the case of Smith, is necessarily going to come up against the reality that undermines those ideals, specifically that property is founded upon disappropriation for many and that the progress brought about by technological inventions and improvements of production often manifests itself as precarity and insecurity for large numbers of workers. That reality, the reality which undermines the egalitarian ideal, does not appear directly but can only manifest itself as a symptom.

In each case these are particular Althusser effects, and I cannot claim that they are adequate or wholly faithful to his thought, but, it was Althusser who argued that a philosophy in some sense exists in its effects, in the openings it makes possible in thought.

For more on Althusser and his theory of ideology see: Immanent Cause: Between Reproduction and Nonreproduction.

Presented in Santiago, Chile

Immanent Cause: Between Reproduction and Nonreproduction

Originally posted in February of 2017.

Of all the various provocations in *Lire le Capital* there is perhaps none more provocative than structural causality. In this case the provocation can be measured in the gap between the implications of the concept, its effects on social relations, subjectivity, and history, and its formulation, which is provisional and partial—mutilated as Spinoza might say. Structural or metonymic causality posits that the economy and society, base and superstructure, is neither a linear transitive cause, nor a relation of expression, but a cause which only exists in and through its effects. Or, put otherwise, the effects of the economy in the spheres of ideology must be thought of as causes as much as effects, as conditions of its reproduction. Framed in this way the concept of "structural (or immanent) causality" is not just a concept limited to its appearance in *Lire le Capital*, but it becomes integral to Althusser's later examination of ideology and reproduction. Reproduction is the necessary condition for seeing ideology as not just an effect of economic structures but their necessary precondition. Reproduction is another way of viewing the immanent nature of the mode of production, how its effects in the sphere of subjectivity and social relations, become necessary conditions. Althusser's writing shows a different trajectory, not only did reproduction become the specific theme of *Sur la Reproduction*, but the manuscripts on "aleatory materialism" also return to reproduction, thinking necessity from contingency, as the becoming necessary of the encounter. It is a matter of thinking the coexistence of reproduction and non-reproduction, which is to say class struggle, without resorting to a voluntarist conception of political action. Non-reproduction must be as immanent as reproduction, the conditions of the unraveling of a given mode of production must be as integral to it as its perpetuation. It is this trajectory which has been taken up by subsequent readers of not only Althusser, but of Spinoza and Marx as well.

From Immanent Causality to Reproduction

In order to make this argument it is necessary to first to think through not just the points of contiguity of structural causality and reproduction, the overlap of their respective problems and articulation, but also the manner in which they redefine and transform each other. In doing so it must acknowledge both the heterogeneity of the different interventions, arguments, and concepts, and the overall organization of their logic. This is true of not only *Lire le Capital*, which is made up of different interventions, and different authors, but of Althusser's later texts, defined as is often the case, by their intervention in a specific conjuncture.

Immanent, structural, or metonymic causality appears in Althusser's contribution to *Lire le Capital*, under a barrage of names and conceptual fields, names and concepts ranging from the history of philosophy to psychoanalysis. This barrage is framed in response to particular problem: "…with what concept are we to think the determination of either an element or a structure by a structure."[1] In some sense the definition here is primarily negative. The mode of production cannot be thought in terms of a transitive causality, as a

---

1 Louis Althusser The Object of *Capital*," trans. Ben Brewster in Louis Althusser et al, *Reading Capital*, New York: Verso, 2015, 343.

linear transmission of cause to effect, or of a whole that is expressed in the entirety of its effects, as kind of cultural zeitgeist, permeating everything in equal measure. Spinoza is named to give this term its clarity and lineage. "…it implies that the structure is immanent in its effects in the Spinozist sense of the term, that the whole existence of the structure consists in its effects, in short that the structure, which is merely a specific combination of its peculiar elements, is nothing outside its effects."[2] Following both the spirit and letter of the invocation of Spinoza, we could say that the mode of production, the economy, does not exist as a simple cause, standing outside and above the social relations that it determines, but exist only in and through its effects.

As much as this section constitutes a rupture, and a theoretical revolution, it is theoretical revolution that is uneven its effects even in terms of Marx's writing, let alone Marxism. Althusser spends the remaining pages of the section detailing the extent to which Marx falls behind his own revolution, returning to concepts of essence and appearance, of a linear distinction between cause and effect. Not the least in this list of uneven and incomplete development is the concept of commodity fetishism. As Althusser argues fetishism is all too often reduced to simply to "subjective effects produced in the economic subjects by their place in the process, their site in the structure."[3] However, Marx also asserts that this appearance is not subjective, but objective through and through, a structure determined by other structures and not simply the effect of the economy, of isolated commodity producers, on subjectivity. To which we could add that not only are they not just subjective, they are not simply effects; the appearance of the commodity, is as much a cause, a condition of the capitalist mode of production, as an effect. Thus, Marx's "immense theoretical revolution" entails not just a rethinking of causality, but also the categories of essence and appearance, subjective and objective. These conceptual categories

---

2 Louis Althusser The Object of *Capital* 344.
3 Louis Althusser The Object of *Capital* 347.

and distinctions come apart in the face of another problem, less to do with the history of philosophy and its concepts, and more specific to the problem at hand, and that is the distinction between production and reproduction.

It is Etienne Balibar's contribution to *Lire le Capital* that makes this connection between reproduction and structural causality explicit. Balibar picks up on one of Marx's most provocative formulations, that the process of production is a double production, producing things, commodities, and producing and reproducing social relations as well. This relation, Balibar argues, must be understood as a disjunction more than a conjunction. Production, the production of things, has a fundamentally different causality and temporality than the production of social relations. As Balibar writes, "There are two concepts, the concept of the 'appearance' and the concept of the effectivity of the structure of the mode of production."[4] Production is what we see, it conforms to our quotidian experience of temporality, it is the temporality and experience of the transitive causality of the working day, which is to say the phenomenological experience in capitalism. In contrast to this reproduction is a different temporality and different causality; it has always already begun, its beginning is its end, Reproduction does not just exceed the temporal conditions of the living present. It also exceeds the confines of the economic instance. Reproduction implies the effects of the non-economic conditions of production, law, the state, the police, etc. on the conditions of production. Reproduction demands thinking the intersection of different elements, different structures, the effect of which also constitutes a cause, and vice versa. It is with respect to reproduction that the extent that the immense theoretical revolution of immanent causality becomes clear.

Everything that Balibar asserts in his contribution to *Lire Le Capital*, reproduction as reproduction of relations, and the temporal and conceptual shift from production, (even Marx's

---

4 Etienne Balibar, "On the Basic Concepts of Historical Materialism," trans. Ben Brewster in Louis Althusser et al, *Reading Capital*, New York: Verso, 2015, 439.

letter to Kugelman), is repeated in Althusser's famous essay on "Ideology and Ideological State Apparatuses" and the manuscript *Sur la Reproduction*. What Althusser stresses in this context is not the theoretical innovation of immanent causality, but the difficulty of arriving at the perspective of reproduction. Every day daily consciousness is mired in the temporal condition of production, and, we could add the causal conditions of transitive causality, seeing only serial repetition and the immediate causality of proximate causes. As Althusser writes:

> "The tenaciously self-evident truths (the empiricist kind of ideological self-evident truths) of the point of view of production alone, or even of simple productive practice (which is itself abstract with respect to the process of production), are so much a part of our everyday consciousness' that it is extremely difficult, not to say practically impossible, to rise to the standpoint of reproduction. Yet, outside this standpoint, everything remains abstract (not just one-sided, but distorted). That holds even at the level of production and, a fortiori, at the level of simple practice."[5]

One could argue that this is the same problem, that of immanent causality, grasped from the other side, not from the concept but from experience. Quotidian experience is defined by its limited perspective in the structure, unable to grasp the structural conditions that situate and determine it. As much as Althusser's writing on reproduction continues and expands the concept, and conceptual revolution, of immanent causality, it also adds, or further extends, a particular structure that reproduces the structure. In *Lire le Capital*, Althusser only made a brief allusion to the "objective," which is to say structural dimension of the subjective attitude of fetishism. Now, in this latter text, ideology, of the ideological apparatus, is the proper name of the objective production of subjectivity, or, to use a less awkward term,

---

5 Louis Althusser, *On the Reproduction of Capitalism* translated by G.M. Goshgarian, New York: Verso, 2014, 47.

the structural effect and condition of other structures. As Etienne Balibar sums up Althusser's innovation as follows.

> Instead of adding a theory of the "superstructure" to the existing theory of the structure, he aims at transforming the concept of the structure itself by showing that its process of "production" and "reproduction" originally depends on unconscious ideological conditions. As a consequence a social formation is no longer representable in dualistic terms—a thesis that logically should lead us to abandon the image of the "superstructure". Another concept of historical complexity must be elaborated, with opposite sociological, anthropological, and ontological prerequisites.[6]

This other concept is perhaps immanent causality, but as we will see below, this is not without further problems and qualifications. In some sense the provocation exceeds its conceptualization. What immanent causality destroys, the division between cause and effect, base and superstructure, before and after, the immense theoretical revolution, exceeds the concepts constructed in its place. The partial and provisional nature of Althusser's own solution, the manuscript on reproduction is only a partial and incomplete response to the problem.

Reproducing Marxist Spinozism

If *Lire le Capital* initiates a generation of Marxist-Spinozists, a list that includes not only direct descendants such as Etienne Balibar and Pierre Macherey, but also two generations of thinkers across Europe, US, and the world, it does so precisely through the provisional and incomplete nature of its formulation. It is possible to see Althusser's remarks on "immanent causality" and reproduction as stretched between two theses, or aspects of Spinoza's thought: the immanent causality of nature, and what Althusser terms the opacity of the immediate, the imagination as the degree zero of thought and

---

6 Etienne Balibar, "The Non-Contemporaneity of Althusser." in *The Althusserian Legacy*, Edited by E. Ann Kaplan and Michael Sprinker. London: Verso, 1993, 8.

perception. These aspects are related, in Althusser's thought as much as Spinoza's, defining the poles of science and ideology. This relation, in all of its aspects, constitutes the defining problem of Althusser's thought throughout the seventies. However, I am interested in diverging from that problem here, and trying to think through the relation between immanent causality, reproduction, and subjectivity.

As something of a belated response to Althusser's provocation, a recent generation of Marxist-Spinozists Frédéric Lordon, and Chantal Jaquet have developed both a Spinozist theory of reproduction and non-reproduction. Starting with Lordon it is possible to see something that is fateful to the spirit, if not the letter of Althusser's provocation. Like Althusser, Lordon sees Spinoza as answering a question posed by Marx, as being the necessary complement rather than influence of Marx's thought. Only this problem is not causality, but reproduction itself: why do workers work for capital rather for their own liberation? Lordon answers this question by turning to what could be roughly called Spinoza's anthropology, the account of the affects and desire developed in Part Three of the Ethics. As much as this turn, this anthropology, can be understood as a turn away from Althusser, placing the question of the human or humanity at the center of its conceptualization of reproduction, Lordon does so in a manner that invokes the spirit if not the letter of immanent causality. As Lordon writes, "We do not merely live in a capitalist economy, but in a capitalist society."[7] (Capital must be understood not just as an economy, a single instance of the social structure that has effects on other elements of society, but is itself the totality of society or the immanent in its effects.) These two conceptions, totality or immanent cause, are not at all identical, but Lordon does not leave much on how to choose which concept is operative. His point is more fundamental. Capital, like every other social structure, can only exist if it reproduces itself not just at the level of economic structure, or even legal and political institutions but at the level of desires.

---

7 Frédéric Lordon, *Willing Slaves of Capital: Spinoza and Marx on Desire*, Translated by Gabriel Ash, New York: Verso 2014, 86.

As Lordon argues, humans beings, like everything else, are defined by a fundamental striving, the conatus, but this striving is intransitive, without a given object or a goal. The determination of the striving, the assigning of particular objects and goals, is the history of the different encounters and relations. If something is perceived to increase joy or sadness it will be either desired or shunned accordingly. Spinoza primarily considered this history as an individual history, or biography; a history of one's encounters and relations defining a particular character or ingenium, to use a word that will become important in the pages to follow. Character, habit, or ingenium, that which we strive for and struggle against is determined in part by a history of an often forgotten and overlooked history of encounters. Lordon adds a historical and social dimension to this formation of character. The reason money, as Spinoza argues, "occupies the mind of multitude more than anything else" is that there is no object, no desire, that is not conjoined with the image or idea of money. Far from a theoretical binary which posits individual striving, or interest, opposed to social forces, Lordon argues that Spinoza's geometry of the affects makes it possible to recognize that social forces exist on in and through individual striving and vice versa, what he terms "energetic structuralism." As Lordon writes,

> Collective human life reproduces itself, or begins to change solely as a consequence of the interplay of people's inter-affections, or, to say this in the simplest way possible, out of the effect they have on one another, but always through the mediations of institutions and social relations.[8]

Society exists only in and through its individualized affects; or, to put it differently, individual striving, the joys and sadness of individual life, exist only in and through social relations.

As much as Lordon's mention of a capitalist society mirrors without invoking a kind of immanent causality, it does so on a terrain that

---

8 Frédéric Lordon, *Willing Slaves of Capital*, 138.

is ambiguously historicist. The center of Lordon's argument is a progressive development of the colinearization of desire. At its first stage, that of primitive accumulation, all that is required for the reproduction of capital is the foreclosure of any non-capitalist alternative, the destruction of the commons or non-commodified conditions of reproduction. It is fear, the fear of starvation that compels the reproduction of capital. The increase of consumer society transforms this condition. One works no longer just to avoid starvation but to acquire objects of desire. Fordism is not just a new method of production, or a new regime of acquisition, but a new organization of desire. Finally, and this is the real object of Lordon's critique, the third organization of desire, that of neoliberalism, organizes happiness and desire, the joyful affects, are no longer found in the consequence of work, the objects of consumption, but are found in the activity itself. This is the mantra of contemporary neoliberalism, that, in the words of Steve Jobs, "the only way to do great work is to love what you do." It is this last regime of desire that tolerates no deviation, no gap between the striving of the individual and that of the capitalist enterprise, reducing every individual to "companies of one" that work harder the more they seek their desire and satisfaction in work itself. It is at this point that capital becomes immanent with the historical field. Lordon, however, is ambiguously historicist on this point. Ambiguous first because his remarks about capital are divided between a general anthropology in which every society, every mode of production, reproduces itself through the organization of desire, and a specific critique of contemporary capitalism as demanding a specific colinearization of desire. This ambiguity can be turn back onto Althusser's text as well. Given Althusser's argument about the historical legacy of Spinoza's discovery of immanent causality, its emergence and eclipse, it is possible to ask why does the concept return in the mid-sixties? Perhaps, and this can only be a provocation, the capitalist mode of production appears more "immanent" more dependent upon its effects in the emergent consumer society of France in the sixties than in Marx's time when capital was still emerging from its pre-capitalist conditions, still dependent on the state to destroy pre-capitalist relations. Immanent causality is not explicitly theorized with respect to its historical moment, the moment of real subsumption, but it bares traces of its historical period.

Without intending to Lordon's schema of three different regimes returns us to Althusser's critique of historicism: it seems both necessary and obvious to argue that the three regimes of desire Lordon articulates must coexist in some sense in the same historical conjuncture, there are obviously people compelled to work out of fear of starvation working alongside individuals motivated by consumer goods as well those searching for their dream job. This is not just true globally, but locally as well: you could find all three in the same coffee shop, where busing tables coexists alongside of networking. Or, more to the point, these same articulations of desire would coexist even in the same individual, in the same compulsion to return to work the same day, which would be another way of asserting the ambivalence of the affects. Which in turn raises the more difficult problem of how to think together immanent causality and the differential temporality of the historical conjuncture: the former suggests a kind of self-identity of capital producing and reproducing itself while the later posits every historical moment as torn between different temporalities, as absolutely not self-identical.

Lordon traverses the same basic problems of Althusser, but with fundamental differences, of what could be called its philosophical anthropology and historicism. Or rather he introduces both an anthropological reading of Spinoza, focusing on conatus and the affects as the articulation of human striving, and a historicist reading of immanent causality, understood in terms of the different historical articulation of desire. It could be possible to see this as a step back of sorts. However, there is a bit at least one step forward in this step back. Lordon's turn towards the affects expands our understanding of the immance of immanent causality, reminding us that such a cause must be extended to its intimately lived effects. Capital is not just immanent to the state, the law, and politics, but to our desires and dreams. Reproduction of the relations of production are as much about the reproduction of desires, as they are ideology or an imagination. The conatus has to be understood as structured and structuring, structured by the history of encounters and affects, and structuring in the sense that its desires are what animate and give rise to institutions, economy, etc. Every child knows that an institution that is not in some sense passionately lived would not last a day. What Lordon foregrounds is the intimacy of immanent causality, the extent to which the economy, capital, is not just an economic structure, or even ideology, but an organization of striving, of desire. Framed in this way it is possible to understand the connection between the step forwards and backwards. The more immanent causality is brought into the intimate space of subjectivity, the more subjectivity is seen as not just an effect but also a cause, the more it seems possible to see this causality as a closed circle, as capital endlessly reproducing itself by producing the subjects that desire it. Immanent causality risks reproducing a historicism that goes far beyond the expressive variety.

Aleatory Reproductions

Here the later Althusser offers something as a response. Althusser's later writing is most often celebrated for its return to the event, to contingency, but as Althusser argues, a reconsideration of contingency of the event cannot be separated from a reconsideration of necessity. As Althusser writes, "Instead of thinking contingency as a modality of necessity, or an exception to it, we must think necessity as the becoming necessary of the encounter of contingencies."[9] Everything would seem to rest then, on how we understand this becoming necessary, how necessity or at least the appearance of necessity emerges in a world of contingency. The political philosophers that Althusser engages with, Machiavelli, Rousseau, and Marx all offer different answers, and these different answers constitute the bulk of their political philosophy. For Machiavelli this necessity

---

9 The Underground Current of the Materialism of the Encounter. " in *The Philosophy of the Enounter: Later Writings*, 1978–1987. Trans. G.M. Goshgarian. New York: Verso, 2016, 193.

is identified with the figure of the prince: the contingent event, the prince seizing power, can sustain itself or maintain itself if the prince possesses sufficient virtú, is skillful enough to manage his appearance amongst the people, the affects of hatred and fear, then his power will last. For Rousseau, whose *Discourse on the Origin of Inequality*, puts forward the audacious thesis of the "radical absence of society as the essence of society," the becoming necessary of society is constituted by the increased specialization and hierarchy constituted by society itself. Once instituted society becomes its own rationale: "[A]s soon as one man needed the help of another, as soon as one man realized that it was useful for a single man to have provisions for two, equality disappeared, property came into existence, labor became necessary."[10] For Marx the becoming necessary of the contingent encounter of workers and capitalists is the transition from the early stage of primitive accumulation, in which force of the state is necessary to turn displaced farmers into workers, to full development of capitalism in which the force of the state is replaced by the mute compulsion of economic relations. As Marx writes, "The silent compulsion of economic relations sets the seal on the domination of the capitalist over the worker. Direct extra-economic force is still of course used, but only in exceptional cases."[11] Commodity production and wage labor become their own reciprocal justifications. Becoming necessary, the transformation of the encounter into something necessary, is considered in terms of social dependency, political strategy, and economic compulsion. Politics, society, and economics, three figures of becoming necessary that in most accounts would be differentiated, distinguished by their relative degrees of necessity, are considered to be simply different versions of the same general problem, of the becoming necessary of the contingent encounter. They are not just the same problem, but they also come together insofar as they are subjectified, internalized.

---

10 Jean Jacques Rousseau, *Discourse on the Origin of Inequality*, Translated by Donald Cress, Indianapolis: Hackett, 1992, 51.
11 Karl Marx, *Capital: A critique of political economy, Volume I*. Translated by Fowkes. New York: Penguin, 1977, 899

Rousseau, Machiavelli, and Marx can also be considered as three different modes and temporalities of reproduction. Rousseau underscores the fundamental fact of social relations reproducing themselves; once one lives in a society, a society defined by the division of labor and dependency, its very existence acts as a compulsion to reproduce itself. The social order, the very division between farmer and blacksmith, is its own reproduction. In contrast to this Machiavelli underscores the political dimension of reproduction, the way in which the state reproduces its own authority. An authority that is reproduced through the figure of the Prince the representation of state power with its corresponding myths and affective constitution of love and fear. Finally, Marx underscores the economic basis of reproduction, the way in which anonymous and seemingly natural institutions of the economy reproduce themselves. If this three aspects can cohere, forming a massive "society effect" in which society, politics, and economy all not only cohere, but also reinforce each other, social norms, political rule, and economic relations all "playing the same score," constituting a massive monolith of reproduction, they do so only insofar as that score is played, individually lived and desired. Or, more accurately, the score is transindividual, constituting the basis for individual and collective experience. It is because the structure must be lived to be reproduced, and reproduced to be lived, that it can always unravel as much as sustain itself.

Chantal Jaquet argues that nonreproduction must be considered as a necessary corollary to reproduction. In order to clarify what she means by nonreproduction it is necessary to clarify that Jaquet takes as her object precisely what is occluded from both sides of a certain ideological divide. On the one side there the various theorists of reproduction, from Althusser to Bourdieu, who examine the way in which social institutions from the school to the family necessarily reproduce the relations of production. Opposed to this there is a different discourse of not only a different political orientation, conservative or right rather than Marxist, but of a different epistemological register, more anecdotal than theoretical, that asserts the non-reproduction of these relations through the stories of individuals of humble beginnings who have made it rich, or have otherwise crossed the divides of the economic, racial, or gendered order. Against this division, which posits non-reproduction as unthinkable on one-side, as something which does not happen, and as the necessary truth of human agency, on the other, Jaquet argues that non-reproduction must be thought not just in its singularity but in terms of its structural conditions. The structural conditions of non-reproduction are the same as the structural conditions of reproduction, but thought in terms of their tensions and conflicts rather than their overlap and intersection.

Non-reproduction must be thought in and in through the singular and overdetermined nature of the particular strivings, the particular complexion that defines not just each individual but their relation to their class. Turning to Spinoza Jaquet borrows the term ingenium to theorize this complexion, the intersection of social relations and individual desires. As Jaquet writes,

> "Ingenium could be defined as a complex of sedimented affects constitutive of an individual, her way of life, judgments, and behavior. It is rooted in the dispositions of the body, and comprises physical and mental ways of being alike."[12]

The different factors that constitute a particular complexion carry with them the particular class relations actualized in multiple different ways of speaking, acting, feeling, etc. Class is not just something that exists as an economic relation, defined by one's relation to the means of production, nor is it simply defined by ideology, it goes much deeper than either term suggests, becoming something felt and carried in the body. It is the effect of and the reproduction of multiple different factors, economic, ideological, social, and political.

---

12 Chantal Jaquet, *Transclasses: A Theory of Social Non-Reproduction*, Translated by Gregory Elliot, New York: Verso, 2023, 76.

But these factors are different, maintaining their distinct relations and causality: ideological, affective, and other aspects of class can cohere and not cohere in a given conjuncture, and a given individual. One finds an echo of Spinoza's assertion that only ideas can determine ideas, and only bodies can determine bodies, and the identity and difference of minds and bodies, ideologies and affects, is central to Jaquet's concept of ingenium. The multiple factors of the ingenium, minds and bodies, ideas and affects, cannot be the effect of a single cause because they have different causal conditions. Thus, Jaquet's work constitutes an important rejoinder to Lordon, rather than see the linear causality of the economy on the conatus of the individual, shaping and determining a particular subjectivity which is nothing other than the reproduction of a particular mode of accumulation, it is necessary to grasp the multiple factors, ideas and comportments as much as affects, that constitute a particular complexion.

Here Althusser's writings on aleatory reproduction and Jaquet on non-reproduction intersect, albeit roughly. Whereas Althusser posits the heterogeneity of the structure, of the different modalities of becoming necessary, a heterogeneity tied to the different instances of social, economic, and political dimensions of reproduction, Jaquet asserts the heterogeneity of the individual complexion or ingenium. These two heterogeneities overlap, but are not identical. Or, to be more precise, structural causality, the causality of structures upon structures, necessitates that the ingenium of the individual must be thought in terms of its relation and nonrelation, the relation and non-relation of ideas and affects, concepts and comportments (thus we see that the reference to Spinoza, and to the different causality of ideas and things, was perhaps not so out of place in Althusser's writing on aleatory materialism) The identity and difference of ideas and affects, social relations and political representations, relates ultimately to the identity and difference of reproduction and nonreproduction of a particular mode of production. To twist a phrase from Antonio Gramsci, we could say that the modern individual is composed of elements of the most primitive social relation, the state form, and the market, as well as elements of oppositions and tensions of all three. The historical heterogeneity of the given conjuncture is also the heterogeneity of the ingenium of individuals composing and sustaining it, and vice versa.

Conclusion

While Lordon's thought can be understood as a particular logical culmination of Althusser, or more to the point, the drawing of a conclusion of the points of Marx and Spinoza that Althusser suggests but does not develop, it does so in a manner that is, to an extent uneven, revealing limits as much as insights. Lordon's energetic structuralism can be understood as the completion of structural causality, positing that the effects of a structure must be thought down to the intimacy of desire. However, in doing so Lordon reveals the tension between structural causality, understood as reproduction, and differential temporality, understood as historical transformation. Jaquet's work offers the necessary corrective. If it is necessary to supplement Spinozist causality with a Spinozist anthropology, that anthropology must be one of the overdetermination of both individual and collective ingenium, or of the transindividual basis of each. The differential historicity does not just encompass those grand institutions and apparatuses, the state, law, and even capital, that carry with them their bloody origins, current contradictions, and future possibilities, but the more mundane and quotidian aspects of desire, knowledge, and comportment that define a particular individual's life as well. Against the apparent monolith that makes capital seem as inevitable as fate we must seek to see the intertwining of reproduction and nonreproduction that defines every conjuncture, every individuation, every social relation.

Images from Black Panther and Crew (Marvel Comics)

Anti-Aesthetics: Or, Towards a Spinozist Theory of Cultural Production

Originally posted in March of 2016.

In all of the various attempts to produce and reproduce Spinozism, creating a Spinozist account of society, economy, and politics, little attention has been paid to Spinoza's aesthetics. Spinoza's aesthetics could be considered more of a meta-aesthetics or even anti-aesthetics, since its fundamental orientation is to put into question the idea of aesthetic judgement, the idea that our ideas of beautiful or ugly, order or disorder, have any autonomous basis or ground. This anti-aesthetics is sketched between a few scattered propositions, scholium, and other remarks that address the basis of judgements of taste and value, at every point it shows that any aesthetics is at best an inadequate idea, making effects into causes, and at worst a kind of alienation.

First, there is Spinoza's reversal of the fundamental nature of value in judgement. As Spinoza writes in the Scholium to Proposition Nine of Part Three of the *Ethics*.

> "From all this, then, it is clear that we neither strive for, nor will, neither want, nor desire anything because we judge it to be good; on the contrary we judge something to be good because we strive for it, will it, want it, and desire it."[1]

This particular Scholium has taken on central importance in the neo-spinozisms of Lordon and Citton. For them it displaces any remnant of methodological individualism, the idea that individual desires have some kind of autonomy or primacy. Desire is as much an effect, a product of other affects and relations, as it is a cause, a fundamental aspect of striving. Or, put in terms related to aesthetics and aesthetic judgement, how and what we judge must be considered an effect not an autonomous origin.

To open a parentheses on Marx and Spinoza (yet again) it is possible to consider this passage on the production of desire, the production of consumption, along with Marx's formulation in the *Grundrisse*. As Marx writes,

> "Hunger is hunger, but the hunger gratified by cooked meat eaten with a knife and fork is a different hunger from that which bolts down raw meat with the aid of hand, nail and tooth. Production thus produces not only the object but also the manner of consumption, not only objectively but also subjectively. Production thus creates the consumer."[2]

Returning to *Ethics* IIIP9 and the reversal of desire and judgement is worth noting that this reversal follows a proposition that asserts that the mind's striving is radically indifferent to the distinction between adequate and inadequate ideas. Spinoza would agree with Aristotle that we all strive for something we call good, but disagree in the sense that "good" for Spinoza is just an effect of previous encounters and relations. As Spinoza writes in the Preface to Part IV, "What is called a final cause is nothing but a human appetite insofar

---

[1] Benedict de Spinoza, *Ethics*, Translated by Edwin Curley, New York, Penguin, 1994, EIII9Schol.
[2] Karl Marx, *The Grundrisse*, Translated by Martin Nicolaus, New York: Penguin, 1973, 92.

as it is considered as a principle, or primary cause, of some thing."

That Proposition does not begin the "anti-aesthetics" that runs throughout the *Ethics*. It actually begins in the Appendix of Part One where Spinoza argues that the fundamental categories of order/disorder, beautiful/ugly, etc. reveal nothing about what we perceive, but reflect the confused desires of the one who judges.

> "And because those who do not understand the nature of things, but only imagine them, affirm nothing concerning things, and take the imagination for the intellect, they firmly believe, in their ignorance of things, and of their own nature, that there is an order in things."

This argument is resumed in the Preface to Part IV, where Spinoza foregrounds the pragmatic dimension of all judgments of value. All judgements of good or bad, order and disorder, perfect and imperfect stem from a model that is either openly asserted or implied.

> "But after men began to form universal ideas, and devise models of houses, buildings, towers, and the like, and to prefer some models of things to others, it came about that each one called perfect what he saw agreed with the universal idea he formed of this kind of thing, and imperfect, what he saw he agreed less with the model he had conceived, even though its maker thought he had entirely finished it."

Anti-Aesthetics

Pierre Macherey's overlooked (and poorly translated) *For a Theory of Literary Production* takes up Spinoza's Anti-Aesthetics, explicitly citing Spinoza's critique of the model as the basis for aesthetic judgement. As Macherey writes,

> "In this sense, all criticism can be summed up as a value judgment in the margin of the book: "could do better." Glimpsing but never attaining this "better," it looks beyond the real work to its dream image. There can be no doubt that this legality is merely reactive, valuable only as a defense, affirming this hypothetical distance between the fact and the law, the work and its norm, solely in order to secure and maintain its own function. But this is only a temporary defeat for empiricism. Both the 'taste' which acts no questions and the 'judgement' which dispenses with scruples are closely related. The naive consumer and the harsh judge are finally collaborators in a single action.
>
> There is only one true difference between them, and this will appear later: the empiricist critic wants to be the author's accomplice, he believes that the work can only emerge under the pressure of participation; the judge on the other hand, would set himself up to instruct the writer, claiming a clearer vision of his intention, pointing out his carelessness, evading the delays of a real production in his impatience for the essential."[3]

I was led to these thoughts by three different causal relations: first, I am teaching Spinoza this semester, second, I picked up Macherey's book off my shelf and started rereading some passages, and lastly, and more aleatory, *Black Panther*. I am not going to blog about *Black Panther*, everything I would say has already been said (and then some), and the last thing the world needs is another white dude's opinion on the film. However, it did strike me that many of the criticisms of the film, and appreciations are framed in response

---

3 Pierre Macherey, *A Theory of Literary Production*, Translated by Geoffrey Wall, London: Routledge, 1978, 16.

to a model (an ideal) that it did or did not live up to A point made clearly and succinctly by the following tweet.

TORMABLAIEFDHZSJKLNBDS...
@Tormny_Pickeals

Black Panther was a fine movie but its politics were a bit iffy. wouldve been way better if at the end the Black Panther turned to the camera & said "i am communist now" & then specified hes the exact kind of communist i am

2/19/18, 9:34 AM

There are of course reasons, which is to say multiple causes, as to why *Black Panther* in particular elicits so many competing models, so many ways it ought to be. First of all there is a kind of narrative scarcity when it comes to black superheroes, or heroes; white superheroes come in multiple modes from the dark and gritty, *Logan*, to the light and family friendly, *Ant-Man*. There is perhaps less variety with respect to politics, most superheroes being part of a fantasy of crime control through private vigilantes, but one could still make a distinction between Batman's privately funded fascism and Spider-Man's friendly neighborhood watch. *Black Panther* is the only film about a black superhero. It is also that situates its narrative firmly within multiple aspects of the black diaspora. The film intersects with so many liberatory desires from the reformist ideals of inclusion and diversity to the more radical possibilities disclosed by its afrofuturistic design and the character's more radical namesake. Given this plurality of desires and ideals it is no wonder that the film has been alternately lambasted and celebrated. Many of the debates and discussions about the film were less about the film as a film than its failure to correspond to some critic's ideal, some model of what it should be. Which is not to simply criticize all these idealizations, these longings and expectations, they are real strivings even if they inadequately expect to glean utopian content from part of the ever expanding Marvel universe.

The question remains, however, is there some other way to think about this film. Macherey's response, and I am simplifying greatly, is to shift from consumption to production, to focus not on the right way to consume a cultural product but how it was produced. Not production in the literal and limited sense of the term, as in the behind the scenes look at effects, rewrites, and rehearsals. Which is not to say that it wouldn't be interesting to learn more about those conditions, finding out if the studio insisted on a bigger role for T'Challa's CIA sidekick, Everett Ross, or if Ryan Coogler had planned to end the film with T'Challa and Killmonger teaming up to overthrow colonialism before the studio panicked. Unfortunately, we do not really have access to those details. We can however think its production more broadly as both determined and detourning (to sues the situationist term) of the larger political, economic, and social environment. In other words, it does not just reproduce this environment but transforms it as well. It is hard not to see *Black Panther* as not so much failing to realize some utopian dream but accurately reworking the ideological constraints of the present. On this point it is interesting to compare it to the recent run of *Black Panther and the Crew* which dealt with the same question (Wakanda's role in the larger struggle for black liberation) in a much less neoliberal vein but also with smaller sales (Marvel cancelled it after two issues). To cite Macherey once again (perhaps all I am doing is make an argument to reread *A Theory of Literary Production*), "The literary work must be studied in a double perspective: in relation to history, and in relation to an ideological version of that history."[4] This point could also be applied to film.

---

4 Pierre Macherey, *A Theory of Literary Production*, 115.

My point is not to simply acquiesce to the way of the world, to state cynically "what did you expect," but to assert that it might be more useful to grasp the real constraints underlying cinematic production rather than the failure to correspond to imagined models, or at the very least consider the two together.

For more on Spinoza, Aesthetics, and Macherey see Imagination, Fiction, Knowledge: Towards a Spinozist Theory of Cultural Production, Part II.

Pierre Macherey
A Theory of Literary Production

Imagination, Fiction, Knowledge: Towards a Spinozist Theory of Cultural Production Part II

Originally posted in March of 2022.

Spinoza is only mentioned in one sustained passage of Macherey's *A Theory of Literary Production* and like many of the passages in that book the significance of the passage in question entails a return to the original French edition.

There is a reference to Spinoza in Chapter 10 on Illusion and Fiction. The first part is as follows:

> "To understand this ordinary condition of language, let us borrow from Spinoza's description of passionate life: desire is applied to an imaginary object and expresses itself fluently, lost in the pursuit of an absence, distracted from its own presence; an inadequate, incomplete, torn and empty discourse flinging itself into the quest for an excluded centre, unable to construct the complete form of a contradiction; a line endlessly extended according to a false perspective. Desire lagging behind its own emptiness, deprived from the first, never appeased. Language in

> flight, running after a reality which it can only define negatively, speaking of order, liberty and perfection, the beautiful and the good, as well as chance and destiny. A delirium, speech bereft of its object, displaced from its own manifest meaning, not spoken by any subject: bewildered, forsaken, inconsistent; despairing throughout its dim fall. Existence comes to the individual in the form of a very primitive illusion, a true dream, which sets up a certain number of necessary images: man, liberty, the will of God. It is spontaneously defined by a spontaneous use of language which turns it into a shapeless riddles with wholes – a text that slides vigorously over itself, doing its utmost to say nothing, since it is not designed actually to say anything."[1]

A few things about this passage, the first but not necessarily the most important is that I had to modify the translation a bit to get it to work, and it could probably benefit from a more thorough translation, as could the whole book. Second, it is worth nothing that Macherey take up a particular dialectical turn of phrase from Althusser in which ideology, or in this case, the imagination, has to be seen as full because it is empty, without an outside because it is nothing but outside, speaks of everything because in the end it is only about its own lack. As with the case of Althusser's famous essay, the reference here is to the Appendix to Part One of the *Ethics*, specifically Spinoza's genealogy of such terms as order and disorder, good and bad, and so on. These terms, these final causes, are nothing other than the fundamental misrecognition of desires and needs, effects taken for causes.

As Macherey goes onto clarify, Spinoza's entire critical project is a matter of overcoming this language of the imagination, this understanding of the world in terms of final causes, replacing it with common notions. In clarifying this critical project Macherey introduces a third term which mediates between the imagination and reason and that is fiction, or aesthetic activity.

---

[1] Pierre Macherey, *A Theory of Literary Production*, Translated by Geoffrey Wall, London: Routledge, 1978, 63.

"Spinoza's notion of liberation involves a new attitude to language; the hollow speech of the imagination must be halted, anchored; the unfinished must be endowed with form, determined (even though the indeterminate depends on a certain kind of necessity, since it can be known). To effect this change, two sorts of activity are proposed: theoretical activity which, in assuring the passage to adequate knowledge, knowledge, affixes language to concepts; for Spinoza there is no other way; however, aesthetic activity, on which he is almost silent, also arrests language by giving it a limited—though unfinished—form. There is a profound difference between the vague language of the imagination and that of the text; within the limits of the text this language is in several senses deposed (at the same time denigrated, abandoned, and contemplated)."[2]

This is the object of Spinoza's theory of literary production; for Macherey literature, or aesthetic activity in general, acts on and transforms the illusions of the imagination by subjecting it to a particular form, or forms. These forms, that of literature itself, its different genres or themes, have a determination that is not that of the concept but nor is it the purely subjective form of the imagination.

Macherey ends that section by invoking the three different forms, three different uses of language, illusion, fiction, and theory, that although they use the same words are worlds apart, separated by an unbridgeable gap. Macherey's division does not correspond to the three types of knowledge in Spinoza; in effect it breaks the first kind of knowledge in two placing immediate experience under illusion and "knowledge from signs" under fiction. In some sense it is closer to Lacan's division between imaginary, symbolic, and real. The effects of this attempt to think of fiction as a third, situated between, ideology and theory continues through Macherey's later work. Macherey continues to consider literature as not just an object for theory, but a way of knowing the world distinct from philosophy and sociology. His studies of the university and everyday life consider the literature

---

2 Pierre Macherey, *A Theory of Literary Production*, 63.

on these topics to have their own specific insights and revelations.

In one of his most recent books *En Lisant Jules Verne*, Macherey opens with a question as to what extent we could understand a "literary mythology." As Macherey explains part of his interest in Verne is because of his role in giving a literary form to some of the defining ideas of modern ideology, tying together progress, technological innovation, exploration, and colonization. In that text Macherey turns to Spinoza again making it clear that even though Spinoza has little to say about aesthetic activity as such, and nothing resembling an aesthetics, he does have a lot to say about a particular literary mythology, that of a particular scriptural authority called superstition.

Illustration from 20,000 Leagues Under the Sea

Of course scripture as a particular mythology, or superstition, had a rather specific and determined set of restrictions and conditions for its dissemination and perpetuation. As Spinoza argues superstition is sustained by a restriction of what can be said. If its object is obedience that is not just because it produces obedience, but is also sustained by it, by the restriction of interpretations and experience that make it possible for the same signs and narratives to have the same resonance and meaning. Ingenium is both the cause and effect of the social order, both an effect of the social structures and conditions and the basis of their reproduction. The question after Spinoza would seem to be to what extent we can understand the production of this mythology in a society no longer sustained by a sacred text or a dominant interpretation. This is Yves Citton's question: what does myth look like in an age defined less by a central mythology than by the dissemination of multiple fictions of the culture industry.

For his part, at least in the book on Verne, Macherey defines modern myth by a kind of dialectic from Marx. First, there is the well-known, albeit somewhat odd statement regarding the end of myth. As Marx writes in the 1857 Introduction:

> "Let us take e.g. the relation of Greek art and then of Shakespeare to the present time. It is well known that Greek mythology is not only the arsenal of Greek art but also its foundation. Is the view of nature and of social relations on which the Greek imagination and hence Greek [mythology] is based possible with self-acting mule spindles and railways and locomotives and electrical telegraphs? What chance has Vulcan against Roberts and Co., Jupiter against the lightning-rod and Hermes against the Crédit Mobilier? All mythology overcomes and dominates and shapes the forces of nature in the imagination and by the imagination; it therefore vanishes with the advent of real mastery over them. What becomes of Fama alongside Printing House Square? Greek art presupposes Greek mythology, i.e. nature and the social forms already reworked in an unconsciously artistic way by the popular imagination. This is its material. Not any mythology whatever, i.e. not an arbitrarily chosen unconsciously artistic reworking of nature (here meaning everything objective, hence including society). Egyptian mythology could never have been the foundation or the womb of Greek art. But, in any case, a *mythology*. Hence, in no way a social development which excludes all mythological,

all mythologizing relations to nature; which therefore demands of the artist an imagination not dependent on mythology."³

This statement about the end of myth has to be read against another less known text, Marx's letter to Kugelmann from 1871. As Marx writes,

> "Up till now it has been thought that the growth of the Christian myths during the Roman Empire was possible only because printing was not yet invented. Precisely the contrary. The daily press and the telegraph, which in a moment spreads inventions over the whole earth, fabricate more myths (and the bourgeois cattle believe and enlarge upon them) in one day than could have formerly been done in a century."⁴

Between these two statements is the dialectic of contemporary myth, the very conditions that make its destruction possible,

---

3 Karl Marx, *The Grundrisse*, Translated by Martin Nicolaus, New York: Penguin, 1973, 110.
4 Karl Marx, Karl Marx to Ludwig Kugelmann 1871, https://www.marxists.org/archive/marx/works/1871/letters/71_07_27.htm#

the mastery of nature and the overcoming of ignorance, make its dissemination possible. This dialectic is possible because the conditions of the dissipation of ignorance are unevenly distributed, not everyone partakes in the same mastery of nature, and some are not only subordinated to it, but to a social world that they do not understand as well. If Marx painted us a picture of the mystery of how Greek myths could coexist with the locomotive then the mystery of our world is that of flat earth theories being beamed around the globe by satellite.

This is not much of a conclusion, and, to be honest, I have not finished the Verne book yet. The provocation that I wanted to retain here is the idea that we have to think of "literary mythology," or to some extent, the imaginary, as situated both between individual imagination and social knowledge, and between the conditions of its destruction, the demythologization of the world, and its remythologization through the culture industry.

For more on myth see Let Me Tell You of the Time That Something Occurred: On Yves Citton's Mythocratie for more on literary production see Anti-Aesthetics: Or, Towards a Spinozist Theory of Cultural Production.

Jason Read

La micropolítica del capital
Marx y la prehistoria del presente

I did not really have an image for this post, so I thought I would just plug the Spanish translation of my first book.

Nexus Rerum: Spinoza and Marx (again)

Originally posted in November of 2016.

> "...in the postindustrial age the Spinozan critique of representation of capitalist power corresponds more to the truth than does the analysis of political economy."
>
> – Antonio Negri[1]

The encounter of Spinoza and Marx is arguably one of the most productive encounters in contemporary philosophy. This encounter has several origins and multiple trajectories, its most recent wave begins with the works of Alexandre Matheron, Gilles Deleuze, and Louis Althusser, continuing into multiple waves, across different variants of Marxism and Spinozism. This encounter is not, as is often the case of the dominant forms of philosophical writing and research, a matter of discerning the influences that connect them, or the arguments that would divide them. It is rather an articulation of their fundamental points of intersection, points that are not simply given but must be produced by a practice of philosophy.

One such point of articulation is their shared materialism, materialism understood as the primacy of action to thought, of

---

1 Antonio Negri, "Reliqua Desiderantur: A Conjecture for a Definition of the Concept of Democracy in the Final Spinoza," translated by Ted Stolze, in *The New Spinoza*, T. Stolze and W.Montag eds. Minneapolis: University of Minnesota, 1997, 246 n. 21.

the order of bodies and relations to consciousness. This perhaps seems obvious in the case of Marx, whose formulation "Life determines consciousness, consciousness does not determine life" can be understood as one fundamental articulation of materialism. It is perhaps less obvious in the case of Spinoza, despite his supposed assertion of the identity of the order and connection of thought and extension, of ideas and things as two expressions of the infinite power of substance. However, Spinoza's materialism is not just to be found in his understanding of the ultimate constitutive order of the universe, but in the secondary status he ascribes to thought. We are, as Spinoza, argues, "born ignorant of the causes of things…and conscious of our appetite." Moreover, it so happens that the causes of our appetite is one of the first things that we are ignorant of, we think that we desire something because it is good, unable to grasp the experiences, the relations that cause us to call one thing good and another evil. There is in both Spinoza and Marx, a secondariness to consciousness, thought is not the act of subject mastering a world, but a secondary and derived effect of practices and relations, fundamentally unaware of its conditions.[2]

This basic materialist principle, "the secondariness of the consciousness," can be found not just at the level of their specific formulations, their ontologies and politics of history, but at the level of their particular practice of philosophy. I am thinking specifically of the end of the first chapter of *Capital*, the famous passage on the "Fetishism of Commodities and its Secret" and the Appendix to Part One of the *Ethics*. These texts are well known. The first has given us the concept of commodity fetishism, reification, and various criticisms that extend far beyond its specific engagement. The latter has been described by Althusser as the matrix of every possible theory of ideology, and has continued to act on the history of philosophy, albeit at a distance. Their influence cannot be ignored, separately and together they have formed the backdrop of much of the intersecting concepts of reification, the

---

2 Franck Fischbach, *Marx with Spinoza: Production, Alienation, History*, Translated by Jason Read, Edinburgh: Edinburgh University, 2023, 79.

imaginary, and ideology. Beyond or prior to this history, however, there is the specific role they play within their respective texts and arguments.

They can both be described as preemptive, preemptive in the sense that as much as they are situated within their particular arguments, discussing the particular problems of the commodity form and of the anthropological-theological imaginary, they necessarily come before their necessary philosophical conditions. Spinoza's text begins to expound something of the human tendency to see ourselves as a kingdom within a kingdom, before developing the fundamental propositions detailing knowledge, affects, and desire, which make up Parts III and IV of the *Ethics*. It is an anthropology that exists prior to the very conditions of developing the fundamental aspects of human intellectual and emotional life. Marx's text presents Robinson Crusoe, the medieval world, and the famous (but cryptic) free association of producers before developing the very idea of a mode of production, the social structure. This preemptive strike is in each case necessary: both Spinoza and Marx recognize that what they asserting goes against the prevailing common sense, the prevailing understanding of God or capitalism. They also recognize that the causes or conditions of this "spontaneous philosophy" are not ideas and propositions put forth by philosophers, but life, understood as causes and conditions for viewing a world in a determinate way. They are the point where each philosophy confronts its absolute enemy, its absolute outside, whether it be in the form of the entire anthropo-theological imaginary of a free subject and a teleologically oriented God or in the reified and ahistorical acceptance of exchange value. They are the point where the concept intersects with polemic, where an argument confronts the world and world view which is opposed to it.

What is confronted by each of these tests is less a specific philosophical position, or a figure from the history of philosophy, than an entire common sense or way of thinking. Both the section on "Commodity Fetishism" and the Appendix of Part One address the way in which the world necessarily appears to everyone, a common sense and not a canonical text. In the first case it appears to be made up of objects, commodities that possess value in and of themselves, independent of any human action. In the second case, that of Spinoza's critique of the anthropomorphic and teleological thought, there is the way in which the world appears, first as something exterior to us, as something that if it is governed at all it is regulated by an unknowable but human—all—too human god. Despite the difference of cause, a different that relates to the critique in each case, religion and political economy, each passage deals with the question of value, with the extent to which the value that a thing embodies in terms of its worth or merit, is itself a quality of a thing or a subjective state, a mode of imagining. Of course this might seem that I am simply equivocating with respect to the concept of value, vacillating between the ethical and economic meaning. (Although it is hardly my problem alone) What sustains this connection in this case is that for Spinoza and Marx value is neither found in the things themselves, as in the case of what Alexandre Matheron calls the objectivity of values, nor is it a purely subjective evaluation. Value is not an intrinsic quality, nor is it a purely subjective state. It is something produced by actions, structures, and relations. For both Marx and Spinoza value has to be thought in terms of its genesis, a genesis that includes the structures and relations that constitute it, and the way that it necessarily appears.

Which is to say that in each case, the world, the necessary appearance of things, encompasses a constitution of subjectivity. Subjectivity is posited at first as a cause. The values of objects, commodities, and the intentions of an unknowable God are initially sought because they meet our needs, or what we perceive to be our needs. However, as soon as they become instituted, as soon as the market and religion are constituted, their values are less the effects of actions than their causes. As Marx argues, to the workers, "their social action takes the form of the action of objects, which rule the producers instead of being ruled by them." A similar logic, in which the effect of an action is transformed into its cause, can be found in Spinoza's account of the progression from prejudice to superstition in the Appendix. Prejudice takes as its starting point the originary consciousness of desire and the ignorance of the causes of things, including our desire. Superstition is the transformation of this initial condition, its constitution into an explicit doctrine that not only reinforces this ignorance, but makes it foundational to the functioning of power, the priests and despots who interpret the signs and powers of this hidden God. As Spinoza argues in his political writings, superstition is not just a matter of doctrines and ideals, but practices, practices that constitute subjectivity in and through subjection. Subjectivity in terms of its needs and desires, is at first a cause, producing the basic conditions in which the economy or religion becomes necessary, but it ultimately becomes an effect, produced by these very institutions and structures.

To generalize perhaps too strongly, we could say that what these two texts offer is a critique of the mutual constitution of subjectivity and a world, or the institutions of the world. It is a matter of what Frédéric Lordon and André Orléan refer to as "immanent transcendance": the production, from the multitude, from collectivity, of a transcendent instance, state or an economy, through the various practices of the collectivity itself.[3] Which is not to say, despite the temptation Marx himself offers with his talk of fetishism and incense, that religion and the economy are the same, that the economy has become a new god, or something to that effect. Rather it is a matter of uncovering what is at stake in the rather forced overlapping of their respective problems, problems that are ultimately that of representation. Immanent transcendence is the way in which the effects of a given practice, of a subjective comportment appear as its cause. It is this, and not just some simple materialism, that is perhaps Marx and Spinoza's strongest point of convergence.

The points of divergence are no less instructive. In Spinoza's text the constitutive illusion is that of individual autonomy, which constitutes a kingdom within in a kingdom. This autonomy is in some sense mitigated by a world of goods, by objects which are seen as a good and bad, and supplemented by God, whose autonomy

---

3 Frédéric Lordon and André Orlean 2008, "Genèse de l'État et Genèse de la monnaie: le modele de la potential multitudios" in Yves Citton and Frédéric Lordon, *Spinoza et les sciences sociales: De la puissance de a multitude à l'économie des affects*, Paris: Éditions Amsterdam, 2008, 246

and intentionality fills the gap of my frustrations. In Marx's text the constitutive illusion is that of the object, of value; if the subject plays any role at all it is secondary, it is an effect of the reification of values and of its own subjective potential. At this point the divergences would appear to outweigh the communality, leaving only the basic, but not inconsequential, materialist priority of practices to representations as the only common ground. Given that Spinoza and Marx's critique is directed alternately at anthropocentrism as much as teleology, the objectivity of value as much as its subjectivity, to what extent could even their materialism be considered similar not at the level of what it critiques, but what it proposes? Cesare Casarino has offered something of a response to this question by focusing on a not inconsequential terminological similarity between the two texts. In the Appendix, Spinoza writes of the way in which the prejudices of anthropocentrism and teleology present an obstacle to men's understanding of the "concatenation of all things [rerum concatenationem]."[4] Casarino argues that this idea of immanence, or immanent causality, as the connection of all things, a connection without a privileged subject, object, or God at its center, matches both the spirit and the letter of Marx's thought. In spirit it matches Marx's general critique of capital, found most specifically in the section on primitive accumulation, where Marx counters the moralizing account of the thrift and greed with the multiple list of causes, from the slave trade to the reformation, that made capitalism possible: capital thought as the contingent encounter of all of world history. To the letter, Casarino indicates Marx's use of nexus of all things [nexus rerum] to describe exchange value. Spinoza and Marx are able to critique the seemingly disparate philosophies of anthropocentrism and bourgeois political economy because both fail to think the nexus rerum, the connection of things, in other words, immanence, by positing the subject, God, or the law like functioning of the economy as something which exists outside the

---

4 Cesare Casarino, "Marx Before Spinoza: Notes Toward an Investigation," in *Spinoza: Now*, Edited by Dimitris Vardoulakis, Minneapolis: Minnesota, 2011, 180.

mutually constitutive connection of things.

The "connection of all things," the immanent order of the world is precisely what the seemingly opposed philosophical positions of subjective volition, theological transcendence, or economic necessity, cannot grasp. Thus, the connection of all things appears negatively, as the dark spot overlooked by these various philosophical perspectives. That is not its only appearance, however: in the opening section of *Capital* Marx's meditations on the expanded form of value in *Capital* argue that value has to be thought of as nothing other than the relation of every commodity with every other commodity, of everything with everything. In a similar way Spinoza ends the first part of the *Ethics* with the proposition, "Nothing exists from whose nature some effect does not follow," a proposition that offers one of the multiple implications of immanent causality. These assertions are only glimpses, only a figuration of the connections of everything with everything. In the first case, that of Marx, value even in its expanded form does not yet get us to the fully developed thought of the interconnections of everything, of immanent causality, a concept which only appears symptomatically as it were in those passages where Marx discusses capitalism as a product of the entire history of mankind down to the present. Similarly we could argue that the full effects, for lack of a better world of Spinoza's assertion that there is nothing that does not produce effects, that everything is a cause as much as it is an effect, does not fully work its difficult logic out until we get to the affects and vicissitudes of the striving of a finite conatus. An immanent ontology cannot just be uttered as a concept, but must be produced. *Capital* and the *Ethics* are two instances of this of this production.

We could argue that what we are offered by both Spinoza and Marx is a gesture towards what we could call a communist ontology, an ontology of immanence and relations. However, this ontology is not yet a politics, or is not immediately given as such. What these two texts underscore is that the immanent ontology must be thought of as not only the condition of our thought and action, but as a condition which as cause is transformed, masked in terms of its effects. The connection of things that is the capitalist mode of production, in its global origin and everyday effects, appears not as social relation, or as a relation at all, but as the value of things. Or, as Spinoza argues, God as nature, God as the immanent cause must be understood as itself the necessary cause of the image of God as a transcendent cause, standing above the world. The immanent relations of causality must themselves be understood as the cause of the human tendency to view oneself as a "kingdom within a kingdom." This is the immanent transcendence I referred to earlier, transcendence itself as an effect of immanence. It is an effect, but it is also a cause. There is no surer guarantee of capital's functioning than its appearance as something necessary and timeless. As Marx writes in the concluding section of *Capital*, "The advance of capitalist production develops a working class which by education, tradition, and habit looks upon the requirements of that mode of production as self-evident natural laws."[5] Capital reproduces itself not just at the level of the economy and politics but also and most importantly at the level of subjectivity. This point is developed even further by Spinoza, whose central political (or theological/political question), "why do men fight for their servitude as if it was salvation," indicates an even deeper grasp of the extent to which political power is reproduced through the practices that create desires, habits, and affects.

Despite the differences we can see that Spinoza and Marx's respective critiques are not only similar in their preemptive form, but in their object as well. The object of their critique may be fundamentally different in its structure and history, from theology to the economy, but it is fundamentally the same in its function. The object of the preemptive critique is not this or that idea, or even ideology, but it is the point where the existing social relations becomes not just an idea but also an entire subjective comportment, a way of life. If these texts get ahead of themselves, expounding a critique that demands concepts and relations that have been not yet developed, they do so only because the ideas, concepts, and world views that they critique are precisely that which stands in the way of their conceptual development. Ideological

---

5 Karl Marx, *Capital: A Critique of Political Economy, Volume I*, Translated by Ben Fowkes, (New York: Penguin, 1977), 899.

intervention is both prior to, and an effect of, theoretical development.

Beyond this overlap, this similarity of the method and object of critique, what might this conjunction of Marx and Spinoza offer for thinking about philosophy about the world and the present? First, we can isolate in the two elements of the critique a general problematic that cuts through several critical terms. First, we have what is referred to as the "connection of all things," nature, capital, or the entire profane history of the world, an object that exceeds any attempt to represent it, to bring it under the concepts of subjective intention, transcendent order, or necessary laws. This is in different cases what both Marx and Spinoza are trying to think. We could call this "the common" only in that it exists only in and through its constitutive relations. The objects of Spinoza and Marx's critique are not entirely misguided: God and Capital are an attempt to represent the absent or immanent totality as the necessary condition of thought and action, but they do so by representing it within the existing imaginary, subordinating it to subjectivity, transcendence, and a reification of existing conditions. Grasping this connection of all things, or absent cause, means taking on the way in which it is represented, as God or the fetish of value, recognizing that these representations or ideas are nothing other than effects of the structures, its modes or necessary appearances, effects that are also simultaneously causes, necessary conditions of its reproduction. Finally, all of this, the connection of things, its representations in Gods and fetishes, and the relation between the two, as cause and effect, can only be developed through a practice of philosophy that I have awkwardly identified as "preemptive." This practice does not see a critique of the existing ideas and representations as something secondary, as a subordinate activity best left to popularizers and pedagogy, but as a constitutive condition of philosophy itself. Philosophy only exists through its engagement with what could be called, for lack of a better word, ideology, the collection of thoughts, representations, and affects that reproduce the world and its structures of domination.

For more on Spinoza and Marx see Economies of Affect/Affective Economies: Towards a Spinozist Critique of Political Economy.

Economies of Affect/ Affective Economies: Towards A Spinozist Critique of Political Economy

Originally posted in November of 2013.

Antonio Negri argues that, "...in the postindustrial age the Spinozian critique of representation of capitalist power corresponds more to the truth than does the analysis of political economy."[1] Many of the contemporary turns to Spinoza in Marxist thought have followed this trajectory, turning away from the critique of political economy towards critiques of ideology or, in Negri's case, the representation of power. This is perhaps not surprising, it is easier to make connections between Spinoza's critique of superstition and theories of ideology than it is to connect his understanding of desires and striving to consumption and production in capitalism. As much Spinoza offered a trenchant critique of the religious, monarchical, and even humanist ideologies of his time, he had little to say, at least directly, about the emerging capitalism. Money is only mentioned once in the *Ethics*,

---

1 Antonio Negri, "Reliqua Desiderantur: A Conjecture for a Definition of the Concept of Democracy in the Final Spinoza," translated by Ted Stolze, in *The New Spinoza*, T. Stolze and W.Montag eds. Minneapolis: University of Minnesota, 1997, 246 n. 21.

where it is defined as the universal object of desire that "occupies the mind of the multitude more than anything else."[2] While such a statement intersects with critiques of greed and the capitalist transformation of desire it remains to partial and incidental to developing a Spinozist critique of political economy.

Frédéric Lordon has argued that the point of intersection between Spinoza's thought and Marx is not to be found in rereading superstition as ideology, or even in the isolated assertion of the affective dimension of money. Instead it is to be found in a more profound intersection between subjectivity and the economy. As Lordon argues Spinoza's theory of the conatus, of the striving that defines each thing, is the connection point between a Spinozist ontology or anthropology, and a Marxist critique of political economy. This is not the connection argued for in some right wing appropriations of Spinoza, or left dismissals, which see in the conatus the assertion of self-interest that underlies all human actions. Spinoza's striving is not the utility maximizing individual underlying contemporary economics. As Lordon argues, the conatus strives, but what it strives for, the objects it considers desirable and relations it pursues, are themselves determined by its capacity to be affected. Desire, the desire to be, is intransitive, which becomes transitive by the way it is shaped by its encounters. This fundamental ontological and anthropological postulate has its corollary a social theory in which every mode of production must be considered as a particular problem of "colinearization," a particular articulation of its striving with the striving of the individuals which comprise it.

An introduction to what Lordon calls "colinearization" can be found in Marx's theory of primitive accumulation, a theory which is much about the transformation of subjectivity of habits and ideas as it is about economic transformation. Marx defined the former with respect to capitalism as follows, 'The advance of capitalist production develops a working class which by education, tradition,

---

[2] Benedict de Spinoza, *Ethics*, Translated by Edwin Curley, New York, Penguin, 1994, EIVAPPXVIII

and habit looks upon the requirements of that mode of production as self-evident natural laws.'[3] This habituation, the reorientation of striving, is, at least at first, based on a reorganization of the basic desire for survival, to persevere in one's being. Even this desire, a desire that is nothing other than self-preservation, must be understood as structured. Spinoza's concept of the conatus is free from any naturalism, any reduction of striving to a struggle for life. It is precisely because of the conatus lack of any teleology, its striving for nothing other than what it is determined to strive, that it is simultaneously singular and relational. The relational basis of the conatus includes, in Lordon's interpretation, not just the immediately present others and their affective composition, but the past strivings that structure and determine institutions. As much as the immediate desire for survival, the need for food and shelter, underlies wage labor, this 'immediate' striving must be turned away from other means of survival, from its connection to other pre-existing forms of survival or the simple act of taking what one needs. Marx's account of 'primitive accumulation' is not just the destruction of any commons and the accumulation of wealth, it is also the destruction of the very idea of an existence not predicated on the commodity and wage form. It is a primitive accumulation of the conatus. The history of every institution, of every practice, is the destruction of certain modes of striving and the creation, or canalization, of other forms. Nature creates neither nations nor economies. No social order is based on some natural striving, or, rather every social order is; the difference is in how that striving is articulated, its objects and activities.

If capitalism has as its defining characteristic the separation of workers from the means of production, then this separation radically alters the immediacy of need and desire. Hunger might drive people to work, but that work will always be out of sync with the immediacy of that desire. Lordon argues that the fundamental

---

3 Karl Marx, *Capital: A Critique of Political Economy, Volume I*, Translated by Ben Fowkes, New York: Penguin, 1977, 899.

transformation necessary to bring Spinoza's affective composition into the present is the fundamental separation between striving, activity, and its object. This separation from the means of production is less a fundamental loss, as it is in accounts of alienation, than it is a fundamental transformation of activity, of what it means to engage in self-preservation or work. There is an indifference to the activity itself, the goals of the particular activity are stripped of their meaning, their particular orientations of good and bad, perfect and imperfect. As much as we might affectively attach ourselves to any particular job, any particular task, developing our potential and relations, becoming the cause of our joy, this is secondary to the desire, and need, for money. Concrete labor is subordinated to abstract labor. There is thus an affective split at the core of the labor process, between the possible love of my own activity, its concrete joys, and its results, its abstract exchangeability. What we could call the affective composition of labor is how, at a given moment in time, these two aspects are valued or devalued, how much joy is sought in the activity of labor itself, or how much is sought in terms of the accumulation it makes possible. This shift between activity and object is complicated, both cause and effect, of the changing relations of hope and fear in a given historical moment.

Lordon offers a sketch of this history of the affective composition of labor, framed in terms of three periods: the first is the period corresponding to primitive accumulation and the advent of formal subsumption, this is followed by Fordism, and then neoliberalism. In the first period, that of primitive accumulation of the conatus, the simple lack of an alternative to wage labor is sufficient, striving is determined by the fear of starving. As Marx writes the capitalist mode of production depends in part on the 'worker's drives for self-preservation and propagation.'[4] At its most fundamental level, all capitalism has to do is destroy any alternatives, curtail the commons, and crack down on those who would strive to realize their existence outside of wage labor. The second, Fordism, is defined by its

---

4 Karl Marx, Capital: A Critique of Political Economy, Volume I, 718.

intersecting transformations of both the separation of activity from any intrinsic joy and the affective investment of consumption. Labor is simplified and fragmented, stripped of the pleasures and mastery. This is the work of the assembly line. At the same time the sphere of consumption is expanded. Ford's famous 'five dollar day' increased the spending power or consumers. The affective composition of Fordism could be described as a fundamental reorganization of conatus, of striving, away from labor, from activity, and towards consumption. The worker's activity is fragmented, made part of a whole that exceeds it, becoming as much passivity as activity. The sadness of work, its exhaustion, is compensated for with the joys of consumption. This transformation from an affective investment in work to an affective investment in consumption could also be described as a shift from active joy, joy in one's capacity to act, and the transformation of action, to passive joy. Passive joyful affects are those that increase our power of acting, while remaining outside of our control. The pleasures of consumption, of consumerism, can be understood as passive joys, they promise some increase of our power, of our joys and strivings, but what they can never give, what can never be sold is the very capacity to actively produce new pleasures.

The Fordist compromise can thus be distinguished from later, post-Fordist or neoliberal, articulations of affects, transformations that can also be described through a transformation of work and consumption. Broadly speaking, these transformations can initially be described by a dismantling of the security and stability of work. The Fordist compromise carried with it a dimension of stability, brought about by collective bargaining and the centrality of the contract. Neoliberalism as it is defined by Lordon, is a first and foremost a transformation of the norms and structures that organize and structure action. As such it is fundamentally asymmetrical, workers are exposed to more and more risk, while capitalists, specifically those concerned with financial capital, are liberated from the classical risks of investment. This loss of security for the worker fundamentally changes the affective dimension of money. It is no longer an object of hope, the possible means of realizing one's desires, but becomes that which wards off fear. Money becomes part of the desire for security, the only possible security: one's skills, one's actions, might have no value in the future, but money always will. One could understand this shift from Fordism to neoliberalism as a shift from a regime of hope (tinged with fear) to a regime of fear (tinged with hope). Hope and fear cannot be separated, but that does not mean that a given affective composition is not defined more by one than the other. Thus, it could be argued that precarity is best understood as an affective concept. It is less of a matter of some objective shift in the status of security than it is a shift in how work and security is perceived. If precarity can be used to adequately describe contemporary economic life it is less because everyone is working under some kind of temporary or part time contract, although these have become significant, than it is because of a constant sense of insecurity infuses every work situation. Precarity affects even stable employment through its technological transformation, it is always possible to be working or at least in touch with work, and a generalized anxiety infuses all of work, as more indirect measures of productivity replace the productivity of the assembly line. Indirect, fragmented, and immaterial work of services, knowledge management, and emotional labor are less subject to direct quantification, the measure of units produced, and are thus subject to review and evaluation. Generalized insecurity, constant contact, and the uncertainty of evaluation define the neoliberal economy of fear.

The shift from Fordism to neoliberalism cannot just be described as a shift from hope to fear, from a desire for money grounded on the expanding terrain of a good life to a desire grounded on insecurity of the future. It is a fundamentally different affective composition, one that transforms the relation to work as much as money. As Luc Boltanski and Eve Chiapello argue in *The New Spirit of Capitalism*, one of the central aspects of neoliberalism, at least at the level of the language of managers and economists, is its presentation of insecurity as opportunity.[5] The breakdown

---

5 Boltanski, Luc and Eve Chiapello, *The New Spirit of Capitalism*, Translated by Gregory Elliot, New York: Verso, 2005, 64.

of the security that functioned as the backdrop of Fordist desire, making possible a linear arrow of accumulation, is presented as liberation as a freedom from bureaucracy and control. The constant movement from project to project, the lack of stability and long-term connections, is attached not to fear, the loss of security, but to hope, to the constant ability to make new connections, to break with the past in the name of a new future. As work becomes more and more insecure, and less and less capable of providing a linear and stable progression, it becomes more and more consuming of time and energy. Neoliberalism is a massive rearticulation of not only the relation to money, becoming both an object of desire and fear, but of risk as well. The new spirit of capitalism revalorizes risk.

Far from being a return to some fundamental fear neoliberalism demands the highest coefficient of colinearization, the correlation of individual striving and the striving of the mode of production. It is no accident that the vocabulary of neoliberalism, terms such as "human capital," "personal brand," "network," etc. all reproduce the idea of an identity of individual and capital. This is a transformation of work as well; work is no longer defined as something endured, as a necessary passivity that is exchanged for money, for the joys of consumption. Work instead becomes the terrain of self-realization and actualization. This transformation is not just a matter of a fundamental different representation of the breakdown of stability, the presentation of insecurity as freedom, itself a variant of the spontaneous philosophy of the sphere of consumption, but also of a breakdown of the boundaries separating work from life. This is in part an effect of the instability of work, as jobs become more precarious, or are even appear to be precarious, work itself becomes a kind of perpetual application for the job.[6] The use of the phrase 'networking' reflects this breakdown, it is a social idea not just for times of unemployment, when making new contacts becomes paramount, but it is an ideal that encompasses all social relations. Weak ties, the ties that connect one to co-workers and colleagues, become invested

---

6 Southwood, Ivor, *Non-Stop Inertia*, Winchester, UK: Zero Books, 2010, 16.

with maximum hope and fear, as any tie, any relation could possible alter ones future. This precarious investment in relations with others is further complicated by the proliferation of technologies of sharing and surveillance that make self-presentation not just an isolated moment, for the workday or job interview, but a constant task. The networking, flexibility, and constant self-surveillance of the job search become a defining characteristic of contemporary labor. All the while this characteristic is purported to be not a repression of one's fundamental self and identity, but its expression. It is not just that the networking and the labor of appearing motivated, engaged, and enthusiastic has to be a kind of deep acting, demanding a great deal of commitment, but that workplace also encompasses those activities and relations that would seem to be outside of it, increasingly trying to make leisure, play, and creativity part of its structure.

Lordon's presentation is schematic, overly so, in his recently published *La Société des Affects*, he augments this schema by turning to two of the final propositions of Part Three of Ethics. In those final passages Spinoza argues that there are as many loves and hates 'as there are species of objects by which we are affected'[7] and 'each affect of each individual differs from the affect of another as much as the essence of one from the essence of the other.'[8] The multiple objects, and multiple strivings, constitute the basis for multiple affective compositions, each shifting and ambivalent as the same object is both the object of love and hate, and the same individual comes to hate what they once loved. Rereading these propositions back into the schematic history of different affective modes of production does not dispense with the latter, shattering it into a pure multiplicity where a thousand flowers bloom. Rather, these differences, variations of love and hate, must be understood as variations on a dominant theme. As Lordon argues there will always be bosses who are kind and generous, work situations that engage a broader range of activity, but these differences and deviations are ultimately just different expressions

---

7 Benedict de Spinoza, *Ethics*, EIIIP56.
8 Benedict de Spinoza, *Ethics*, EIIIP57.

of the same fundamental relation. The nicest boss in the world cannot fundamentally alter the fundamental structure of the Fordist or neoliberal labor conditions, the affective engagement at the level of individual intention does nothing to alter the basic relation with the activity and object. This affective veneer, the work of human relations, is not inconsequential: the real work it does it producing the appearance of difference, a society of individual actions rather the persistent structures, it makes workplaces and companies look different, obscuring the common nature of the wage relation. Much of the quotidian criticism of work, or of capitalism in general, focuses on the differences: we complain about this boss, or protest this big corporation for being particularly offensive, but do not address the fundamental relation of exploitation or the profit motive which exceeds the different ways in which it is instantiated. The plurality, a plurality dictated by what Spinoza would call the spontaneous order of nature, the different ways in which things have affected us, takes precedence over the perception of common relations.

To this emphasis on plurality as a perpetual alibi, we can add another thesis from Spinoza. As Spinoza argues, we are more likely to hate or love an act that we consider to be free than one which is considered necessary. On this last point Spinoza's affective economy intersects with one of the central points of Marx's critique of political economy, that of fetishism, which could in part be summed up as perceiving the capitalist mode of production as necessary and natural rather than the product of social relations. The naturalization of the economy, its existence as self-evident natural laws, makes it difficult for us to hate it, to become indignant. The affective economy of capitalism is one in which it is easy to become angry and grateful at the deviations, the cruel bosses and the benevolent philanthropists, while the structure itself, the fundamental relations of exploitation, are deemed too necessary, too natural, to merit indignation. The naturalization of the economy, its fetishization, is coupled with its complexity, which makes it difficult for us to recognize its determination of our striving. We might be able to trace the causes which have determined us to like this or that thing, have this or that taste, but it is so hard to grasp the causes which have channeled our striving into wage labor and our grafted our desires onto the purchasing of commodities, so much so that work and consumption seem to be a natural conditions rather than historical institutions.

The production of indignation is a difficult task, it goes against not just the perceived necessity of the capitalist mode of production but the ways in which our very desires, our most intimate strivings, have been produced by capitalism. From this perspective Spinoza's central provocation to a critique of political economy is not the isolated remark about the power of money, but the fundamental thesis that men "believe themselves free because they are conscious of their own actions, and ignorant of the causes by which they are determined."[9] This assertion cuts against any assertion of the supposed desire for capitalism, the desire for consumer goods, etc., as its justification, such desires are merely effects taken as causes. Its destructive dimension, its pars destruens, is quite clear; what is less clear, however, is how it constitutes a positive political project. The starting point, beyond the difficult recognition of the way in which we are already determined, is Spinoza's recognition that we endeavor to of those things that increase our joy, and shun those thoughts which weaken and sadden us. This affective tendency not only explains why we "fight for our servitude as if it was salvation," but also why we continue, against all evidence to believe that the current economic system will eventually come around, reward us for our efforts. Moreover, not only must any radical transformation break the lines of articulation that weave together striving with labor, happiness with consumption, it must produce other joys, other ways to strive. A revolution is as much a reorientation of our affective relations as it is of social relations and cannot be one without the other.

For More on Spinoza and Marx see Nexus Rerum: (Spinoza and Marx, again).

---

9 Benedict de Spinoza, *Ethics*, EIIIP2S.

The Imaginary Institution of Society: Spinoza's Version

Originally posted in January of 2023.

When I was in graduate school "the imaginary" was one of those words that circulated all the more readily often because it was untethered to any specific theoretical source. It borrowed bits from Lacan and bits from Castoriadis to suggest some historically specific articulation of the very capacity to imagine. There were multiple imaginaries, political, social, technical etc., As someone who was getting interested in Spinoza at the time I tried to connect his writing on the imagination with this idea to no avail.

Now, thinking about Spinoza again, it might make sense to think about the way in which Spinoza's particular idea of the imagination is useful for thinking about social and political life. I should be clear that on this point I mean "imagination" as it is described as a particular kind of necessarily incomplete and inadequate knowledge in the *Ethics*, and not superstition as it is developed in Spinoza's political writings. Any such separation is artificial, superstition is nothing other than a particular organization of the imagination, however, it is still worth at least heuristically focusing on the more spontaneous dimension of the imagination as separate from and prior to superstition.

For Spinoza the imagination, images formed by the body, always involve both the body that affects us and how we are affected. As Spinoza writes,

> "Next, to retain the customary words, the affections of the human body whose ideas present external bodies as present to us, we shall call images of things, though they do not reproduce the figure of things. And when the mind regards bodies in this way, we shall say that it imagines."[1]

It is not representation but presence that is central to the imagination. To imagine something is to regard it as present. This presence is a confused amalgamation of the qualities of the thing affecting us, and the way we are affected. To imagine is to treat our own associations and connections as if they were part of what we are perceiving.

> "For example, a soldier, having seen traces of a horse in the sand, will immediately pass from the thought of a horse in the sand will immediately pass from the thought of a horse to the thought of a horseman, and from that to the thought of war and so on. And so each one, according as he has been accustomed to join and connect the image of things in this or that way, will pass from one thought to another."[2]

As I have argued in my post on Spinoza and conspiracy theories, the imagination can be both complex and highly mediated, involving a chain of associations from hoof print to horse, and horse to war, and immediate, directly lived as something present. As Althusser stresses for Spinoza the imagination is nothing other than the phenomenological world of lived experience as such. All of our perceptions and evaluations of the world as it is lived, or tendency to view some aspects of nature as good or bad, useful or harmful,

---

1 Benedict de Spinoza, *Ethics*, Translated by Edwin Curley, New York, Penguin, 1994, EIIP17Schol.
2 Benedict de Spinoza, *Ethics*, EIIP18Schol.

organized or disorganized, are the imagination, which is to say are confused perceptions of our own desires and the way that the object affects us.

I was thinking of this mediation of the immediate or the immediacy of mediation when reading about theories of race. First, and not surprising, is this line from Etienne Balibar's "Is there a Neo-Racism?" As Balibar writes "I shall therefore venture the idea that the racist complex inextricably combines a crucial function of misrecognition (without which the violence would not be tolerable to the very people engaging in it) and a 'will to know', a violent desire for immediate knowledge of social relations."[3] In other words, part of the appeal of racism is that it makes social relations immediately legible. It provides a geography, dividing towns into the "good" and "bad" part, a morality, telling us (people who believe ourselves to be white) who to trust and who to fear. As much as this imagination is immediate, registered in somatic markers such as skin, hair, and eye color, the immediacy is a product of associations and connections that we are constantly subject to, media, entertainment, etc., and, like Spinoza's soldier, we have forgotten in focusing on the immediate present nature of the image.

Or, to take another version of the argument, this time from Stuart Hall,

> "Race is only one element in this struggle to command and structure the popular ideology: but it has been, over the past two decades, a leading element: perhaps the key element. Since it appears to be grounded in natural and biological "facts," it is a way of drawing distinctions and developing practices which appear, themselves, to be "natural," given and universal...Race provides the structure of simplifications which make it possible to construct plausible explanations of troubling developments and which facilitates the application of simplifying remedies. Who now wants to begin to explore the complex of economic and political forces which have perpetuated and multiplied the poverty of the working-

---

3 Etienne Balibar, "Is there a Neo-Racism?" Translated by Chris Turner in Etienne Balibar and Immanuel Wallerstein Race, *Nation, Class: Ambiguous Identities*. London: Verso, 1991, 19.

class districts of the inner cities? Who will have time for that complicated exercise—which may require us to trace connections between structures of our society which is more convenient to keep apart: when a simple, obvious, "natural" explanation lies to hand."[4]

A few hasty connections/conclusions.

One of the thing that should not be overlooked is how the racist, or "race realist" explanation offers a quick an easy explanation of a variety of phenomena. We drive through the poor inner city and see black people living there, hear stories of the crimes that happen there, and all of this just seems to be given to us as a fact. The connection between race, poverty, and crime is immediately apparent. An actual, or to use the Spinozist term, adequate understanding of the actual factors that have made the inner city the way it is would have to take into consideration the history of slavery, Jim Crow, redlining, deindustrialization, etc. etc. etc., Of course it is important to point out that what appears here as immediate, race as an explanation, is itself the product of a long history of associations. It took us a long time to see race, and it takes a lot of work, political and ideological, for us not to see everything about social, economic, and political life that is effaced in the immediacy and simplicity of seeing race.

So this is what it might mean to consider what "the imaginary institution of society" might mean from a Spinozist perspective. It is the dominance of a particular set of immediate associations of bodies and qualities, associations that are themselves the product of a complex articulation (in Hall's sense), that disappears in the immediacy of the association. I have focused here on race as one such mediated immediacy. It would be wrong to think it is the only one. As Alexandra Minna Stern argues in her book *Proud Boys and the White Ethnostate: How the Alt-Right is Warping the American Imagination*, "Transphobia is the butter on the bread of much alt-

---

[4] Stuart Hall, *Selected Writings on Race and Difference*, Edited by Paul Gilroy and Ruth Wilson Gilmore, Durham: Duke, 2021, 68.

right and alt-light vlogging."⁵ As with race there is an appeal to a kind of natural immediacy, that of sex, gender, and gender roles, one that is the product of many mediations, right down to the latest explosion at a gender reveal party. The natural order of sex and gender is in some sense the entry point to a larger sense of a natural order. Of course the relation between these two different images of nature, racial and sexual, is complex, overdetermined, and in some sense always shifting.

As much as there is an epistemic tendency towards the imagination predicated on its immediacy and self-evident nature, there is a practical one as well: the order and connection of bodies being the same as ideas and all. For many, especially those with advantages in the existing order, there are reasons to hold unto and act within the horizon described by its imagination. I recently finished reading Jeremy Gilbert and Alex William's *Hegemony Now: How Big Tech and Wall Street Won the World (and How We Win it Back)*. In the midst of that book there is a long discussion to retrieve the idea of interests in politics. One of the things that Gilbert and Williams stress that one's interest is related to both one's position and one's horizon. As they write,

> "From this perspective, workers who vote for immigration restrictions are acting against their interests when conceived within a liberal, communist, or even expansively social democratic horizon, but not when conceived within a conservative horizon. What is it that defines the particular characteristics of the horizon within which interests are perceived, computed, and acted upon? In part it must be a question of the scale—in terms of space and time—of that horizon. When horizons of interest are operating at a small scale, this will mean a focus on the hyperlocal (my immediate family) and the hyper-present (today and tomorrow and

---

5 Alexandra Minna Stern, *Proud Boys and the White Ethnostate: How the Alt-Right is Warping the American Imagination*, Boston: Beacon, 2019, 134.

perhaps next year). What is reasonable within one horizon is unreasonable in another."[6]

If we want to change and expand the horizon of people's interest we must first recognize the horizon that they already operate within even if that horizon is defined by imaginations that seem irrational to us. "Inadequate and confused ideas follow with the same necessity as adequate, or clear and distinct ideas." (EIIP36).[7] To put this in Spinozist terms, we all strive to maintain our existence, but we do so according to what we understand, rightly or wrongly, to be in our interest according to our given level of imagination or understanding. All of which is a very long way of saying that any politics of radical change has to start with understanding the epistemic and practical attachments that most have to the existing imaginary institution of society.

For more on Spinoza and the imagination see Reduction to Ignorance: Spinoza in the Age of Conspiracy Theories and Imagination, Fiction, Knowledge: Towards a Spinozist Theory of Cultural Production, Part II.

---

6 Jeremy Gilbert and Alex Williams, *Hegemony Now! How Big Tech and Wall Street Won the World (and how we win it Back)*, New York: Verso, 2022, 144.
7 Benedict de Spinoza, *Ethics*, EIIP36.

The General Intellect Personified: Capitalism as a Social Relation

Originally posted in March of 2011.

For brevity's sake, I am not going to go through the myriad problems and paradoxes of that strange thing called "Marxist Philosophy": the interminable debate of "interpreting" versus "changing" the world. However, as a short introduction to what I want to discuss, I will say that one way to understand the relation between Marx and philosophy is as a series of both provocations and critiques. What Etienne Balibar, in *The Philosophy of Marx*, called simultaneously "falling short of" and "going beyond philosophy"; the first takes the form of fragments of philosophical speculation, often presented as conclusions without premises, and the later takes the form of a critique of philosophy's claim to autonomy. It is the first of these that I would like to focus on.

The unstated center of Marx's thought is a thought of social existence, of community, that is something more than, or other than, a collection of individuals. Without this, the critique of the egocentric rights of man;" of the Robinsonades of political economy; and of the illusions of "Freedom, equality. and Bentham" that make up the spontaneous ideology of the market would not make any sense. Or, more fundamentally, without this communism would be the empty utopia that its critics accuse it of being.

However, when it comes to theorizing the grounds of this community though some understanding of social existence, Marx often falls short. At times Marx asserts it as a fact, without giving the ground of this fact, as in the following passage from *Capital*.

> "Whether the combined working day, in a given case, acquires this increased productivity because it heightens the mechanical force of labor, or extends its sphere of action over a greater space, or contracts the field of production relatively to the scale of production, or at the critical moment sets large masses of labor to work, or excited rivalry between individuals and raises their animal spirits, or impresses on the similar operations carried on by a number of men the stamp of continuity and many-sidedness, or performs different operations simultaneously, or economizes the means of production by use in common…whichever of these is the cause of the increase, the special productive power of the combined working day, is under all circumstances, the social productive power of labor, or the productive power of social labor. This power arises from cooperation itself. When the worker co-operates in a planned way with others, he strips off the fetters of his individuality, and develops the capabilities of this species [*Gattungsvermögen*]."[1]

This passage, and the entire section on cooperation, is important for at least two reasons. First, within the logic of *Capital*, it precedes the sections on "The Working Day," thus illustrating the struggle and antagonism that animates and transforms the capitalist mode of production. Second, the reference to Gattungsvermögen, species capacity, suggests another way of reading the relation of the young Marx to the old Marx. It offers a way of thinking species being, not as some metaphysical notion of the essence of man, but as part of a social ontology, as the historically existing capacity and powers of

---

1 Karl Marx, *Capital: A Critique of Political Economy, Volume I*, Translated by Ben Fowkes, New York: Penguin, 1977, 447.

social relations. Despite this provocation, there is also the strange indifference to the ultimate conditions of this increased value of cooperation: it could be the effect of the uniformity imposed by the machine, animal spirits, or whatever.

So, one of the philosophical tasks left in the wake of Marx, an answer to a question posed but not answered, would be to theorize cooperation itself. This is not to be confused with the altruism that moralists and evolutionary psychologist concern themselves with; cooperation, and the sociality it implies, is not a moral category but simply the effects that individual actions have on each other. Or, more to the point, that there are no such thing as purely individual actions, whenever we act we act in relation to each other. There is a social surplus to all action.

This social surplus relates to surplus value as well. At this point in *Capital* Marx has already made his fundamental argument that surplus value stems from the difference between the cost of labor power, the wage, and its productivity. This is true for every worker, but cooperation increases this surplus. Marx argues that the simple fact of adding the forces of labor together, of combining the efforts of workers, increases the productivity of labor. The whole is greater than the sum of its parts. There is thus a surplus above and beyond the surplus value grounded in the exploitation of labor.

Marx also argues that this cooperation, this collective worker, is itself the genesis of the increasingly specialized and technological work of manufacture, large-scale industry, and the factory. It is only once that a group of workers are brought together in one place, in one productive process, that it becomes possible to begin to fragment the labor process, assigning different tasks to different individuals. This specialization gives rise to specialized tools through an analysis of the component elements of the labor process. Marx's argument in the middle section of *Capital* is an argument about technology, arguing that technology is itself a product of social relations. Machines emerge from the cooperative and fragmented labor process, even responding to its crises and conflict. As Marx writes,

"It would be possible to write a whole history of the inventions made since 1830 for the sole purpose of providing capital with weapons against working class revolt."[2]

Beyond what this might mean for a philosophy of technology it is worth pointing out that the social surplus then gives rise to the technological surplus. Science, like cooperation, is not paid for, it becomes part of the generalized productive force of society. This is, after all, the initial definition of the "general intellect."

Social relations and science, or technology, both create a surplus, a surplus above and beyond the exploitation of the individual. It could also be said that these surpluses are above and beyond labor, at least abstract wage labor. It could be said, and if we did we would be very close to some of the concepts and problems of autonomist Marxism, all of which start from the idea of a surplus produced by immaterial labor or the general intellect. However, it is important to underscore that unlike autonomist Marxism, at least in some assertions, Marx does not give this surplus a prefigurative dimension, it is not a harbinger of a communist future. Quite the contrary, he identifies it with an increased fetishization of capitalism itself. The more that capital utilizes the combined energy of the collective worker and the more that it puts to work science and knowledge the more that it appears that capital itself is productive. As Marx writes:

> "This entire development of the productive forces of socialized labor (in contrast to the more or less isolated labor of individuals), and together with it the uses of science (the general product of social development), in the immediate process of production, takes the form of the productive power of capital. It does not appear as the productive power of labor, or even of that part of it that is identical with capital. And least of all does it appear as the productive power either of the individual workers or of the workers joined together in the process of production."[3]

---

2 Karl Marx, *Capital*, 536.
3 Karl Marx, *Capital*, 1024.

Marx even takes this a step further, suggesting that it appears as not just as the productive power of capital in general but the attribute of a specific capitalist. One could perhaps interpret this as an argument that the more these surpluses of cooperation and science enter into production the more the person of the capitalist is fetishized, seen as the source of wealth. This might be an interesting thesis to examine, a dialectic of abstraction and concretization in which abstraction leads to concretization. Anecdotal evidence of this can be found by surveying the companies of contemporary capitalism. The more wealth is produced by knowledge and cooperation, the more it appears to be the attribute of a talented individual. Bill Gates, Steve Jobs, Mark Zuckerberg, these are all household names. Contrast this to corporations such as BP, Toyota, Boeing, etc., their CEOs are known only to a select few, perhaps reflecting the fact that in their case the source of value is not so readily obscured. The more cooperative and knowledge based the production process is the more readily it is fetishized in the genius of an individual.

That might be one direction to pursue, but I would rather suggest that these observations point to a necessary corrective of autonomist theory. It is not enough to champion the productive power of the general intellect, it is necessary to explore the fetishization of this power in capital, and in the supposed "great men" that make up the history of the present. In previous writings I have focused on Deleuze and Guattari's use of the "socius" to theorize this relation. Deleuze and Guattari develop this concept from Marx's fetish, stressing that society itself is a fetish. As Deleuze and Guattari write,

> "...the forms of social production, like those of desiring production, involve an unengendered nonproductive attitude, an element of anti-production coupled with the process, a full body that functions as a socius. This socius may be the body of the earth, that of the tyrant, or capital. This is the body that Marx is referring to when he says that it is not the product of labor, but rather appears as its natural or divine presuppositions.

In fact, it does not restrict itself merely to opposing productive forces in and of themselves. It falls back on [il se rabat sur] all production, constituting a surface over which the forces and agents of production are distributed, thereby appropriating for itself all surplus production and arrogating to itself both the whole and the parts of the process, which now seem to emanate from it as a quasi-cause."[4]

Just as the despot appears to be the cause and not the effect of subjection, capital appears to be the cause and not the effect of labor. Once disconnected from the conditions of production, from the virtual relations that make it possible, society, the socius, not only appears to be autonomous, in the form of money making money, but is an effect that appears as a cause. Society not only appears to exist prior to the differential relations, the production and desire that constitute it, it also appears to stand above these relations as their necessary condition. The fetish has become common sense in that we see society, with its structures, rules and goals, as something that exists prior to and is constitutive of the social relations of desire, perception and production.

For Deleuze and Guattari this distortion stems from an almost categorical difference between representation, including the representation of capital, and production. Capital is not produced in the same way it is represented. To argue that capital, or individual capitalists, represent the productive power of capital based on an almost metaphysical divide between production and representation, becoming and being, is to miss the specific relations that constitute this appearance for Marx. These relations are the relations of cooperation and the productivity of science, sources of surplus that cannot be phenomenally located in the individual's exertion and labor. The more abstract and relational labor becomes, the more it appears to be concretized in the genius of an individual. Just as the real abstraction of value is concretized in money, the real abstraction

---

4 Gilles Deleuze and Félix Guattari, *Anti-Oedipus: Capitalism and Schizophrenia*, Translated by Robert Hurley et al, Minneapolis: University of Minnesota, 1983, 10.

of cooperation is concretized in the figure of the genius capitalist, the CEO or entrepreneur. Some individuals are real abstractions. That would be the polemical provocation of this line of thought, but still much needs to be done to examine the specific ways that the productive power of cooperation and science is represented.

For More on the representation of capitalism see "The Spontaneous Ideology of Conspiracy: This One on Marx".

The Universe Spends Too Much Time on Me. By Jon Read

Negative Solidarity: Towards the Definition of a Concept

Originally posted in August of 2013.

Even though it is not a recent post, I was struck by this post on "negative solidarity" on the blog *Splintering Bones Ashes*. To cite from the blog:

> "More than mere indifference to worker agitations, negative solidarity is an aggressively enraged sense of injustice, committed to the idea that, because I must endure increasingly austere working conditions (wage freezes, loss of benefits, declining pension pot, erasure of job security and increasing precarity) then everyone else must too. Negative solidarity can be seen as a close relation to the kind of 'lottery thinking' the underpins the most pernicious variants of the American Dream. In lottery thinking we get a kind of inverted Rawlsian anti-justice- rather than considering the likelihood of achieving material success in an unequal society highly unlikely and therefore preferring a more equal one, instead the psychology of the million-to-one shot prevails. Since I will inevitably be wealthy in the future, this line of thinking runs, I will ensure that the conditions when I become wealthy will be as advantageous to me as

possible, even though on a balance of realistic probabilities this course of action will in fact be likely to be entirely against my own interests. More than lottery thinking, which is inherently (if misguidedly) aspirational in nature, negative solidarity is actively and aggressively anti-aspirational, utterly negative in the most childish fashion, and drives a blatant "race-to-the bottom". Negative solidarity operates under the invisible, though clearly contradictory and self-refuting, assumption of reflexive impotence. I will endeavor to campaign for the lowering of working standards since I must suffer the same lowered standards, because there is only one direction in which the thermodynamic system of socio-economics can run: towards the abject exploitation of sump-end post-Fordist (faux-free market) Neoliberalism. When the Tories talk of social solidarity in the face of the consequences of the financial crisis, it is clearly negative solidarity they have in mind."[1]

There is something about this formulation that seems unavoidable to me. There is no shortage of this evidence for this perspective. Just look at this article in the New York Times about the prospect of a BART strike titled "Changing Attitudes on Labor Color Bay Area Transit Dispute". The whole point of this piece is to argue that the traditionally liberal and union friendly Bay Area is not friendly to the idea of a BART strike. The article is filled with quotes that demonstrate this "negative solidarity" in which opposition to the union is framed in terms of the precarious and vulnerable position of those without such protections. To cite one of the "man on the street" interviews from the article, "Given the economy, I think the unionized people should be breaking even, not necessarily getting ahead," she said. "There are a lot of workers out there who don't even have a union or a pension or health care benefits."[2]

---

1 Alex Williams, "On Negative Solidarity and Post-Fordist Plasticity," January 2010 https://splinteringboneashes.blogspot.com/2010/01/negative-solidarity-and-post-fordist.html
2 Norimutu Onishi, "Changing Attitudes on Labor Color Bay Area Transit Dispute," *The New York Times*, August 10, 2013, https://www.nytimes.com/2013/08/11/us/changing-attitudes-on-labor-color-bay-area-transit-dispute.html

This perfectly illustrates the negative solidarity outlined above. Lack of a pension, or of health care, becomes an argument against those who still maintain such basic standards of living, a case against them, not an argument for everyone to be given the same basic rights. There is no aspiration, no hope for a better condition, the only we can collectively move is down. I think that one can argue negative solidarity has become the dominant ideological and affective response to the current economic crisis. As the promises and fantasies of neoliberalism fell apart the result was not, as many hoped, widespread anger against the system, but generalized fear coupled with anger towards anyone who seemed too stable, too secure, too content. Teachers, public workers, and the few who have union protections became the villains of this story.

Adam Kotsko has critiqued the logic of this argument recently on his blog.[3] I am less interested, however, in pointing out the flaws in this logic of negative solidarity than understanding its particular genesis and causal conditions. I am interested in moving beyond a "descriptive theory," a concept that seems to match up with our experience, or the experience cited in the Times towards a more comprehensive theory. Specifically, I am interested in thinking this along the lines of what could be called "the affective composition of labor."

The contemporary composition of labor that defines negative solidarity is one dominated by fear rather than hope, by the pervasive uncertainty of one's position and future. The institutional dimension of this composition are fairly clear, a loss of the institutional conditions of solidarity, such as unions, parties, etc., but even this explanation seems too simplistic. If negative solidarity means anything it indicates a transformation of not only the general affective sensibility, but also the imagination. Its causal conditions must be sought not just in the change of institutions, but the change of ideology. Here it is useful to cite the generation of negative solidarity in the myths of the "welfare queen" or her son

---

3 Adam Kotsko, "Privilege and the rhetoric of Austerity," August 10, 2013, https://itself.blog/2013/08/10/privilege-and-the-rhetoric-of-austerity/

and daughters, the lazy teacher or union protected worker, which have channeled anger and ressentiment towards the powerless through fictions of their supposed enjoyment. To grasp negative solidarity is to understand the way in which the institutional transformations of the recent decades (the order and connection of forces) and the ideological dimensions (the order and connection of the imagination) have combined to create a pervasive sense of hopelessness, powerlessness, and misdirected hostility. I have not offered much towards this here, just a provocation for future research. It does seem that negative solidarity needs to be understood, and transformed. I am not advocating a return to the old institutions, just that a recognition of collective power requires some organization, some solidarity, in order to be something more than an abstract idea. The task is to go from a negative solidarity towards a solidarity of negation, towards a collective transformation of our economic and political condition rather than a collective acquiescence to its most virulent dimensions.

For more on Negative Solidarity see Personalized Ideology (or Ideology Personified): On Silva's Mood Economy for more on the economy of affects see Economies of Affect/Affective Economies: Towards a Spinozist Critique of Political Economy.

Red May Seattle

The Original Sin of Accumulation: Trying to Say Something Original About Ursprüngliche Akkumulation

Originally posted in May of 2017.

A bit of context: last weekend I was asked to participate in Red May Seattle, contributing to both its Marx-a-thon, a day long reading group on *Capital* and the *Grundrisse*, as well as discussing neoliberalism, science fiction, and the current struggles. What follows here is neither the text of what I presented on primitive accumulation, nor a kind of self-critique after the fact; it is an attempt to jot down some thoughts that were generated in collective discussion and reflection before they dissipate. It is red in practice and in theory, or, at the very least red in theoretical practice. What follows owes a great deal to all of those present at Red May. Names are withheld because I may have completely misunderstood what they were saying.

One way to understand primitive accumulation is it is theorized by Marx is in terms of the question of how the economy functions, reproduces itself. Contrary to the idea that the economy, that capital, functions on its own working as a self-reproducing process, it posits a necessary supplement to exploitation. How the economy functions on its own differs according to theoretical orientation and context. For Adam Smith it was a matter of mankind's tendency to "barter, truck, and exchange," but one could argue that such an image of the economy functioning on its own, reproducing itself, underlies even historical accounts of capital. In the first we are dealing with an anthropology, even an essentialism, while in the second we are dealing with economism. What the chapter on primitive accumulation (as well as the chapter on Colonization) reveal is that there is no capitalist economy without a capitalist state, no accumulation without dispossession. Part of the popularity of primitive accumulation is that it brings violence and cruelty of the periphery into the core of the apparently clean and well-regulated functioning of capital.

Such a reading, especially in its tendency to find primitive accumulation everywhere from the colonies to privatization to Uber's assault on the common possession of the automobile risks overlooking Marx's own understanding of capitalism. As much as capital emerges in the extra-economic violence of the state it cannot be reduced to it. To quote from my own *The Micro-Politics of Capital*:

> "Marx is somewhat ambiguous with respect to the closure of primitive accumulation and its relation to the mode of production it engenders. At times, Marx appears to argue that primitive accumulation and the overt violence it involves ends in the day-to-day relations of exploitation; while at other times it appears that the violent lawmaking power of primitive accumulation is merely privatized and brought indoors into the factory. Marx emphatically illustrates the order of discipline imposed by the factory codes: "The overseer's book of penalties replaces the slave-driver's lash. All punishments naturally resolve themselves into fines and deductions from wages, and the law-giving talent of the factory Lycurgus so arranges matters that a violation of this laws is, if possible, more profitable to him than the keeping of them" (CI 550/447). Marx suggests that there is a qualitative difference between primitive accumulation and the

capitalist economy it engenders, in terms of the former's bloody discontinuity and the latter's continuity and silent functioning. At the same time, however, Marx would suggest that this qualitative change is best understood perhaps as a change in the form of violence itself, capitalist accumulation is nothing other than primitive accumulation continued onto the shop floor, and thus nothing other than a continuation of the modification of violence begun with "bloody legislation" and the enclosure acts. The violence of law and the police gives way to the coercive force of the shop supervisor and the rhythm of machines."[1]

It is perhaps Will Roberts who offers the most trenchant critique of all of those who insist on the ubiquity of primitive accumulation. As Roberts writes in *Marx's Inferno*,

> "The point of Marx's account of primitive accumulation is not that capital has its origin in acts of violence and theft, but that capital has is origin in the opportunistic exploitation of the new forms of freedom created by acts of violence and theft. Violence and theft cannot give rise to capital directly. There must be a displacement from the acts of violence and theft to the process of capitalizing upon the conditions thereby created. Part and parcel of capital's treachery is that it requires others to create its conditions of existence."[2]

Following Roberts on the point that an overemphasis on the state and violence leads to an underemphasis on capital itself, on the domination internal to the reproduction of capital, it might be possible to argue for a different supplement. One of the most striking characteristics of Marx's chapter on primitive accumulation is that it stresses the story, the narrative and myth, of primitive accumulation. Primitive accumulation is a story, a just-so story, told about the origins of capital. As Marx writes:

---

[1] Jason Read, *The Micro-Politics of Capital: Marx and the Prehistory of the Present*, Albany: Suny Press, 29.
[2] William Clare Roberts, *Marx's Inferno: The Political Theory of Capital*, Princeton: Princeton University, 2017, 207.

> "This primitive accumulation plays approximately the same role in political economy as original sin does in theology. Adam bit the apple, and thereupon sin fell on the human race. Its origin is supposed to be explained when it is told as an anecdote about the past. Long, long ago there were two sorts of people; one the diligent, intelligent, and above all frugal elite; the other lazy rascals, spending their substance, and more, in riotous living. The legend of theological original sin tells us certainly how man came to be condemned to eat his bread by the sweat of his brow; but the history of economic original sin reveals to us that there are people to whom this is by no means essential. Never mind! Thus it came to pass that the former sort accumulated wealth, and the latter sort finally had nothing to sell except their own skins."[3]

To pull a Zizek and cite myself again:

> "Thus, as much as so-called primitive accumulation posits a theory of the formation of the capitalist mode of production, albeit one predicated on a presupposed division between the diligent and the lazy, it turns this explanation toward the present in the form of a moral tale. The origin provides the present with a moral alibi, dividing the capitalist and the worker along the lines of the good and the bad."[4]

Ok, finally, here is where I get to saying something new, or at least try to do so. Primitive accumulation is an account of the original constitution of the capitalist relation. As such it is a story of the destruction of the commons and the social relations that preceded capital. It explains how the very imperative to work is itself necessitated by the destruction of any other possible condition for reproduction. Or, as Marx writes, from this point forward it is possible to rely on the "worker's drives for self-preservation and propagation" in order to reproduce capital. However, Marx's inclusion

---

3 Karl Marx, *Capital: A Critique of Political Economy, Volume I*, Translated by Ben Fowkes, New York: Penguin, 1977, 873.
4 Jason Read, *The Micro-Politics of Capital*, 21.

of primitive accumulation as a moral story suggests that such a brute assertion of economic necessity has never taken place, that capital always required a supplement, not, in this case, of state violence (although that is needed as well), but of ideological justification. From its origin capital has always needed stories about itself in order to justify its existence. The idea of the capitalist as job creator, as the origin and source of wealth is just as important to capitalism as the accumulation of wealth; the idea of work as a moral activity, as defining one's worth is just as important as work as economic activity. There is no brute economic activity without its mythology.

These stories interpellate workers in ways that are historically specific. It is not just the fear of starvation that brings people to the factory gates but the desire to escape the patriarchal home, the peasant village, or other conditions, desires that are fueled as much by fantasies of wealth and escape as the material conditions of need. On this point I am very much indebted to everyone at Red May.

One cannot separate structural conditions, surplus value and the wage form, from the stories and narratives of capitalist desire and worker's striving, because they are always already intermingled. Striving, desire, is always already determined by both the economic relations and their "mythic" representation. Second, to end on a point that is less infra-philosophical and more practical, one could then think about the way in which capital to this day continues to tell stories about itself, and how these stories function as a condition of its reproduction. The best evidence against the idea of mute compulsion is the simple fact that capital never ceases to talk about itself. Part of this seems to be intertwined with the problem of neoliberalism, which as much as it involved new spaces of market relations and a new conception of economic activity, it is also is the era in which capital becomes more thoroughly narrativized, or, to paraphrase Lordon, capital becomes not just our economy but also our culture.

For more on the representation of capitalism see "The General Intellect Personified: More on Capitalism as a Social Relation."

TRANSLATIONS

-

Vengez-moi : The Avengers et l'industrie culturelle

Translated by David Buxton. Published in September of 2017.

Je ne comptais pas écrire sur *The Avengers*, car le film ne m'inspirait pas. J'y ai passé un bon moment dans un état de régression absolue. Hulk cassait tout, Thor maniait son marteau, des quolibets marrants furent prononcés, et ça pétait dans tous les sens. Pour citer Adorno : « *ce n'est pas pour rien que l'on peut entendre en Amérique de la bouche des producteurs cyniques que leurs films doivent tenir compte du niveau intellectuel d'un enfant de onze ans. Ce faisant, ils se sentent toujours plus incités à faire d'un adulte un enfant de onze ans* »[1]. Selon ce critère-là, le film est une réussite.

Dans le prolongement de cette remarque d'Adorno, une appréciation première du film serait de dire qu'il représente le point culminant de la tendance de l'industrie culturelle à transformer tout en publicité. Les livres deviennent des annonces pour les films, les films deviennent des annonces pour les bandes sonores, les bandes sonores deviennent des annonces pour les jeux vidéo, etc., tout produit est une publicité pour un autre. *The Avengers* poussent cette logique à un autre niveau. À partir d'*Iron Man* en 2008, on a vu une série de films dont les brèves apparitions de vedettes et les séquences post-génériques se retrouvent dans le film dont il est question ici. Je cite à ce propos les remarques faites par Fredric Jameson sur le devenir film de la bande-annonce :

> « *Or, la bande-annonce doit non seulement montrer quelques images des vedettes, et quelques échantillons des scènes d'action, mais aussi récapituler pratiquement tous les coups de théâtre, dévoilant ainsi toute l'intrigue à l'avance. À terme, le consommateur invétéré et forcé de ces spectacles à venir (dont cinq ou six précèdent le film principal, et remplacent les anciens courts-métrages) finit par faire une découverte*

---

1 Conférence en français pour l'université radiophonique internationale, 21 et 28 septembre, 1963 : https://www.le-terrier.net/adorno/industrie.htm

capitale, à savoir que la bande-annonce suffit. On n'a plus vraiment besoin de voir le film entier (à moins que l'objet soit de tuer le temps) »[2]

La convergence de séquences aboutissant à *The Avengers* va à l'encontre de cette logique dans la mesure où c'est le film lui-même qui existe désormais pour promouvoir la suite, en dehors d'une bande-annonce. Les scènes décisives se retrouvent souvent après le générique de la fin. (La remarque de Jameson, datant de 1997, pourrait être elle-même « historicisée »).[3] Dans le cas des films comme *The Avengers*, la bande-annonce pointe vers une autre bande-annonce, devenue une véritable forme culturelle en elle-même. Il faudra contextualiser cette évolution par rapport à la dynamique du capital financier.

Rien n'empêche de voir *The Avengers* comme le point culminant de cette tendance au marketing multiplateforme. Il existe, néanmoins, deux arguments qui nuancent ce point de vue. D'abord, la tendance dominante dans la production de blockbusters reste la stratégie de « gonflage et largage » (*pump and dump*). Un film de ce type fait l'objet d'un battage médiatique (*hype*) sur tous les supports possibles, il est projeté en ouverture simultanément sur plusieurs milliers d'écrans, et il en tire des revenus conséquents, avant que la réponse critique sur les réseaux sociaux puisse le faire couler. Il s'agit toutes proportions gardées d'un cycle expansion-récession (*boom and bust*). Mais l'idée de passer quatre ans à développer un film qui formerait la base de films futurs est du moins une longue arnaque, à défaut d'être un investissement à long terme.

Deuxièmement, pour apogée de la culture publicitaire qu'il soit, ce marketing transversal est aussi et surtout le prolongement de la culture des *comics*, qui met en scène un univers autant que des

---

[2] Fredric Jameson, « Culture and Finance Capital », *The Cultural Turn : Selected Writings on the Postmodern 1983-1998*, Verso (London, New York), 1998, 2009, p. 155 (je traduis).

[3] Référence à la célèbre première phrase (« *Il faut toujours historiciser !* ») de l'un des ouvrages majeurs de Jameson, *L'Inconscient politique* (Questions théoriques, 2012, édition originale, 1981). Remarquons le décalage important entre la date de la publication américaine (chez Cornell University Press) et la traduction française, due à Nicolas Vieillecazes. (Compte-rendu intéressant de l'édition française par Stéphane Haber ici sur le site *La Vie des Idées*).

personnages. Autrement dit, il faut voir *The Avengers* comme un film *comic book* plutôt qu'un film de super-héros. Il s'agit moins du « voyage (initiatique) de super-héros » que de la représentation d'un monde où des dieux scandinaves se battent contre des guerriers aux pouvoirs exceptionnels. Ce sont des références intertextuelles familières depuis longtemps aux lecteurs des *comics*. La construction d'un univers a toujours été une stratégie de marketing, et une intrigue avec un personnage Marvel est systématiquement prolongée ailleurs.

Il semble, toutefois, que *The Avengers* puissent toujours s'appréhender à travers ce croisement d'une forme marketing et du contenu issu de la *pulp culture*. On peut voir cela dans le choix du réalisateur Joss Whedon, qui bénéficie d'une forte réputation auprès des « fans » (série culte, blogs, tee-shirts), et qui est amateur des *comics*. Ce choix a un sens dans le contexte d'un renversement culturel, où les créateurs de télévision comme Joss Whedon (*Buffy*), David Simon (*The Wire*), Matt Wiener (*Mad Men*) sont étudiés comme des auteurs avec des styles singuliers.

Ce qui est intéressant dans le choix de Whedon, c'est que *The Avengers* viennent juste après son travail de scénariste sur *Cabin in the Woods* (*La cabane dans les bois*), qu'il faut voir comme une allégorie de tournage. Dans ce film, un groupe d'hommes, recroquevillés autour de moniteurs de surveillance, activent des touches et tournent des boutons afin de construire des scènes pour plaire à des dieux invisibles. Il se trouve, comme par hasard, que le désir de ceux-ci se porte sur des nymphomanes nubiles poursuivies par des monstres. De même, le film *The Avengers* a aussi ses dirigeants invisibles, le « Conseil » et un groupe d'hommes penchés sur des moniteurs dans un héliporteur. Les échanges entre Nick Fury et le Conseil révèlent finalement la structure du film. La scène où le Conseil exprime ses doutes quant au groupe bizarre rassemblé par Fury fait penser à une réunion d'investisseurs avec des managers de Disney : « *vous voulez dire qu'on va tout miser sur un film avec un dieu scandinave, un héros de la Deuxième Guerre mondiale, et un homme-robot ?* ». La construction de *The Avengers* serait donc un livre ouvert. Le grand moment libérateur qui donne aux Vengeurs quelque chose à venger s'avère être orchestré autant à l'écran que hors écran. De même pour le dénouement grandiose. Ces moments métaphysiques prennent souvent la forme d'un débat entre Nick Fury, qui défend les idéaux d'héroïsme et de pureté, et le Conseil qui préfère l'efficacité assurée par la technologie. Difficile de ne pas y voir une externalisation des premières réunions entre créateurs et financiers (pitch meetings), ainsi que celle du conflit entre le geek devenu réalisateur, et sa boîte de production. Dans ce cas, la scène post-générique représente la victoire du premier sur la dernière.

Au-delà de cet angle métaphysique, le film ressemble à un *comic book* porté à l'écran. Certains vont jusqu'à affirmer qu'il s'agit du premier film à avoir pleinement assimilé les implications de la destruction des Tours jumelles le 11 septembre 2001. Pour ma part, je pense qu'il serait plus intéressant d'examiner la façon dont il normalise certaines tendances qui se sont manifestées depuis, à savoir le recours à la torture et à l'utilisation généralisée de la surveillance. La première n'y figure pas, mais elle est constamment sous-entendue. Il y en a même quelques allusions dans la scène introduisant la Veuve noire, et dans celle où le méchant Loki est prisonnier à bord de l'héliporteur. Certes, Thor refuse de torturer son frère (et finalement le rend à la planète Asgard pour être traduit devant une sorte de tribunal intergalactique). Plus intéressante est la manière dont le film traite de la surveillance. *The Dark Knight Rises* fait de celle-ci le thème principal de l'intrigue, accompagné comme il se doit par des lamentations éthiques. Batman accepte d'y avoir recours dans un « état d'exception » pour vaincre le Joker, et détruit la technologie après.

Dans *The Avengers*, un agent du Shield déclare en passant qu'on est en train de scanner tous les caméras, mobiles, portables, etc., afin de localiser Loki. La surveillance totale fait désormais partie de la toile de fond. On pourrait prolonger ce constat en affirmant que la question soulevée dans le film, à savoir, vaut-il mieux combattre une menace par un groupe d'individus aux compétences supérieures, ou par de la technologie et des armements, peut se comprendre comme une référence voilée à la stratégie militaire américaine après le 11 septembre.

French Translation of Avenge Me: Avengers and the Culture Industry.

L'accumulation primitive de la préhistoire : sur les films de dinosaurs

Translated by David Buxton. Published in June of 2018.

Une diversité de prémisses dans les films de dinosaures

Gamin, j'étais obsédé par les dinosaures, rien d'unique à cela. Mais mon obsession n'avait pas de débouché populaire adéquat pour l'exprimer. C'était bien avant la franchise de *Jurassic Park* (1993). Alors, je regardais tous les films de dinosaures lorsqu'ils étaient diffusés dans l'après-midi, ou tard dans la nuit : *Le Sicième Continent* (1975), *The Last Dinosaur* (1977), etc. Ces films n'étaient pas nombreux, et en général ils étaient assez médiocres. Je me souviens en particulier de *The Valley of Gwangi* (1969), qui a bénéficié des effets spéciaux crées par Ray Harryhausen. C'était une autre époque, définie par la rareté des produits culturels, et non leur prolifération.

On trouve une diversité de prémisses dans les films des années 1950–70 pour expliquer l'existence des dinosaures. Le problème de tous ces films est le même : comment faire coïncider les dinosaures et les humains dans l'espace et dans le temps ? On pouvait tout simplement passer outre la réalité préhistorique en réunissant les dinosaures et les hommes des cavernes dans le même film (*Un million d'années avant J.C.*, 1966). Une meilleure solution était de situer l'intrigue sur une île inconnue (*King Kong*, 1933, 1976, 1986, 2005) ou dans une vallée isolée (*Le Monde perdu*, 1960), préservées du processus d'évolution, prémisse qui devenait de moins en moins tenable avec les progrès en cartographie dans le monde entier.

Une autre option encore était d'introduire les dinosaures dans un film historique, de l'époque du Far West (*The Valley of Gwangi* ou le nettement inférieur *Beast from Hollow Mountain* (1956)), ou lors des derniers jours de la conquête coloniale pendant la Première

Guerre mondiale (*Le Sixième Continent*), ce qui nous ramène à une époque où l'on pouvait croire encore en l'existence d'un monde perdu. En désespoir de cause, on pouvait transférer le genre sous terrain (*Voyage au centre de la Terre* (d'après Jules Verne), 1959, 1999, 2008, 2012), ou sur une autre planète (*Planet of Dinosaurs*, 1977). Si ma mémoire est bonne, le voyage dans le temps n'a jamais existé dans le genre (1). L'histoire des films de dinosaures suit largement l'histoire du colonialisme et de l'appropriation primitive des ressources jusqu'au Pôle nord et au-delà. Il n'est pas surprenant que Thomas Jefferson, troisième président des États-Unis, fût amateur de la paléontologie, et que de nos jours les frères Koch le soient aussi. On doit au spécialiste des études visuelles W. J. T. Mitchell un livre passionnant sur le dinosaure en tant qu'icône de l'entreprise moderne ainsi que de l'État.[1]

Ce qui minait cette diversité de prémisses, c'était la distribution limitée, répétitive de dinosaures. Presque tous les films faisaient figurer en vedette un tyrannosaure, avec un tricératops, un ptérodactyle et quelques autres pour faire bonne mesure. Création riche d'un point de vue fantasmatique, les dinosaures se situaient à mi-chemin entre des animaux réels et des monstres irréels. En tant que création culturelle, ils faisaient partie d'une culture commune, du moins pour les enfants du vingtième siècle. Le tyrannosaure pouvait se voir et dans les musées et dans les films ; il n'appartenait à personne.

Une réserve culturelle inexploitée

Sur la page IMDB IMDB qui lui est dédiée, Michael Crichton, auteur du roman original et du scénario, parle explicitement de la renommée (ou, comme on le dit maintenant, de la reconnaissance de marque) du dinosaure comme source d'inspiration. « *Au musée aujourd'hui, il y avait une petite attraction avec un garçon d'environ six ans dont les pieds ne touchaient même pas le sol. Chaque fois qu'on*

---

[1] W.J.T. Mitchell, *The Last Dinosaur Book: The Life and Times of a Cultural Icon*, University of Chicago Press, 1998.

lui a montré un dinosaure, il criait « tyrannosaure », « stégosaure » pendant une heure. Je me demandais pourquoi les dinosaures fascinent à ce point-là. C'est alors que j'ai décidé d'écrire Jurassic Park. » Il s'agissait pour Crichton d'une sorte de moment eurêka, la découverte non d'une réserve de pétrole, mais d'une réserve culturelle massive et inexploitée.

Il faut comprendre *Jurassic Park* de prime abord comme une remise à jour du problème générique spécifique aux films de dinosaures que j'ai évoqués ci-dessus. La manipulation génétique devient la nouvelle frontière à être explorée et commercialisée. La cartographie du génome rend possible ce que la cartographie de la Terre interdisait, à savoir le retour des dinosaures dans le monde actuel. Cette innovation diégétique va de pair avec l'innovation technique présidant à la production du film. Ce ne serait pas la seule fois que les images de synthèse et la manipulation génétique se combinent dans une informatique de la domination, l'une sur l'écran, l'autre derrière celui-ci. Si l'original *Jurassic Park* retient encore l'attention, c'est pour la qualité de ses effets spéciaux. Situé entre la fin des effets animatroniques et l'émergence des effets numériques, le film atteint un point esthétique idéal, plus convaincant que l'animation image par image (*stop motion*) ou les créatures mécaniques, mais sans l'aspect jeu vidéo du film numérique moderne.

L'original *Jurassic Park* coïncide avec l'émergence d'une cinématographie organisée autour de scènes imposées (*set pieces*). L'adjectif « spielbergien » a des sens multiples : des liens de famille sentimentaux, la commercialisation d'une forme particulière d'émerveillement enfantin, etc., mais je dirais qu'il s'applique aussi à la fragmentation du film en une série de scènes imposées mémorables reliées par des intrigues maigrichonnes (le plus souvent concernant justement des liens de famille). On peut avoir l'impression que les films de Spielberg ont été conçus pour être découverts au hasard sur une chaîne de câble, regardés pour les grandes scènes excitantes comme l'évasion du tyrannosaure, et puis zappés. Il n'y a que quelques films de Spielberg que j'envisagerais de revoir du début à la fin : *Les Aventuriers de l'Arche perdue, Dents de la mer, Rencontres du troisième type*. Pour les autres, le tout est moindre que la somme de ses parties. Je me souviens à peine du remake de *La Guerre des mondes*, mais j'aimerais revoir la scène de l'attaque sur le ferry. On associe plus le réalisateur Michael Bay (*Armageddon, Transformers*) avec cette logique de fragmentation et de chaos, mais Spielberg représente à sa façon la préhistoire de la destruction de l'attention. Cela reflète un paysage médiatique transformé, défini moins par la rareté que par la surabondance de choix.

Une expérience de marque particulière

On peut aussi comprendre *Jurassic Park* comme une sorte de film nostalgique, qui exploite la fascination enfantine pour les dinosaures. À la différence d'autres films nostalgiques, qui commercialisent tel dessin animé, telle bande dessinée, telle ligne de jouets, *Jurassic Park* profite de quelque chose de générique, l'histoire naturelle de la Terre. Cela fut un défi pour la marchandisation inéluctable de jouets et d'autres produits dérivés du premier film. À la différence des Stormtroopers de *La Guerre des Étoiles* ou des Transformers de la franchise du même nom, n'importe qui peut vendre un jouet tyrannosaure (par exemple, la société allemande Schleich en fabrique un qui est vendu dans beaucoup de musées). *Jurassic Park* a contourné cela en mettant sa marque (*brand*) de façon voyante sur chaque jouet, assorti d'une campagne publicitaire qui encourageait les enfants à l'identifier. Les films et la campagne de marketing représentent une tentative de transformer l'histoire naturelle en expérience de marque particulière, qui fait partie d'une autre sorte d'empire. Dans une grande mesure, cela a bien marché, bien plus que pour les jouets de dinosaures avant *Jurassic Park*. On n'a pas vu d'autres films de dinosaures depuis. Si vous voulez des dinosaures, en pixels ou en caoutchouc, désormais c'est *Jurassic Park* ou rien.

Dans les films suivants de la franchise, ce problème particulier de marquage se déplace du domaine du marketing vers l'intrigue du film elle-même. On n'a plus besoin de la caution scientifique des musées et des paléontologues. Une grande partie de la narration des films récents concerne la création à des fins mercantiles de nouveaux dinosaures, qui font assurément partie de la propriété intellectuelle d'Universal et d'Amblin Entertainment (Spielberg). Cette inflation du nombre de dinosaures complique la donne au niveau de la narration. En revanche, les dinosaures génétiquement modifiés, l'Indominus Rex et l'Indoraptor, résolvent un autre problème interne à ce genre de film, la séparation du monstre de l'animal. Tout film qui transforme un animal en monstre doit affronter cette difficulté. Comment expliquer pourquoi un animal continuerait à chasser des humains avec tant de zèle quand il existe d'autres sources de nourriture ? Les animaux ne se comportent pas comme des tueurs en série. Ce problème est encore plus aigu dans le cas des dinosaures qui, à la différence des requins, sont autant adorés que craints. Dans les films plus récents, on assigne le rôle du méchant au monstre génétiquement modifié, et les autres dinosaures deviennent alors relativement sympathiques. Un élément récurrent dans ces derniers films est l'intervention jouissive et bienvenue d'un tyrannosaure qui dévore un manager sans scrupules qui n'en mérite pas moins.

S'il y a une chose de positive à dire du dernier film *Jurassic World 2 : Fallen Kingdom*, c'est qu'il retourne cette logique contre elle-même. Alors que chaque film de la franchise a pour toile de fond un bien communal et son aliénation, à savoir le dinosaure comme élément d'une culture historique d'une part, et l'expérience d'une marque de l'autre, le dernier de la série rend explicite cette opposition. Les dinosaures aimeraient tout simplement retourner dans leur monde, et être laissés en paix. Les méchants capitalistes veulent par contre les transformer en marchandises, en armements, alors que les protagonistes, amis des dinosaures, veulent briser leurs cages.

Sur ce dernier point, on peut faire un parallèle avec un autre remake d'une intrigue de Michael Crichton, *Westworld*, qui raconte le même scénario d'un parc à thème qui dérape. Cette fois, ce sont des robots et non des dinosaures qui s'échappent. Les deux fictions convergent dans un monde où les formes de vie artificielles s'émancipent complètement de leur lieu d'origine, celui-ci devenant alors moins un cauchemar qu'un salut utopique. On a rencontré l'ennemi, c'est nous-mêmes. Le corollaire est la prise de conscience que, par comparaison, les monstres ne sont pas si monstrueux que cela.

French Translation of The Primitive Accumulation of Prehistory: On the Jurassic Park Films

Blockbusters et mèmes à l'ère de l'effondrement viral

Translated by David Buxton. Published in 2020.

En ce moment, je réfléchis à une question d'une naïveté désespérante : à quoi sert la culture populaire ? Ou plus précisément, comment fonctionne-t-elle comme culture, en donnant du sens au monde et en exprimant nos désirs ? J'ai été incité à poser cette question pour deux raisons sans rapport. D'abord, je monte un séminaire en première année sur « la politique et la culture » qui m'oblige à passer en revue quelques arguments classiques concernant l'usage et le mésusage de la culture de Williams et d'Adorno à de Certeau. Ensuite, quand je ne travaille pas sur ce cours (ou sur une autre activité contraignante), je fais comme tout le monde, à savoir rechercher un film ou une série qui pourrait faire passer le temps du confinement.

« *Les restaurants s'ouvrent de nouveau : l'ambiance (vibe)* » *(plan du film Alien détourné)*

En réalité, je me demande comment mieux faire passer ce temps. Parfois, j'ai juste envie d'être diverti (j'ai regardé tous les épisodes du *Prisonnier* et pas mal d'épisodes du classique *Star Trek*), et parfois j'ai envie d'aborder le moment actuel, mais à distance, à travers la sécurité apportée par des médiations (évitant toute fiction qui évoque directement les pandémies et les apocalypses). Il m'est assez pénible de tomber sur une intrigue faisant brusquement revenir le présent. Les sous-intrigues d'infection virale dans *The Host* et dans *La Planète des singes : L'Affrontement* ont été un peu difficiles à supporter, surtout le début du dernier. Tout cela pour dire que je me pose des questions habituellement éludées quand on regarde un film pour tuer le temps dans un avion, ou chez soi : que veux-je de la culture populaire ? Est-ce simplement une question de divertissement ? Ou faudrait-il qu'elle nous donne quelque chose de plus, qui nous aide à affronter tout ce qui nous bombarde plus que jamais : la peur, l'anxiété, le bouleversement social, la perte, et même la mort ?

Schématiquement résumé, l'un des aspects de la critique de Horkheimer et d'Adorno de « l'industrie culturelle » est que les impératifs de la production de masse et du profit produisent une « culture » qui n'en est pas une, qui ne nous offre rien de nourrissant. En témoignent les trois passages suivants :

> « *L'aspect prédigéré du produit [culturel] prévaut, se justifie et s'établit de façon d'autant plus marquée qu'il renvoie constamment à ceux qui ne peuvent rien digérer qui n'a pas été déjà prédigéré. C'est de la nourriture pour bébé : la réflexion permanente sur soi-même ancrée dans la compulsion infantile vis-à-vis de la répétition des besoins que [le produit culturel] a créés en premier lieu.* »[1]

> « *La culture qui d'après son propre sens non seulement obéissait aux hommes, mais toujours aussi protestait contre la condition sclérosée*

---

[1] T. W. Adorno, « The Schema of Mass Culture », in *The Culture Industry*, Routledge, New York, 1991 (je traduis de l'anglais), p. 100. (Une traduction française de l'allemand original (1943) existe, due à Christophe David : « Le Schéma de la culture de masse », *Mortibus* 10/11, automne 2009, devenue introuvable).

dans laquelle ils vivent et par là leur faisait honneur, cette culture, par son assimilation totale aux hommes, se trouve intégrée à cette condition sclérosée ; ainsi elle avilit les hommes encore une fois. Les productions de l'esprit dans le style de l'industrie culturelle ne sont plus aussi des marchandises mais le sont intégralement. »[2]

« *Ce qu'on pourrait qualifier de valeur d'usage dans la réception des biens culturels est remplacé par la valeur d'échange ; au lieu de rechercher la jouissance on se contente d'assister aux manifestations « artistiques » et « d'être au courant », au lieu de chercher à devenir un connaisseur on se contente donc d'un gain de prestige. Le consommateur devient l'alibi de l'industrie du divertissement aux institutions de laquelle il ne peut échapper. Il faut avoir vu* Mrs. Miniver, *tout comme il faut avoir chez soi* Life *et* Time. *Tout est perçu sous ce seul aspect : pouvoir servir à autre chose, même si cet autre chose est aussi vague que possible. Tout objet n'a de valeur que comme objet d'échange et n'a aucune valeur en soi.* »[3]

Si tout cela vous semble excessif, accusation récurrente levée contre Horkheimer et Adorno, pensez au jugement courant « *il a bien vieilli* » à propos d'un vieux film, et au constat étonné qu'il y avait quelque chose, appelons-le un usage, alors que le film en question ne circule plus, son moment de « faut avoir vu » étant passé depuis longtemps. La culture devient non seulement une marchandise, mais aussi une forme de monnaie qui s'échange chaque fois qu'on bavarde, ou qu'on va sur les réseaux sociaux. On ne l'utilise que pour échanger, et si on manque de monnaie ou ignore la dernière tendance, on est rejeté du marché, abandonné sans un sou. Cela dit, c'est en se penchant sur les réseaux sociaux qu'on peut déceler un autre usage. Je pense en particulier aux mèmes qui réorientent les éléments d'intrigue des

---

[2] T. W. Adorno «L'industrie culturelle », *Communications* (Paris), 3 : 1964, p. 13 (traduit de l'allemand par Hans Hildenbrand et Alex Lindenberg).
[3] Horkheimer et Adorno, *Kulturindustrie*, Editions Allia, 2012, p. 85-6 (traduit de l'allemand par Eliane Kaufholz). (La même version est disponible aussi comme chapitre de *La Dialectique de la Raison*, Gallimard, collection « Tel », 1974). Pour un résumé du mélodrame sentimental *Mrs. Miniver* : https://en.wikipedia.org/wiki/Mrs._Miniver. Les magazines *Life* et *Time* servirent de modèles en France pour *Paris Match* et *L'Express* respectivement.

films, dévalorisant ainsi la « circulation de la monnaie », ou tout au moins, la faisant travailler avec une valeur différente.

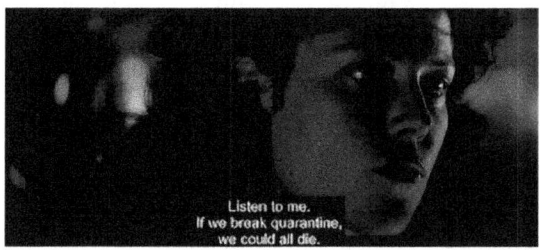

Prenons le cas des mèmes qui exploitent des blockbusters hollywoodiens comme Alien (1979) et Les Dents de la mer (1975) pour comprendre, et pour commenter la réponse du gouvernement à la pandémie du Covid-19. S'agissant d'Alien, certains de ces mèmes (comme celui ci-dessus) ne font que citer le dialogue original et les éléments de l'intrigue, qui prennent un autre sens dans l'ère du confinement et de la quarantaine. D'autres (comme celui au début de cet article) entament une autre lecture du film, qui focalise moins sur la créature du titre que sur l'employeur privé qui met en danger l'équipage du vaisseau Nostromo. L'affirmation que « l'équipage est sacrifiable » a une autre pertinence à un moment où les gens retournent au travail en pleine pandémie. Nous sommes tous à bord du Nostromo maintenant, inquiets pour nos primes, et considérés comme sacrifiables aux yeux de nos employeurs.

<

Alors que le Premier ministre britannique Boris Johnson désigne le maire Vaughan (*Les Dents de la mer*) comme un héros[4], sûrement la mésinterprétation la plus bizarre dans l'histoire de la culture populaire, nous autres voyons le maire comme l'incarnation de tout politicien qui place le maintien des bénéfices et l'intérêt du capital

---

4 Stuart Heritage, "Boris Johnson's Hero is the Mayor Who Kept The Beaches Open in Jaws. That is Fine by Me." *The Guardian*, March 13, 2020. https://www.theguardian.com/film/2020/mar/13/boris-johnson-coronavirus-hero-mayor-larry-vaughn-jaws

devant la préservation de la vie, bref tout(e) homme ou femme politique. La focalisation sur le maire comme figure du Mal nous offre une lecture différente de celle, plus idéologique, originalement proposée par Fredric Jameson. Lisant le film contre le roman, Jameson centre son analyse sur la façon dont la survie du policier Brody et de l'océanographe Hooper au détriment du chasseur de requins Quint énonce l'idée d'une Amérique en transformation. Il affirme :

> « *Or, le contenu du partenariat entre Hooper et Brody projeté par le film peut être précisé, socialement et politiquement, comme l'allégorie d'une alliance entre la force de la loi et la nouvelle technocratie de l'entreprise transnationale : une alliance qui doit être cimentée, non seulement dans le triomphe fantasmé sur la menace mal définie du requin lui-même, mais surtout dans la précondition indispensable de l'effacement de l'image traditionnelle d'une Amérique plus vieille qu'il faut éliminer de la conscience historique et de la mémoire sociale avant qu'un nouveau système de pouvoir ne prenne sa place. On pourrait continuer de lire cette opération en termes d'archétypes mythiques si on veut, mais alors dans ce cas ce serait une vision utopique et rituelle qui est aussi tout un programme – très inquiétant – politique et social. Cela touche des contradictions sociales et des anxiétés actuelles seulement pour les exploiter dans sa nouvelle tâche de résolution idéologique, nous exhortant symboliquement à enterrer les vieux populismes, et à réagir à une image de partenariat politique qui projette une stratégie de légitimation entièrement nouvelle ; il déplace efficacement les antagonismes de classe entre riches et pauvres qui perdurent dans la société de consommation (et dans le roman duquel le film fut adapté) en les remplaçant par une sorte de nouvelle fraternité, fallacieuse, dans laquelle le spectateur se réjouit, sans se rendre compte qu'il ou elle y est exclu(e).* »[5]

Jameson pense fournir une corrective dialectique à l'argument de Horkheimer et d'Adorno. Pour lui, il faut que l'industrie

---

5 Fredric Jameson, « Reification and Utopia in Mass Culture », in *Signatures of the Visible*, Routledge, New York, 1990, p. 38-9 (je traduis).

culturelle serve à quelque chose, qu'elle nous offre autre chose que les références échangées en bavardant. Nous ne mangerions pas de la nourriture pour bébé s'il n'y avait rien à goûter ou à digérer, un contenu utopique sous la forme d'une résolution de contradictions et de conflits existants. Cette dimension utopique est elle-même déformée et réifiée au point où on se retrouve en train d'applaudir le sacrifice de Quint face à l'alliance entre Brody et Hooper, entre les ordres policier et technocratique.

La focalisation dans les mèmes sur le maire comme figure représentant l'appât du gain donne une lecture moins sophistiquée, mais chargée d'une autre orientation politique. Il n'est plus question d'une alliance entre la police et la technocratie en tant que force d'ordre nouvelle, mais de la façon dont l'alliance entre la politique et le commerce constitue l'ordre sous lequel nous vivons tous, même dans les bons vieux temps de l'Amérique des petites villes (d'autant plus que le film élimine la sous-intrigue dans le livre sur la corruption mafieuse).

<

On ne peut parler tout à fait d'un détournement de ces films, car le message antientreprise a toujours été là dès le début. D'une certaine manière, *Alien* et *Les Dents de la mer* ont toujours été plutôt axés sur la lutte « humain contre humain » qu'« humain contre animal », d'autant qu'il faut que l'entreprise commerciale soit présente pour pousser les humains dans un conflit avec un animal qui finalement ne veut que manger, vivre et survivre. On pourrait également avancer l'argument que les deux films étaient au seuil de l'émergence de la forme blockbuster, et étaient ainsi plus riches en narrativité, en personnages et même en thèmes sous-jacents que le dernier lot de films de franchise ; il semblerait que l'industrie culturelle de nos jours fonctionne du moins en partie par la création constante de la nostalgie pour ce qui apparaît comme une version antérieure, meilleure, d'elle-même. C'est là un point que même Horkheimer et Adorno n'avaient peut-être pas vu.

Malgré ces réserves, je m'intéresse à la façon dont les mèmes filmiques en prolongent le contenu anticapitaliste existant, c'est-à-dire comment un mème peut à la fois produire et refléter une nouvelle sensibilité moins pacifiée par l'industrie culturelle, et en mesure d'exprimer la colère et l'indignation à travers elle. (Bien entendu, cette observation n'est pas limitée à ces deux films. *Jurassic Park* a aussi été l'objet de plaisanteries et de mèmes, et on pourrait facilement imaginer une grande relecture des films hollywoodiens en termes d'entreprises plus intéressées par les bénéfices que par la préservation des vies).

Quand j'ai revu récemment *Alien* et *Les Dents de la mer* au prisme de leur nouvelle vie virale en tant que mèmes critiques de la réponse à la pandémie, je pensais un moment écrire un post réaffirmant leur côté anticapitaliste. Je n'ai pas eu besoin de le faire ; on l'avait déjà fait à travers divers mèmes et blagues en ligne. Ces deux films me semblaient déjà réécrits par le contexte nouveau, qui les a transformés en commentaires sur ce contexte. Il se pourrait que la culture populaire ne nous donne pas grande chose à retravailler ; après tout, peut-être n'est-elle que de la nourriture pour bébé. Mais même celle-ci peut être jetée contre le mur dans un accès de rage. Et cette rage va être nécessaire non seulement pour se sortir du moment politique actuel, mais aussi pour construire quelque chose de nouveau. Comme l'affirma Mark Fisher à propos de l'anticapitalisme de *Hunger Games*, il est parfois utile de se rappeler qui est l'ennemi, et de prendre le message antientreprise dans la culture populaire au pied de la lettre.[6] Même les produits de l'industrie culturelle peuvent être utilisés non pas uniquement pour renforcer des idéologies existantes, mais pour forger de nouveaux mythes. Quant à moi, je sais que je ne regarderai plus jamais *Alien* ou *Les Dents de la mer* de la même façon.

French Translation of The Use and Abuse of Blockbusters for Life: Movies and Memes in the Age of Viral Collapse.

---

6 Mark Fisher, "Dystopia Now" https://markfisherreblog.tumblr.com/post/39217506447/dystopia-now

Le diable est dans les détails : la démonologie du capital dans « La Quatrième Dimension »

Translated by David Buxton. Published in March of 2019.

Impossible d'exagérer à quel point, enfant, j'étais fan de *The Twilight Zone* (*La Quatrième Dimension*). J'ai regardé tous les épisodes de l'ancienne série (CBS, 1959–64) lors des rediffusions dans les années 1980, c'est pourquoi j'avais un petit téléviseur en noir et blanc dans ma chambre. En outre, j'étais abonné à la revue du même nom qui publait des nouvelles originales de science-fiction. J'ai également vu le film éponyme (1983) et la nouvelle version de la série la nouvelle version de la série (1985–87).[1]

L'intrigue la plus iconique de la série originale est le pacte avec le Diable pour obtenir de la richesse, du pouvoir ou de la santé, avant de se retrouver subitement face à une conséquence imprévue. Le diable est dans les détails, et chaque tentative faite par un individu de réaliser ainsi son désir se retourne fatalement contre lui. Qui veut être le dirigeant d'un pays puissant devient Hitler caché dans son bunker ; qui veut avoir un million de dollars en liquide en perd tout en impôts, etc. (Ces exemples sont tirés de « The Man in the Bottle » (épisode 38, 1960), où il s'agit non du Diable, mais d'un génie).

Il est tentant de voir le Diable comme l'incarnation de l'ironie de la série, de son amour du dénouement inattendu. Après tout, le présentateur Rod Serling (image ci-dessus) est célèbre pour avoir écrit ce qui serait le meilleur exemple de celui-ci dans l'histoire du

---

1 En français, la version de 1985 s'appelle *La Cinquième Dimension*, ce qui est plus logique d'un point de vue scientifique. *Twilight* en anglais veut dire « crépusculaire », mais peut aussi désigner une zone urbaine périphérique où les constructions sont dilapidées, une condition ou zone transitoire ou indéfinie, ou encore toute période de vie qui voit la lente diminution des forces. Le titre original en français est aussi plat que faux (il ignore la théorie de la relativité, où le temps constitue la quatrième dimension).

cinéma : la dernière image de *La Planète des Singes* (1968). Qu'un pacte avec le Diable puisse mal tourner est un risque que les personnages dans la série n'ignorent pas ; tous essayent, cependant, d'être plus malins que Lui. Prenons l'épisode « Escape Clause » par exemple (épisode 6, 1959). Hypocondriaque, amer et coléreux, Walter Bedecker conclut un pacte avec le Diable en échange de la vie éternelle en bonne santé. Mais il ne semble pas heureux pour autant, se croyant toujours malade, et agressant son médecin, et sa femme ; il exemplifie l'avare décrit par Aristote (*Éthique à Nicomaque*), moins intéressé par la qualité de la vie que par l'accumulation incessante.

Bedecker ne manque pas d'intelligence, cependant. Dans un premier temps, le Diable, un petit gros jovial nommé Cadawaller, semble perdant : quelqu'un d'immortel n'aura jamais une âme à prendre. Bedecker assume sa nouvelle immortalité avec une insouciance totale, se jetant sous un train, buvant du poison, etc. Sa femme le retrouve sur le point de se jeter dans le vide depuis un grand immeuble, et meurt en essayant de l'empêcher. Accusé de meurtre, Bedecker avoue dans l'idée qu'un passage sur la chaise électrique sera encore une expérience amusante. Hélas pour lui, son avocat consciencieux lui obtient une condamnation à la prison à vie. L'Enfer est un lieu sur Terre. Heureusement, le pacte contient une clause de sauvegarde. Bedecker peut renoncer à la vie éternelle à tout moment, et mourir rapidement, cédant ainsi son âme au Diable. Décidément, le diable est dans les petits caractères.

Les diables de *La Quatrième Dimension* peuvent exploiter les péchés de la vanité et de la cupidité, mais leurs méthodes sont plus bureaucratiques que théocratiques. Le pacte respecte les détails à la lettre ; ce sont les conséquences imprévues qui restent voilées. Il est approprié qu'une société capitaliste qui vénère celles-ci y trouve l'image du Diable. Alors que la théologie du marché serait la main invisible, notre dieu terrestre, qui transforme les conséquences imprévues en bénéfices sociaux, sa démonologie consiste dans la manière dont la poursuite de l'intérêt égoïste bute sur les limites de la connaissance individuelle. Personne ne peut anticiper toutes les ramifications possibles d'une action singulière, même d'un simple vœu, et la vie éternelle a ses inconvénients inconnus. Le dieu du marché nous rassure que nos actions intéressées seront bénéfiques pour la société, mais le diable de la responsabilité nous rappelle que nous devrons répondre de celles-ci, même de ce que nous n'aurions jamais pu prévoir.

L'épisode qui illustre le mieux cette théologie du capital est « Of late, I think of Cliffordsville » (épisode 116, 1963). Pour la petite histoire, cet épisode est vraisemblablement la source de l'un des meilleurs exemples de fausse citation dans la culture populaire contemporaine. Dans le film *Die Hard* (1988), le personnage Hans Gruber cite le vers : « *Le grand Alexandre, voyant l'étendue de son empire, pleura car il ne lui restait plus de mondes à conquérir* ». Il l'attribue à Plutarque, mettant en valeur son éducation classique. Mais cette phrase n'existe nulle part dans Plutarque. Elle apparaît bien, en revanche, dans *La Quatrième Dimension*. Peut-être Gruber a confondu éducation classique et télévision classique !

Un sentiment similaire se trouve dans un autre classique, Le Capital de Marx : « *Cette contradiction entre limite quantitative et absence de limite qualitative de l'argent plonge et replonge le thésauriseur dans son destin de Sisyphe de l'accumulation. Il lui arrive ce qui arrive au conquéreur du monde qui, à chaque nouveau pays, ne conquiert en fait qu'une nouvelle frontière.* »[2] Ce n'est pas Alexandre qui a besoin de nouveaux territoires à conquérir, mais l'exigence moderne d'accumulation capitaliste. La phrase de Marx s'accorde bien avec l'épisode en question.

Celui-ci s'ouvre dans le bureau de William Feathersmith, un magnat du pétrole, en train de détruire son dernier concurrent. L'achèvement de son empire correspond à l'épuisement de son but. C'est le concierge de l'immeuble qui lui fait la référence à Alexandre le Grand. Dans la prochaine scène, Feathersmith se retrouve dans le bureau de l'Agence de Voyages Devlin. La propriétaire à cornes,

---

2 Karl Marx, *Le Capital, livre 1*, traduction sous la responsabilité de Jean-Pierre Lefebvre, Quadrige/PUF, 1993 (1983), p. 150.

Mademoiselle Devlin, ne fait aucun effort de cacher sa nature démoniaque. Feathersmith s'attend que Devlin lui propose d'acheter son âme, mais il s'avère que celle-ci est déjà en sa possession ; il n'y a presque pas de pactes faustiens classiques dans *La Quatrième Dimension*. Au cours de la vie de Feathersmith, entièrement consacrée à l'accumulation, de nombreuses vies ont été détruites, ce qui vaut comme peine la damnation éternelle. En échange de pratiquement tout son patrimoine, Mademoiselle Devlin, qui ne traite qu'en liquide, fait réaliser le rêve de Feathersmith : remonter le temps jusqu'à la petite ville de sa jeunesse, Cliffordsville, en 1910, afin qu'il puisse se mettre à rebâtir son empire. La répétition contient cependant une différence de taille. Feathersmith sait maintenant ce qu'il ne savait pas à l'époque : la localisation exacte des gisements de pétrole en dehors de la ville, le destin boursier des entreprises existantes, et toutes les inventions des cinquante dernières années. Tout en exaltant les vertus de la compétition, Feathersmith entend se lancer dans un jeu entièrement truqué en sa faveur.

Malgré tout, ses tentatives de manipulation du marché échouent lamentablement. Les gisements de pétrole ne pourront être exploités avant quelques décennies, car ils sont trop profonds pour la technologie de 1910. De plus, sa connaissance des inventions comme le moteur à démarrage automatique, la radio et l'aluminium est celle du consommateur ou de l'investisseur, non de l'ouvrier ou de l'ingénieur. Autrement dit, sa connaissance de ces technologies est limitée à de vagues généralités, et manque totalement de détails concrets qui seraient nécessaires pour les fabriquer. Il essaye de discuter avec des mécaniciens, mais savoir que quelque chose existera dans l'avenir ne permet pas de le créer dans le présent.

On dirait que l'épisode est tiré de l'essai de Lukacs, « La Réification et la Conscience du Prolétariat », adapté à la télévision par Rod Serling. La bourgeoisie ne peut comprendre l'histoire, le processus réel de transformation historique, car elle est nécessairement absente du lieu où cela se fait, le lieu de production. À la place de celui-ci, n'existe que la mythologie de grands individus, ou bien la certitude de Feathersmith que lui, comme Alexandre le Grand, fait partie de ces individus qui font l'histoire, et que le progrès historique est objectif. Le pétrole fut découvert aux environs de Cliffordsville dans les années 1930, donc il eût pu aussi bien être découvert en 1910 selon cette logique. Lukacs écrit : « *Car les deux extrêmes où se polarise l'incapacité de l'attitude bourgeoise contemplative à comprendre l'histoire, « grands individus » comme créateurs souverains de l'histoire, et « lois naturelles » du milieu historique, se trouvent dans la même impuissance – qu'ils soient séparés ou réunis – devant l'essence de la nouveauté radicale du présent, essence qui exige qu'on lui donne un sens.* »³ Ce qui est absent de ces deux extrêmes est le véritable travail de « fabrication de l'histoire ».

Comme le dit après coup Mademoiselle Devlin à Feathersmith, ruiné et réduit à être concierge à son tour : « *Bien sûr ça n'a pas marché. Ça ne pouvait jamais marcher pour vous. Voulez-vous savoir pourquoi ? Parce que vous êtes un magouilleur. Un financier et un arriviste. Un cerveau, un manipulateur, un pilleur. Parce que vous êtes un preneur et non un bâtisseur. Un intrigant et non un concepteur. Un exploiteur et non un inventeur. Un utilisateur et non un messager.* »

Un redémarrage (*reboot*) de la série a été lancé en avril 2019 sur CBS sous la houlette du comédien Jordan Peel comme présentateur, producteur, et du moins en partie, scénariste et réalisateur. Je me demande quand même si l'histoire sera aussi difficile à maîtriser pour lui qu'elle ne fut pour le pauvre Feathersmith. *La Quatrième Dimension* est presque trop iconique pour être refaite. J'espère que ça marchera, mais j'espère aussi qu'on n'a pas fait de pacte avec le Diable à cette fin !

French Translations of The Devil is in the Details: The Twilight Zone's Demonology of Capital.

---

3 Györgi Lukacs, *Histoire et Conscience de classe*, Éditions du Minuit, 1959 (1923), traduit par Kostas Axelos et Jacqueline Bois, p. 217.

Le capital « woke » et le crépuscule de la bourgeoisie

Translated by David Buxton. Published in April of 2021.

Pour qui possède un minimum de mémoire historique, les controverses concernant l'esprit « *woke* » ressemblent à un remake, ou à un redémarrage de la panique autour du « politiquement correct » vécue par la génération précédente.[1] Il s'agit des mêmes peurs, des mêmes fulminations, des mêmes figures de vertu, des mêmes coupables, bref, des mêmes traditions sacrées soi-disant menacées. Le postmodernisme et les universités qui l'abritent sont de nouveau mis en cause. Selon cette interprétation tout à fait plausible, ce n'est qu'une reprise. La seule raison pour le changement de vocabulaire (« *woke* » remplaçant « politiquement correct ») serait le désir de ne pas admettre que la nouvelle menace est en réalité plutôt ancienne. Nouveau logo, même emballage. Il existe, cependant, quelques différences qui témoignent de la nature changeante du rapport entre la culture et le pouvoir.

Ce qui vient d'abord à l'esprit, c'est qu'il y a eu un déplacement fondamental quant à l'objet des attaques. Il n'est plus question de classiques consacrées comme Shakespeare, Dickens et Milton, mais de Mr Potato Head (jouet), de Trader Sam (vendeur de têtes dans une attraction « exotique » à Disney World) et de quelques

---

[1] *Prolongeant le politiquement correct, le* woke *(éveillé) désigne aux États-Unis la prise de conscience (mâtinée d'une forte dose d'empathie culpabilisante) de l'oppression « systémique » subie par les Noirs et d'autres groupes ethniques (*Black Lives Matter, *apparu en 2013), par les femmes (le mouvement #MeToo), et par les minorités sexuelles (les LGBTQ+) qui intègrent désormais les identités « non binaires ». Il ne faut pas le réduire, comme certains le font en France, à ses excès puritains comme la cancel culture et l'humiliation des individus (*shaming*). Comme l'affirme Jason Read, le woke est tout à fait soluble dans un capitalisme « libéral » qui se veut non patriarcal, non raciste, au point d'y être naturalisé (mais non sans heurts). La vertu ostentatoire (*virtue signalling*) devient un acte de communication inclusive à peu de frais, et pour les entreprises, une opération de marketing rentable, les diverses revendications identitaires provenant de consommateurs comme les autres. Et l'annulation de Trader Sam (ci-dessus) ne représente aucunement une perte pour qui que ce soit.*

vieux livres pour enfants du Dr Seuss. La culture « *woke* » émerge quand les guerres autour du canon universitaire visent plus bas, ciblant dorénavant la vile culture commerciale. Par conséquent, la nature de la défense contre cet assaut se modifie. Alors qu'autrefois un partisan des classiques comme Allan Bloom pouvait écrire *The Closing of the American Mind* (1987), et revendiquer l'universalité de la culture occidentale, les défenseurs contemporains des jouets et des parcs à thème se doivent d'embrasser la particularité irréductible d'une telle prétention. Les plaisanteries sur les chasseurs de têtes, les « Esquimaux » et les sauvages en Afrique semblent innocentes seulement si on n'est pas concerné. Dans la plupart des cas, on ne fait que défendre les plaisirs d'un racisme désinvolte.

En second lieu, bien que les universitaires et leurs étudiants « dupés » soient toujours les pourvoyeurs primaires de la culture « *woke* », la liste des coupables comprend désormais les entreprises. Les exemples d'annulation cités ci-dessus (Mr Potato Head, etc.) proviennent justement des mesures prises par les entreprises elles-mêmes. En réalité, ce qui est souvent critiqué comme décision « *woke* » relève plutôt du marketing. Ce que le fan de base des parcs à thème ne semble pas comprendre, c'est que Disney va produire un film fondé sur son expérience, et que la réorganisation de celle-ci correspondra à ce film à vocation universelle. Disney excelle en ce type de recyclage culturel, produisant des films d'action qui sont des adaptations de ses films animés et ainsi de suite, devenant du coup une sorte de machine de mouvement perpétuel.

Souvent déploré pour ses excès, le capitalisme « *woke* » n'est rien d'autre qu'une tentative de développer des marchés. C'est l'aspect universalisant du capital que Marx a reconnu comme révolutionnaire :

> *Là où elle est arrivée au pouvoir, la bourgeoisie a détruit tous les rapports féodaux, patriarcaux, idylliques. Elle a impitoyablement déchiré la variété bariolée des liens féodaux qui unissaient l'homme à ses supérieurs naturels et n'a laissé subsister d'autre lien entre l'homme et l'homme que l'intérêt tout nu, le dur « paiement comptant ». Elle a noyé dans les eaux glacées du calcul*

égoïste les frissons sacrés de l'exaltation religieuse, de l'enthousiasme chevaleresque, de la mélancolie sentimentale des petits-bourgeois. Elle a dissous la dignité personnelle dans la valeur d'échange et substitué aux innombrables libertés reconnues par lettres patentes et chèrement acquises la seule liberté sans scrupule du commerce. En un mot, elle a substitué à l'exploitation que voilaient les illusions religieuses et politiques l'exploitation ouverte, cynique, directe et toute crue.[2]

À la lumière de cela, allons au-delà d'une simple défense de la basse culture. Les limitations récentes du droit de vote promulguées en Géorgie, touchant de manière disproportionnée les citoyens issus des minorités, ont fait l'objet de boycotts et de condamnations de la part des entreprises aussi diverses que la Major League Baseball, Coca-Cola et Delta Airlines. Cela crée un effet bizarre quand certains élus de droite, les mêmes qui reçoivent quantité de dons des entreprises, se permettent de critiquer l'Amérique *corporate* pour son influence sur la vie politique.[3]

Pris ensemble, ces deux aspects de la charge actuelle contre « le complexe industriel outragé » (pour reprendre la formule apte du sénateur républicain Mitch McConnell) signifient le crépuscule de la bourgeoisie. Par cette expression, je ne veux pas dire le déclin du pouvoir du capital, ou de ceux qui possèdent les moyens de production ; je ne parle pas non plus d'un néoféodalisme, concept avancé récemment par Jodi Dean. Suivant Étienne Balibar, je veux dire plutôt la création d'une « *classe des super-riches qui n'ont pas d'autre prétention à la distinction que la consommation.* »[4] A cela, j'ajouterais que le déclin de la prétention à la distinction est aussi le déclin de l'universalisme. Ce qui a soutenu en partie la bourgeoisie en tant que classe dirigeante, c'est non seulement sa distinction

---

2 Marx, Engels, *Manifeste du parti communiste*, traduction par Émile Bottigelli, Aubier, 1972.
3 Bess Levin, "Mitch McConnell Doesn't Have a Problem With Corporations Getting Involved in Politics When He's Suckling at the Corporate Teat," *Vanity Fair*, April 6, 2021. https://www.vanityfair.com/news/2021/04/mitch-mcconnell-corporate-donors
4 Etienne Balibar, "Sur les interpretations de Mai 68" in *Histoire Interminable: D' un siècle l'autre, Écrits I*, Paris: La Découverte, 2020, 109.

améliorative, mais aussi son universalisme, l'idée que n'importe qui pourrait acquérir sa culture et ses normes. D'où l'importance de l'éducation et de l'idéologie méritocrate pendant son âge d'or. La classe dirigeante de nos jours ne prétend à aucune distinction particulière. Bien que je déteste parler de lui, je pense que Donald Trump a été le premier président post-bourgeois, ou du moins celui du déclin de l'efficacité symbolique de la culture bourgeoise.

On était bien reçu chez (Big Mac) Donald !

Trump a fait fi des normes et des conventions du goût bourgeois à chaque occasion possible, contrairement à Obama qui a ouvertement embrassé celles-ci comme quelque chose que n'importe qui pouvait acquérir, quelle que soit sa race ou son origine sociale. Barack Obama a été en même temps le premier président noir, et le dernier souffle de la bourgeoisie, le dernier à cause du premier. Ce contraste a mené certains, bizarrement, à voir en Trump un représentant de la classe ouvrière, mais il y a une différence importante entre le déclin de l'efficacité symbolique des « marqueurs bourgeois de distinction », et la transformation réelle des classes sociales. Trump, bien entendu, n'a jamais prétendu être autre chose qu'un richard, et son patrimoine n'est jamais passé par la médiation du capital culturel. Sa fortune était de toute évidence vulgaire, sans la moindre trace de distinction. On pourrait même affirmer que cela comportait un message encore plus universalisant, passant non par des institutions culturelles, de l'éducation et de l'État, mais par l'universalité du *fast food*, qui offre le même produit à tout le monde. Une table à manger jonchée de burgers marie l'opulence et l'accessibilité, c'est ce à quoi beaucoup de gens peuvent s'identifier. Mais associer Trump, et la classe dirigeante actuelle avec cet ersatz d'universalité qu'est le Big Mac serait d'oublier mon argument du début. Les critiques du « capital *woke* », ou pour employer un terme plus absurde, du « communisme *corporate* », n'épousent pas l'universalité des marques comme Disney et Mr Potato Head, mais réclament à cor et à cri le droit d'en jouir dans leur particularité irréductible, raciale et sexuelle.

Voilà ce qui caractérise le moment actuel, où les entreprises ont davantage investi dans de l'universalité et de l'égalité (même si ce n'est que l'universalité de l'exploitation et l'égalité d'accès aux mêmes marques) que l'État et ses élus, lesquels embrassent ouvertement une hiérarchie raciale et des normes patriarcales. C'est un moment régressif ; la tâche pour la gauche serait non seulement d'éviter les reprises mercantiles de « liberté, égalité et Bentham » (John Stuart Mill), mais aussi de construire un universalisme réel venu d'en bas, opposé à la fois à celui du marché et de l'État bourgeois.

French Translation of Woke Capital and Twilight of the Bourgeoisie (How is that for a title?).

En attendant les robots : Benanav et Smith sur les illusions d'automation et les réalités d'exploitation

Translated by David Buxton. Published in December of 2020.

L'année 2020 a vu la parution de deux livres remarquablement similaires : *Automation and the Future of Work* d'Aaron Benanav et *Smart Machines and Service Work* de Jason E. Smith. Sans couvrir exactement le même terrain, les deux livres se chevauchent trop pour qu'on puisse provoquer un débat entre eux. Il est mieux alors de les appréhender ensemble, non pour leur charge commune contre des idées fantaisistes sur l'automation, mais pour la manière dont ils mobilisent la thèse notoire de la baisse tendancielle du taux de profit.

Quand j'ai commencé à étudier Marx dans les années 1990, aucun élément de sa pensée n'était plus discrédité que cette thèse. On considérait généralement qu'elle faisant partie du mauvais côté téléologique de Marx, à approcher avec prudence en passant par une litanie de contre-tendances. Les prédictions de l'avenir relevaient des résidus hégéliens, voilà pour la critique philosophique. Qui plus est, la baisse tendancielle du taux de profit ne correspondait pas au monde de l'époque : l'Union soviétique n'était plus, et le capitalisme semblait être revigoré par le *dotcom boom*. Il est possible de voir toute la vague post-opéraïste (Negri et Hardt, Virno, Lazzarato) comme une tentative d'imaginer une transition vers le communisme fondée non sur les contradictions du capitalisme, mais sur les forces de celui-ci, autrement dit, un post-capitalisme fondé sur l'abondance plutôt que sur la paupérisation, sur l'action plutôt que sur l'exclusion. La remarque vaut aussi pour le courant accélérationniste, qui conçoit un monde post-capitaliste à partir de la capacité du capital à produire du progrès technologique (quand bien même ce progrès a été largement gaspillé).

Les livres de Smith et de Benanav peuvent être lus comme une contre-tendance forte à ces deux courants. Leur publication rend plus visible cette nouvelle orientation contestataire, qui conteste non seulement certaines lectures de Marx, mais aussi l'idée dominante que l'automation soit l'impulsion principale derrière le capitalisme, son idéologie spontanée à l'ère d'Uber et de smartphones.

Benanav prétend que l'image spontanée d'un remplacement des humains par l'automation, conduisant à la précarité et au chômage, n'est pas la bonne façon d'interpréter la réalité. Selon lui, la précarité des emplois n'est pas le produit de la révolution à venir des machines, mais la conséquence de la stagnation et du déclin du capital. Il décrit cette illusion ainsi :

> « Le sens collectif que le rythme des innovations économisant de la main-d'œuvre s'accélère est une illusion. C'est comme la sensation qu'on peut avoir en regardant par la fenêtre d'un train qui se ralentit à l'approche d'une gare, dépassant les trains de l'autre côté des voies qui semblent s'accélérer. Les innovations économisant de la main-d'œuvre semblent se produire à un rythme plus rapide seulement quand on les aperçoit de l'autre côté des voies, c'est-à-dire du point de vue d'une économie dont la croissance est toujours plus lente ».[1]

Ce n'est donc pas l'automatisation qui impulse le chômage et le sous-emploi, mais la baisse générale des profits. Le train où on se trouve n'avance pas vers un avenir post-travail. La vitesse et l'instabilité qu'on voit viennent en réalité du train sur l'autre voie, celle de la profitabilité qui se ralentit, qui mène au licenciement ou à la précarisation des employés. Voilà pourquoi les plus grands changements des vingt dernières années ont eu lieu non dans l'industrie et les services, mais dans la surveillance et dans le traçage. Ces derniers sont moins caractérisés par la productivité accrue que

---

1 Aaron Benanav, « Automation isn't wiping out jobs. It's that our engine of growth is winding down », *The Guardian*, 23 janvier 2020, https://www.theguardian.com/commentisfree/2020/jan/23/robots-economy-growth-wages-jobs

par la surexploitation, la possibilité d'extirper plus de travail de moins de travailleurs.

Pourquoi l'idée d'automation, d'une révolution technologique, a-t-elle continué de prévoir de manière quasi cyclique la montée des robots et la fin du travail ? Peut-être parce qu'une grande part des innovations des dernières décennies n'ont pas eu lieu dans les usines ni même dans les restaurants, mais ont plutôt visé la consommation et le divertissement, aboutissant à l'appareil qu'on tient dans la main. Comme le dit Smith dans un entretien qui reprend l'argument de son livre :

> « Le smartphone se propose comme l'innovation indicative de notre ère, sa marchandise « star ». Son omniprésence – dans les rues, les réunions, les cours, les salles à manger - confirme son statut emblématique. Mais il ne fait que combiner quelques appareils plus anciens comme le téléphone mobile et l'ordinateur personnel. Offrant l'accès à une panoplie de divertissements (le *shopping*, les plateformes de musique et de vidéo, la communication interpersonnelle) à travers un seul écran interactif, ces appareils parachèvent une confluence en cours depuis quelques décennies : la fusion du commerce et de l'information, du divertissement et de la vie sociale, de la stylisation de soi et de la vie civique, tout cela sur un écran tactile d'une taille unique. L'utilisateur est tiraillé entre ces registres, les activant tous en même temps : sans repères, sa réaction oscille entre le divertissement anecdotique et la rage inarticulée. Mais la main libre sur le marché boursier qu'ont eu les entreprises « numériques », et leur force de frappe apparente sur les loisirs, la consommation, l'identité personnelle, le discours public – tous depuis longtemps en décomposition – ont donné lieu à des affirmations concernant cette technologie de base qui dépassent de très loin son impact réel sur les habitudes de consommation, de réception, et d'interaction. Quant au travail, ces innovations promettaient de déclencher un décollage exponentiel de la productivité. C'est précisément ce qui n'est pas arrivé. Au lieu de cela, on a eu droit à des réseaux

de plus en plus serrés de surveillance et de traçage, dans les rues et sur les lieux de travail. »[2]

Les livres de Smith et de Benanav se complètent bien. Benanav consacre plus de temps aux aspects économiques de la stagnation, alors que Smith se dédie davantage à expliquer pourquoi l'idéologie spontanée de l'automation est si persistante, et comment l'expérience quotidienne de la technologie—consultant nos smartphones en permanence—nous fait croire en une transformation révolutionnaire à venir, qui ne pourrait certes se réaliser dans les conditions sociales et économiques actuelles. La consommation apparaît plus radicale, justement en raison des profits manufacturiers déclinants. Le smartphone représente moins une nouvelle force de production qu'une sorte de contraction des marges de profit, où on essaie d'extraire plus de consommation et de travail des conditions existantes de production. Cet appareil représente aussi l'impasse des gains de productivité, car même s'il devient moins cher à produire, la plupart des consommateurs n'en ont besoin que d'un seul. Steve Jobs ne fut jamais en mesure d'être le nouveau Henry Ford, car le smartphone, en dépit de son ubiquité culturelle, est loin d'avoir l'influence à grande échelle de l'automobile. Comme l'indique Smith, personne ne le sait mieux qu'Apple, qui consacre la plupart de ses profits au rachat de ses propres actions, plutôt que d'investir dans la prochaine génération de smartphones.

Sur ce dernier point, il faut évoquer Uber, et la proposition 22 en Californie qui a classé les conducteurs d'Uber (et d'autres plateformes) comme des autoentrepreneurs et non des employés. Alors que le visage public d'Uber est l'application désignant les voitures à notre disposition, ce qui l'impulse vraiment—en attendant de faire le moindre bénéfice—est sa capacité à contourner les exigences minimales des lois du travail. Quant à la productivité, Uber ne change pas grand-chose ; s'il met plus de voitures sur

---

[2] Jason E. Smith, entretien avec Tony Smith, « Machines intelligentes et travail tertiaire », *Variations*, 24, 2021, https://journals.openedition.org/variations/2028/

les routes aux heures de pointe, ce sont les mêmes voitures privées et les mêmes routes existantes. Au fond, c'est un logiciel de hélage électronique, où l'innovation véritable est sa manière de profiter des chômeurs cherchant du travail ou des travailleurs sous-employés cherchant des heures supplémentaires. C'est de la surexploitation déguisée en innovation technologique.

On pourrait dire la même chose des autres entreprises de l'économie numérique supposément à la pointe ; quand elles n'utilisent pas la richesse accumulée pour racheter leurs propres actions, elles investissent non dans l'augmentation de la productivité, mais dans de nouvelles façons de vendre de l'espace publicitaire (Facebook) ou dans l'amélioration des formes de surveillance (Google). Même le distributeur automatique de billets est moins un caissier robot qu'un moyen d'externaliser le travail ordinaire de la banque. Les innovations technologiques n'ont pas augmenté la productivité. Là où elles ne ciblent pas l'attention du consommateur, elles sont principalement utilisées pour l'organisation et pour la surveillance des travailleurs, créant un état d'anxiété permanente.

Que conclure de tout cela ? Benanav et Smith, tous les deux, suivent l'ouvrier militant James Boggs en affirmant que la question de la révolution a moins à voir avec la classe ouvrière traditionnelle qu'avec les précaires et les chômeurs. Les travailleurs dans une économie stagnante sont de plus en plus isolés, et de surcroît, divisés entre surexploités et précaires cherchant désespérément à les rejoindre. Ils ont plus de rapports avec leurs employeurs (qui les surveillent en permanence) et avec les publicitaires (qui visent à exploiter chaque instant de leur « temps libre ») qu'ils ont avec d'autres travailleurs. Comme le dit Smith, la classe ouvrière de nos jours est fortement infusée de valeurs managériales, se surveillant mutuellement dans des postes où la frontière entre encadrement et travail est floue. Cela crée des barrières monumentales à son organisation, ce qui explique peut-être pourquoi nous vivons dans un âge de contestations sporadiques qui n'évoluent jamais en mouvements politiques. Dernièrement, comme le dit Benanav, surmonter la peur de l'automatisation, du remplacement des travailleurs par des machines, implique aussi l'abandon des fantaisies correspondantes d'un « communisme de luxe pleinement automatisé » (Aaron Bastani).[3] Le capital n'est pas en train de produire ses propres fossoyeurs automatisés, mais d'acheminer les creuseurs de la terre plus rapidement vers leurs propres tombes. Il n'y aura pas d'avenir post-travail, mais il reste la possibilité de lutter pour un monde dans lequel le travail (et la créativité et la recherche) est davantage orienté vers les besoins humains.

French translation of Waiting for the Robots: Benanav and Smith on the Illusions of Automation and the Realities of Exploitation.

---

1 Aaron Bastani, *Communisme de luxe. Un monde d'abondance grâce aux nouvelles technologies* (traduction : Hermine Hamon), Diateino, 2021 (2019).

Te debo una explicación: Graeber y Marx sobre las historias de origen

Translated by Javier Sainz Paz y Jaime Ortega.
Published in December of 2020.

La historia de la llamada acumulación originaria es bien conocida por los lectores de Marx. Esta historia fue la forma en que la economía política entendió los orígenes del capitalismo, explicando cómo el mundo fue dividido entre trabajadores y capitalistas. Aquella historia evoca la fábula del saltamontes y la cigarra, entre aquellos que ahorran y aquellos que despilfarran, aunque Marx le da un giro literario diferente. Como escribe Marx:

> "Los orígenes de la primitiva acumulación pretenden explicarse relatándolos como una anécdota del pasado. En tiempos muy remotos—se nos dice—, había, de una parte, una minoría trabajadora, inteligente y sobretodo ahorrativa, y de la otra un tropel de descamisados, haraganes, que derrochaban cuánto tenían y aún más. Es cierto que la leyenda del pecado original teológico nos dice que el hombre fue condenado a ganar el pan con el sudor de su frente; pero la historia del pecado original económico nos revela por qué hay gente que no necesita sudar para comer. No importa. Así se explica que mientras los primeros acumulaban riquezas, los segundos acabaron por no tener ya nada que vender más que su pellejo"[1]

Marx sostiene que esta historia es inadecuada para explicar el origen del capital. Para aquellos que sólo poseen su fuerza de trabajo para vender, no es suficiente ahorrar dinero, porque la acumulación en nada sirve para los que solo tienen su fuerza de trabajo para veneder. Para

---

[1] Carlos Marx. "Capítulo XXIV. La llamada acumulación originaria. 1. El secreto de la acumulación originaria" en El Capital I. Trad. Wenceslao Roces. México, FCE. p. 607.

conseguir trabajadores, una gran población debe ser despojada de los medios de producción, despojada de la tierra y de los bienes comunes. El origen del capitalismo no es una historia moral de ahorro, sino una sangrienta historia de expropiación; una historia que abarca la esclavitud, el colonialismo e incluso la reforma protestante.

Marx terminó primer volumen de *El capital* con esta crítica y David Graeber abre su libro, *Debt: The first 5,000 Years* con una crítica a otra fábula contemporánea que alude al origen del dinero. Esta historia, que puede ser rastreada hasta Aristóteles, comienza con una economía basada en el trueque, pero, como puede decir cualquiera que haya llevado su vaca al mercado y vuelto con frijoles mágicos, el trueque es increíblemente inconveniente. El dinero, afirma la historia, surge para resolver las deficiencias del trueque, la dificultad de llevar objetos al mercado y reducir el tiempo que pasamos esperando a alguien que tenía lo que uno deseaba y a alguien que deseara lo que uno tenía. Más importante aún, el dinero es un asunto de iguales, basado únicamente en la conveniencia y el interés. Es por eso que esta historia es tan popular entre Adam Smith y los libros de texto contemporáneos de economía.

Graeber considera que hay algo erróneo en esta historia: nunca sucedió. Utiliza una gran cantidad de evidencia arqueológicas y antropológicas para argumentar que esta delicada transición del trueque al dinero nunca existió. Toda esta evidencia histórica toma sustento en un simple problema: el trueque presupone una tipo de sociabilidad entre personas que están completamente desconectadas, sin vínculos y enfrentadas en un conflicto directo. Marx diría que ello presupone sujetos burgueses, sujetos conectados solo por el interés propio. Lo que sostiene Graeber es que la historia, o más bien la antropología, ha documentado todo tipo de formas en las que circulan los bienes, en las que también circulan lazos de todo tipo, tanto amistades como deudas.

Graeber da más *crédito* (en realidad no sé si pretendí, o no, ese juego de palabras) a una versión diferente del dinero: la teoría de la deuda primordial, que sostiene que el dinero surgió de los impuestos, de la necesidad del Estado de generar dinero. Esta teoría comienza no con una equivalencia, sino con una asimetría fundamental que a menudo esta fundada en la religión, en el sentido de deuda con el mundo. (Los lectores de Deleuze y Guattari reconocerán gran parte de este énfasis en la deuda primordial que atraviesa *El Anti-Edipo* y las *Mil Mesetas*).

Graeber resume esta dicotomía de estos dos puntos de vista de la siguiente manera:

> *"Se trata de una gran trampa del siglo XX: por un lado está la lógica del mercado, en la que nos gusta imaginarnos que comenzamos como individuos que no deben nada a nadie. Por el otro lado está la lógica del Estado, donde todos comenzamos con una deuda que nunca podemos pagar del todo. Se nos dice continuamente que son opuestos, y que entre ellos se contienen todas las posibilidades humanas reales. Pero es una falsa dicotomía. Los Estados crearon los mercados. Los mercados necesitan Estados. Ninguno puede continuar sin el otro, al menos, de manera parecida a las formas en que los conocemos hoy en día."*[2]

Lo que ilustran estas dos cuentas es que la deuda es siempre una combinación de igualdad y jerarquía. La falsa dicotomía de la cuenta de los orígenes del dinero los presenta como alternativas, pero eso pasa por alto el hecho de que siempre están entrelazados en la deuda. Para citar a Graeber nuevamente:

> *"La deuda es algo muy específico, y surge de situaciones muy específicas. En primer lugar requiere una relación entre dos personas que no se consideren seres fundamentalmente diferentes, que sean al menos potencialmente iguales, que son iguales en las cosas que en realidad importan y que no se encuentran en ese momento en un estado de igualdad, pero para los que hay alguna manera de arreglar las cosas."*[3]

---

[2] David Graeber. *En deuda: Una historia alternativa de la economía.* Barcelona, Ariel, 2012. p. 95.
[3] David Graeber. *En deuda: Una historia alternativa de la economía.* Trad. de Joan Andreano Weyland. Barcelona, Ariel, p. 160

Graeber dedica gran parte del libro a analizar la historia de esta lógica particular de jerarquía e igualdad, jerarquías que determinan quién se espera que pague sus deudas y quién puede retenerlas. Esta jerarquía continúa hasta el presente, hasta el momento actual de rescates para unos y austeridad para otros. Sin embargo, el libro de Graeber no pretende realizar ser una historia del tema; si bien cubre los cinco mil años de deuda, la esclavitud, la estandarización del oro, el sistema fiduciario y cada de ellos es discutido, primordialmente se les ve como diferentes transformaciones de esta lógica. A Graeber le interesa principalmente la forma en que la deuda monetizada se cruza y se separa de los lazos y obligaciones sociales.

En el centro de esta antropología se encuentra el siguiente axioma sobre la sociedad humana:

> *"En realidad, el comunismo es la base de toda sociabilidad humana. Es lo que hace posible la sociedad. Existe siempre la noción de que, de cualquiera que no sea un enemigo, se puede esperar que actúe según el principio de «cada cual según sus posibilidades», al menos hasta cierto punto: por ejemplo, si uno necesita saber cómo llegar a un lugar y el otro conoce el camino".*[4]

El punto de Graeber está bien tomado, hay mucho que decir sobre este comunismo de la vida cotidiana, en la forma en que las relaciones de cooperación impregnan nuestras acciones diarias. Es importante refutar la antropología del neoliberalismo, la afirmación de que siempre y naturalmente estamos inmersos en una competencia feroz, en busca de la máxima ganancia por el mínimo gasto. Una antropología así simplemente no tiene en cuenta todas nuestras tendencias a ofrecer ayuda en distintas formas. No describe la vida diaria real, ni siquiera en el capitalismo.

Como conclusión algo abrupta, permítanme decir que emparejé a Graeber con Marx por dos razones que no tienen nada que ver con revivir algún debate entre el anarquismo y el comunismo. Primero,

---

[4] David Graeber. *En deuda: Una historia alternativa de la economía.* Trad. de Joan Andreano Weyland. Barcelona, Ariel, p. 126.

creo que la fantasía del trueque, del dinero que surge del trueque, es una ideología tan falsa y perniciosa como la moralización de la historia de la llamadaacumulación originaria. Estas historias son perniciosas no por lo que dicen sobre el pasado, sino por por su forma de operación en el presente. La idea moral del capitalista ahorrativo y del trabajador furtivo continúa en nuestras discusiones contemporáneas sobre los "creadores de empleo" y los perezosos receptores del desempleo, así como la idea del dinero como un factor igualitario que respalda el ideal del mercado libre como una relación social sin subordinación. La crítica de Graeber al trueque debe colocarse junto con la explicación de la acumulación originaria de Marx. Sin embargo, y esta es la segunda razón, leí la crítica de Marx a la llamada acumulación originaria para también hacer una crítica, de una explicación de la historia, basada enteramente en motivos e intenciones humanas. El capitalismo no es una cuestión de ahorro, despilfarro o codicia, es una cuestión de plusvalor, fuerza de trabajo y otras abstracciones reales. Así, el comunismo puede ser la base de toda sociabilidad, pero el capitalismo es a menudo indiferente a la sociabilidad o, peor aún, la explota.

Como tema de investigación, la deuda va y viene de lo económico a lo moral y, por lo tanto, es tentador ubicar su historia en actitudes e ideas, pero una verdadera historia de la deuda también debe examinar la estructura que es indiferente a esas ideas.

Spanish Translation of I Owe You an Explanation: Graeber and Marx on Origin Stories.

Colpi preventivi: Marx e Spinoza

Translated by Gigi Roggero. Published in November of 2022.

Nell'età postindustriale la critica spinoziana della rappresentazione del potere capitalistico si avvicina alla verità più dell'analisi dell'economia politica.
– Antonio Negri[1]

In principio è la pratica

L'incontro tra Spinoza e Marx è probabilmente uno dei più produttivi nella filosofia contemporanea. Esso ha diverse origini e molteplici traiettorie, l'ondata più recente inizia con le opere di Alexandre Matheron, Gilles Deleuze e Louis Althusser, proseguendo in modi differenti, attraverso diverse varianti del marxismo e dello spinozismo. Questo incontro non riguarda, come spesso accade per le forme dominanti della scrittura filosofica e della ricerca, la necessità di distinguere le influenze che derivano dall'una all'altra, o gli argomenti che le dividono. È piuttosto un'articolazione dei loro punti di intersezione fondamentali, punti che non sono semplicemente dati, ma che devono essere prodotti da una pratica filosofica.

Uno di questi punti di articolazione è il loro comune materialismo, inteso come primato dell'azione sul pensiero, dell'ordine dei corpi e dei rapporti sulla coscienza. Ciò forse appare ovvio nel caso di Marx, la cui affermazione «non è la coscienza che determina la vita, ma la vita che determina la coscienza» va intesa come un'articolazione fondamentale del materialismo. È invece meno ovvio nel caso di Spinoza, nonostante la sua affermazione dell'identità dell'ordine e della connessione di pensiero ed estensione, di idee e cose come due espressioni dell'infinita potenza della sostanza. Tuttavia, il materialismo di Spinoza non va cercato nella sua comprensione dell'ordine costitutivo ultimo dell'universo, ma nello statuto

---

1 F. Fischbach, *La production des hommes: Marx avec Spinoza*, Vrin, Paris 2014, p. 29.

secondario che attribuisce al pensiero. Noi siamo, sostiene Spinoza, «nati ignoranti delle cause delle cose... e consapevoli del nostro appetito». Inoltre, accade che le cause del nostro appetito siano una delle prime cose di cui siamo ignoranti: pensiamo al fatto che desideriamo qualcosa perché è buono, incapaci di cogliere le esperienze e i rapporti che ci fanno chiamare una cosa buona e un'altra cattiva. C'è sia in Spinoza che in Marx una secondarietà della coscienza: il pensiero non è l'atto di dominio del soggetto sul mondo, ma un effetto secondario e derivato delle pratiche e dei rapporti, fondamentalmente inconsapevole delle sue condizioni.

La secondarietà della coscienza

Questo principio materialista di base, «la secondarietà della coscienza», si trova non solo a livello delle loro specifiche formulazioni, delle loro ontologie e politiche della storia, ma a livello della loro particolare pratica filosofica.[1] Penso in particolare alla fine del primo capitolo del *Capitale*, al famoso passo sul «carattere di feticcio della merce e il suo arcano», e all'«Appendice» alla prima parte dell'*Etica*. Sono testi ben noti. Il primo ci ha fornito il concetto di feticismo della merce, di reificazione e varie critiche che vanno ben oltre il suo specifico utilizzo. Il secondo è stato descritto da Althusser come la matrice di ogni possibile teoria dell'ideologia, e ha continuato ad agire nella storia della filosofia. La loro influenza non può essere ignorata, separatamente e insieme hanno fatto da sfondo a gran parte dei concetti tra di loro intersecantesi di reificazione, immaginario e ideologia. Al di là o prima di questa storia, tuttavia, vi è il ruolo specifico che svolgono nei loro rispettivi testi e argomentazioni.

Entrambi i principi possono essere descritti come preventivi, nel senso che, per quanto si collochino all'interno di particolari argomentazioni, discutendo i particolari problemi della forma-merce e dell'immaginario antropologico-teologico, vengono necessariamente prima delle loro necessarie condizioni filosofiche. Il testo di Spinoza comincia a esporre qualcosa della tendenza umana a vederci come un regno dentro un regno, prima di sviluppare le proposizioni fondamentali che dettagliano la conoscenza, gli affetti e il desiderio, che costituiscono le parti III e IV dell'*Etica*. Il testo di Marx presenta Robinson Crusoe, il mondo medievale e la famosa (ma criptica) libera associazione di produttori prima di sviluppare l'idea stessa di un modo di produzione, la struttura sociale. Questo colpo preventivo è in ogni caso necessario: sia Spinoza che Marx riconoscono che ciò che affermano va contro il senso comune prevalente, ovvero la coscienza prevalente dell'economia o del cosmo. Riconoscono anche che le cause o le condizioni di questa «filosofia spontanea» non sono idee e proposizioni ma la vita, intesa come cause e condizioni per vedere un mondo in forma determinata. Sono il punto in cui ogni filosofia si confronta con il suo nemico assoluto, il suo assoluto fuori, sia nella forma dell'intero immaginario antropo-teologico di un soggetto libero e di un Dio teleologicamente orientato, sia nell'accettazione reificata e astorica della forma del valore. Sono il punto in cui il concetto si interseca con la polemica, dove un argomento si confronta con il mondo e la visione del mondo che gli si oppone.

Ciò con cui ciascun testo si confronta non è tanto una specifica posizione filosofica, o una figura della storia della filosofia, quanto un intero senso comune o modo di pensare. Sia la sezione sul «feticismo della merce» che l'«Appendice» della prima parte dell'opera spinoziana affrontano il modo in cui il mondo appare necessariamente a tutti, un senso comune e non un testo canonico. Nel primo caso sembra essere costituito da oggetti, merci che possiedono un valore in sé e per sé, indipendentemente da qualsiasi azione umana. Nel secondo caso, la critica di Spinoza al pensiero antropomorfo e teleologico, c'è il modo in cui il mondo appare, prima di tutto come qualcosa di esterno a noi, come qualcosa che agiamo e che, se è governato, lo è da un Dio inconoscibile ma umano. Nonostante la differenza di causa, che riguarda comunque la critica, della religione e dell'economia politica, ogni passaggio affronta la questione del valore, la misura in cui il valore che una cosa incarna è essa stessa una qualità di una cosa o di uno stato soggettivo, un modo di immaginare.

Naturalmente potrebbe sembrare che io stia semplicemente equivocando rispetto al concetto di valore, vacillando tra il significato etico e quello economico. Il che non è solo un mio problema. Ciò che sostiene questa connessione è, in questo caso, che per Spinoza e per Marx il valore non si trova nelle cose stesse, come nel caso di quella che Alexandre Matheron chiama l'oggettività dei valori, né è uno stato puramente soggettivo. Il valore delle cose, il loro statuto buono o cattivo, non è una qualità intrinseca, né uno stato puramente soggettivo. È qualcosa prodotto da azioni, strutture e rapporti. Per Marx e Spinoza il valore deve essere pensato nei termini della sua genesi, che comprende la struttura e i rapporti che la costituiscono, e il modo in cui necessariamente appare.[2]

La costituzione della soggettività

Ciò significa che in ogni caso il mondo, l'aspetto necessario delle cose, comprende una costituzione di soggettività. La soggettività è posta innanzitutto come causa. I valori degli oggetti, delle merci e delle intenzioni di un Dio inconoscibile vanno inizialmente ricercati nel fatto che soddisfano i nostri bisogni, o ciò che percepiamo essere i nostri bisogni. Tuttavia, non appena vengono istituiti, non appena il mercato e la religione si costituiscono, i loro valori sono meno gli effetti delle azioni che le loro cause. Come sostiene Marx rispetto agli operai, «il loro proprio movimento sociale assume la forma d'un movimento di cose, sotto il cui controllo essi si trovano, invece che averle sotto il proprio controllo». Una logica simile, per cui l'effetto di un'azione si trasforma nella sua causa, si ritrova nell'analisi di Spinoza della progressione dal pregiudizio alla superstizione nell'«Appendice». Il pregiudizio assume come punto di partenza la coscienza originaria del desiderio e l'ignoranza delle cause delle cose, compreso il nostro desiderio. La superstizione è la trasformazione di questa condizione iniziale, la sua costituzione in una dottrina esplicita che non solo rafforza questa ignoranza, ma la

---

2 A. Matheron, *Individu et communauté chez Spinoza*, Editions de Minuit, Paris 1969, p. 90.

rende il fondamento del funzionamento del potere, dei sacerdoti e dei despoti che interpretano i segni e i poteri di questo Dio nascosto. Come sostiene Spinoza nei suoi scritti politici, la superstizione non è solo una questione di dottrine e di ideali, ma di pratiche che costituiscono la soggettività dentro e attraverso la sottomissione. La soggettività, in termini di bisogni e desideri, è in un primo momento una causa, che produce le condizioni di base in cui l'economia o la religione diventano necessarie, ma in ultima analisi diventa un effetto, prodotta proprio da queste istituzioni e strutture.[3]

Generalizzando, forse troppo, potremmo dire che ciò che questi due testi offrono è una critica della reciproca costituzione della soggettività e di un mondo, ovvero delle istituzioni del mondo. Si tratta di ciò che Frédéric Lordon e André Orléan definiscono «trascendenza immanente»: la produzione, da parte della moltitudine, della collettività, di un'istanza trascendente, di uno Stato o di un'economia trascendenti, attraverso le varie pratiche della collettività stessa.[4] Il che non vuol dire, nonostante la tentazione che Marx stesso offre parlando di feticismo e incenso, che religione ed economia siano la stessa cosa, che l'economia è diventata un nuovo Dio, o qualcosa del genere. Si tratta invece di scoprire cosa c'è in gioco nella sovrapposizione piuttosto forzata dei rispettivi problemi, che in definitiva sono quelli della rappresentazione. La trascendenza immanente è il modo in cui gli effetti di una determinata pratica, di un comportamento soggettivo, appaiono come la sua causa. È forse questo, e non un semplice materialismo, il punto di convergenza più forte di Marx e Spinoza.

Comunanze e divergenze

I punti di divergenza sono non meno istruttivi. Nel testo di Spinoza l'illusione costitutiva è quella dell'autonomia individuale, che forma

---

3 Matheron descrive questa particolare causalità circolare nei seguenti termini: «è vero che lo Stato è forte perché gli obbediamo, ed è anche vero che gli obbediamo perché è forte» (ivi, p. 327).
4 Y. Citton – F. Lordon, *Spinoza et les Sciences Sociales*, Amsterdam, Paris 2010, p. 246.

un regno dentro un regno. Questa autonomia è in qualche modo mitigata da un mondo di oggetti che sono visti come un bene e un male, e completata da Dio, la cui autonomia e intenzionalità colma il vuoto delle mie frustrazioni.[5] Nel testo di Marx l'illusione costitutiva è quella di un mondo di oggetti, di valori; se il soggetto gioca un ruolo esso è secondario, un effetto della reificazione dei valori e delle proprie potenzialità soggettive. A questo punto le divergenze sembrerebbero prevalere sulla comunanze, lasciando come solo terreno comune la fondamentale—ancorché non irrilevante—priorità materialistica delle pratiche sulle rappresentazioni. Dato che la critica di Spinoza e di Marx è rivolta alternativamente all'antropocentrismo e alla teleologia, all'oggettività del valore quanto alla sua soggettività, in che misura anche il loro materialismo potrebbe essere considerato simile non a livello di ciò che critica, ma di ciò che propone?

Cesare Casarino ha offerto una risposta a questa domanda, concentrandosi su una non trascurabile somiglianza terminologica tra i due testi. Nell'«Appendice», Spinoza scrive del modo in cui i pregiudizi dell'antropocentrismo e della teleologia rappresentano un ostacolo alla comprensione da parte degli uomini della «concatenazione di tutte le cose [*rerum concatenationem*]».[6] Casarino sostiene che questa idea di immanenza, o causalità immanente, in quanto connessione di tutte le cose, una connessione senza un soggetto, un oggetto o un Dio privilegiato al suo centro, corrisponde sia allo spirito che alla lettera del pensiero di Marx. Nello spirito corrisponde alla critica generale di Marx al capitale, che si trova in particolare nel capitolo sull'accumulazione originaria, dove Marx contrappone il racconto moralizzatore della parsimonia e del risparmio alla lista delle molteplici cause, dalla tratta degli schiavi

---

5 Sostiene Warren Montag: «Il Dio che si trova al di là del mondo (materiale) ed è libero di dirigerlo secondo la sua volontà incondizionata è quindi l'immagine speculare dell'uomo che trascende il mondo fisico e governa il proprio corpo con assoluta maestria, esso stesso immagine speculare di Dio: un circolo vizioso teologico e antropologico».

6 C. Casarino, *Marx before Spinoza: Notes towards an Investigation*, in D. Vardoulakis, a cura di, *Spinoza Now*, University of Minnesota Press, Minneapolis 2011, p. 7.

alla riforma, che hanno reso possibile il capitalismo: il pensiero del capitale come incontro contingente di tutta la storia del mondo. Alla lettera, Casarino indica l'uso di Marx del nesso di tutte le cose [*nexus rerum*] per descrivere il valore di scambio. Spinoza e Marx sono in grado di criticare le filosofie apparentemente disparate dell'antropocentrismo, della teleologia e della reificazione, perché tutte queste non riescono a pensare il *nexus rerum*, la connessione delle cose, in altre parole l'immanenza, ponendo il soggetto, Dio o la legge come funzionamento dell'economia, come qualcosa che esiste al di fuori della connessione mutualmente costitutiva delle cose.

La «connessione di tutte le cose», l'ordine immanente del mondo è proprio ciò che le posizioni filosofiche apparentemente opposte della volizione soggettiva, della trascendenza teologica o della necessità economica non riescono a cogliere. Così, la connessione di tutte le cose appare in negativo, come il punto oscuro trascurato da queste diverse prospettive filosofiche. Tuttavia, non è la sua unica apparenza: nel capitolo iniziale del *Capitale*, Marx analizza la forma allargata del valore capitalistico, sostenendo che deve essere pensato come nient'altro che il rapporto di ogni merce con ogni altra merce, di ogni cosa con ogni altra cosa. In modo simile Spinoza conclude la prima parte dell'*Etica* con la proposizione secondo cui non esiste nulla dalla cui natura non consegue alcun effetto, una proposizione che offre una delle molteplici implicazioni della causalità immanente. Queste affermazioni sono solo degli scorci, una figurazione delle connessioni di tutto con tutto. Nel primo caso, quello di Marx, il valore, anche nella sua forma allargata, non ci porta ancora al pensiero pienamente sviluppato delle interconnessioni del tutto, della causalità immanente, concetto che appare solo sintomaticamente, come in quei passaggi in cui Marx parla del capitalismo in quanto prodotto dell'intera storia dell'umanità fino al presente. Allo stesso modo potremmo sostenere che gli effetti completi, in Spinoza, non funzionano pienamente rispetto alla sua difficile logica fino a quando non si arriva agli affetti e alle vicissitudini della ricerca di un *conatus* finito. Un'ontologia immanente non può essere pronunciata solo come concetto, la maggior parte di essa deve essere prodotta. Il *Capitale* e l'*Etica* sono due esempi di questa produzione.

Verso un'ontologia comunista

Possiamo sostenere che ciò che ci viene offerto sia da Spinoza che da Marx è un gesto verso ciò che chiamiamo un'ontologia comunista, un'ontologia dell'immanenza e dei rapporti. Tuttavia, questa ontologia non è ancora una politica, e non è immediatamente data come tale. Ciò che questi due testi sottolineano è che l'ontologia immanente deve essere pensata non solo come la condizione del nostro pensiero e della nostra azione, ma come una condizione che in quanto causa è trasformata, mascherata nei suoi effetti. La connessione delle cose che forma il modo di produzione capitalistico, nella sua origine globale e nei suoi effetti quotidiani, appare non come rapporto sociale, o come rapporto in generale, ma come valore delle cose. Oppure, come sostiene Spinoza, Dio come natura, Dio come causa immanente deve essere inteso come la causa necessaria dell'immagine di Dio in quanto causa trascendente, che sta al di sopra del mondo. I rapporti immanenti di causalità devono essere intesi essi stessi come la causa della tendenza umana a vedersi come un «regno dentro un regno». Questa è la trascendenza immanente a cui mi riferivo prima, la trascendenza stessa come effetto dell'immanenza. È un effetto, ma è anche una causa.

Non c'è garanzia più sicura del funzionamento del capitale se non la sua apparenza come qualcosa di necessario e senza tempo. Come scrive Marx nel capitolo sulla «cosiddetta accumulazione originaria» del *Capitale*: «*Man mano che la produzione capitalistica procede, si sviluppa una classe operaia che per educazione, tradizione, abitudine, riconosce come leggi naturali ovvie le esigenze di quel modo di produzione*».[7] Il capitale si riproduce non solo a livello economico e politico, ma anche e soprattutto a livello di soggettività. Questo punto è ulteriormente sviluppato da Spinoza, la cui questione

---

7 Karl Marx, *Capital: A Critique of Political Economy, Volume I*, Translated by Ben Fowkes, (New York: Penguin, 1977), 899.

politica (o teologico-politica) centrale, «perché gli uomini lottano per la loro servitù come se fosse la salvezza», indica una comprensione ancora più profonda della misura in cui il potere politico si riproduce attraverso le pratiche che creano desideri, abitudini e affetti.

Nonostante le differenze, possiamo constatare che le rispettive critiche di Spinoza e Marx sono simili non solo nella loro forma preventiva, ma anche nel loro oggetto. L'oggetto della loro critica può essere fondamentalmente diverso nella sua struttura e nella sua storia, dalla teologia all'economia, ma è fondamentalmente lo stesso nella sua funzione. L'oggetto della critica preventiva non è questa o quella idea, o addirittura l'ideologia, ma è il punto in cui l'esistente divisione dei poteri diventa non solo un'idea bensì un intero comportamento soggettivo, una forma di vita. Se questi testi consentono di anticipare, esponendo una critica che richiede concetti e rapporti non ancora sviluppati, lo fanno solo perché le idee, i concetti, le visioni del mondo che criticano sono proprio ciò che blocca il pensiero e l'azione.

Al di là di questa sovrapposizione, della somiglianza di metodo e oggetto della critica, cosa potrebbe offrire questa congiunzione di Marx e Spinoza per pensare la filosofia del mondo e del presente? Possiamo isolare nei due elementi della critica una problematica generale che taglia trasversalmente diversi termini critici. Abbiamo innanzitutto ciò che viene chiamata la connessione di tutte le cose, la natura, il capitale, o l'intera storia profana del mondo, un oggetto che supera ogni tentativo di rappresentarlo, di condurlo ai concetti di intenzione soggettiva, di ordine trascendente o di leggi necessarie. Questo è, in casi diversi, ciò che sia Marx che Spinoza cercano di pensare. Potremo chiamarlo il «comune», solo in quanto esiste nei e attraverso i suoi rapporti costitutivi. Gli oggetti della critica di Spinoza e di Marx, Dio e il Capitale, pongono la totalità assente come condizione necessaria del pensiero e dell'azione, ma lo fanno rappresentandola all'interno dell'immaginario esistente, subordinandola alla soggettività, alla trascendenza, alla legge.

Non è qualcosa che può essere immediatamente dato o celebrato.[8] Cogliere questa connessione di tutte le cose, o causa assente, significa assumere il modo in cui è rappresentata, come Dio o feticcio del valore, riconoscendo che queste rappresentazioni o idee non sono altro che effetti delle strutture, dei suoi modi o delle apparenze necessarie. Effetti che sono anche contemporaneamente cause, condizioni necessarie della sua riproduzione.

Infine, la connessione delle cose, le sue rappresentazioni in Dio e nei feticci, e il rapporto tra i due, come causa ed effetto, può essere sviluppata solo attraverso una pratica filosofica che ho approssimativamente identificato come «preventiva». Questa pratica non vede una critica delle idee e delle rappresentazioni esistenti come qualcosa di secondario, un'attività subordinata che è meglio lasciare ai divulgatori e alla pedagogia, ma come una condizione costitutiva della filosofia stessa. La filosofia esiste solo attraverso il suo impegno in ciò che si potrebbe chiamare, per mancanza di una parola migliore, ideologia, la raccolta di pensieri, rappresentazioni e affetti che riproducono il mondo e le sue strutture di dominio.

Italian translation of a modified version of Nexus Rerum: (Spinoza and Marx, again).

---

[8] «È infatti il nuovo sistema mondiale, il terzo stadio del capitalismo, che è per noi la totalità assente, il Dio o la Natura di Spinoza, l'ultimo (anzi, forse l'unico) referente, il vero terreno dell'Essere del nostro tempo» (F. Jameson, *The Geopolitical Aesthetic*, Indiana University Press, Bloomington 1995, p. 82).

Economías del afecto / economías afectivas: hacia una crítica spinozista de la economía política

Translated by Sebastian Touza.
Published in November of 2013.

Antonio Negri sostiene que "en la era posindustrial la crítica spinozista de la representación del poder capitalista corresponde más a la verdad que el análisis de la economía política".[1] Muchas de los retornos contemporáneas hacia Spinoza dentro del pensamiento marxista han seguido esta trayectoria, alejándose de la crítica de la economía política en dirección hacia las críticas de la ideología o, en el caso de Negri, de la representación del poder. Tal vez esto no es sorprendente; es más fácil hacer conexiones entre la crítica de Spinoza a la superstición y las teorías de la ideología que hacer conexiones entre su comprensión de los deseos y de la voluntad de consumo con la producción. Así como Spinoza ofreció una crítica incisiva de las ideologías religiosas, monárquicas e incluso humanistas de su época, tuvo poco que decir, al menos directamente, sobre el capitalismo emergente. El dinero sólo es mencionado una vez en la *Ética*, donde es definido como el objeto universal de deseo que "suele ocupar el alma de la multitud con la mayor intensidad."[2] Mientras que semejante enunciado se cruza con las críticas de la codicia y la transformación capitalista del deseo, sigue siendo parcial e incidental al desarrollo de una crítica spinozista de la economía política.

---

[1] Antonio Negri, "Reliqua Desiderantur: A Conjecture for a Definition of the Concept of Democracy in the Final Spinoza," translated by Ted Stolze, in *The New Spinoza*, T. Stolze and W.Montag eds.
[2] Benedict de Spinoza, *Ethics*, Translated by Edwin Curley, New York, Penguin, 1994, EIVAPPXVIII.

Frédéric Lordon ha sostenido que el punto de intersección entre el pensamiento de Spinoza y Marx no debe buscarse en la relectura de la superstición como ideología, o incluso en la afirmación aislada de la dimensión afectiva del dinero. Se encuentra en cambio en una intersección más profunda entre la subjetividad y la economía. Como sostiene Lordon, la teoría spinozista del conatus, del esfuerzo por permanecer en su ser que define a cada cosa, es el punto de conexión entre la ontología o antropología spinozista y una crítica marxista de la economía política. Esta no es la conexión sostenida en algunas apropiaciones de derecha de Spinoza, o en rechazos desde la izquierda, que ven en el conatus la afirmación del interés propio que subyace a todas las acciones humanas. El esfuerzo de las cosas por permanecer en su ser que plantea Spinoza no coincide con el individuo que maximiza utilidades subyacente en la economía contemporánea. Como sostiene Lordon, el conatus se esfuerza, pero aquello por lo que se esfuerza, los objetos que considera deseables y las relaciones que busca están ellas mismas determinadas por su capacidad de ser afectadas. Este postulado ontológico y antropológico fundamental tiene como corolario una teoría social en la que cada modo de producción debe ser considerado como un problema particular de "colinearización", una articulación particular de su esforzarse con el esforzarse de los individuos que lo componen.

Una introducción a lo que Lordon llama "colinearización" puede encontrarse en la teoría de la acumulación primitiva de Marx, una teoría que trata en la misma medida sobre la transformación de los hábitos de la subjetividad y sobre la transformación económica. Marx definió lo primero con respecto al capitalismo de la siguiente manera: "El avance de la producción capitalista desarrolla una clase obrera que, por educación, tradición y hábito, considera a los requisitos de ese modo de producción como leyes naturales y autoevidentes."[3] Esta habituación, la reorientación del esforzarse está, al menos al principio, basada en una reorganización del deseo

---

[3] Karl Marx, *Capital: A Critique of Political Economy, Volume I*, Translated by Ben Fowkes, New York: Penguin, 1977, 899.

básico de supervivencia, de perseverar en el propio ser. Incluso debe entenderse que este deseo, un deseo que no es otra cosa que autopreservación, está estructurado. El concepto del conatus en Spinoza está libre de todo naturalismo, de cualquier reducción del esforzarse a una lucha por la vida. Es precisamente porque el conatus carece de una teleología, no se esfuerza más que por aquello a lo que está determinado a esforzarse, que es simultáneamente singular y relacional. El fundamento relacional del contatus incluye, en la interpretación de Lordon, no sólo a los otros inmediatamente presentes y su composición afectiva, sino a todo esforzarse pasado que estructura y determina las instituciones. En tanto que el deseo inmediato de supervivencia, la necesidad de comida y refugio, subyace al trabajo asalariado, este esforzarse "inmediato" debe ser apartado de otros medios de supervivencia, de su conexión con otras formas preexistentes de supervivencia o del simple acto de tomar cada uno lo que necesita. La descripción que hace Marx de la "acumulación primitiva" no es sólo destrucción del común y acumulación de riqueza, es también la destrucción de la idea misma de una existencia no fundamentada en la mercancía y la forma-salario. Se trata de una acumulación primitiva del conatus. La historia de cada institución, de cada práctica, es la destrucción de ciertos modos de esforzarse y la creación, o la canalización, de otras formas. La naturaleza no crea naciones ni economías. Ningún orden social está fundado en un esforzarse natural o, mejor dicho, todos los órdenes sociales lo están; la diferencia está en cómo se articula ese esforzarse, en sus objetos y actividades.

Si el capitalismo tiene como característica distintiva separar a los trabajadores de los medios de producción, entonces esta separación altera radicalmente la inmediatez de la necesidad y el deseo. El hambre puede impulsar a la gente a trabajar, pero ese trabajo siempre estará desfasado con respecto a la inmediatez de ese deseo. Lordon sostiene que la transformación fundamental necesaria para traer al presente la composición afectiva de Spinoza es la separación fundamental entre el esforzarse, la actividad y su objeto. Esta separación de los medios de producción es menos una pérdida fundamental, como ocurre en las descripciones de la alienación, que una transformación fundamental de la actividad, de lo que significa dedicarse a la autopreservación o al trabajo. Hay una indiferencia a la actividad en sí, los objetivos de la actividad particular están despojados de sus sentidos, sus orientaciones particulares al bien y el mal, lo perfecto y lo imperfecto. En tanto podemos unirnos afectivamente a cualquier trabajo particular, cualquier tarea particular, que desarrolle nuestro potencial y nuestras relaciones, que se convierta en la causa de nuestra dicha, esto es secundario con respecto al deseo y la necesidad de dinero. El trabajo concreto se subordina al trabajo abstracto. Existe así una escisión afectiva en el corazón del proceso de trabajo, entre el posible amor por mi propia actividad, sus dichas concretas, y sus resultados, su intercambiabilidad abstracta. Lo que podríamos llamar la composición afectiva del trabajo es cómo, en un momento dado, estos dos aspectos son valuados o devaluados, cuánta dicha se busca en la actividad del trabajo misma, o cuánta se busca en términos de la acumulación que hace posible. Este desplazamiento entre actividad y objeto es complicado, tanto causa como efecto, de las relaciones cambiantes de esperanza y miedo en un momento histórico dado.

Lordon ofrece un boceto de esta historia de la composición afectiva del trabajo, enmarcada en tres períodos; primero el período correspondiente a la acumulación primitiva y el advenimiento de la subsunción formal; seguido por el fordismo y el neoliberalismo. En el primer período, el de la acumulación primitiva del conatus, la simple falta de una alternativa es suficiente, el esforzarse es determinado por el miedo a padecer hambre. Como escribe Marx, el modo capitalista de producción depende en parte de "los impulsos del trabajador a la autopreservación y la propagación".[4] En el nivel más fundamental, todo lo que tiene que hacer el capitalismo es destruir cualquier alternativa, restringir el común [commons] y tomar medidas enérgicas contra aquellos que se esfuerzan en realizar su

---

4 Karl Marx, *Capital: A Critique of Political Economy*, Volume I, 718.

existencia fuera del trabajo asalariado. El segundo, el fordismo, está
definido por la intersección de dos transformaciones: la separación
de la actividad de toda dicha intrínseca y el investimiento afectivo
del consumo. El trabajo es simplificado y fragmentado, despojado
de los placeres y del virtuosismo. Este es el trabajo de la línea de
montaje. Al mismo tiempo se expande la esfera del consumo. El
célebre "día de cinco dólares" de Ford aumentó la capacidad de gasto
de los consumidores. La composición afectiva del fordismo podría
describirse como una reorganización fundamental del conatus, del
esforzarse, desde el trabajo, de la actividad, y hacia el consumo. La
actividad del trabajador es fragmentada, hecha parte de un todo que
la excede, para convertirse tanto en pasividad como en actividad. La
tristeza del trabajo, su agotamiento, es compensada por las dichas
del consumo. Esta transformación de un investimiento afectivo en el
trabajo a un investimiento afectivo en el consumo podría describirse
también como un desplazamiento de la dicha activa, la dicha de la
capacidad propia de actuar y de la transformación de la acción, a la
dicha pasiva. Los afectos dichosos pasivos son aquellos que aumentan
nuestra potencia de actuar, mientras que permanecen fuera de
nuestro control. Los placeres del consumo, el consumismo, pueden
comprenderse como dichas pasivas, prometen cierto aumento de
nuestra potencia, de nuestras dichas y deseos, pero lo que nunca
pueden brindar, lo que nunca puede venderse, es la capacidad misma
de producir activamente nuevos placeres.

El compromiso fordista puede así distinguirse de las posteriores,
posfordistas o neoliberales, articulaciones de afectos, transformaciones
que pueden también describirse por medio de una transformación del
trabajo y el consumo. En términos generales, estas transformaciones
pueden describirse inicialmente como un desmantelamiento de
la seguridad y la estabilidad del trabajo. El compromiso fordista
acarreaba consigo una dimensión de estabilidad, producida por
las negociaciones colectivas y la centralidad del contrato. El
neoliberalismo, tal como lo define Lordon, es primero que nada
una transformación de las normas y estructuras que organizan y

estructuran la acción. Como tal es fundamentalmente asimétrico, los trabajadores están expuestos cada vez a más riesgos, mientras que los capitalistas, específicamente los que se ocupan del capital financiero, son liberados de los riesgos clásicos de la inversión. Esta pérdida de seguridad para el trabajador cambia fundamentalmente la dimensión afectiva del dinero. Ya no es un objeto de esperanza, el medio posible para realizar los propios deseos, sino que se convierte en aquello que repele el miedo. El dinero se convierte en parte del deseo de seguridad, la única seguridad posible: las habilidades y acciones propias no tendrán ningún valor en el futuro, pero el dinero siempre lo tendrá. Puede entenderse este desplazamiento del fordismo al neoliberalismo como un desplazamiento de un régimen de esperanza (matizada con miedo) a un régimen de miedo (matizado con esperanza). La esperanza y el miedo no pueden separarse, pero eso no significa que una determinada composición afectiva no esté definida por una más que por el otro. De este modo, es posible sostener que la precariedad se comprende mejor como un concepto afectivo. Es menos una cuestión de cierto desplazamiento objetivo en el estatus de la seguridad que un desplazamiento en cómo se perciben el trabajo y la seguridad. Si la precariedad puede ser usada para describir adecuadamente la vida económica contemporánea es menos porque todos están trabajando con algún tipo de contrato temporario o de media jornada, aunque estos son significativos, que porque un sentido constante de inseguridad impregna a todas las situaciones laborales. La precariedad afecta incluso al empleo estable por medio de su transformación tecnológica; siempre se puede estar trabajando o al menos en contacto con el trabajo y una ansiedad generalizada impregna la totalidad del trabajo, a medida que las mediciones más indirectas de la productividad reemplazan a la productividad en la línea de montaje. El trabajo indirecto, fragmentado e inmaterial de los servicios, la gestión del conocimiento y el trabajo emocional están menos sujetos a la cuantificación directa, la medición de unidades producidas, y por consiguiente están sujetos a la inspección y la evaluación. La inseguridad generalizada, el contacto constante y la inseguridad de la evaluación definen la economía del miedo neoliberal.

El desplazamiento del fordismo al neoliberalismo no puede solo ser descripto como un desplazamiento de la esperanza al miedo, de un deseo por el dinero fundado en el terreno en expansión de una buena vida a un deseo fundado en la inseguridad del futuro. Se trata de una composición afectiva fundamentalmente diferente, que transforma la relación tanto con el trabajo como con el dinero. Como sostienen Luc Boltanski y Eve Chiapello en *El nuevo espíritu del capitalismo*, uno de los aspectos centrales del neoliberalismo, al menos al nivel del lenguaje de los gerentes y los economistas, es la presentación de la inseguridad como oportunidad.[5] La descomposición de la seguridad que funcionaba como telón de fondo del deseo fordista, que hacía posible un vector lineal de acumulación, es presentada como una liberación de la burocracia y el control. El movimiento constante de un proyecto a otro, la falta de estabilidad y de conexiones a largo plazo, está unida no al miedo, la pérdida de seguridad, sino a la esperanza, la capacidad constante de hacer nuevas conexiones, de romper con el pasado en nombre de un nuevo futuro. A medida que el trabajo se hace cada vez más inseguro, menos capaz de proporcionar una progresión estable, consume más tiempo y energía. El neoliberalismo es una rearticulación masiva no sólo de la relación con el dinero, que se convierte en objeto de deseo y de miedo, sino también del riesgo. El nuevo espíritu del capitalismo revaloriza el riesgo.

Lejos de ser un retorno a cierto miedo fundamental, el neoliberalismo exige el más alto coeficiente de colinearización, la correlación del esfuerzo por permanecer en su ser del individuo y el esfuerzo por permanecer en su ser del modo de producción. No es un accidente que el vocabulario del neoliberalismo, términos como "capital humano", "marca personal", "red", etc., reproduzcan la idea de una identidad del individuo con el capital. Esta es también una transformación del trabajo; el trabajo ya no se define como algo que se soporta, como una pasividad necesaria que se intercambia

---

5 Boltanski, Luc and Eve Chiapello, *The New Spirit of Capitalism*, Translated by Gregory Elliot, New York: Verso, 2005, 64.

por dinero, por las dichas del consumo. El trabajo en cambio se convierte en el terreno de la autorrealización y la actualización. Esta transformación no se refiere sólo a una representación fundamentalmente diferente de la descomposición de la estabilidad, la presentación de la inseguridad como libertad, que es una variante de la filosofía espontánea de la esfera del consumo, sino también una descomposición de los límites que separan al trabajo de la vida. Esto es en parte un efecto de la inestabilidad del trabajo; a medida que los empleos se hacen más precarios, o incluso parecen precarios, el trabajo mismo deviene una suerte de proceso perpetuo de solicitud de empleo.[6] El uso de la frase "establecer contactos" [networking] refleja esta descomposición; es una idea social no sólo para las épocas de desocupación, cuando hacer nuevos contactos es primordial, sino que es un ideal que abarca todas las relaciones sociales. Los lazos débiles, los lazos que nos conectan con los compañeros de trabajo y colegas, son investidos con un máximo de esperanza y de miedo, ya que cualquier lazo, cualquier relación, puede alterar nuestro futuro. Esta inversión precaria en relaciones con otros se complica más por la proliferación de tecnologías del compartir y la vigilancia que convierten a la autopresentación que deja de ser un momento aislado, de la jornada laboral o la entrevista de trabajo, para convertirse en una tarea constante. El establecimiento de contactos, la flexibilidad y la constante autovigilancia de la búsqueda de trabajo se convierten en una característica propia del trabajo contemporáneo. Al mismo tiempo se pretende que esta característica no sea una represión del sí mismo y de la identidad, sino su expresión. No se trata sólo de que el establecimiento de contactos y el trabajo de aparecer motivado, comprometido y entusiasta tenga que ser una suerte de actuación profunda, que exija un gran compromiso, sino de que el lugar de trabajo también incluye a aquellas actividades y relaciones que parecerían estar fuera de él, y trata cada vez más de convertir al ocio, el juego y la creatividad en parte de su estructura.

La presentación de Lordon es abiertamente esquemática; en su

---

6 Southwood, Ivor, *Non-Stop Inertia*, Winchester, UK: Zero Books, 2010, 16.

recientemente publicado *La société des affects*, aumenta este esquema recurriendo a dos de las proposiciones finales de la Parte Tres de la *Ética*. En esos pasajes finales Spinoza sostiene que existen tantos amores y odios "cuantas son las especies de los objetos por los cuales somos afectados" (E. III, p. 56) y "cualquier afecto de un individuo se diferencia tanto del afecto de otro, cuanto la esencia del uno difiere de la esencia del otro" (E. III, p. 57). Los objetos múltiples, y los múltiples esfuerzos en perseverar en su ser, constituyen el fundamento de las múltiples composiciones afectivas, cada una cambiante y ambivalente puesto que el mismo objeto es tanto objeto de amor y de odio, y el mismo individuo llega a odiar lo que una vez amó. Una relectura de estas proposiciones a la luz de la historia esquemática de los diferentes modos afectivos de producción no deja de lado a estos últimos, destrozándolos en una pura multiplicidad en la que florecen mil flores. Por el contrario, estas diferencias, variaciones del amor y el odio, deben entenderse como variaciones de una melodía dominante. Como sostiene Lordon, siempre habrá jefes amables y generosos, situaciones laborales que involucran una más amplia gama de actividades, pero estas diferencias y desviaciones son en definitiva sólo distintas expresiones de una misma relación fundamental. El jefe más agradable del mundo no puede alterar significativamente la estructura fundamental de las condiciones de trabajo fordista o neoliberal, el compromiso afectivo a nivel de la intención individual no hace nada por alterar la relación básica con la actividad y el objeto. Este revestimiento afectivo, la tarea de las relaciones humanas, no es intrascendente: más que el papel que juega en motivar a los trabajadores individuales, el trabajo verdadero que realiza es producir la apariencia de diferencia, una sociedad de acciones individuales y no de estructuras persistentes. Buena parte de la crítica cotidiana del trabajo, del capitalismo en general, se concentra en las diferencias: nos quejamos de este jefe, o protestamos contra esta gran corporación por ser particularmente repudiable, pero no abordamos la relación fundamental de explotación o la razón de lucro que excede los diversos modos en que se presenta. La pluralidad, una pluralidad prescripta por lo que Spinoza llamaría el orden espontáneo de la naturaleza, los diferentes modos en que las cosas nos han afectado, tienen prioridad sobre la percepción de las relaciones comunes.

A este énfasis en la pluralidad como coartada perpetua, podemos agregar otra tesis de Spinoza. Como sostiene Spinoza, es más posible que odiemos o amemos un acto que consideremos libre que uno que consideremos necesario. En este último punto la economía afectiva de Spinoza se interseca con uno de los puntos centrales de la crítica de Marx a la economía política, el fetichismo, que puede en parte resumirse como percibir el modo capitalista de producción como necesario y natural, no como un producto de las relaciones sociales. La naturalización de la economía, su existencia como leyes naturales autoevidentes, hace difícil para nosotros odiarla, indignarnos. La economía afectiva del capitalismo es tal que es fácil enojarse o agradecer las desviaciones, los jefes crueles y los filántropos benévolos, mientras que la estructura misma, las relaciones fundamentales de explotación, son consideradas demasiado necesarias, demasiado naturales, como para que ameriten indignación. La naturalización de la economía, su fetichización, está acoplada a su complejidad, que hace que nos resulte difícil reconocer su determinación de nuestro esforzarnos. Podríamos ser capaces de rastrear las causas que nos han determinado a que nos guste esto o aquello, a tener este o aquel gusto, pero es tan difícil aprehender las causas que han canalizado nuestro esforzarnos en el trabajo asalariado y aferrado nuestros deseos a la compra de mercancías, tanto que el trabajo y el consumo parecen condiciones naturales más que instituciones históricas.

La producción de la indignación es una tarea difícil, no va sólo contra la necesidad percibida del modo de producción capitalista sino contra los modos en que nuestros deseos mismos, nuestros esfuerzos más íntimos en perseverar en nuestro ser, han sido producidos por el capitalismo. Desde esta perspectiva, la provocación central de Spinoza a una crítica de la economía política no es el comentario aislado sobre el poder del dinero, sino la tesis fundamental de que los hombres "se creen libres porque son conscientes de sus propias acciones e ignorantes de las causas por las cuales están determinados" (E. III, p. 2, e.). Esta afirmación contrasta con cualquier afirmación del supuesto deseo por el capitalismo, el deseo de consumir bienes, etc. como su justificación; tales deseos son meramente efectos tomados como causas. Su dimensión destructiva, su *pars destruens*, está bien claro; lo que no está tan claro, sin embargo, es cómo constituye un proyecto político afirmativo. El punto de partida, más allá de la dificultad de reconocer el modo como ya estamos determinados, es el reconocimiento por parte de Spinoza de que en aquellas cosas que aumentan nuestra dicha, y alejamos aquellos pensamientos que nos debilitan y entristecen. Esta tendencia afectiva no sólo explica por qué "luchamos por nuestra servidumbre como si fuera la salvación", sino también por qué continuamos, contra toda prueba, creyendo que llegará el momento en que el sistema económico actual recapacitará y nos recompensará por nuestros esfuerzos. Además, toda transformación radical no sólo debe romper las líneas de articulación que entrelazan al esforzarse con el trabajo, la felicidad y el consumo, debe producir otras dichas, otras formas de esforzarse. Una revolución es tanto una reorientación tanto de nuestras relaciones afectivas como de las relaciones sociales y no puede ser una cosa sin la otra.

Spanish translation of "Economies of Affect/Affective Economies: Towards A Spinozist Critique of Political Economy."

www.ingramcontent.com/pod-product-compliance
Lightning Source LLC
Chambersburg PA
CBHW060827190426
43197CB00039B/2527